PRIDE OF THE INLAND SEAS

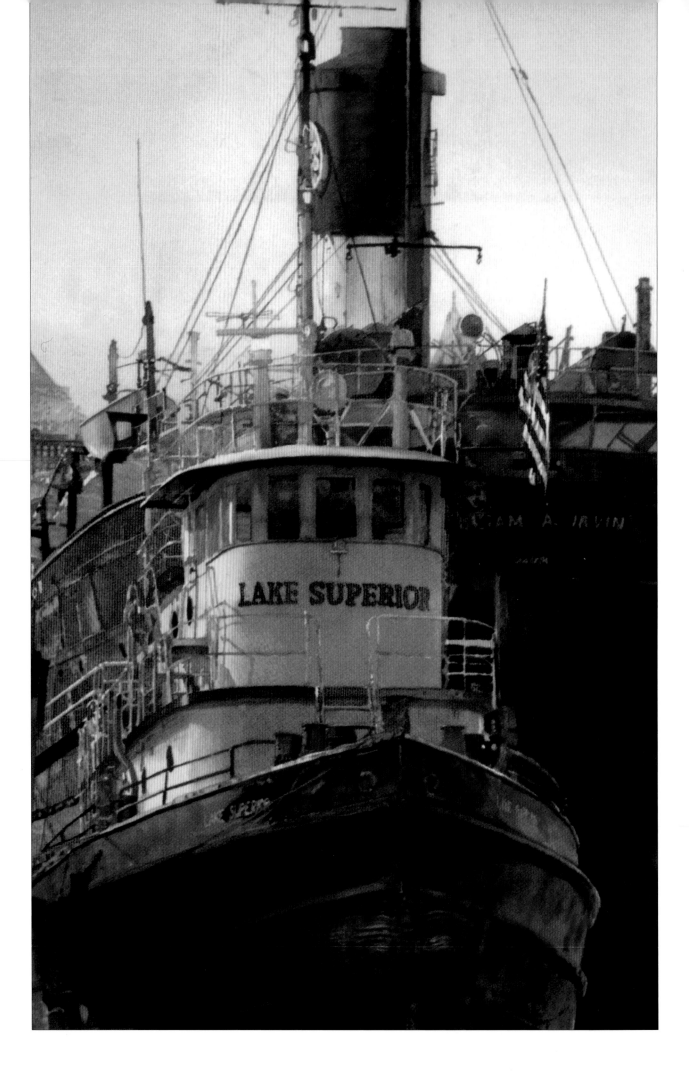

PRIDE OF THE INLAND SEAS

An Illustrated History
of the Port of
Duluth — Superior

SEAS

BILL BECK

AND

C. PATRICK LABADIE

C. Patrick Labadie

AFTON HISTORICAL SOCIETY PRESS

Publication of

PRIDE OF THE INLAND SEAS

*An Illustrated History of the
Part of Duluth-Superior*

was made possible with
financial support from the

Duluth Seaway Port Authority.

Additional funding was provided by:

American Steamship Company

Cleveland-Cliffs, Inc.

Cutler-Magner Company

Fraser Shipyards, Inc.

Hallett Dock Company

The Interlake Steamship Company

Lake Superior Magazine

Lake Superior Port Cities, Inc.

Lake Superior Warehousing Co., Inc.

Midwest Energy Resources Company

Afton Historical Society Press

P.O. Box 100

Afton, MN 55001

800-436-8443

aftonpress@aftonpress.com

www.aftonpress.com

Front cover: The Interlake Steamship Company's Charles M. Beeghly *approaches Duluth–Superior (Tim Slattery, Harbor Reflections).*

Page 2: Former flagship of the USS Great Lakes Fleet, the William A. Irvin *shares a permanent berth next to the Duluth Entertainment and Convention Center with the retired U.S. Army Corps of Engineers tug* Lake Superior *(watercolor by John Salminen).*

Back cover: The Nonsuch, *replica of a bygone era on the Great Lakes, visits Duluth–Superior on a celebratory tour during the early 1970s (Basgen Photography, DSPA Collection).*

Edited by Michele Hodgson

Graphic layout by Mary Susan Oleson

Production assistance by Beth Williams

Printed by Pettit Network, Inc., Afton, Minnesota

Library of Congress Cataloging-in-Publication Data

Beck, Bill.
Pride of the inland seas : an illustrated history of the Port of Duluth/Superior / Bill Beck and C. Patrick Labadie.—1st ed.
p. cm.
Includes index.
ISBN 1-890434-55-8 (alk. paper)
1. Harbors—Minnesota—Duluth—History. 2. Harbors—Wisconsin—Superior—History. I. Labadie, C. Patrick. II. Title.

HE554.D8B43 2004
386'.8'09776771—dc22

2003027412

Printed in China

Afton Historical Society Press publishes
exceptional books on regional subjects.

W. DUNCAN MACMILLAN
President

PATRICIA CONDON JOHNSTON
Publisher

CONTENTS

PRESIDENT'S NOTE 7
FOREWORD 9
ACKNOWLEDGMENTS 10

1   The Voyageurs' Highway 13
THE FIRST SHIPS APPEAR 20

2   The Locks and La Pointe 23
SAILS ON THE HORIZON 30

3   Steel Rails to the Head of the Lakes 33
DIGGING THE DULUTH SHIP CANAL 42

4   Wheat to Feed the World 45
IN THE EYE OF THE BEHOLDER 54

5   Iron Port, Coal Port 57
AMERICA'S STEEL DISTRICT EMERGES 70

6   Timber Port 73
THE ERA OF LUMBER HOOKERS 82

7   Passengers and Package Freight 85
THE AUTOMOBILE TRADE 96

8   A World-Class Port 99
COMMERCIAL FISHING 108

9   The Shipbuilders 111
STILL A DANGEROUS LAKE 124

10   Zenith City of the Unsalted Seas 127
PEAVEY'S FOLLY 138

11   The Golden Age of Cruise Ships 141
THE PETROLEUM BUSINESS IN THE TWIN PORTS 146

12   The Lean Depression Years 149
DULUTH-SUPERIOR IN 1939 158

13   The Twin Ports at War 161
THE *WOODRUSH*, THE *SUNDEW*, AND THE "180s" 172

14   The Range Resurgent 175
VESSEL REPAIR AND FRASER SHIPYARDS 186

15   From Tidewater to Bluewater 189
THE HERITAGE OF THE MODERN ELEVATORS 200

16   Growth of an International Port 203
THE *ROGER BLOUGH* 214

17   Revolutions in Commerce 217
THE WRECK OF THE *EDMUND FITZGERALD* 228

18   Retrenchment and Rebirth 231
THE GREAT LAKES TOWING COMPANY 242

19   The Go-Go Nineties 245

NOTES 260
ILLUSTRATION CREDITS 282
INDEX 284

Built in Duluth in 1944 and stationed in the port since 1980, the Sundew *will be decommissioned in 2004.*

PRESIDENT'S NOTE

AFTON PRESS is proud and pleased to bring to print *Pride of the Inland Seas,* the fascinating story of the birth, growth, and often erratic development of one of North America's largest ports, in a place 600 feet above and more than 2,000 miles away from the nearest ocean. I am the great-grandson of Will W. Cargill, the founder of Cargill, Inc., whose company fortunes have been long entwined with those of the Port of Duluth-Superior, and this book is close to my heart.

At the extreme western tip of mighty Lake Superior, the world's largest expanse of surface freshwater, the harbor that would become the Port of Duluth-Superior was a gift of the last Ice Age. Scoured from igneous rock by receding glaciers and protected from the fury of periodic lake storms by a narrow, nine-mile-long sand peninsula, the sprawling natural harbor would be reconfigured into forty-nine miles of shoreline and scores of commercial properties—among them, one of Cargill's earliest grain terminals.

This is the first historical narrative of the Port of Duluth-Superior in at least fifty years, and certainly the most comprehensive ever published as a book for scholars, marine buffs, and general readers. It is the story of how a place once inhabited by Native Americans became a French fur-trading post and, eventually, a major commercial trade artery in the middle of a continent.

But it is far more than a tale of two northern Minnesota and Wisconsin cities and their freshwater ships and cargoes. It is a compelling human drama of fortunes made or lost, and dreams fulfilled or shattered, as entrepreneurs and public officials strove to capitalize on the building of America and the development of the Great Lakes navigation system.

In many ways, the history of Duluth-Superior is the history of Great Lakes shipping and its parallel relationship with the growth of Midwest agriculture, the timber industry, and the North American iron and steel industry. Throughout

the decades, the port has linked the world to the region's abundant natural resources: flourishing fields of wheat, vast forests of pine, spruce, and tamarack, and ranges so rich in iron ore that one writer called Superior "a great cold lake in an iron collar."

It is also a history of the vagaries of global trade. Authors Bill Beck and C. Patrick Labadie skillfully describe the impact of politics and macro-economics on local and lakes-wide shipping. In some cases, distant events created huge surges of business, as in World War II and the Korean War, when shipments of iron ore from Minnesota's Vermillion and Mesabi Ranges, as well as manganese from its Cuyuna Range, hit all-time highs. In others, external forces had negative effects, as in the advent of "containerization," which virtually dried up the port's general cargo business.

One underlying theme is the sheer unpredictability of human and commercial fate. There is the story of how the Merritt brothers, on the verge of becoming giants in the iron ore industry, lost nearly everything in the panic of 1893 and forfeited their budding empire to eastern money interests. And how a score of coal docks that once lined the Duluth-Superior harbor disappeared—along with millions of tons of inbound coal cargoes—only to be replaced by one mammoth facility that today moves prodigious volumes of coal *outbound.*

While these subjects may ignore day-to-day port activities, the book does not. The authors flavor the text with firsthand anecdotes from archival sources as well as from nearly fifty interviews with port officials, sailors, dockworkers, and others for whom Great Lakes shipping was or is a way of life.

This is a wonderful and important book indeed about the people, events, and geological riches that have made Duluth-Superior an enduring world port and, yes, the undisputed "pride of the inland seas."

W. Duncan MacMillan
PRESIDENT, AFTON HISTORICAL SOCIETY PRESS
RETIRED DIRECTOR, CARGILL, INC.

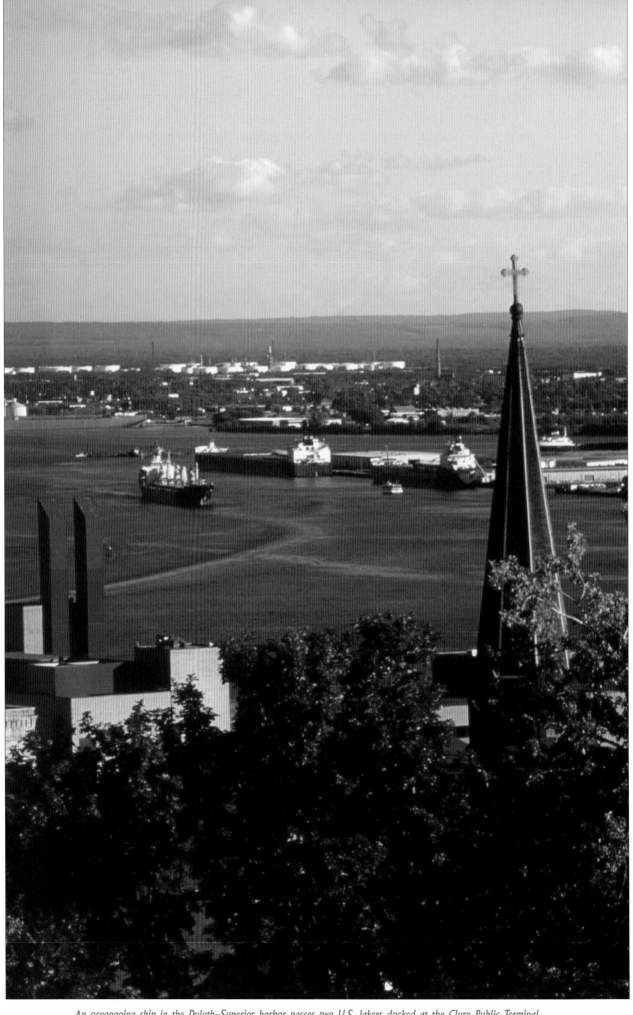

An oceangoing ship in the Duluth–Superior harbor passes two U.S. lakers docked at the Clure Public Terminal.

FOREWORD

THE WORLD OF waterborne transportation—"the shipping business," as it was known before the advent of trains and trucks and airplanes—is a world apart from the one where most folks reside.

Its uniqueness is not easily described, probably because the only constant is that it involves the carriage of goods on the water. Otherwise, it's a world—one might say a universe—with so many diverse players and professions, so many different types of vessels, so many varied kinds of cargo that even the people who spend their lives there have difficulty trying to explain it to others.

Capturing it in words and pictures through the birth and development of one port—the largest on North America's Great Lakes—was the monumental task the Duluth Seaway Port Authority assigned to regional authors and historians Bill Beck and C. Patrick Labadie.

In the judgment of this writer, who's been on hand for nearly one-third of the Port of Duluth-Superior's recorded history, they nailed it.

Because the history of a port is reflective of the history and commercial development of its hinterland, *Pride of the Inland Seas* is far more than a story about the building of docks and the opening of navigation channels. This port's true history, in fact, began long before there were two cities and two states sharing a common harbor at the westernmost tip of Lake Superior, long before there was a United States.

When the first European explorers and missionaries arrived in the seventeenth century, they found Native American settlements in the sheltered waters just upriver from today's sprawling harbor. Then came more Europeans, including the legendary voyageurs as exploiters of the beaver whose fur pelts were prized in Europe. Next were American entrepreneurs, large and small, making or sometimes squandering fortunes as the fledging Duluth and Superior communities rode through cycles of boom times and bad times.

Meanwhile, through tenacity, fate, faith, timing, dumb luck—call it what you will—the natural harbor attracted the railroads, warehouses, grain elevators, lumber mills, coal docks, and shipyards that gave the cities their economic underpinnings. Then, little more than 100 years ago, came the iron ore docks that would catapult Duluth-Superior into a port of national significance. And in 1959, Duluth-Superior became more than a lakes port when the St. Lawrence Seaway opened direct trade with nations around the globe.

It's all brought together here—or most of it, at least. The story is so rich, so compelling, that numerous related anecdotes could not be squeezed between these covers. They, consequently, are available on a companion Web site: www.duluthport.com.

This cross-use of media was one of Bill Beck's brainstorms for *Pride of the Inland Seas*. He proposed it at a time when he and I had nearly exasperated the patience and affability of the remarkable Patricia Johnston, publisher of Afton Historical Society Press, because of our insistence that we could not reduce an already late manuscript more than we already had. To her enduring credit, Patricia agreed to the novel approach.

So here it is (and on the Web site)—a story of far-sighted visionaries and pie-in-the-sky dreamers, of sailing schooners and thousand-foot lake carriers, of roughneck rowdies and hardboiled investors. The Port of Duluth-Superior has seen them all in its colorful history . . . and they now live on through these pages.

A final note: This book would not have been possible without the support of the Duluth Seaway Port Authority board of commissioners and staff, the cooperation of maritime professionals who shared stories and donated photographs, the donations of various companies (see copyright page), and the willingness of Afton Historical Society Press to participate in this project.

Davis Helberg
EXECUTIVE DIRECTOR 1979–2003
DULUTH SEAWAY PORT AUTHORITY

ACKNOWLEDGMENTS

When I started writing *Pride of the Inland Seas* five years ago, my wife, Elizabeth, noted that it was less a job than a labor of love. Chronicling the history of this greatest of Great Lakes ports—beginning long before it was called Duluth-Superior, when Native Americans portaged their birch bark canoes up past the Dalles of the St. Louis River—*is* most definitely a labor of love. Like any such undertaking, it could not have been accomplished without the help of dozens of people who share the same love for ports and boats and the Great Lakes.

Although not listed as a coauthor, Davis Helberg, former executive director of the Duluth Seaway Port Authority, was instrumental in getting *Pride* conceived, researched, written, edited, designed, and published. I've been privileged to know Dave for a quarter-century, and rarely have seen him more enthusiastic about a project. He helped line up scores of interviews that unearthed the great stories that enrich this book. He submitted to hours of interviews, downloading his encyclopedic knowledge of the Great Lakes since the 1950s. He read, and often challenged, every word of the manuscript. He selected and approved every illustration you see in this magnificent volume. Without his full commitment, this book would never have happened. All I can say is, thanks, Dave.

C. Patrick Labadie, my coauthor, may know more about the Great Lakes in the nineteenth century than anyone alive. Pat's research skills and amazing recall of arcane maritime trivia consistently enlivened the manuscript. The Labadie library, one of the more remarkable Great Lakes archival collections, was an unbelievable resource for reconstructing the port's early history and a source of many of the wonderful photos that grace these pages.

Laura Jacobs of the Great Lakes Maritime Collection of the University of Wisconsin–Superior Library was indefatigable in tracking down faded newspaper clippings as well as making available dozens of photographs. When Laura was tied up with other duties, Eric Bonow was the designated tracker-downer.

Old friend Pat Maus steered me toward forgotten labor and business files in the Northeast Minnesota Historical Center collection at the University of Minnesota–Duluth. Pat's knowledge of the region's history is unparalleled, and her assistance, as always, was much appreciated.

Dick Bibby and Wes Harkins invested countless hours selecting photographs and memorabilia from their private collections for the book. These key players in the Twin Ports maritime industry have spent years preserving Duluth-Superior's maritime heritage.

I can't begin to recount, let alone thank, the hundreds of people who shared stories about the Great Lakes after I arrived in Duluth in 1979 as a business and financial reporter for the *Duluth News-Tribune and Herald.* But I'd be remiss if I didn't mention at least a few. Donn Larson always had stories about the lakes, and Ray Erickson enjoyed them as much as I did. Ed Ruisi arrived in Duluth about the time the first salties did, and Sven Hubner, Chuck Hilleren, and Chuck Ilenda could pretty much by themselves reconstruct the history of the grain trade in the Twin Ports during the past half-century. I spent an enchanting afternoon with Germaine Guthrie, who painted a word picture of her husband, Alastair, legendary dean of Duluth-Superior shipping agents.

Cliff Grindy, Ken Fossum, Howard Hagen, and the late Keith Yetter spent hours discussing the Twin Ports' heavy industry, and Gary Nicholson told of how Duluth reclaimed a reputation for warehousing and intermodal excellence. Bill Buhrmann talked about fleet operations, and Dick Amatuzio acquainted a novice with the vagaries of line-handling. Jay Van Horn and Hollie Graves covered a century of grain elevator history, and Wally DeBruyne described the complex world of supplying ship provisions.

The history of maritime labor in the Twin Ports is steeped in legend. I only wish I had taped fellow Duluth port commissioner Edward L. Slaughter when I served with him in the 1980s. "Buster" Slaughter was the voice and image of the International Longshoremen's Association and its predecessors in the Twin Ports for nearly seventy-five years. Fortunately, Pat Maus of the Northeast Minnesota Historical Center located a tape-recorded interview with Slaughter in the 1970s. Russ Wedin, Bob Picard, and Kenneth Stringer told me about more recent ILA history.

Captain Tony Rico is another Twin Ports legend I wish I had subjected to an oral-history interview in the 1980s. Rico was a founder of today's Great Lakes pilotage system in the 1960s and few early contemporaries survive, but Captains Dennis Aho, Skip Skuggen, Bill Jeffery, and Gil Porter all had distinguished careers on the Great Lakes, plus many years in the pilots' fraternity. Porter, especially, told fascinating stories of his years aboard the U.S. Coast Guard cutter *Woodrush*. Captain Armand Johnson reminisced about his days as a lakes sailor, mate, and master.

The "hidden port" is an intriguing slice of Duluth-Superior life, comprising the hundreds of men and women who work in such fields as U.S. Customs, grain inspection, cargo stowage, and ship fueling. Frank Missine, Milt Eng, John Wuotila, and Captains Sencer Under and Dick McLean spent hours explaining intricacies of the hidden port.

The Duluth Seaway Port Authority is the public face of maritime activities at the head of the lakes. I started covering port authority board meetings in 1979 and spent six years during the 1980s as a City Council appointee to the board. *Pride of the Inland Seas* allowed me to renew many acquaintances with those past and present who have made the port authority such a success. David Oberlin told of his days as port director in the 1960s. Don Ireland reminisced about port governance in the 1980s. Robert C. Maki explained the underpinnings of maritime law. Captain Ray Skelton walked me through shipboard propulsion in the twentieth century, and Andy McDonough brought me up to date on industrial development. Sam Browman, once the port's marketing guru, shared his incredibly detailed knowledge of commercial transportation patterns. Lisa Marciniak coordinated searches through the port authority's voluminous records. Becky McMillan, Shellie Golden, and Anne Mann expedited the busy two-way FedEx traffic between Duluth and Indianapolis during the editing and caption-writing process.

My successors as port commissioners supported the project from the start. Helena Jackson and Janet Nelson took a keen interest, while Bill Kron and Steve Raukar saw the inherent wisdom of telling the definitive story of the Twin Ports. The late Tom Grosser would have loved *Pride of the Inland Seas*.

Former Hoosiers Larry and Jerilyn Fortner always threw open the doors of the church or the cabin for a visiting writer from Indianapolis. Wayne Brandt, himself an organizer for the Seamen's International Union in his early days, was always good for an enlightening dinner in Duluth or Indianapolis. Kathleen Curley really learned her history as an intern, tracking down obscure articles from *National Geographic*, *Inland Seas*, and *The Nor'Easter*.

Patricia Johnston, publisher of Afton Historical Society Press, took a chance on the project, ably shepherding *Pride of the Inland Seas* from start to finish. Michele Hodgson copyedited the manuscript while old friend Marian Lansky of Duluth-based Clarity lent her special skill to the creation of the book's maps and graphics. Mary Susan Oleson melded text and images into the book's gorgeous design.

Like all of my previous thirty or so books, *Pride of the Inland Seas* would never have seen the light of day without the efforts of my wife. Betty is editor, bookkeeper, scheduler, friend, scold, motivator, and cheerleader. Somewhere along the line I did learn how to become chief cook and bottle-washer (ask me about my homemade lentil and sausage soup) and I did manage to get out a first draft. When it comes to books, however, Betty does just about everything else.

But don't blame her, Helberg, or Labadie for the inevitable errors, misstatements, omissions, and other screw-ups. Those are usually mine. -B.B.

Voyageurs in Montreal canoes disappear into the mists of Lake Superior in this 1873 painting by Frances Ann Hopkins.

CHAPTER ONE

The Voyageurs' Highway

THE WAY WEST TO the heart of the continent and its bounteous trade lay by water rather than by land. And the French, Dutch, and British explorers who colonized outposts along the East Coast of North America in the fifteenth and sixteenth centuries soon discovered what the original inhabitants had known for a hundred generations: the trackless forest was just that.

A squirrel could have left the tiny French settlements in the valley of the St. Lawrence River in 1610 and traveled west to the Great Plains nearly three thousand miles distant without ever once touching the ground. The boreal forest that covered eastern North America in the seventeenth century stretched from the permafrost around Hudson Bay to the waters of the Gulf of Mexico. The broad canopy of deciduous trees and conifers posed a barrier to settlement that was perhaps more perceived than genuinely insurmountable.

Samuel de Champlain, the first European to venture into the wilderness of the North American continent, described the height of the forest, the bountiful chestnut trees, and the numerous vines as "more beautiful than I have seen in any other place."[1] Champlain's fateful 1609 accompaniment of a Huron Indian war party against their traditional enemies, the Iroquois, to the lake that bears his name in upstate New York was significant in two respects. It marked the first, tentative steps by Europeans into the wilderness, and it created an enmity between the French and the Iroquois that had immense implications for North American history during the next century-and-a-half.

Champlain didn't know it at the time, but barely a month after his harquebus killed two Iroquois war chiefs on the shores of Lake Champlain, somewhere between what are now Crown Point and Ticonderoga, New York, a third event that would affect the future of North America took place fewer than 100 miles south. Henry Hudson, a British navigator sailing for the Dutch West Indies Company, piloted his *Half Moon* up the river named after him and stopped at present-day Albany to trade with the Native Americans.[2]

NORTHWEST PASSAGE

Henry Hudson, like most of the European explorers of the era, had been looking for a passage to China and the Orient. Setting out from tiny ports on the Dutch North Sea, England, the Bay of Biscay, and Portugal, the adventurers sailed west in leaky caravels, many smaller than modern-day yachts and cabin cruisers, looking for the riches of the Indies. The intrepid sailors discovered a landmass they initially took to be Asia, but soon found to be two uncharted continents where none was known to exist. Actually, the Europeans probably just rediscovered the North American landmass.

Viking sailors in the Middle Ages had pushed westward from Greenland during a centuries-long warming period and likely established short-lived settlements in what is now New-foundland. As early as the late 1300s, Basque fishermen were reportedly making the perilous Atlantic crossing from ports in northern Spain to the codfishing grounds of the Grand Banks. When Jacques Cartier discovered the Gulf of St. Lawrence in 1534 and planted a cross dedicated to the king of France on Quebec's Gaspé Peninsula, he laconically noted that he had to sail through a Basque fishing fleet of some 1,000 boats to get there.[3]

In the early 1600s, when settlements were being established in the valleys of the St. Lawrence and the Hudson, and along the Atlantic coast in Massachusetts and Virginia, it began to occur to the royal courts and the merchant empires of Europe that the new continent was not, after all, anywhere near the court of the Great Khan in China. That didn't preclude royal expeditions chartered by half a dozen nations from searching for a Northwest Passage to Asia during the next two centuries. But the new colonies were relaying reports back to Europe that the interior of this new continent was blessed with riches that made the search for China irrelevant. Cartier and John Cabot, an Italian sailing for the British, in the 1500s observed that the native inhabitants were dressed in the furs of beaver, otter, and fox, pelts that were reputedly in great supply in the interior. Champlain heard rumors of gold and silver deposits of inestimable value far to the west.

Getting there was the problem. The British colonies hugging the shores of the Atlantic were, in most cases, coast-bound. The rivers of the New England and Middle Atlantic states were short, steep, and riddled with rocks. The rivers rose in the Appalachian Mountains, which essentially paralleled the coast from Maine to Georgia. Getting across the Appalachians would take the English colonists the better part of two centuries to achieve. But there were no Appalachians to bar the way of the French into the interior of North America. There were broad rivers flowing west and south from the first French settlements of Quebec, Mont Royal, and Trois-Rivières in eastern Canada. The St. Lawrence River drained the eastern third of the continent and opened the Great Lakes to French penetration and trade.

BIRCH BARK AND BEAVER

From the time of the earliest settlement of New France, Champlain had heard the native inhabitants' stories of sweet-water seas far to the west and southwest. Through his friendship with the Huron, Champlain had learned that the *mer douce* to the west were accessible by water, either southwest via the St. Lawrence past Lake Ontario and the thundering gorge of Niagara or west up the River of the Ottawas to Lake Nipissing, Georgian Bay, and Lake Huron.

Champlain had been among the first to realize that the birch bark canoe of the Native Americans was the key to unlocking the trade potential of French North America.[4] Native Americans had used the canoe for centuries for hunting and trading across much of eastern North America. They traded buffalo robes from the prairies west of the Great Lakes, clay for pipes from Minnesota, and copper from the south shore of Lake Superior. When Jacques Cartier discovered the mouth of the St. Lawrence River for France in 1535, he noted that the native inhabitants sported copper amulets and knives that came, they said, from a freshwater sea far to the west.[5]

The cargo from the beginning of the French regime was trade goods going upriver and furs going down. As early as the 1630s, furs regularly left New France for Europe. For more than 150 years, Europe had relied on the czars of Russia to supply furs for gentlemen's and ladies' fashions. Chief among the furs most sought by Europeans in the 1600s was beaver. "Seldom has an animal exercised such a profound influence on the history of a continent," explained Peter Newman in his history of the Hudson Bay Company. "Men defied oceans and hacked their way across North America; armies and navies clashed under the Polar moon; an Indian civilization was debauched—all in the quest of the pug-nosed rodent with the lustrous fur."[6] At the time of Charles I of England in the 1630s and 1640s, beaver hats trimmed with ostrich feathers were the height of sartorial elegance. Beaver was also popular in hatmaking because it didn't look like fur. Beaver hairs had little hooks on the end, not unlike Velcro, which would interlock when pressed to create a solid fabric. Hatters called the process "felting," and the felted pelt was easily formed into a hat.[7]

The rivers, lakes, and wetlands of North America contained a beaver population to rival that of Russia and Siberia. Beaver populated every stream from northern Mexico to the Arctic Circle. In the 1600s, an estimated ten million beaver existed in present-day Canada alone. The birch bark canoe, in its many sizes, would help French traders to tap that market.

Fur traders cook breakfast in the country north of Lake Superior in this painting by Cornelius Krieghoff.

THE UPPER LAKE

Samuel de Champlain arrived in French North America in 1603. For the next thirty years, he pushed the boundaries of the French colony ever westward. Champlain sent young French nobles and merchants to live among the indigenous tribes of the valley of the St. Lawrence to learn their languages and customs. Then he dispatched these coureurs de bois to the interior with their Native American hosts. Another contingent of Frenchmen accompanied the Huron and the voyageurs into the wilderness. Missionary fathers of the Jesuit, Recollet, and Franciscan orders set out from Montreal with the express intent of saving souls. Highly educated, deeply committed to their faith, and intensely curious, the missionaries recorded in their journals and reports much of what we now know of the exploration of the Upper Great Lakes in the 1600s and 1700s.

By 1615, Champlain and Etienne Brulé, one of the first missionaries to live among the Huron, had reached the eastern shores of Lake Huron, the sweet-water sea Champlain had been hearing about for twelve years. Sometime later, Brulé pressed north and west to the *sault,* or rapids, that separated Lakes Huron and Superior.[8] The first missionaries were quick to name the river that fed the rapids the St. Mary's, in honor of the Mother of Christ. The rapids became known as the Falls of St. Mary, or the Sault. According to Gabriel Sagard, a Recollet lay brother, Brulé and his companion canoed at least thirty days along the south shore of the big lake west of the Sault, and brought back reports of copper boulders not far inland from the shores.

Jesuits Charles Raymbault and Isaac Jogues visited the Anishinaabe fishing village at the Sault between Lakes Superior and Huron in 1641 and established a mission there.[9] Fifteen years later, two of the more intrepid voyageurs explored much of Lake Superior and the country to the south and west. Pierre Esprit Radisson and Medard Chouart—Sieur de Grosseilliers, a son of the minor French nobility—set off from Montreal to the upper lake. Between 1656 and 1660, they wintered on Green Bay of Lake Michigan, crossed what is now Wisconsin to Prairie Island on the

Upper Mississippi, explored much of what is today the Upper Peninsula of Michigan, and established a fur trading post on Chequamegon Bay of Lake Superior near present-day Ashland, Wisconsin. When Radisson and Groseilliers returned to Montreal with fur-laden canoes in the summer of 1660, they were hailed as heroes.[10]

Radisson and Groseilliers—"Radishes and Gooseberry" to a generation of Minnesota and Wisconsin schoolchildren—returned to Chequamegon Bay from 1661 to 1663. During the next twenty years, they spent much of their time in the wilderness, switching their allegiance between New France and the Hudson Bay Company. But in the process, they opened Lake Superior and the rich beaver-trapping grounds between Lake Nipigon and Hudson Bay. Whether they discovered the site of what is now Duluth-Superior is shrouded in the mists of time. That honor is traditionally awarded another minor French nobleman, Daniel Greysolon, Sieur DuLhut.

Born at St. Germain-en-Laye near Paris in about 1654, Greysolon chose the army as a career and arrived in New France with the King's Guards in the early 1670s. He returned to France in 1674 to fight for King Louis XIV against the Dutch Republic, but was back in Montreal in the spring of 1675.[11] Like so many young noblemen of the time, he formed a trading company to make his fortune in the fur trade.

In September 1678, Greysolon, his brother Claude, six voyageurs, and a handful of Christian Hurons set out from Montreal for the upper lake. They wintered at the Sault and then pushed west in the spring. Historians still differ on whether Greysolon actually landed at the head of the lakes or cut inland from Wisconsin. But legend credits him with stepping ashore at Minnesota Point in Duluth on or about June 27, 1679.[12]

Greysolon's mission was to bring about peace between the Anishinaabe of Lake Superior and the Sioux, who lived west of the lake in what is now central Minnesota. His route west from the head of the lakes was one that countless thousands of fur traders would take during the next century-and-a-half. He followed the rocky and sometimes rough St. Louis River from its mouth and portaged around the Thomson Falls some fifteen miles inland. The party continued west on the St. Louis above the falls to the Savannah Portage, where they carried their canoes into the Upper Mississippi River drainage.[13] They then paddled to Izatys, a Sioux village on Lake Mille Lacs.

For much of 1679–1680, Greysolon explored the canoe routes west and south of the head of the lakes and dispatched at least one convoy of Montreal canoes laden with furs back east to New France. He spent the winter of 1679–1680 some two hundred miles to the north at the mouth of the Kaministiquia River near what would become Fort William, Ontario.[14] In the summer of 1680, he met Father Louis Hennepin, a Recollet missionary to the Sioux, on the Upper Mississippi.[15] Greysolon crossed Wisconsin in the fall of 1680 to Green Bay and wintered at the Jesuit mission at Michihilimackinac before returning to Montreal in the spring of 1681.[16]

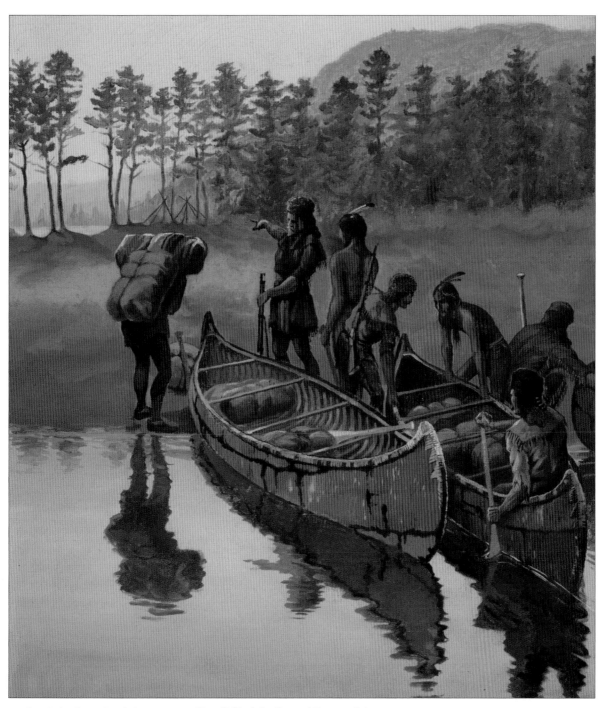

Francis Lee Jaques's painting re-creates Sieur DuLhut's landing at Minnesota Point.

fought the French for control of the lucrative beaver trade in the interior of North America. When Quebec fell in 1759, all of the trading rights and privileges that had formerly accrued to the merchants of Montreal became British rights and privileges. All pelts were sent to London instead of Paris. But the British and the Hudson Bay Company wrestled with competition from unlicensed traders.

By 1765, Hudson Bay Company's Alexander Henry and Jean-Baptiste Cadotte had established a post at Chequamegon Bay and were sending traders into the Fond du Lac area on the St. Louis River. Construction began on a fort at Grand Portage on the north shore of Lake Superior, but the licensed trappers faced unrelenting competition in the Rainy Lake and Lake of the Woods country northwest of Pigeon River. Hudson Bay Company trappers, meanwhile, were traveling as far west as the Saskatchewan River.[18]

An engraving from Robert Ballantyne's 1876 history Hudson Bay *shows the spirited exchange of fur and trade goods.*

For most of the next twenty-five years, Greysolon contributed his military skills to the governors of New France, commanding its forts in the northwest and battling its enemies, the Iroquois and the British. He died in Montreal in 1710, a decorated war hero and "an honest man" to his peers and colleagues.[17] Daniel Greysolon, Sieur DuLhut, went to Lake Superior to trade for beaver pelts, and, by all accounts, oversaw the first shipment of cargo from the great port that would bear his name in the future.

NEW REGIMES

The British victory at the Plains of Abraham in Quebec City in September 1759 brought to an end France's dream of a colonial empire in the new world. The establishment of the Hudson Bay Company in 1670 had trumped New France's strategy of flanking the growing English colonies to its south and east by blocking trade routes to the north and west. With the establishment of company trading factories and military posts on Hudson Bay and James Bay, the British, in effect, blocked French penetration to the north and west.

For most of the ninety years between 1670 and 1760, the British and their Iroquois allies

The American Revolution coincided with the creation of the North West Company, the trading firm formed by Montreal merchants to compete with the Hudson Bay Company. The Treaty of Versailles that ended the American Revolution in 1783 awarded the new American Republic much of the land north and west of Lake Superior. Although subsequent treaties gave British and American traders reciprocal rights in each other's territory, the Hudson Bay Company gradually concentrated more and more on the trapping potential of the Canadian Rockies.[19]

During the 1790s, the North West Company controlled much of the fur trade in northern Minnesota west of Lake Superior. Jean Baptiste Perrault built a trading post at Fond du Lac, as well as smaller posts on the St. Louis River, Leech Lake, Pine Lake, and Ottertail Lake. In 1800, the North West Company dominated the fur trade of the Great Lakes and its hinterlands, with more than one thousand traders and clerks shipping pelts back along the traditional canoe routes to Montreal.[20] But infighting among the partners led to the creation of the XY Company in 1795. Further competition came from the Hudson Bay Company, which still controlled much of the trade in the country north of Lake Superior.

The last major competitor to arrive on the scene was John Jacob Astor's American Fur Company. Founded in 1808, the company served the Lake Superior trade from posts at Fond du Lac, Minnesota; La Pointe on Madeline Island, Wisconsin; and Mackinac Island, Michigan. Following the War of 1812, Astor accelerated his efforts to control the fur trade in the United States. Congress obliged his grandiose plans in 1816 by passing legislation that essentially prohibited foreigners from trading on American soil.[21] Astor immediately began hiring North West Company traders to work for American Fur, and for the next four years the two companies engaged in out-and-out warfare. Exhausted by its battles with American Fur, the North West Company agreed in 1821 to a merger with its longtime rival, the Hudson Bay Company. Both the North West Company and the Hudson Bay Company had concluded that the transportation costs of canoeing and portaging pelts back to Montreal were becoming prohibitive.[22] For the next twenty years, the American Fur Company had the Lake Superior country to itself. But beaver were rapidly becoming trapped out, and when Prince Albert, Queen Victoria's consort, took to wearing a silk topper in public in London in 1843, it spelled the beginning of the end for beaver hats.[23]

American Fur Company founder John Jacob Astor.

Astor retired in 1833. Ramsay Crooks, who served as Astor's vice president, took over management of a reorganized American Fur Company. Nine years later, American Fur was bankrupt. The era of the beaver on the Great Lakes was over, two centuries after French voyageurs and missionaries opened the upper lake to commerce.

The American Fur Company's Fond du Lac post in 1827 commanded the rich fur trapping region north and west of Lake Superior.

THE FIRST
SHIPS APPEAR

W. H. Bartlett's 1842 steel engraving Working a Canoe Up a Rapid *shows the labor necessary to portage a Montreal canoe in the north country.*

THE EARLIEST TRAVEL by Europeans in the Lake Superior region was done in canoes. There is no doubt that the lake was preferred to the tortuous overland trails forged millennia earlier by native peoples. The explorers were interested in getting from one end of Lake Superior to the other, while the Anishinaabe traveled from winter homes to seasonal hunting grounds or to areas with specific resources like copper, fish, forest products, and wild rice. The needs of the two groups were distinctly different.

With the advent of the fur trade in the seventeenth century, French and British traders and voyageurs resorted more and more to ancient trails and portages for access to furs, but their principal routes east and west were still over the lake, still using birch bark canoes. Not surprisingly, the burgeoning transportation requirements of the trade brought larger vessels. Between 1770 and 1840, fur companies built no fewer than sixteen ships on Lake Superior, varying from 20 tons to 135 tons. While most of these vessels were the same two-masted schooners common on the Lower Great Lakes, there were also two barges, two single-masted sloops, and a square-rigged brig.

The first large vessel known to have been employed on Lake Superior was built at Pointe-aux-Pins (Pine Point) near Sault Ste. Marie, Michigan, in 1735 by Frenchman Denis de la Ronde. Yet this pioneer craft was not built for the fur trade at all. Described as a "decked vessel of 25 tons, carrying at least two sails," la Ronde's ship was intended to carry copper from mines he established at Ontonagon. It was about 100 years before its time.

Representing a syndicate of British mineral speculators, Alexander Baxter Jr. also built a barge and a 40-ton sloop at Pointe-aux-Pins in 1771–1772, but that venture failed when a copper mining venture at Ontonagon collapsed financially and a vein of silver at Pointe Mamainse petered out. Baxter sold the sloop in 1774. The time had not yet come to exploit the mineral resources of the remote region; indeed, it would be nearly seventy-five years before conditions were right to mine and ship the copper, silver, and iron ore profitably.[24]

The fur companies of the Lake Superior region began expanding operations before the eighteenth century was over. They had long been running ships on Lake Michigan between Detroit and Mackinaw, but goods were inefficiently transported from there to the Sault and Grand Portage by flat-bottomed bateaux.

To speed the process, the three-year-old North West Company built the 40-ton schooner *Athabasca* at Pointe-aux-Pins above the Sault in 1786. The fur company next built the larger sloop *Otter* in 1793, followed by the *Perseverance, Invincible,* and *Fur Trader* in 1802, the *Recovery* in 1809, and the *Mink* around 1811. The latter two or three were constructed at Fort William, Ontario. The older Hudson Bay Company seems to have persisted in using canoes and bateaux until years later.

Some of the old sailing craft were dismantled after 1830, and others were sent down the rapids at the Sault for service on the lower lakes. At least two were lost in the attempt.[25]

In the early 1830s, following the collapse of the European market for beaver pelts, fur companies turned to commercial fishing on Lake Superior, taking advantage of their existing infrastructure. Their posts at La Pointe, Grand Portage, Grand Marais, Fond du Lac, Isle Royale, and Michipicoten all proved to be productive fishing stations during the next years.

To serve the far-flung stations, the American Fur Company built the brig *John Jacob Astor* in 1835, named for the outfit's colorful head; rival Hudson Bay Company constructed the smaller *Whitefish* the following year. During 1837 American Fur Company added the new schooners *Madeline* and *William Brewster* (the former constructed at La Pointe), while Hudson Bay Company portaged the *Mary Elizabeth* around the rapids at the Sault to Lake Superior.

A financial panic engulfed the nation in 1837, and within four years the Lake Superior fishery collapsed almost as spontaneously as it had begun fewer than ten years before. During its brief zenith, the industry had nearly depleted the stocks of several fish species, and it would be decades before healthy stocks were restored. Meanwhile, other, more significant changes were coming to the Lake Superior basin that would change its character forever.[26]

Landscape of Superior, Wisconsin, *was sketched by artist Eastman Johnson from George Stuntz's trading post on Minnesota Point in 1857. The large building emitting smoke in the background is a sawmill run by Johnson's brother, Reuben, at the lumber yard at Detroit Pier. The steamer on the left is the* Lady Elgin, *which foundered with five hundred persons on board in 1860.*

CHAPTER TWO
The Locks and La Pointe

IN THE 1840S, traders of the American Fur Company's Northern Outfit at Fond du Lac, Minnesota, were as likely to meet geologists and surveyors on Lake Superior as other fur traders. As the fur trade on Lakes Superior and Huron waned, the young American republic and its constituent states were exploring the Great Lakes for their timber, mineral resources, and agricultural potential. Cities were already growing and bustling on the south shore of the most accessible of the Great Lakes. Moses Cleaveland's outpost on the shore of Lake Erie was developing into the metropolis that would later bear his misspelled name. The completion of the Erie Canal in 1825 connected Lakes Ontario, Erie, Huron, and Michigan with the Hudson Valley and made Buffalo, New York, on Lake Erie the first Great Lakes port.[27] Four years later, the Welland Canal would bypass Niagara Falls, providing a direct link between Lakes Erie and Ontario. By the early 1840s, entrepreneurs in Chicago on the south shore of Lake Michigan were discussing the feasibility of building a canal to link the lake with the Illinois River just miles to the west across the prairie and connecting Chicago to the Mississippi River system.[28]

Civilization in the form of cities, farms, and roads had been coming to the Great Lakes frontier since passage of the Northwest Ordinance in 1787 carved political jurisdictions out of the old Northwest Territory. Ohio, Indiana, and Illinois all had gained statehood before 1820. Michigan followed in 1837, and Wisconsin would be recognized in 1848. Settlers pushed into the new states from the south and east. Many came up the rivers in search of land, farms, and fortune. Many more arrived on the lower lakes by way of steamboats that began plying Lakes Ontario, Erie, Michigan, and Huron after 1825.

The Canadian-owned *Frontenac* had begun service on Lake Ontario in 1816, and the Buffalo-built *Walk-in-the-Water* had appeared on Lake Erie two years later. Emitting copious plumes of smoke from their wood-fired boilers, these primitive steamboats transported the first wave of immigrants and settlers to the developing ports studding the lower lakes.[29] Until the coming of the railroads in the 1840s and 1850s, Great Lakes steamboat traffic would be the primary method of reaching what was then referred to as the West.

THE FIRST MINING BOOM
Europeans had known of mineral riches in the country south and west of the upper lakes since the time of New France. The first French explorers had commented on the native copper amulets and knives worn by the Native Americans, who claimed that the red metal came from huge boulders on the shore of a freshwater lake far to the northwest of the valley of the St. Lawrence River. British investors had attempted to mine copper along the Ontonogan River, emptying into the south shore of Lake Superior, at the time of the American Revolution. And travelers traversing Lake Superior east and south of the Keweenaw Peninsula portage had long noted that their compasses spun erratically in the vicinity of the River of the Dead. It was lead that sparked the first mining boom in the Upper Midwest. French explorers as early as the 1690s had been aware that easily worked galena deposits were scattered on the surface east of the Mississippi River in what is today southwestern Wisconsin, northeastern Iowa, and northwestern Illinois.

When the United States negotiated the purchase of the Louisiana Territory from Napoleon in

1804, the lead mining region of the Upper Mississippi became American territory. The new republic was in desperate need of lead for munitions for its young army and state militias, and lead also was the basic ingredient of paint. The result was a mining boom that engulfed the lead district after 1825. Within four years, more than thirteen million pounds of refined lead were being produced from government-licensed lead smelters in the three-state region.

"THE INDIAN PROBLEM"

The rush to profit from Wisconsin's mineral resources revealed two problems that would have to be solved before the new nation could safely develop the mineral and timber resources of the Great Lakes hinterland. Policy-makers in Washington, D.C., had to come to terms with the Native American population of the region, which in the early nineteenth century was becoming impoverished by the gradual decline of the fur trade. And venture capitalists and politicians had to work together to reduce the crippling transportation costs that accompanied the shipment of bulk commodities back to the population centers in the East.

The lead mining boom had helped precipitate full-scale hostilities between Native Americans and the settlers of Wisconsin, Illinois, and Iowa in 1832. Bands of Sac and Fox, alarmed by the rush of settlers, took to the warpath under Black Hawk, an aging leader who had fought against the Americans in the War of 1812. Federal troops and Illinois militia put down the uprising with the help of Native American allies and relocated the hostiles west of the Mississippi River.[30]

The resettlement policy was a keystone of congressional efforts to deal with what was commonly called the "Indian problem" in the decades following the War of 1812. Although European Americans often possessed superior weaponry, their opponents were much more comfortable in the woods of eastern North America.

The weaponry that decided the fate of a continent was microscopic. Smallpox and measles killed far more Native Americans during the first two centuries of European colonization than muskets and cannon. "The main killers were Old World germs to which Indians had never been exposed, and against which they therefore had neither immune nor genetic resistance," explained Jared Diamond in his groundbreaking *Guns, Germs, and Steel.*[31] Smallpox raged through North America in the 1770s and 1780s, adding to the death toll of the Revolutionary War.[32] In 1837, the year that Michigan became a state, a smallpox epidemic swept through Mandan and Hidatsa villages on the Upper Missouri River; more than 90 percent of the population died that pestilent summer.[33]

THE TREATY OF LA POINTE

The federal resettlement program was designed to relocate Native Americans west of the Mississippi River and open the land between the Allegheny Mountains and the Mississippi River for American settlement. In the thirty years between 1815 and 1845, the federal government concluded more than thirty treaties with tribes east of the Mississippi.[34] For the future development of the Lake Superior country, two of the more important treaties came in 1837 and 1842.

The Anishinaabe of the Lake Superior hinterlands had been among the most accommodating tribes on the continent. They had been exposed to Europeans since voyageurs and missionaries arrived at the Falls of St. Mary (the Sault) in the 1600s, and the Anishinaabe had been willing participants in the fur trade for two centuries. Many Anishinaabe in the area had converted to Catholicism, and a not insignificant number had intermarried with French traders.

In the summer of 1854, the commissioner of Indian Affairs called all of the Anishinaabe bands of the Lake Superior and Mississippi River country to the small settlement of La Pointe on Madeline Island, Wisconsin. The largest of the Apostle Islands protecting Chequamegon Bay, Madeline had been a center for Anishinaabe commerce since the French arrived on Lake Superior two centuries earlier. Anishinaabe bands trickled into La Pointe in early and mid-September. For two weeks, they haggled among themselves and with the American commissioners. When the negotiations were completed on September 30, the

La Pointe on Madeline Island, Wisconsin, the great homeland of the Anishinaabe, or Ojibwe, people.

bands had signed the Treaty of La Pointe, ceding to the United States much of the land in Minnesota east of a line from International Falls to Hibbing and south to Mille Lacs Lake.[35] In return, the commissioners confirmed the earlier reservations established under the terms of the 1837 and 1842 treaties at Fond du Lac, Grand Portage, Nett Lake, Vermilion Lake, and Grand Fork River in the ceded territory.[36]

Included in the 1854 cession was the tiny village of Duluth, founded that summer at the base of the bluff that framed the far western end of Lake Superior. Superior City, Wisconsin, founded the year before, was laid out on land that had been ceded by the Anishinaabe in 1842. Between the two tiny settlements was the finest natural harbor on Lake Superior.

BOOM COPPER
The United States had a secondary but more compelling reason than halting Native American warfare in its desire to negotiate treaties with the Lake Superior and Mississippi bands of Anishinaabe. By the time of the second cession, in 1842, it was becoming apparent to politicians

in Washington, D.C., and Lansing, Michigan, that the barren south shore of Lake Superior was rich in mineral and timber resources.

When Michigan approached statehood in the mid-1830s, it wanted a strip of land along the western shores of Lake Erie included in state boundaries. The Toledo Strip contained what would become one of the busiest harbors on the Great Lakes, but Ohio laid competing claims to the strip. The Buckeye State had been a state for twenty years, and Ohio's delegation in Congress carried the issue. Although the move was unpopular in Michigan, Congress awarded the Toledo Strip to Ohio. In recompense, Michigan's new statehood boundaries would include most of what is today the Upper Peninsula.[37]

Michigan's governor, Stevens T. Mason, resolved to make the best of a bad situation. Shortly after Michigan achieved statehood, Mason appointed Douglass Houghton as the first state geologist. Houghton, a New York native, had accompanied Henry Rowe Schoolcraft to Lake Superior in 1830 as the Schoolcraft expedition's surgeon and had related his adventures in a series of popular lectures in Detroit. Houghton went north to Lake Superior in the summer of 1840 and found copper on Michigan's isolated Keweenaw Peninsula. He noted copper-bearing rock at Copper Harbor on the tip of the peninsula, and actual mass copper further inland and south. He reported his findings in early 1841 to Governor Mason and the legislature and returned in the summer of 1843 to begin surveying the rocky peninsula jutting northwest into the frigid lake.[38] News of Houghton's discoveries precipitated the first great land rush to Lake Superior.

By 1845, Boston and Pittsburgh investors had formed the Cliff Mining Company to mine for mass copper along the bluffs running up the Keweenaw Peninsula's spine.[39] By 1850, three mines—the Cliff, the Delaware, and the Minesota—were on their way to establishing Michigan's Keweenaw Peninsula as the preeminent copper-producing region of the nineteenth century. Ironically, Douglass Houghton never made a dollar from his 1840 discovery. Returning from a surveying trip on a stormy October evening in 1845, he and four companions attempted to beach their canoes at the mouth of the Eagle River, halfway down the Keweenaw Peninsula. Houghton and one of his companions drowned in attempting to make the perilous landfall.[40]

A SPINNING COMPASS

No sooner had the rush to the copper district begun than surveyors made the second great mineral discovery along the south shore of Lake Superior. In the fall of 1844, William Burt and a party of ten men were running transit lines for a survey near Teal Lake south of the mouth of the Carp River near present day Marquette, Michigan. Suddenly, the magnetic compass the crew was using to check their azimuth readings began spinning wildly. Burt, the inventor of a solar compass, compared the reading of the magnetic compass against his solar compass and immediately surmised that something was afoot. "Boys," he shouted to the surveyors, "look around and see what you can find."[41] A cursory inspection of the nearby ground revealed outcrops of iron ore jutting from beneath the spruce and tamarack trees. The crew gathered

specimens and that fall reported their find to state officials in Lansing.

Philo Everett, a merchant in downstate Jackson who had planned to invest in copper properties on the Keweenaw, heard of the iron discovery the following summer when he and his party disembarked at the Falls of St. Mary (the Sault) for the trip west across Lake Superior. They purchased a mackinaw boat from a local trader who told them he could find the iron deposits south of the Carp River. He couldn't, and the party continued on to Keweenaw Bay to carry out the original plan. Near L'Anse, they met Marji Gesick, an Anishinaabe chief, who said he could find the iron ore. Two members of Burt's party returned to the mouth of the Carp River with Marji Gesick, who promptly took them to the iron outcrops.[42] Everett filed on the claim, which lies in present-day Negaunee, and formed the Jackson Iron Company. The next year, he and his partners returned to the site, collected three hundred pounds of the iron, and packed it out to the Carp River and then east to the Sault. They engaged the services of a downstate smelter, who made the first bar of iron mined on Lake Superior from the sample.[43]

That same summer of 1846, the Cleveland Iron Mining Company was formed to mine an iron deposit west of the Jackson property near present-day Ishpeming, Michigan. A third company, the Marquette Iron Company, was formed by Massachusetts venture capitalists in 1848 to mine deposits located west of Ishpeming.

The first three mines on what was to become the Marquette Iron Range proved the existence of a fabulously rich ore body. But getting that iron to market kept all three properties unprofitable during the first ten years of the range's existence. In 1850, one producer shipped ore to Pittsburgh, where it was refined and commanded a price of $80 a ton. But shipping and handling costs came to more than $200 a ton.[44]

MR. HARVEY'S CANAL

It was perfectly obvious to everyone on the south shore of Lake Superior, and to the investment community in Michigan and out East, that

Sailing for the Chicago and Lake Superior Line, the wooden propeller Cuyahoga *passes through the original Soo lock, circa 1860.*

the Upper Peninsula would never realize its mineral potential until the bottleneck at the Sault was eliminated. The drop from Lake Superior to Lake Huron was twenty-one feet, but that twenty-one-foot drop was contained in a mile of white water at the Sault. The rapids were impassable for ships. The solution to eliminating the blockage was to build a canal and locks bypassing that mile of rapids. In actuality, the North West Company had built a small lock and canal at the Sault in 1797 to accommodate Montreal canoes and mackinaw boats passing through. But the canal and lock, as well as the fur trading post, had been destroyed by American troops in one of the last actions of the War of 1812.[45] By the 1840s, mackinaw boats, schooners, and a few small steamers plied the south shore between the Sault and the copper and iron districts. But those vessels had been laboriously portaged around the falls and were, in essence, captive to Lake Superior. In 1850, every bit of cargo, equipment, and supplies destined for Carp River, Copper Harbor, or Ontonogan had to be unloaded from one vessel at the lower falls, portaged a mile around the rapids, and then reloaded on a second vessel at the upper end of the cataract. Similarly,

every barrel of copper or bloom of iron underwent the same portage downbound.

Michigan's legislators and public officials had realized at statehood that a canal and locks at the Sault could open the potential for establishing a fisheries industry on Lake Superior. The Michigan legislature appropriated $25,000 for a feasibility study and in 1839 authorized the construction of a canal and locks. In 1840, Henry Clay of Kentucky ridiculed the measure in the U.S. Senate. A canal at the Sault, the "Great Compromiser" thundered, was "a work beyond the remotest settlement of the United States, if not the moon."[46]

Matters remained stalemated for more than a decade. In 1850, promoters built a short-line, horse-drawn railroad around the falls, which speeded the transfer of cargo but didn't eliminate the core problem. With the acceleration of copper and iron mining in the late 1840s and early 1850s, Michigan again put pressure on Congress to rectify the situation. With the sectional crisis between North and South over slavery beginning to build, and investment in far-off

Lake Superior increasingly coming from New York, Ohio, and Pennsylvania, support in Congress for a canal at the falls broadened. Copper and iron, after all, had military applications.

On August 26, 1852, President Millard B. Fillmore signed into law the bill authorizing construction of a canal and locks system at the Sault. The legislation established precedence for a federal-state share for improvements at the Sault that exists to this day. Instead of appropriating funds from the budget, the federal government transferred 750,000 acres of the Upper Peninsula that had been ceded to the United States by the 1842 treaty with the Lake Superior Anishinaabe. The land grant to Michigan, which was equal to 2 percent of the total land area of the state, was to be used to defray construction costs of a canal.[47]

The St. Mary's Falls Ship Canal Company proposed to dig a canal a mile long with two accompanying locks, each 350 feet in length and 70 feet wide. The bid price was slightly more than $400,000.[48] Named to head the project was twenty-four-year-old Charles T. Harvey, a Connecticut native who had landed by ship at the Sault in late 1852 as a salesman for the Fairbanks Scale Company of Vermont. Laid low by an attack of typhoid fever, Harvey had followed the 1853 debate in the Michigan legislature with keen interest. That spring, he persuaded his employers to submit a construction bid. Erastus Fairbanks and his brother already had interests in iron lands on the Marquette Range, and they persuaded New York manufacturer Erastus Corning and railroad builder John W. Brooks to join them in forming the Ship Canal Company.[49] Harvey was given unlimited authority to complete the project. He arrived at the Sault in June 1853 with a shipload of equipment and a $50,000 line of credit at a Detroit bank. Within a week, he had hired four hundred laborers to begin digging and blasting the canal around the falls.[50]

The Ship Canal Company had a two-year state deadline to complete the canal and locks. Construction continued year-round, even though temperatures at the falls dropped to thirty-five degrees below zero during the winter months.

Cholera struck the camp in the summer and early fall of 1854. By that time, Harvey had more than two thousand laborers on the payroll, and he organized burial parties to dispose of the bodies secretly at night to avoid panic in the camp.[51]

Costs escalated rapidly. Every bit of foodstuffs, tools, and supplies had to be shipped to the Sault from Detroit.

"EVERY STATE HAS BENEFITED"
The Fairbanks brothers and Corning watched the mounting costs with growing concern. In the summer of 1854, they dispatched Brooks to the Sault to take over superintendency of the actual construction. Harvey retained his title, but Brooks oversaw the project's completion.[52] On April 19, 1855, water began flowing down the canal from Lake Superior to Lake Huron. Two months later, on June 18, Captain Jack Wilson locked through upbound with the steamer *Illinois*.[53] Minutes later, the steamer *Baltimore* locked through going down.[54] On August 14, 1855, the brig *Columbia* passed through the locks downbound with a cargo of 132 tons of iron ore from the Marquette Range.[55]

When all accounts were settled, Harvey and Brooks had spent almost $1 million to build the canal and locks, more than double the original cost estimate.[56] But the investors became multimillionaires because much of the land they received in payment contained valuable iron and copper deposits. What they had accomplished was of inestimable value. The canal at what would become known as the Soo opened the vast mineral resources of Lake Superior to commercial development. Within half a century, the Soo was referred to as "the busiest mile on earth" because of the nonstop traffic through the locks.[57]

In 1905, Peter White, one of the Clevelanders who dominated the Lake Superior iron ore trade, traveled to the Soo with President Teddy Roosevelt to celebrate the fiftieth anniversary of the opening of the locks. White told the crowd that the "opening of the Sault Canal has been of the largest benefit to the whole U.S. of any single happening in its commercial or industrial history. Every state has benefited from it."[58]

A wooden freighter locks through sometime in the 1880s.

The 1905 celebration of the fiftieth anniversary of the opening of the Soo Lock attracted thousands of tourists, including President Theodore Roosevelt, and a parade of boats.

SAILS ON
THE HORIZON

Built in 1839 and portaged around the rapids of the St. Mary's River to Lake Superior, the schooner Algonquin *was the first vessel to trade at the head of the lakes. She was abandoned at Superior in 1865.*

EVERY APRIL DURING THE LATE 1840S and early 1850s, when the ice started breaking up on Lake Superior, miners in Michigan's Keweenaw copper towns and on the Marquette Iron Range began watching for the first ship of the season. Before the locks were opened at the Falls of St. Mary's River in 1855, the lake's residents depended on steamers and sailing vessels to replenish their essential supplies. Only the hardiest travelers attempted to reach the copper and iron districts via the few military and game trails south to Green Bay on Lake Michigan.

The steamboats and schooners that plied the lake in the decade before 1855 were captive to Lake Superior. Most had been laboriously portaged around the rapids at the Sault, which posed an impassible barrier to navigation.[59] The ships ferried supplies and passengers to the mines and returned with their decks weighted down by barrels of copper and iron.

The sight of sails or a wisp of smoke on the horizon was occasion for rejoicing along the lake at Copper Harbor, Eagle River, Ontonagon, and Carp River. The winters there were long and hard and unlike anything the miners had experienced in the East or in their native Cornwall, England. Blizzards frequently immobilized the diggings for days, and on the Keweenaw Peninsula it was not uncommon to register twenty feet of snow in a winter. Temperatures plunged to well below zero for weeks at a time. By March or April, the tiny settlements were often scraping the bottoms of the flour barrels. Ice on Wisconsin's Whitefish Bay or spring storms could delay resupply missions for up to a month.

For a few years after the collapse of the fur companies' commercial fishing ventures in the mid-1830s, no ships at all sailed on Lake Superior. Then in 1840, the Cleveland North Western Lake Company brought the 56-foot schooner *Algonquin* to Sault Ste. Marie and hauled it overland on rollers to launch it in the big lake and to inaugurate a whole new era of commerce. For the next several years, the inauspicious little ship bore the entire burden of the lake's commercial traffic.[60]

The copper boom on the Keweenaw Peninsula and reports of rich iron deposits in 1844 near the Carp River at present-day Marquette were all the incentive shipowners needed to begin sending other vessels to Lake Superior. In the summer of 1845, the schooners *Fur Trader, Merchant, Napoleon, Ocean, Siskiwit, Swallow,* and *Uncle Tom*

and the "propeller" *Independence* (a steam-powered vessel that used a screw propeller instead of paddle wheels) all made the laborious portage past the rapids into Lake Superior. Other vessels followed during the next several seasons as well.[61]

Some ships had remarkably short lives on the big lake. On June 12, 1847, the *Merchant* departed the Sault with seven passengers and seven crew, bound with supplies for Copper Harbor. The next night, a summer storm descended on the lake with gale-force winds from the northwest. The *Merchant* vanished, likely lost with all hands off Grand Island on the South Shore.[62] The propeller *Monticello*, brought to Lake Superior in 1847, was wrecked on Keweenaw Point in 1851, and the propeller *Independence* blew up at the Sault in 1853.

Copper and iron drew others to Lake Superior. Horace Greeley, editor of the *New York Weekly Tribune,* was actually referring to the copper districts when he exhorted his readers to "go west, young man." His urgings weren't entirely altruistic. Like many journalists in the mid-nineteenth century, Greeley was an active participant in some of the stories he covered. When he visited Lake Superior in the summer of 1847 and again in 1848, he wanted to acquaint his readers with the splendor of the Upper Great Lakes, but he also invested in a Keweenaw copper mine at Eagle Harbor.[63] Happily, Greeley's two trips were instrumental in forcing Washington, D.C., to revisit its opposition to locks and a canal at the Sault. The *Tribune* was a leading Whig journal and widely read in the halls of Congress. When Greeley wrote that "a large portion of our vast Internal Commerce is daily exposed to destruction and those employed in it to death for want of proper Harbors, Piers, Breakwaters, etc.," Congress was bound to listen.[64] His strong voice for federal improvements on the upper lakes bore fruit four years later when Congress passed an act to authorize construction of locks and a canal at the Sault.

Gilbert Munger's 1871 View of Duluth from the Heights *shows the impact the Minnesota Ship Canal was having on the Zenith City.*

CHAPTER THREE

Steel Rails to the Head of the Lakes

THE OPENING OF THE SAULT (St. Mary's Falls) ship canal in the summer of 1855 had an immediate and salutary effect on commerce from the Lake Superior mining districts.

Costs of transporting cargo dropped rapidly. In 1855, mine operators on the Marquette Range paid $3 a ton to get their ore from the mines just twelve miles to the mouth of Carp River at present-day Marquette and aboard vessels bound for the Sault. It cost another $5 a ton to get the ore from Lake Superior to the Lake Erie receiving ports.[65] Only 1,449 tons of Marquette Range ore went down the Great Lakes the first season the locks were opened. Three years later, in 1858, more than 31,000 tons of Marquette ore were locked through downbound. By then, the cost of getting the ore from the mines in Negaunee to the docks in Marquette was only 87 cents a ton, and shipping the ore from Marquette cost only $2.09 a ton to Lake Erie, 40 percent of the cost in 1855.[66]

The opening of the locks at the Sault—called "the Soo" by area residents—brought competition to Lake Superior. Shipowners who had hesitated to confine their vessels above the St. Mary's rapids before 1855 now gladly dispatched whole fleets to compete for the ore trade on Lake Superior. The locks also alleviated the isolation that many settlers in the mining districts had felt in the 1840s and early 1850s. With the introduction of regular service from Ontonagon, Copper Harbor, Eagle Harbor, and Marquette to Detroit, Cleveland, Buffalo, and Chicago, residents of the Lake Superior country could look forward to mail, supplies, and a connection with the outside world.

A SUPERIOR HARBOR

The 1855 completion of the locks did not

obscure the fact that Lake Superior was a great lake with a rockbound shore. Few natural harbors where vessels could tie up to load and off-load cargo existed along the lakeshore. Copper Harbor required nerves of steel to enter or leave in high wind. Marquette faced the open lake. Ontonagon suffered from persistent shoaling. Perhaps the finest natural harbor occurred at the western end of the lake. Thomas L. McKenney, who

An ad placed by the Cleveland, Detroit, and Lake Superior Line in the Cleveland Daily Forest City Democrat *boasts its many stops on Lake Superior during its 1857 sailings between Cleveland and the head of the lakes.*

Marquette's first gravity ore dock, viewed from Ripley's Rock, was built in 1859.

accompanied Michigan territorial governor Lewis Cass on a trip to the American Fur Company post at Fond du Lac, Minnesota, in 1826, described his reaction at first sighting the harbor.

"When within about 10 miles of the end of the lake," he wrote, "we noticed a line stretching from shore to shore, the north and south shores being about 10 miles distant, that seemed like a narrow shadow—not very well defined. As we approached nearer, it became more substantial, and when four miles off, it was a well-defined beach with trees, pine and aspen, scattered infrequently over it from one end to the other, and this was the *Fond,* or bottom—or, more properly, Head of Lake Superior. The River St. Louis enters it through this beach, which is of sand, and which is from thirty to two hundred yards wide, and diagonally—the mouth of the river being not more than two hundred yards wide."[67]

What McKenney was describing would become known to generations of residents of the Twin Ports of Duluth and Superior as the Superior entry. Deep and sandy-bottomed, the mouth of the St. Louis spilled billions of gallons of tea-colored water and sediment into the lake each year. But in swinging east from the enclosed bay, the river scoured a channel between the narrow shadow spied by McKenney and the actual shoreline. That sand beach fronting the lake, built up over many millennia, is now known as Park Point, or, to mapmakers, Minnesota Point. It protected the river channel from the wind and waves of Lake Superior and created one of the finest natural harbors on the entire Great Lakes.

In its natural state, the harbor was far from perfect. The St. Louis River had a tendency to wander as much as half a mile from its channel. The mouth was prone to shoaling, and the channel was shallow, rarely more than eight feet deep. Islands of matted vegetation floated in the bay. But it was sand and it was protected, something few other natural harbors on Lake Superior could boast. And once the new locks and canal were completed at the Soo, that fact alone made the head of the lakes a potential spot for development.

When development came, it was tied up with land speculation. George R. Stuntz is accorded the honor of being the first settler of the modern era in what is now Duluth-Superior. A surveyor with the Iowa, Wisconsin, and Minnesota district of the federal government's survey force, Stuntz was dispatched north from Davenport, Iowa, in the spring of 1852 to draw the boundary between Minnesota and Wisconsin at the head of the lakes. Stuntz liked what he saw and returned for good the next year.

"I saw as surely then as I do now," he wrote in 1892, "that this was the heart of the continent commercially, and so I drove my stakes."[68]

Investors in far-off New York and Washington, D.C., were studying maps of the Lake Superior region and noting that the head of the lakes was a mere 150 miles from the Minnesota territorial capital of St. Paul. With the completion of the canal and locks at the Soo expected in 1855, and with the fine natural harbor at the mouth of the St. Louis River, the head of the lakes looked to be an ideal place to plat a town that would perhaps serve as the terminus of a rail system that could tap the growing grain commerce of Minnesota Territory.

In 1853, Henry M. Rice, one of the dominant figures of Minnesota politics in the 1850s, put together a consortium of investors to found a town site on the Wisconsin side of the harbor. Rice, who had made a fortune in the fur trade on the Upper Mississippi, had friends in high places. His investment syndicate included Senator John Breckenridge of Kentucky, Senator Stephen A. Douglas of Illinois, and William Wilson Corcoran, a prominent banker in the nation's capital.[69] Douglas introduced a bill in the U.S. Senate that called for the construction of a railroad from the proposed town site of Superior to St. Paul and then south to Dubuque on the Upper Mississippi River, but the legislation's estimated $50 million price tag effectively killed the proposal.

The settlers quickly set about securing land claims on the Wisconsin side of the boundary, and entrepreneurs established supply stores and primitive sawmills on the site. The steamer *Napoleon* was a frequent visitor from the Soo and the copper district farther east, and the tiny settlement at the head of the lakes grew through 1854. By the end of the year, the population had swelled to six hundred people. In the early summer of 1855, a small steam sawmill on the banks of the Nemadji River was busily producing sawtimber for the expected housing boom at the town site.[70]

Meanwhile, the signing of the Treaty of La Pointe in 1854 sparked a similar land boom across the harbor on the Minnesota side. The Reverend Edmund F. Ely, one of the first Protestant missionaries to Lake Superior, purchased a land claim in what is now West Duluth and moved his family to a group of lots that was quickly incorporated as the Oneota town site.[71] Samuel Wheeler of St. Paul established a sawmill at Oneota in 1855, and about twenty people were living on the West Duluth hillside by the end of the year.[72] Among Ely's neighbors were Lewis Merritt and his son, Napoleon. In 1856, the Merritts returned to their hometown of Ashtabula, Ohio, for the rest of the family. In late October, Hephzibah Merritt, five of her seven sons, and assorted daughters-in-law and grandchildren stepped ashore at Superior.

"I wish you could have seen how beautiful the Head of the Lakes looked at that time," nine-year-old Alfred Merritt recalled later in life. "It was practically in a state of nature."[73]

Settlers began spreading up Lake Superior's North Shore from Oneota in 1855 and 1856. By the end of the decade, eleven town sites had been platted on the Minnesota side of the lake. Perhaps two thousand people were living in Superior and the Minnesota town sites when the ice retreated from western Lake Superior in the spring of 1857.

THE PANIC OF 1857

In the twentieth century, it became fashionable to refer to upheavals in the American economy as recessions or depressions. People in the nineteenth century didn't have that semantic luxury. Economic dislocations a century-and-a-half ago

By the spring of 1871, work was nearing completion on the breakwater extending into Lake Superior from Fourth Avenue East in Duluth. Here, a scow schooner is alongside as a brigantine departs, and the passenger steamer Meteor *ties up. Elevator A is under construction at left.*

were referred to as panics. It was an apt word. People panicked when they no longer had faith that the currency, stocks, or bonds in their possession were worth their face value.[74] Wall Street would be rocked by three major panics in the last half of the nineteenth century—in 1857, 1873, and 1893—and a fourth in 1907. Each of the nineteenth-century panics had a negative effect on the commercial developments at the head of the lakes.

As residents at Superior awaited the first steamers of the 1857 navigation season, the panic sped unchecked through the American economy. Grain companies and flour mills, banks and insurance companies, even the giant Illinois Central Railroad failed. Farmers couldn't get paid for their crops. Factories closed. The panic decimated the Great Lakes shipping industry. Much of the cargo in 1857 consisted of passenger traffic plying the lakes between Buffalo, Cleveland, Toledo, Chicago, and Milwaukee. Immigration dropped drastically in the summer of that year and didn't pick up again until after the Civil War. Most of the lower lakes passenger and package freight fleets laid up early in the fall of 1857 rather than run until nearly Christmas, as had been the rule in the past. Eight of the largest steamboats on the lakes, including the newly built *City of Buffalo* and *Crescent City,* were either

withdrawn from the lakes or dismantled.[75] The *City of Superior,* the head of the lakes' first namesake, came down the launch ways in Cleveland in July 1857. The steamer was dashed to pieces on the rocks at Copper Harbor in a November storm, sparing her owners the cost of dismantling her.[76]

The panic of 1857 had been a cruel blow to the residents of the head of the lakes. It would take a decade for Duluth and Superior to recover, and their rebirth would be predicated on the existence of the natural harbor shared by the two communities.

THE LAKE SUPERIOR & MISSISSIPPI RAILROAD

The seeds of economic recovery were planted in 1857, the panic year. Minnesota was approaching statehood and was already on its way to becoming the nation's granary. Settlers had pushed up the Mississippi and Minnesota River valleys. Irish, German, and Scandinavian immigrants had populated much of the southern third of the territory with farms and small towns.[77]

In the 1850s, spring wheat had become a staple crop in a fertile crescent stretching from the Minnesota River valley south to the Iowa border and back northeast again across Wisconsin to Lake Michigan.[78] For Minnesota farmers, the transportation lifeline for their crop was the Upper Mississippi River south to St. Louis and New Orleans.

Minnesotans had long dreamed of tying the sprawling territory together with steel rails. An 1857 federal land grant sent the territorial legislature into a frenzy of planning for a network of railroads across the soon-to-be-state. That same year, the legislature approved land grants and a $5 million bond issue to finance no fewer than five railroads in Minnesota. Each would have its terminus in the capital of St. Paul.[79]

None of the proposed railroads would run north from St. Paul to Lake Superior. The territory's timing was atrocious, and the panic of 1857 ensured that the territory or the proposed railroads would not be able to raise the investment capital needed to finance construction.[80] Four of the railroads did begin construction work in 1858, but the new state—which joined the union that year—was able to raise less than half of the originally proposed bond issue. Late

An 1870 map shows the route of the Lake Superior & Mississippi Railroad into Duluth. Note the breakwater, center, and Superior Entry, lower right.

in 1859, Governor Henry Hastings Sibley reported to the legislature that the ambitious railroad construction project was a bust; only 239 miles had been even graded to that date, and the amount of track laid was minimal.[81]

Sibley's successor as governor, Alexander Ramsey, proposed a rescue plan that would reward the railroads for construction of trackage. Ramsey, a Pennsylvanian who had been Minnesota's first territorial governor in 1849,

A Great Lakes barkentine loads cargo at the Lake Superior & Mississippi Railroad freight wharf in the summer of 1872.

AN 1867 PREDICTION

In 1857, the federal government appropriated $15,000 for the construction of a small, red brick lighthouse on Minnesota Point at the natural entry to the Duluth-Superior harbor.[83] The appropriation called for equipping the light-house with state-of-the-art, French-made Bardou lenses.[84] Four years later, William H. Hearding of the U.S. Topographical Corps locked through the Soo on the iron side-wheeler *Search,* and spent ten weeks during the summer and fall of 1861 charting the Duluth-Superior harbor from the natural entry twenty miles upriver to Fond du Lac.[85] Hearding's survey, undertaken during the first bleak summer of the Civil War, reflected the federal government's increased interest in the Union's ports and harbors. Six years later, Congress backed up the interest with money. An appropriation of $28,691.02 funded the start of what would be eight years of harbor improvements, including the construction of two wooden, rock-filled crib piers across the Superior entry bar and stabilizing the riverbanks with rock and gravel. In 1873, the renamed U.S. Army Corps of Engineers awarded the first contract for dredging in the harbor.[86]

Philadelphia financier Jay Cooke helped underwrite the Union during the Civil War. His ambitious postwar rail expansion west of the head of the lakes spurred rapid settlement of the Twin Ports in the late 1860s and early 1870s.

also proposed that a fifth railroad be built, this one from St. Paul to the settlements clinging to the hillside above Lake Superior. Ramsey's 1861 message to the legislature pointed out that the proposed Lake Superior & Mississippi Railroad would provide the new state and its citizens a trade outlet to the east. Even more important, Ramsey noted, was the fact that the impending Civil War might well sever Minnesota's trade lifeline to the Lower Mississippi River.[82]

The Minnesota legislature accepted Ramsey's 1861 recommendation and chartered the Lake Superior & Mississippi. But the onset of the Civil War that spring, and Minnesota's aggressive participation in all theaters of the conflict, put railroad development plans on the back burner. Control of an uprising by Sioux Indians in western Minnesota during 1862 consumed much of the state's resources for more than a year, and it wasn't until 1864 that interest revived in a rail link to Lake Superior. By that time, the first improvements to the harbor had been made.

In the first annual report to Colonel J. B. Wheeler of the corps' Chicago district, Henry Bacon, assistant civilian army engineer, foresaw the bright possibilities of the natural harbor at the western end of Lake Superior. "As a depot for forwarding and reception of wheat from places of production," Bacon wrote in the summer of 1867, "the bay of Superior may eventually be one of the greatest in the world."[87]

MR. COOKE'S RAILROAD

At the time Bacon penned his prescient statement, construction on the Lake Superior & Mississippi Railroad was already under way. In 1863, William L. Banning, a prominent St. Paul banker, resurrected the railroad concept. He persuaded the city of St. Paul to raise $250,000 in a bond issue to construct a southern terminus for the railroad and sent lobbyists to Congress to push for a specific land grant for the railroad. On May 5, 1864, as Generals Ulysses S. Grant and Robert E. Lee slugged it out in the Battle of the Wilderness in northern Virginia,

Congress appropriated five alternate sections of land to Minnesota on each side of the proposed 150-mile right-of-way from St. Paul to Lake Superior.[88] The land grant eventually came to more than 1.5 million acres.[89]

With the land grant in hand, Banning wrote to eastern investors to line up financing for the railroad. One of his correspondents, Jay Cooke of Philadelphia, politely declined the opportunity to invest. But the next year, Cooke acquired an interest in a substantial acreage of pinelands in northern Minnesota. In 1868, he decided to visit his holdings.[90] At the time, Cooke was a legend in national financial circles. He was considered the nation's first investment banker, and had founded Jay Cooke and Company in 1861 after working for other Philadelphia banks for much of the 1850s. He had almost single-handedly financed the Civil War for the Union side, selling more than $360 million in war bonds from 1861 to 1865.[91]

With the end of the war, Cooke cast about for new investment venues. Railroads were an obvious choice. The war had proved the ability of rail networks to move huge volumes of cargo and troops, and the federal government was actively promoting transcontinental railroads to tie together the reunited nation. Nor was Cooke a stranger to the Great Lakes. He had been born and raised near Sandusky, Ohio, on the south shore of Lake Erie, and he had purchased nearby Gibraltar Island as a summer retreat in 1864.[92]

That fall, Jay Cooke and Company and another Philadelphia investment banking house, E. W. Clarke and Company, bought into the Lake Superior & Mississippi.[93] Banning remained president of the railroad, but Philadelphia associates of Cooke were brought aboard as executives and directors. By 1869, Jay Cooke and Company had sold more than $2.5 million of the railroad's bonds.

On his inspection tour, Cooke initially had thought that Superior was the more likely terminus for the proposed rail venture. The Wisconsin city had ample acreage along the flat bottomlands of the St. Louis and Nemadji Rivers fronting the harbor. But since Minnesota was administering the federal land grant for construction of the Lake Superior & Mississippi, the northern terminus was a quid pro quo.

A view of Lake Avenue in 1873 from the Duluth hillside. The most visible alteration to the landscape is the addition of the Duluth Ship Canal at far left.

Workers dig foundations for the Lake Superior & Mississippi Railroad's wharf on Lake Superior in the summer of 1870. In the background is the People's Line propeller Norman, *which provided scheduled service between Chicago and Duluth.*

The route north was to be through Minnesota, and the northern terminus was to be Duluth.[94]

The news that Jay Cooke, the Philadelphia financier, was backing the railroad sent an electric jolt through Duluth. When Cooke had visited in June 1868, only fourteen families were living on Minnesota Point and the adjacent hillside. Thomas P. Foster, editor of the *Duluth Minnesotian,* saw clearly what Cooke's participation in the railroad venture foretold. Duluth, Foster said, would become "the Zenith City of the unsalted seas."

Overnight, Duluth turned into a boomtown, reminding pioneer settlers like the Elys, Merritts, and George Stuntz of the heady days of 1856. The city's population swelled to an estimated thirty-five hundred by the time Fourth of July celebrations rolled around in 1869. Most of the new arrivals were immigrants, Swedes and Norwegians booking passage on lake steamers from

Buffalo or Detroit. Newcomers slept in tents and waded in ankle-deep mud along what is now Superior Street. The old-timers called the new arrivals "69ers" for the year of their appearance. All around the town was tangible proof of the promise that Foster had described the year before. Clapboard buildings were springing up everywhere, although not a few of the hastily erected wooden structures catered to the baser instincts of the town's citizens.

"The lifeless corpse of Duluth, touched by the wand of Jay Cooke, now sprang full-armed from the tomb," said one 69er.[95]

Every day that summer and fall of 1869 and into the following spring and summer, word filtered back to Duluth about the progress of the rail construction crews working south from Duluth and north from St. Paul. By June 1870, the tracks of the Lake Superior & Mississippi were at

Shipping lines quickly saw the appeal of rail connections to the Upper Great Lakes, as this 1870 advertisement in the Detroit Daily Advertiser *demonstrates. Legendary captain Thomas Wilson of the* Meteor *was a mentor for Alexander McDougall.*

Thomson on the St. Louis River, fifteen miles distant. Crews frantically worked for the next six weeks to build timber bridges to cross the difficult rocky valley of the St. Louis and bring the long awaited railroad to the Zenith City.

Just before midnight on August 1, 1870, Engine No. 3 of the Lake Superior & Mississippi Railroad tooted its whistle and headed down the grade into Duluth. The first train consisted of a baggage car, two passenger cars, and two freight cars.[96]

There was general rejoicing in Duluth, but a more muted response in Superior, which had lost its bid to be the northern terminus. Yet nobody could deny that the coming of the railroad heralded a bright future for both cities.[97] Railroad president William Banning came up on a special train three weeks later to inaugurate the formal opening of the line, and Duluth was receiving daily service by the fall of 1870.[98] Trevanion Hugo, who would be a popular Duluth mayor at the turn of the century, described the cacophony of the railroad whistle and the more familiar steamboat whistle that summer of 1870 as "a Wagnerian chant of commercial triumph."[99] That it was. The Lake Superior & Mississippi provided the missing element that would make the Twin Ports actual twin ports. Rail service from the Mississippi River to Lake Superior was one of the best investments the state of Minnesota ever made. It opened new trade routes to the east for Minnesota's farmers and ensured the dominance of Minneapolis as a grain milling center.

Jay Cooke never looked back east. His eyes were firmly fixed on the western horizon. He dreamed big dreams, and Duluth was part and parcel of those dreams.

The scow schooner Chaska, *docked at Oneota circa 1870 or 1871, was the first ship built at the head of the lakes in 1869.*

DIGGING THE
DULUTH SHIP CANAL

The dredge Ishpeming, *used to dig the Duluth Ship Canal in 1871, at a dock in Duluth alongside the steam yacht* Frank C. Fero.

IN THE 150-YEAR EXISTENCE of the Duluth-Superior harbor, no event has been so mythical as the 1871 digging of the Duluth Ship Canal. It's a fanciful tale: Duluth residents, desiring an entry on the Minnesota side of the harbor, began to dig a channel from St. Louis Bay into Lake Superior. Superior residents, alarmed that the digging would alter the course of the St. Louis River on the harbor's Wisconsin side, sought an injunction to stop them. But just as the process server arrived, the Duluthians unleashed the trickle that became the Duluth Ship Canal.

In reality, the ship canal had been studied for years before digging began. Minnesota had in 1857 chartered the Minnesota Point Ship Canal Company to dig a channel from St. Louis Bay to the lake. But the proposal fell victim to the panic of 1857.[100] An 1861 harbor survey for the U.S. Topographical Corps subsequently revealed that the natural entry was less than ideal. The river channel meandered anywhere from 50 to 600 feet wide and from 5 to 15 feet deep.[101]

When the Lake Superior & Mississippi Railroad reached Duluth in August 1870, it solved the problem of getting cargo from the rail terminus to ships by building a breakwater from the foot of Fourth Avenue East. By October, wheat from its new Elevator A was shipped down the lake on the *R. G. Coburn*.[102] But the solution was temporary.[103] LS&MR financier Jay Cooke thus formed the Minnesota Canal and Harbor Improvement Company "to construct a ship canal ... through Minnesota Point."[104] The Army Corps of Engineers had refused in 1869 to fund a second canal, but the LS&MR was willing to bear the cost.[105] In the summer of 1870 the *Ishpeming* began dredging a channel 150 feet wide and 16 feet deep.[106] The site selected was Little Portage, supposedly used by Daniel Greysolon nearly two centuries before, and located 200 feet south of Howard's Dock.[107]

No two Duluth histories agree on when the canal was completed. What is known is that Superior requested an injunction against further dredging.[108] In September 1870, Wisconsin governor Cadwallader C. Washburn asked the corps to stop dredging. In March 1871, chief of engineers A. A. Humphreys wrote D. C. Houston, who oversaw harbor improvements, to alert him if digging resumed.[109] (Humphreys copied his letter to Washburn.[110]) Dredging did resume April 24, Houston said, breaching the point into the lake April 30.[111] In fact, he said, a steamer had passed that day through the canal.[112]

On April 24, Cushman K. Davis, U.S. attorney for Minnesota and Wisconsin, filed suit to halt

the dredging; a process was served on Duluth May 4. Judge R. R. Nelson of the U.S. District Court in St. Paul remanded the case to a colleague in Topeka, Kansas, on May 24.[113] Davis and Wisconsin attorney general S. S. Barlow represented the plaintiffs; Minnesota attorney general F. R. E. Cornell and Duluth city attorney James J. Egan argued the case for Duluth.

The judge issued a temporary injunction June 13, but wrote that if the canal "can in any other manner be completed without injury to the government works," he would dissolve the order.[114] An officer from nearby Fort Leavenworth traveled to Duluth to serve the injunction.[115] As the story goes, Duluth mayor Joshua Culver, banker George B. Sargent, and canal construction supervisor R. S. Munger marshaled volunteers to help finish digging before the injunction arrived Monday morning.[116] By then, however, the cut had been made and the tug *Frank C. Fero* had passed through the channel.

Yet Judge J. D. Ensign and Duluth historian Walter Van Brunt agree that the first cut was achieved April 30. Egan wrote to Humphreys in early June that the canal was already 50 feet wide and 8 feet deep and protected by 75 feet of rock and timber crib on the north side.[117] In actuality, Egan had left Topeka for St. Paul to work a compromise with attorneys for Duluth railroads, then took an offer to the U.S. War Department stating that Duluth was prepared to put up a $100,000 bond to complete a dike from Rice's Point to Minnesota Point.[118] Built at the insistence of Humphreys in 1871–1872, it "soon proved in every other way an absolute debacle."[119] But the two openings increased tidal flow and reversible currents, and the river's scouring action deepened the Superior entry to 12 feet by 1873, something the corps had not been able to accomplish.[120] A hole was blasted through the dike in 1873 and the last of the barrier removed in 1896.[121] By August, the canal was 150 feet wide and 16 feet deep. The steamer *Norman* became the first commercial vessel to use the new entry.[122]

With a 1,500-ton capacity, the D. M. Wilson, *built in 1873, was typical of the first generation of bulk freighters on the Great Lakes.*

CHAPTER FOUR

Wheat to Feed the World

FOR FARMERS IN THE RICH bottomlands of the Mississippi and Minnesota River valleys, completion of the Lake Superior & Mississippi Railroad to Duluth was a godsend. Within weeks of the first train to the head of the lakes, the price of shipping wheat to market plummeted. When William Banning, the St. Paul banker who had helped secure the state charter for the LS&MR, visited Duluth on August 22, 1870, his special train included two boxcars loaded with ten thousand bushels of southern Minnesota wheat. The golden grain was loaded aboard the steamer *Winslow* of the Lake Superior Transit Company, even though the port's first grain elevator was still weeks away from completion.[123] The railroad's completion to Duluth-Superior also sparked the first attempt by other Upper Midwest railroads to quash the competitive advantages offered by the new port. The LS&MR charged farmers 11 cents a bushel to ship their wheat to Duluth from southern Minnesota. All-rail rates from Minnesota to Chicago had been 24 cents at the beginning of the summer, although for many southern Minnesota wheat growers, the all-rail route to Chicago and the lower Midwest was still preferable to shipping wheat north to Lake Superior.[124] Directors of the Milwaukee & St. Paul Railroad vowed to meet and beat the prices of their northern competitors.

Minnesota was wheat country in 1870. In 1858, the year of its statehood, Minnesota had imported grain. Twelve years later, the state was exporting nearly seventeen million bushels of wheat and ranked fifth in the United States in wheat production.

Jay Cooke and his managers tried to break the Milwaukee & St. Paul Railroad's iron grip on southern Minnesota. In the summer of 1871, the Duluth-based railroad leased a steamer and a fleet of barges on the Mississippi River to haul grain to its terminus in St. Paul. The river operation was abandoned after one season because it simply added to the cost of the grain movement northward.[125]

THE NORTHERN PACIFIC

By the fall of 1871, Cooke was deeply involved in another railroad venture. The Northern Pacific Railway embodied his hopes of tying together his Minnesota termini at St. Paul and Duluth with the Pacific Ocean. The land grants received by the LS&MR would be dwarfed by the federal land grants available to any railroad entrepreneur who could push steel rails across the northern tier of states from the Great Lakes to the Pacific Northwest. Congress had appropriated funds in 1853 to ascertain the best route from the Mississippi River to the Pacific Ocean.[126] In 1864, Maine and Vermont railroad interests secured congressional passage of "a bill granting lands to aid in the construction of a railroad and telegraph line from Lake Superior to Puget Sound, on the Pacific coast, by the northern route" across Dakota Territory, Montana Territory, Idaho Territory, and Washington Territory.[127]

Cooke was not part of the original consortium to build the Northern Pacific Railway, but the investors selected his Philadelphia investment banking firm in 1868 to handle the $100 million in bonds estimated necessary to complete the line. His involvement with the LS&MR made his firm a natural choice to handle the financing, and by February 1870, when crews began building the line westward across Minnesota from an LS&MR junction near Carlton, Cooke was the effective general manager of the Northern Pacific Railway.[128]

Construction proceeded rapidly. By the end of 1871, Cooke's crews had reached the Red River at Moorhead, Minnesota. As crews stayed behind to bridge the Red, other crews pushed west, reaching Jamestown in Dakota Territory by the end of 1872. By the next June, the trackage stretched from Duluth to Bismarck, Dakota Territory, on the east bank of the Missouri River, some 450 miles in total.[129]

Railroad historian Albro Martin notes that Cooke's selection of Duluth rather than St. Paul for the eastern terminus of the Northern Pacific was a strategic mistake. "Duluth, on the westernmost reaches of Lake Superior, had been Cooke's choice of the N. P.'s eastern terminus, having as he did the outdated concept of the railroad as a means of connecting navigable bodies of water," Martin wrote in *Railroads Triumphant*.[130] But Cooke saw in Duluth the fulcrum for the perpetuation of his postwar fortune. At the time he committed to the construction of the Lake Superior & Mississippi Railroad, he had put

A shroud of ice covers the wood and iron lighthouse at the end of the outer breakwater, circa early 1870s.

together a syndicate of investors in Philadelphia and London to buy more than seventy thousand acres of land in Duluth and surrounding St. Louis County. The Western Land Association was predicated on the idea that Duluth would become a second Chicago, sending forth a flood of golden grain from the Minnesota and Dakota Territory hinterlands.[131] There also is evidence that Cooke was aware of the potential of iron ore in the low range of hills north of the city, news that was likely conveyed to the Philadelphia banker by veterans of the Vermilion Lake gold rush of 1864.

In September 1873, Jay Cooke and Company became the most noted victim of the prevailing financial panic. Banks and railroads in the United States and Europe tumbled into insolvency as investors fled railroad stocks. Construction halted on the Northern Pacific as Cooke's investments in Minnesota and the Dakota Territory were suddenly worthless.[132] For Duluth, the collapse of Cooke's empire was nearly as catastrophic as the panic of 1857. The city rapidly defaulted on more than $50,000 in bonds and gave up its charter, reverting to village status. More than half of the city's 1873 population of 5,000 left during the next two years. Many of the remaining 2,500 people eked out a living in the mid-1870s in commercial fishing.[133]

The final blow of the panic of 1873 came the following year when the state of Wisconsin again sued to remove the dike across the harbor and plug the Duluth Ship Canal.[134] It had appeared the previous year that the litigation of the Duluth canal had been put to rest. The Northern Pacific had agreed to build a branch line from Duluth to Ashland, Wisconsin, through Superior, and Wisconsin had agreed to drop any further claims against the new canal. More important, the agreement had paved the way for Congress to appropriate $100,000 for improvements to the harbor during the 1874 and 1875 construction seasons.[135] That tacit recognition by Congress of the fait accompli presented by the Duluth Ship Canal was key to the final settlement of the litigation with Wisconsin. When the case finally came before the U.S. Supreme Court in 1877, the justices

Two of Duluth's younger residents tie up a skiff on a summer day in the early 1870s.

fixed on one minor component of Duluth's defense. The Minnesota city claimed that the case was moot because the federal government had taken responsibility for the harbor with its 1873 appropriation. The justices agreed.

NEW MARKETS

Veterans of the panics of 1857 and 1873 could have been forgiven for believing that Duluth and Superior were jinxed towns. But long-term trends set into motion by the spate of rail construction in Minnesota and Dakota Territory in the early 1870s were about to effect a spectacular change in fortune at the head of the lakes. The Northern Pacific and St. Paul & Pacific Railroads had never stopped operating following the 1873 panic, and, in fact, both were profitable. The 1864 Homestead Act attracted thousands of immigrants to the unsettled river valleys of northwestern Minnesota and Dakota Territory. Bisecting the two political jurisdictions was the Red River Valley, perhaps the most fertile farmland on the

North American continent. Flowing north to Lake Winnipeg, the Red River drained a forty-mile-wide strip of rich glacial till that was awaiting the plow.

The coming of the railroads created a land boom in the Red River Valley and adjacent counties of Dakota Territory. An estimated 16,000 people were living in what is today eastern North Dakota in 1878. By 1890, the population of the new state was 190,000.[136] By the late 1870s, "bonanza farms" financed by eastern capital and worked by Scandinavian immigrants dotted the length and breadth of the Red River Valley.[137] The climate of the valley was conducive to raising hard red spring wheat. Planted in the spring and harvested in the fall, spring wheat required new milling methods to gain widespread acceptance on consumers' tables. Most Americans of the late nineteenth century were used to eating bread baked from flour milled from winter wheat, which was planted in the

Midwest and on the southern Great Plains. Winter wheat had a soft shell, and the bran separated easily from the wheat kernel, milling into a fine white flour.[138]

Following fires and explosions at their mills in Minneapolis in the late 1870s, both Cadwallader Washburn and Charles A. Pillsbury built new, state-of-the-art mills in Minneapolis.[139] Both mills were equipped with the latest in European inventions that included ceramic, porcelain, or chilled steel rollers instead of millstones. In a decade's time, flour production in the Mill City zoomed from 850,000 barrels in 1875 to more than 5 million barrels in 1885.[140]

For Duluth, the demographic and technological trends of the late 1870s and early 1880s proved to be a reprieve from the economic troubles of the early 1870s. The best spring wheat grew along the main line of the Northern Pacific Railway, and much of that wheat flowed back

east to Duluth. From 1876 to 1880, the Northern Pacific shipped a yearly average of 1.7 million bushels of spring wheat to the head of the lakes. The average jumped to 9.2 million bushels annually from 1881 to 1885.[141]

"THE CHEAPEST ELEVATORS EVER BUILT"

The opening of the wheat lands in the Red River Valley and the eastern part of Dakota Territory gave Duluth new opportunities for its commerce. No longer was the harbor held hostage to predatory rail rates in southern Minnesota. The bounty of the wheat harvest in the newly opened farmland to the west of the head of the lakes ensured that a solid percentage of that grain would go through Duluth, and later Superior, and thence down the Great Lakes.

In the 1880s, the bulk of the wheat passing through Duluth and Superior was destined for transshipment down the Great Lakes, with most of it consigned to grain elevators and flour

The hillside of Duluth seen from Minnesota Point in the early 1870s. Note the Citizen's Wharf behind the spruce tree (at center) and Elevator A in the background.

mills in Buffalo, New York. In the half century between the completion of the Erie Canal in the 1820s and the beginning of the flood of spring wheat from the Red River Valley and Dakota Territory, Buffalo had established itself as the nation's greatest grain-handling facility. Located at the eastern end of the Great Lakes and the western terminus of the Erie Canal, Buffalo handled the lion's share of the grain shipped from such lower lakes ports as Cleveland, Toledo, Chicago, Detroit, and Milwaukee. By 1850, Buffalo had become the largest grain market in the United States.[142]

At the time the Northern Pacific pushed westward from Duluth in the 1870s, Buffalo was a true transshipment facility. It unloaded grain downbound from Duluth and other Great Lakes ports, stored it in waterfront elevators, and loaded it into Erie Canal boats or railroad cars for delivery to flour mills in Albany, New York City, Boston, Baltimore, and Philadelphia.[143] Up until the late 1830s, an army of Irish immigrants unloaded Great Lakes grain vessels at the Buffalo docks. Bulk grain was shoveled out of the ships' holds into hundred-pound sacks or equally heavy boxes strapped to the backs of hod carriers, who staggered down the gangplank with their loads to the dockside grain warehouses. "Irishmen's backs are the cheapest elevators ever built," one Buffalo grain warehouse owner boasted in 1842.[144] They may have been cheap, but Irishmen's backs were a decidedly slow and inefficient way to unload a vessel. In 1842, vessels were clogging the Buffalo docks because of the length of time it took to unload one schooner or propeller loaded with grain. In the previous six years, the city's grain receipts had jumped from 112,000 bushels to more than 2 million bushels a year.

Joseph Dart, a Buffalo grain merchant, built a six-story grain storage building at the foot of Commercial Street on Buffalo Creek that would revolutionize the grain-handling industry.[145] Dart's first grain elevator had a capacity of 50,000 bushels. In the roofed wooden elevator, the grain was kept clean, dry, and free of pests. Dart later gave credit for his invention to Oliver Evans, an eighteenth-century American inventor who had devised a bucket-and-pulley system for flour mills.[146] But Dart's adaptation of the earlier invention brought about a revolution in the grain-handling industry.

By 1863, twenty-seven grain elevators dotted Buffalo's waterfront. Together, they had a capacity of 5.8 million bushels and a transfer capacity of 2.7 million bushels per hour.[147] Increasingly during the 1870s and 1880s, more and more of that grain came down from the Upper Lakes.

THE BEGINNINGS OF ELEVATOR ROW

The completion of the Northern Pacific Railway west to the Missouri River made Duluth the terminus for much of the spring wheat that would flow east from Dakota Territory in the late 1870s and early 1880s. Until 1878, however, Duluth's grain elevators were located on the unprotected lake side of the harbor.

Elevator A, which had been built by the Union Improvement and Elevator Company in 1870 at the foot of Fourth Avenue East, remained the largest elevator through most of the decade. With a capacity of 350,000 bushels and an hourly throughput of approximately 1,500 bushels, Elevator A was the mainstay of the harbor's grain trade until 1879.[148] In 1872, Elevator A was joined by Elevator No. 1, which was located along the lakefront two blocks west at the foot of Second Avenue East. Built by the Duluth firm of Munger and Markell, Elevator No. 1 had an original capacity of 200,000 bushels.[149]

The collapse of Jay Cooke's financial empire in the panic of 1873 and the rate wars with southern Minnesota railroads kept grain tonnage from increasing dramatically through the head of the lakes. Duluth had recorded 43,542 net tons of grain through Elevator A in 1871, but only 26,658 tons the following year. Tonnage rebounded to 44,376 tons in 1873 and 46,588 tons in 1874, but fell off sharply to 30,306 tons in 1875.[150] Grain shipments recovered to 1872–1873 levels the following year, and stayed in the 41,000-ton range for both 1876 and 1877. The latter year saw the last grain shipments from southern Minnesota arrive at the Duluth-Superior

Elevator A with the ruins of the outer breakwater shortly after the November 1872 storm. The modern two-story brick building on Superior Street is Branch's Hall, Duluth's first brick structure.

harbor. After that date, they were diverted to the Mississippi River route, but the loss of the market to the south no longer mattered.[151] In 1878, the first trainloads of hard red spring wheat from the west arrived at the head of the lakes, and the harbor's grain business never looked back.

In 1878, Elevator A and Elevator No. 1 handled nearly 50,000 tons of wheat from western Minnesota, the Red River Valley, and Dakota Territory.[152] The two lakefront elevators were nearing the limits of capacity with the 1878 tonnage, but plans were already afoot for a major expansion of the harbor's grain-handling facility. For most of the next seven years, the harbor was abuzz with activity as workers erected eleven elevators on the east side of Rice's Point in Duluth. The elevator construction workforce swelled to more than 3,000 people each summer, and sawmills were set up adjacent to the construction site to provide the crews with dimension lumber.[153] The first of the elevators constructed was the Northern Pacific's Elevator B. Leased to the Lake Superior Elevator Company, Elevator B opened in 1879, and its 1-million-bushel capacity immediately tripled the ele-

vator capacity of the harbor.[154] What would become known as "Elevator Row" would constitute the greatest elevator capacity on the Great Lakes outside of Buffalo by the mid-1880s.

The new capacity came on line in the nick of time. Grain tonnage through Duluth doubled in 1879 to 101,378 tons and increased another 15 percent in 1880 to 118,133 tons.[155] Although grain tonnage dropped slightly in 1881, it reached 128,571 tons in 1883. There seemed to be no end to the flow of grain from the prairies to the west. Elevator construction kept pace with the increase in tonnage. The Northern Pacific built Elevator C in 1881, the second million-bushel elevator in the harbor, and Elevator D in 1881, which had a capacity of 1.25 million bushels.[156] The fourth and final Northern Pacific elevator, Elevator G, was built in 1885 with a capacity of 1.3 million bushels. Elevator capacity was further expanded by the 1880 construction of Elevator No. 4 and Elevator No. 5 by the Duluth Imperial Milling and Capitol Elevator Company off Birch and Cedar Streets perpendicular to the harbor. Together, the two elevators added 1.25 million bushels of capacity to Elevator Row. The next to be built was Elevator I just south of the

Northern Pacific complex. Built in 1884 by the Lake Superior Elevator Company, Elevator I had a capacity of 750,000 bushels.[157] The Elevator Row complex on the east side of Rice's Point gave Duluth the storage capacity to stockpile much of the grain from the western prairies. By 1885, Elevator Row had a storage capacity of nearly 9 million bushels.[158]

The increased capacity contributed to a dramatic increase in grain tonnage through the harbor. In 1884, the U.S. Army Corps of Engineers deepened the Soo Locks to sixteen feet, which allowed deeper draft vessels to carry larger tonnages of grain down from Lake Superior. In 1884, grain tonnage from Duluth nearly tripled from the year before at 327,791 tons. Grain shipments through the harbor just missed topping 400,000 tons in 1885 and jumped to more than 530,000 tons in 1886. By 1887, grain tonnages were flirting with the 700,000-ton mark. By that time, too, the Duluth side of the harbor had serious competition from its Wisconsin neighbors.

"TO CLASP THE COMMERCE OF A CENTRAL WORLD"

Superior's failure to attract a railroad terminus to the Wisconsin side of the harbor in the 1870s had retarded development of the community. In many ways, Superior had never really recovered from the panic of 1857. But with the

James J. Hill's Great Northern Railway made Superior its eastern terminus in the mid–1880s. The penetration of the Great Northern into the rich wheat lands of western Minnesota and Dakota Territory at the time made the Twin Ports one of the nation's premier grain exporting ports.

Northern Pacific firmly ensconced on the Duluth side of the harbor, railroad builder James J. Hill of St. Paul saw opportunities for growth across the state line in Wisconsin. In 1888, Hill extended his Eastern Railway from

An Upham, Williams, and Company dredge (at left) sends up clouds of steam as it dredges a slip for Great Northern's Elevator S in West Superior in 1888. Note the logs (at center) used for piling.

Hinckley, Minnesota, north to Superior. The Eastern Railway Company of Minnesota was part of what would become Hill's Great Northern Railway empire. By the turn of the century, the Great Northern, with its mountain goat logo, would haul even more grain to Superior from Montana, North Dakota, and western Minnesota than the Northern Pacific delivered to Duluth.[159] The Great Northern joined the Chicago, St. Paul, Minneapolis, & Omaha Railroad with terminal facilities in Superior. The "Omaha Road" had arrived in Superior in 1883 and immediately gave the Wisconsin port city a rail link south to Chicago.

Hill's vision for Superior was rather grander. Even before the Eastern Railway Company of Minnesota completed its trackage to the city in 1888, Great Northern construction crews were building a massive elevator complex on Superior's St. Louis Bay. Work got under way in 1886 on Great Northern's Elevator S and Elevator X on the west side of the Northern Pacific Wisconsin Drawbridge, with a combined capacity of 5 million bushels. Three annexes built between 1888 and 1893 added another 7.5 million bushels of grain storage capacity.[160] Just across the drawbridge to the east, the Omaha Road began construction on Elevators No. 1, 2, and 3. Unlike other elevators in the harbor, the new complex contained a workhouse and two annexes laid out parallel to the Omaha tracks. Built by A. J. Sawyer, a Duluth grain merchant, and Joseph Moulton, who had been building elevators at the head of the lakes since 1871, the Omaha Road's new elevator complex had a capacity of nearly 3 million bushels.[161] Shortly after its construction, the railroad leased the new facility to the Duluth Elevator Company.[162]

By 1892, ten elevators lined the Superior harbor. Among them they boasted storage capacity of 15 million bushels, 3 million more than the elevators on the Duluth side of the harbor.[163] In 1891, for the first time, the Duluth-Superior facilities surpassed 1 million tons of grain handled.[164]

An anonymous poet in 1889 surveyed the growth of Superior during the previous decade. He wrote in flowering terms of the miracle that had been achieved on the shores of the Superior harbor and St. Louis Bay:

> Where throned by the pine in forest old,
> Superior thrusts up her conquering hand,
> To clasp the commerce of a central world,
> And sow thick cities on an ancient strand.[165]

Indeed, in little more than a decade, the Duluth-Superior harbor had become one of the great grain ports of the world. In the next decade, it would become one of the world's great iron ore ports.

The St. Paul & Duluth Railroad's World's Fair grain car readies to leave Duluth in 1893 for the fairgrounds at Jackson Park in Chicago.

A bird's-eye view of the Duluth harbor in 1883 by J. J. Stoner. Note Lake Superior Elevator Company's Elevator C and B on Rice's Point at center.

Elevator Row, circa 1895, with a package freighter tied alongside Elevator D. Note the first Duluth steam electric plant in foreground.

IN THE EYE
OF THE BEHOLDER

The wooden bulk freighter Superior *and her consort* Sandusky *tied up at Elevator A in the mid–1870s. Sailing for the Western Transportation and Coal Company of Detroit, the duo hauled grain down from the Twin Ports and coal up from Lake Erie.*

SERENDIPITY PLAYED AN IMPORTANT role in Duluth's ascendancy as the Great Lakes' foremost grain port in 1870. Not only was the Lake Superior & Mississippi Railroad completed and the Red River Valley settled at that time, but advances in shipbuilding also brought to the iron ore and grain trades an efficiency undreamed of a decade earlier. The transshipment of "prairie gold" from new Elevator A in Duluth—and ultimately the Twin Ports—was the principal result of those convergent factors.

The bulk freight of the Great Lakes was traditionally carried in schooners, two- and three-masted sailing ships that hauled 250 to 800 tons of cargo. More valuable cargoes—passengers, cattle, manufactured goods, perishables—were transported on fast steamboats, including side-wheelers and screw propellers. Less valuable commodities like lumber, coal, and iron ore were often relegated to slower schooners. But the fastest ships moved grain because they could deliver the products quicker.

In the late 1860s, the government began eliminating a bottleneck in the Great Lakes system with construction of the St. Clair Flats Ship Canal, bypassing a notoriously shallow part of the St. Clair River between Lakes Huron and St. Clair. The canal would mark completion of 12-foot channels throughout the lakes and permit construction of larger, deeper-draft ships.[166]

About fifty schooners were built between 1869 and 1874 to take advantage of the new channel depths, each carrying 1,000 or 1,200 tons of cargo. They were magnificent but slow and wind-dependent, and had to be towed through the St. Clair and Detroit Rivers that connected Lake Huron with Lakes St. Clair and Erie.

Using lumber steamers as a model, Elihu M. Peck of Cleveland designed a more efficient vessel in 1868 for iron ore and grain cargoes. His bulk freighter had large deck hatches for ease of loading and unloading at ore docks and grain elevators, a double deck so cargoes below would be protected from the weather, and engines that could tow one or two cargo-laden barges. The introduction of bulk freighters and their consort system, as it was called, signaled the beginning of the end for sailing ships.[167]

When Peck launched the *Robert J. Hackett* in November 1869, the 210-foot wooden steamer was an instant success. In 1870, he built the 220-foot barge *Forest City* as a consort to the *Hackett;* two years later he refitted the *Forest City* as a bulk freight steamer. Peck also built two barges to be towed by the *Hackett* and *Forest City.* Within ten years, sixty-five ships of the new design ran on the lakes, and a fleet of consort barges was employed as their tows.

Freight ships grew not only in number but in dimension and capacity, thanks to deepened channels and better shipbuilding. Builders experimented with iron components in framing wooden ships, which made for longer, larger hulls. The average gross tonnage for new ships in the early 1870s was 1,059 tons. By 1890 it had surpassed 2,200 tons. By 1900, the average new Great Lakes freighter stood at 5,224 tons.[168] Larger hulls meant more efficient, more profitable ships. The quest for ever larger vessels led to the adoption of iron and steel in shipbuilding. Iron had been used in Scottish and English shipyards since the 1840s, first for small vessels and by 1860 for larger craft. After 1870, iron shipbuilding plants emerged at Buffalo, New York, and at Wyandotte and Detroit, Michigan.

The first bulk freight vessel made of iron was the 287-foot *Onoko,* built at Cleveland by Globe Iron Works in 1882.[169] Steel replaced the more brittle iron frames and shell plates when the *Spokane* was built in 1886, and it soon became the material of choice. With strong metal frames and tough but thin shell-plating, the hulls of iron and steel vessels were lighter than the two-foot-thick hulls of wooden ships, and so they carried much more cargo for their dimensions. Though more costly to build, they were far cheaper to operate and maintain.

Shipbuilders soon discovered that, with the proper design, they could build ships of almost any size with steel, limited only by the channels and harbors they frequented. As a result, a new generation of bulk freighters debuted on the Great Lakes every time the locks and channels were improved. The first 400-foot "bulker" appeared in 1894. Five years later the first 500-footer was launched, followed in 1912 by a 600-foot giant. The growth in size and efficiency continued unabated throughout the century.[170]

A quarter–century after this photo was taken in 1895, the Hull–Rust–Mahoning open–pit iron mine would be one of the world's largest.

CHAPTER FIVE

Iron Port, Coal Port

BY THE MID-1880S, the Duluth-Superior harbor had established a reputation for being one of North America's great grain ports. Terminal grain elevators dotted both sides of the harbor, and a din resounded as workers built elevator annexes and laid railroad track to serve the ever-growing spring-wheat business. Upbound vessels disembarked passengers and unloaded "package freight" at the increasing number of merchandise and passenger docks jutting into the bay. Many passengers were immigrants, westward bound from the Erie Canal and lured by the siren of cheap land in Dakota Territory along the main line of the Northern Pacific.

The Duluth-Superior harbor played its role in the pacification of the Native Americans of the High Plains. Alexander McDougall, who was then just starting his career in shipbuilding at the head of the lakes, recalled that in 1882, as many as ten thousand tons of wild animal skins were piled up on the wharves of Duluth, awaiting passage downbound to tanneries. "Part of this lot was 150,000 buffalo skins," McDougall wrote in 1894. "All the warehouses and cars available for storage were used, and still there were lots more waiting room. In the country west of this great port, the Indians and wild beasts were being driven back."[171] But to become a truly great port, Duluth-Superior needed diversified cargo flows. Animal skins were a one-time phenomenon, reminiscent more of the era of the voyageurs, and were a cargo of the past by the early 1890s.[172] Additional downbound and upbound bulk cargoes were critical to the future success of the head of the lakes.

GRAIN DOWN, COAL UP

In 1885, it was becoming increasingly obvious

that the back-haul cargo that would dominate trade at Duluth-Superior for many years to come was eastern coal. Coal was the fuel of choice for the industrial revolution of the late nineteenth century. America in the 1870s and 1880s had boundless reserves of anthracite and bituminous coal. At a time when the vast forests of the eastern half of the United States had already been cleared and cut for farming, coal was the obvious choice for firing steam boilers as well as home and commercial furnaces. By the mid-1880s, most of the nation's mills, mines, factories, and elevators were powered by coal.[173]

Much of the bituminous coal in production at the time was located in western Pennsylvania and eastern Ohio, easily accessible by rail to Lake Erie ports.[174] In the 1880s, Sandusky, Conneaut, Ashtabula, and Toledo all became coal transshipment ports, handling the flow of upbound coal to the Upper Great Lakes.

For much of the first twenty-five years of bulk commerce on the upper lakes, cargo flow was nearly all downbound, with vessels usually returning empty to Lake Superior ports. It is not entirely clear who first proposed back-hauling coal from lower to upper lake ports, but Minnesota's W. W. "Will" Cargill can perhaps lay claim to being the first to do it on a large scale. Cargill was a La Crosse, Wisconsin, grain dealer who began buying country elevators in Wisconsin and Minnesota in the years following the Civil War. In 1878, Cargill and a partner began purchasing property in Green Bay on Lake Michigan where they leased a terminal from the Chicago & Northwestern Railway. Cargill's plan was to ship grain from Green Bay to lower lakes ports and then back-haul anthracite from Buffalo

A bulk freighter steams outbound through the Duluth Ship Canal in 1908 and the steamer S. R. Kirby pulls away from the Northwestern Fuel Company docks as the America remains tied up at the Booth Dock, around the corner from the Aerial Bridge.

to Green Bay. Cargill then shipped the anthracite west on the Green Bay & Minnesota Railroad to his network of elevators in Wisconsin and Minnesota.[175]

COAL IN THE TWIN PORTS

Duluth and Superior were not too far behind Green Bay in becoming a back-haul destination for coal. The coming of the railroad in 1870 had attracted the first cargoes of coal shipped to the head of the lakes. In the small sailing vessels and steamers of the day, coal frequently was carried upbound as ballast, with lumps of anthracite shoveled into the holds or even carried on deck. The coal was unloaded in wheelbarrows until the Sargent Coal Company built a sizable coal dock just inside the Duluth Ship Canal late in 1871, where vessels could be unloaded by horses pulling wooden dock hoists.[176]

The 1880s brought about a surge in coal movement through the head of the lakes. With the boom in terminal grain elevator construction came a corresponding burst of growth in coal dock construction. In 1881, the Northern Pacific built its first coal dock near downtown Duluth, the same year that the Lake Superior Coal and

Iron Company built the first coal wharf at the end of Connors Point on the Superior side of the harbor. In 1882, the Northern Pacific built a 150,000-ton-capacity coal dock at the foot of Twenty-third Avenue East in Superior. A year later, the Ohio Central Coal and Barge Company built a 200,000-ton capacity coal dock just south of the Northern Pacific's elevator dock on the east side of Rice's Point in Duluth.[177] The spate of coal dock construction, coupled with the deepening of the harbor and the Soo Locks, created a veritable explosion of coal shipments through the Twin Ports. Coal movements doubled, and doubled again during the 1880s. In 1880, 183,000 tons of coal arrived in Duluth or Superior. Two years later, the figure was slightly more than 420,000 tons. In 1886, nearly 913,000 tons moved through the Twin Ports. In 1888, Duluth-Superior was handling 1.4 million tons of coal.[178]

In the coal trade, supply begat demand and vice versa. As the spring-wheat trade increased throughout the decade of the 1880s, the number of vessels visiting the Duluth-Superior harbor continued to grow, from 524 in 1880 to more than three times that number in 1889.[179] And many of those upbound vessels were hauling coal from Buffalo or the Lake Erie ports.

The harbor witnessed another spurt of coal dock construction in the late 1880s and the early 1890s. The Northwestern Fuel Company, one of the major coal handlers on the upper lakes, built a coal dock with a 460,000-ton capacity between Birch and Ash Streets on the Duluth side of the harbor in 1888. The Great Northern built an 800,000-ton-capacity coal dock half a mile west of the Northern Pacific Wisconsin Drawbridge in 1889 on the Superior side of the harbor, and promptly leased the facility to the Philadelphia and Reading Coal and Iron Company.[180] Four more coal docks were built in the harbor in the first half of the 1890s. The Pennsylvania and Ohio Coal Company built a 785,000-ton dock at the foot of Thirty-seventh Avenue West in Duluth in 1892. The next year, the Youghiogheny and Lehigh Coal Company erected an 860,000-ton-capacity dock in Superior's St. Louis Bay near the Northern Pacific Grassy Point Bridge. The Northwestern Fuel Company built a massive 850,000-ton dock

on Superior's Allouez Bay in 1895, and the next year, the Lehigh Valley Coal Sales Company built a small anthracite dock on the west side of Superior's Tower Bay slip.[181]

Hauling coal to Duluth-Superior was less expensive than hauling it by water to Chicago or Milwaukee and shipping west by rail. In 1885, it cost coal companies less than fifty cents a ton to ship coal up the lakes from Buffalo or the Lake Erie ports.[182] And with competing rail systems from Duluth and Superior, Minneapolis rapidly became the Twin Ports' major coal customer. By the mid-1890s, even Will Cargill was shipping coal from Duluth-Superior to the Twin Cities, mainly because it was the least expensive option available to his growing grain company.

THE COST ADVANTAGE
Three factors played into the profitable nature of coal as a back-haul cargo in the 1880s and 1890s. Mechanization of the coal docks and their attendant loading and unloading process reduced the demand for manual labor. Larger vessels constructed of iron and steel began to

7558. Unloading Coal, Duluth, Minn. McKenzie, Photo.

Dockworkers unload coal at a Duluth dock in the early 1900s. Note the clamshell buckets dangling from the pulleys of the bridge crane.

appear on the scene in the 1880s. And the discovery of rich new iron deposits in the Lake Superior region between 1880 and 1900 created a demand for more and more vessels plying the route between Lake Superior and the lower lakes steel ports.

Mechanization of the coal docks in the Duluth-Superior harbor became commonplace in the late 1880s. Coal-fired steam donkey engines were set up on the docks to run conveyor belts from the vessel to the coal stockpile. Laborers still had to shovel the coal onto conveyors, but the moving belts greatly simplified the task of unloading the vessels.

By the mid-1890s most of the larger coal docks in the harbor were dominated by electrically operated bridge cranes. Among the first customers for Niagara Falls power in 1896 were the grain elevators and coal docks dotting the Buffalo waterfront. Within fifteen years, the vast majority of waterfront docks and elevators on the Great Lakes had been electrified. In the Duluth-Superior harbor, most of the electrified facilities before the mid-1890s were run by what

were then called isolated plants. Essentially an isolated plant was a steam boiler hooked to a small dynamo, or generator, and served one or two industrial customers in the immediate area of the generator. In 1884, the Scott and Holston sawmill on Lake Avenue South in Duluth installed the first isolated plant in the Twin Ports to power a band saw and accompanying sash-and-door factory.[183]

The electrically operated traveling bridge cranes, which became an increasing part of the Twin Ports' environmental landscape in the early years of the twentieth century, created efficiencies undreamed of just a quarter-century before. Clamshell buckets carried between 3 and 12 tons. Hoist grab buckets with a capacity of 2 to 6 tons could unload 10,000 tons of coal from a vessel in hours instead of days at a rate of 500 or more tons per hour. Electric boxcar loaders, capable of loading 44 tons of coal in ten minutes, began to appear at the docks in the late 1890s.[184]

The vessels being unloaded of their coal cargoes had grown larger as a result of the 1884 dredging

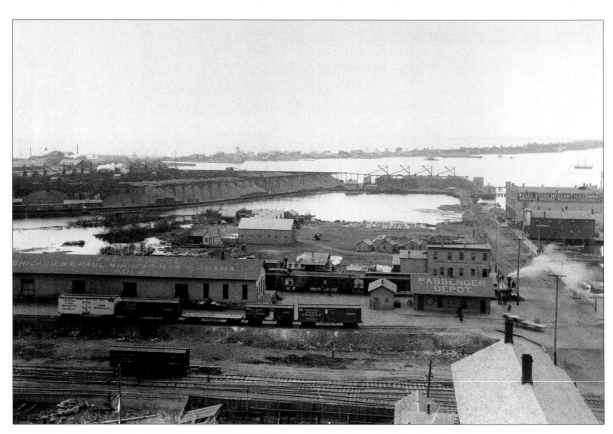

A view of the harbor from Fifth Avenue West in Duluth in the mid–1880s. Note the piles of coal at left center.

of the Soo Locks and St. Mary's River to sixteen feet. By 1890, the typical bulk freighter on the lakes was steam-powered, measuring 2,200 gross tons and averaging 260 feet in length. That was nearly double the gross tonnage of the *Robert J. Hackett,* the largest bulk freighter sailing the Great Lakes in 1871, the year the Duluth Ship Canal opened.[185] A local journalist observed in the spring of 1888 that "year by year the class of vessels coming to Duluth grows better . . . where a few years ago a vessel of 800 tons and capable of taking 30,000 bushels of grain, was considered a monster, a 2,000-ton carrier is now not at all remarkable."[186]

At the dawning of the grain and coal trade in the Twin Ports, most of the vessels were still of wooden construction. By the middle 1890s, wooden bulk freighters were also becoming a thing of the past. Because of the weight of the oaken timbers and keel, hull lengths were limited to about 300 feet. About the time that grain and coal shipments through the head of the lakes began to increase exponentially, marine engineers on the lakes were abandoning wooden-hulled bulk freighters for those built of iron and steel. In 1882, Cleveland's Globe Iron Works launched the *Onoko,* the first true iron-hulled bulk freighter.[187] At 287 feet, it could carry more than 3,000 tons at a fourteen-foot draft. *Onoko*'s triple-expansion steam engine developed more than 1,700 horsepower, and she was fitted with double-bottoms with water ballast tanks. She was nearly thirty feet longer than the largest wood-hulled bulk freighter then afloat. And the beauty of iron- and steel-hulled bulk freighters is that they could be built to a much greater length than their wooden predecessors. With half-inch shell plating, the iron and steel vessels had much greater longitudinal strength than wooden bulk freighters. Iron and steel plating was up to fifteen times lighter than the heavy oaken keels and keelsons of the wooden-hulled freighters.[188]

Onoko made a fortune for her owners, averaging more than $30,000 a year in profits from the time she slipped down the ways in 1882 until the September day in 1915 when a hull plate beneath the engine compartment failed and sent the *Onoko* to the bottom of the lake, sixteen

miles northeast of Duluth.[189] By that time, iron- and steel-hulled bulk freighters were hauling virtually all of the Great Lakes' commodities.

IRON BOTTOMS, IRON CARGO

The third factor that played into the Duluth-Superior harbor emerging as a truly diversified bulk cargo port was the discovery of new and rich deposits of iron ore in the hills north of Duluth. Marquette, Michigan, dominated the iron ore trade through the 1870s and 1880s because the port on the south shore of Lake Superior was closest to the Marquette Range. After enjoying sole claim to the Lake Superior iron ore trade for more than a third of a century, however, the Marquette Range was joined in quick succession by three other iron ranges in the years between 1877 and 1885. Two were in Michigan and nearby Wisconsin. Wisconsin investors began digging exploratory shafts on the Menominee Range south of the Marquette in the mid-1870s. In 1877, the Chicago & Northwestern Railway laid trackage east across the southern half of the Upper Peninsula of Michigan from the Menominee Range communities of Iron River and Iron Mountain to the Lake Michigan port city of Escanaba. Within five years, Escanaba was shipping more than 1.1 million tons of high-grade Menominee Range Bessemer ore to the Lake Erie iron ports.[190]

The Upper Peninsula iron ore commanded $8 a ton at Lake Erie iron ports in the early 1880s, an incentive to develop more deposits on Lake Superior's south shore. Wisconsin geologists had explored westward from the Menominee Range in the 1850s and suspected that additional rich iron deposits were to be found. In the early 1880s, Joseph Sellwood, a Duluth mining engineer, helped form the Penokee and Gogebic Development Company to dig the first iron shaft on what would become known as the Gogebic Range. The Colby Mine, the first on the newly developed range, was located near Bessemer, Michigan, just north of the Wisconsin border.[191] Sellwood and his partners initially planned to ship iron ore from the Gogebic Range to Milwaukee by rail. In 1885, however, the Milwaukee, Lake Shore, & Western Railway Company laid trackage from Bessemer west to

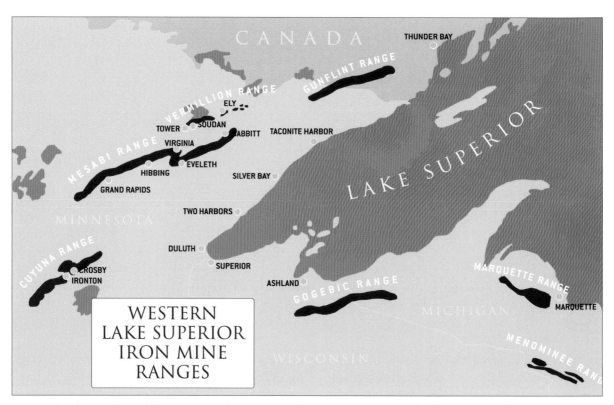

WESTERN
LAKE SUPERIOR
IRON MINE
RANGES

Lake Superior was ringed with huge deposits of iron ore, prompting one twentieth-century American writer to call it a "great cold lake in an iron collar."

the port of Ashland, Wisconsin, on Lake Superior's Chequamegon Bay. Within two years, twenty-four mines on the Gogebic Range were producing more than 1.3 million tons of iron a year, all of it shipped by rail the fifty miles to Ashland for transshipment down the Great Lakes. The Gogebic Range soon surpassed the Menominee Range as the number-two producer in the Lake Superior region.[192]

NORTH TO THE VERMILION

Geologists had long suspected the existence of more rich deposits of iron ore in the rugged hills north and west of Duluth. Surveyors Richard and Henry Eames had touched off the Vermilion gold rush in 1864 when they discovered sulfur and iron pyrites on the south shore of Lake Vermilion. The short-lived rush obscured the fact that what the brothers had found was a substantial bed of extremely hard iron ore.[193] In late 1865, George Stuntz trudged up the Vermilion trail from Duluth and explored much of the country the gold-seekers had tramped not so long before. Stuntz packed sixty pounds of ore samples back to Duluth, convinced that iron ore deposits could be found along the shores of Lake Vermilion. He began lobbying

Duluth friends and acquaintances to exploit the suspected valuable natural resource.[194] "When this country is developed," Stuntz told anyone who would listen, "that big mountain of iron will do it. When they get to hauling that iron out, they will haul in its supplies cheap."[195]

George C. Stone was one who listened to the rumors of a mountain of iron in the hills to the north and west. Duluth's first banker, Stone had arrived at the head of the lakes in 1869 as an assistant to George B. Sargent, financier Jay Cooke's representative in Lake Superior country. Cooke himself had grandiose plans for building iron furnaces and rolling mills for the track of his Northern Pacific Railway at Duluth, and he continued to direct Sargent and Stone to buy northern Minnesota timberlands in the early 1870s. The panic of 1873 derailed all of those plans, and Duluth's promise seemed shortchanged once again by the vagaries of national economics. Eager to rebuild his shattered personal and banking finances, Stone headed east in the late fall of 1874 to interest investors in developing the iron ore resources south of Lake Vermilion. Stone got polite refusals in Chicago, Cleveland,

and Detroit. Stone was about to return to Duluth when he stopped in at the Philadelphia offices of Charlemagne Tower in the spring of 1875.

An 1830 graduate of Harvard University, Tower had made a fortune in the anthracite fields of eastern Pennsylvania.[196] He had cashed out his investments in 1871 and was seeking suitable investment vehicles for his fortune. Tower was no stranger to Cooke and Duluth. He had invested nearly $250,000 in Northern Pacific bonds in the two years before the panic, and he had been named to the railroad company's board of directors in early 1873. Tower was interested in Stone's proposition; he had kept abreast of the rumors about iron ore in northern Minnesota and told Stone that he felt the deposits were potentially developable. Tower agreed to dispatch Albert H. Chester, a geology professor at Hamilton College in New York and an old friend from the anthracite days, to Lake Vermilion.[197] Chester found ore, but Tower hesitated to invest.

By 1875, the situation had changed dramatically. Iron ore prices had nearly doubled to $9.25, and policy-makers were forecasting that the Marquette Range might not have enough reserves to fuel a rapidly expanding steel industry.[198] It would not be the last time that government and business officials predicted a looming domestic iron ore shortage, but the 1880 alarm served to galvanize Tower into action. In early 1880, he engaged Stone to begin purchasing mineral lands south of Lake Vermilion. Much of the land was acquired under the terms of the 1862 Homestead Act, and a majority probably was purchased fraudulently by having settlers claim they had improved the land and then sell to the iron investors. By 1883, Stone had assembled the necessary acreage for a mining operation.

Stone was instrumental in two critical measures: getting the Minnesota legislature to approve 1881 tax legislation that would not penalize the new mining venture during start-up, and acquiring a charter for a railroad from the new mining range to Lake Superior. Tower had committed to developing the new iron deposit after Stone

A Pennsylvania coal and iron millionaire after the Civil War, Charlemagne Tower Sr. provided much of the investment capital for the development of the Vermilion Range. He later served as U.S. ambassador to czarist Russia.

While his father tended to financial and political matters back in Pennsylvania, young Charlemagne Tower Jr. kept an eye on the family's investment in iron mining on the Vermilion Range in northeastern Minnesota.

persuaded the legislature to essentially levy a property tax on mining companies, and not a tax on land or property.[199]

Tower incorporated the Duluth & Vermilion Railroad to haul ore out of the proposed Lake Vermilion mining district. When the Philadelphia entrepreneur discovered that the new railroad would not be eligible for land grants from the state of Minnesota, he quickly authorized Stone to gain stock control of the Duluth & Iron Range Railroad, which had been formed by a syndicate of Minnesota and Upper Peninsula speculators nearly a decade before.[200] Despite its use of the name "Duluth," the railroad would cross sixty-eight miles of muskeg and tamarack swamp and reach Lake Superior at Two Harbors, twenty-seven miles northeast of the Twin Ports. Named for Burlington Bay and Agate Bay, the two best anchorages on Lake Superior's north shore, Two Harbors had been a commercial fishing settlement for more than thirty years. Construction on the new rail line began in July 1883, and the contract specified completion by August 1884.[201] In early 1884, piling work began on the first of two ore docks jutting into Burlington Bay.[202] Meanwhile, crews feverishly built a mining camp at Stuntz Bay on Lake Vermilion. Plans called for stripping off the overburden at the site, digging an open pit, and then following the ore body downward with a deep shaft mine.

Two towns quickly sprang up at the mine site. Tower was named in honor of the Philadelphia financier who was fronting the money for development of the Minnesota Iron Company and its new diggings. The adjacent community was named Soudan. D. H. Bacon, Tower's mine manager, reportedly named the place Soudan because it was as cold during the winter as the Anglo-Egyptian Soudan (now Sudan) was hot in the summer.[203]

Charlemagne Tower and his investors sunk more than $2 million into constructing the railroad to Two Harbors and setting up the mining operation at Tower-Soudan. But their efforts were rewarded in the summer of 1884 when the first load of iron ore from the Vermilion Range made the rail journey to Two Harbors. Minnesota Iron

Company crews had shipped the locomotive *Three Spot* to Two Harbors in June 1884, and then the engineers had wrestled her up over the escarpment to Tower-Soudan on July 31.[204] That first load of iron ore from the Vermilion Range totaled 220 tons. Charlemagne Tower's multimillion-dollar gamble was about to pay off. Just over 62,000 tons of Vermilion Range ore went down the lakes in 1884, and more than 225,000 tons departed Two Harbors in 1885. By 1889, when new mines had been opened at Ely on the eastern edge of the Vermilion, the range was producing and shipping almost 845,000 tons of ore.[205]

THE SLEEPING GIANT AWAKENS

Tower's Duluth & Iron Range Railroad completed a twenty-six-mile spur to Duluth in the summer of 1886, which was scant consolation to those who had hoped the Twin Ports would become the terminus for the nation's newest iron range. The reality, however, was that the opening of the Vermilion Range generated the hope that other iron ranges existed north and west of Duluth. The opening of the Marquette Range on the Upper Peninsula had been followed by the opening of the Menominee and Gogebic Ranges, and residents of Duluth and Superior could take heart by the possibility of lightning striking twice.

The early 1880s were a time of vast movement in the timber industry, as Michigan loggers moved west into the upper lakes country. Cruisers set out daily from Duluth to estimate the volume of timber in northern Minnesota. The Anishinaabe called the one-hundred-mile hilly area from Pokegema Falls on the Mississippi River to south of Lake Vermilion *Mesabi,* or "giant."[206] The granite hills were covered with white and red pine, and the low spots flanking the hills were blanketed with spruce and tamarack.

The Merritt family of Duluth had arrived in the Twin Ports in the year before the panic of 1857 and had multiplied and prospered. Like George Stuntz, Lewis Merritt, the patriarch of the family, was a surveyor and timber cruiser. Five of Merritt's sons took up timber cruising and surveying. Lewis Jr., Alfred, Napoleon, Leonidas, and Cassius Merritt were actively exploring

Hephzibah and Lewis Merritt are surrounded by their sons and nephews in this 1871 photo. The Merritt family of Duluth almost single-handedly opened the Mesabi Range in the early 1890s.

northwest of Duluth in the 1880s and early 1890s. In March 1889, the Merritts struck out southwest from Pike River near Tower-Soudan. They dug test pits that spring, looking for iron ore. What they found was a reddish, crumbly ore that could be pried from the earth with pick and shovel. They were disappointed that their find didn't approximate the harder ore of the Vermilion Range, but when they had the ore tested, they were astounded to discover that it assayed at 60 percent iron content.[207]

News of the ore discoveries set off a veritable land rush across northern Minnesota. The Merritts managed to buy more than 140 land leases, and they immediately set about raising the capital to develop their find.[208] Building an infrastructure to exploit the Mesabi ore would take immense amounts of money. The ore was located in a trackless wilderness sixty miles north and west of Duluth. To successfully develop mines would require the creation of mining communities on the Mesabi, construction of a railroad from the range to Duluth, and erection of ore docks along the shores of the Duluth-Superior harbor.

Leonidas Merritt traveled east to Pittsburgh to interest financier Henry Clay Frick in bankrolling the development work. Frick refused Merritt's proposal, but the Merritt brothers found willing investors in St. Paul, and in early 1891 they incor-

porated the Duluth, Missabe, & Northern Railway Company with a capital stock of $5 million. The DM&N would build a line from the Mountain Iron Mine nearly fifty miles south to the main line of the Duluth & Winnipeg Railway at Stony Brook Junction.[209] The Merritts signed an agreement with the Duluth & Winnipeg whereby the ore from the Mesabi Range would be hauled to Stony Brook Junction and then carried the rest of the way to Lake Superior on the tracks of the Duluth & Winnipeg. The older railroad also agreed to build an ore dock at Allouez Bay on the Superior side of the harbor.[210]

Construction on the railroad and ore docks got under way just after the first of the year in 1892. Meanwhile, the Merritts had entered into agreements with Pittsburgh steel interests to lease the output of the mines being developed on the Mesabi Range. Henry W. Oliver was in Minneapolis during the summer of 1892, attending the Republican national convention that nominated Benjamin Harrison for president. Oliver, an associate of Andrew Carnegie, had built an iron and steel empire in Pittsburgh, and he was intrigued by reports of the richness of the Mesabi ore. He took a train north to Duluth, met several of the Merritts, and toured the new range with them. Oliver quickly committed to take a minimum of 200,000 tons of ore from the range in 1893, and 400,000 tons a year thereafter.[211]

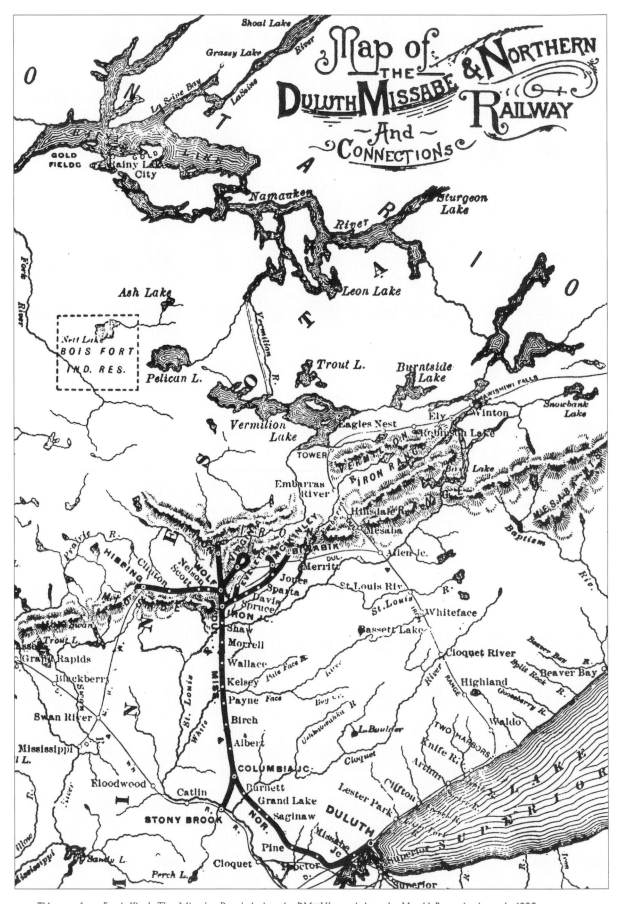

This map from Frank King's The Missabe Road *depicts the DM&N's reach into the Mesabi Range in the early 1900s.*

Work on construction of the DM&N went on around the clock through the spring and summer of 1892. In early October, the first trainload of Mesabi ore came down the hill from Mountain Iron to Stony Brook Junction and east to the new ore dock on Allouez Bay.[212] The Merritts had seemingly defied the odds and opened the Mesabi. They controlled Mountain Iron and several other Mesabi mines. They owned the railroad, and all of Pittsburgh was talking about their ore. In late 1892, Charlemagne Tower approached the brothers through an intermediary. The Minnesota Iron Company, he told them, was prepared to pay the Merritts $8 million for their railroad and Mesabi holdings.[213] The Merritts refused Tower's offer. Leonidas Merritt, in particular, was becoming more convinced that the family could develop the range without outside help. The agreement with the Duluth & Winnipeg Railway had been plagued with problems from the start. The Merritts claimed that the older railroad was reneging on its promise to provide the Merritts with railcars for their DM&N line. Then too the Merritts were evidently affronted by the fact that the ore dock was located in Superior and not in their native Duluth. In early 1893, Leonidas Merritt persuaded his brothers to go it alone. He arranged a loan

from Charles L. Wetmore, a Wall Street financier, and the DM&N began laying tracks from the end of its line at Stony Brook to Fortieth Avenue West in Duluth. Other crews began building a massive new ore dock that would jut nearly a half-mile into St. Louis Bay on the Duluth side of the harbor.[214]

THE DREAM DENIED

It might all have worked, and the Merritt family would have entered the pantheon of American business heroes. But as they had in 1857 and again in 1873, national economic conditions shaped the future of the Duluth-Superior harbor. The panic of 1893 was perhaps the most severe economic dislocation of the nineteenth century. Historian John Steele Gordon called it "the other great depression," and before the panic of 1893 had run its course, more than fifteen thousand companies and nearly five hundred banks had failed.[215] The panic began in the spring of 1893 with the collapse of the Philadelphia & Reading Railroad. Within weeks, the Merritts found themselves fatally overextended. Wetmore, their Wall Street financier, had not been able to secure the full amount of the loan he had promised the fall before. The Merritts were soon unable to pay the contractors they

The pit at Mountain Iron where Duluth's Merritt family discovered the first commercial deposits of iron ore on the Mesabi Range in the fall of 1890. Note the steam shovel stripping overburden in the background.

The first carload of iron ore from Mountain Iron is ready for transport to the docks in the Twin Ports by the Duluth, Missabe, & Northern Railroad in October 1892. Note the spruce tree propped atop the load of ore, signifying the first carload.

had hired to extend the railroad and build the ore docks. Because the contractors were not able to pay their work crews, most of their mines were shut down.

One of the investors Wetmore had lined up for the loan to the Merritts was John D. Rockefeller. Already a legend in American business, the Cleveland-based Rockefeller had by this time created the underpinnings of the American oil industry. Since at least the mid-1880s, he had been quietly investing in iron ore properties in Michigan and Wisconsin as well as Cuba. Rockefeller agreed to underwrite the completion of the Merritts' ambitious iron ore project in Duluth. In June 1893, he lent them $100,000, and later that year, Rockefeller and the Merritts set up a holding company to own and operate the mine, railroad, and dock properties. Rockefeller originally controlled only 20 percent of the Lake Superior Consolidated Iron Mines, but the Merritts' insatiable need for cash ballooned Rockefeller's investment to more than $2 million by the fall of 1893.[216]

In early 1894, Rockefeller gained effective control of the Lake Superior Consolidated Iron Mines. A year later, he had complete control of the company. Leonidas Merritt and his brothers and cousins cried foul. They sued Rockefeller for fraud in federal court in Duluth and won, but the Cleveland industrialist won on appeal. Eventually, Rockefeller and the Merritts settled out of court. Rockefeller paid the family $525,000, and the Merritts publicly retracted the fraud charges they had made.[217] By 1896, Rockefeller was out of the mining end of the business on the Mesabi Range, although he retained lake shipping interests well into the twentieth century. Andrew Carnegie and Henry Oliver gained control of much of the mining and railroad infrastructure of the Mesabi Range, although James J. Hill completed a rail line to the Mesabi in 1899.

By the last year of the nineteenth century, the flow of ore through the Duluth-Superior harbor had increased dramatically. In 1896, a third ore dock was built adjacent to the original Duluth & Winnipeg Railway dock on the Superior side of the harbor.[218] Two more ore docks were built in 1900 and 1901. Mesabi ore flowed across the docks in the 1890s. More than half a million tons went down the lakes in 1893, the panic year, and by 1896, the Twin Ports were handling more than 2 million tons.[219] Already by 1895, more Mesabi ore was leaving Duluth and Superior than coal arriving. In 1899, almost 5 million tons of ore went downbound from Duluth-Superior, nearly twice the volume of coal received at the Twin Ports.[220]

The effect of the opening of the Mesabi Range on Duluth and Superior was magical. The Twin Ports weathered the panic of 1893 remarkably well. The railroads and docks were controlled by Minneapolis, Pittsburgh, and Cleveland interests rather than local capital, but jobs were plentiful. Duluth's population doubled from 1885 to 1890 to more than 33,000 people. Ten years later, in 1900, Duluth was a city of nearly 53,000, with another 10,000 people living across the bay in Superior.[221] More important, the Twin Ports in 1900 were handling nearly 12 million tons of cargo, four times the tonnage of ten years before. Nearly two-thirds of the cargo passing through Duluth-Superior was iron and coal. The head of the lakes had become a truly diversified port at the dawn of the twentieth century.

German-born entrepreneur and timber cruiser Frank Hibbing opened much of the central Mesabi Range and platted the town that bears his name in the summer of 1893. He sold a half-share in his mining interests to Rockefeller associates before the panic of 1893 descended upon northern Minnesota.

A 1910 postcard shows six steel bulk freighters taking on Mesabi ore at the DM&N docks in Duluth. The George H. Russell *is at left, and the* William Davock *is at right.*

69

AMERICA'S STEEL DISTRICT EMERGES

Andrew Carnegie's 1901 decision to sell his steel holdings in Pennsylvania and Illinois to J. Pierpont Morgan paved the way for the formation of U.S. Steel Corporation, the nation's first billion-dollar company.

THE DEMAND FOR IRON ORE in the 1870s and 1880s was fueled by the increasing demand for steel. For much of its first century of existence, the United States was a steel-importing nation. As late as the Civil War, U.S. steel imports, mostly from Great Britain, were greater than domestic production. But by the 1870s, thanks to Andrew Carnegie's realization that the future of railroads depended on the existence of steel rails, America began manufacturing enough steel for its own purposes. The country also found its place as a world leader in steel production.

American foundries had made pig wrought iron since before the American Revolution, mostly by heating the iron ore and then removing oxygen from it. Beehive iron furnaces sprouted in Pennsylvania's Lehigh Valley, upstate New York, and parts of New England during the late eighteenth and early nineteenth centuries.

Englishman Henry Bessemer solved one of the nineteenth century's most difficult metallurgy problems in 1856 when he patented his process for making steel. Blowing air into molten iron ore resulted in steel with tensile strength, flexibility, and malleability into many forms, including blooms, an early type of molded iron, and rods. Within a decade, Bessemer's pear-shaped converters began replacing the iron industry's beehive furnaces.[222] Over many of the next twenty years, the American steel industry used a trial-and-error process to perfect its Bessemer converters. Bessemer had used low-phosphorous ore from Wales in his process, and the higher phosphorous ores from Pennsylvania and New York made unacceptable steel. The lowest phosphorous iron on the continent came from Michigan's Marquette Range, and it soon became the ore of choice for the Bessemer converter.[223]

Pittsburgh rapidly took the lead in America's nascent steel industry. Located at the confluence of the Allegheny, Monongahela, and Ohio Rivers, the western Pennsylvania metropolis was ideally situated for its role as America's leading steel producer. Fuel to fire the converters led to Monongahela Valley's emergence in the 1870s as the nation's first great steelmaking district. By the end of the Civil War, most of the forests south and east of the Great Lakes had been removed or cut, either for fuel or to open agricultural land. Coal was the obvious solution for firing Bessemer converters. For maximum efficiency in the converters, coking coal had to have a high-BTU rating and relatively low ash content. It was baked in brick ovens to produce an almost pure form of carbon, which was an ideal fuel for the Bessemer converter.[224]

Located just fifty miles southeast of Pittsburgh was the Connellsville seam of low-sulfur coking coal. Pittsburgh also had a solid manufacturing base in the 1870s, and that allowed the steel city to capture investment capital. Scotsman Andrew Carnegie had made his fortune as an executive with the Pennsylvania Railroad and had invested his earnings in Pittsburgh's iron furnaces and rolling mills during the Civil War era. Carnegie saw clearly that the future of U.S. railroads was tied to steel rails, and in 1873, he assembled a consortium of Pittsburgh investors to build the most modern steelmaking plant in America at Braddock, eight miles up the Monongahela from Pittsburgh.[225] The Edgar Thomson Works, named for Carnegie's boss, then president of the Pennsylvania Railroad and a $100,000 investor in the mill, poured its first heat on August 26, 1875.[226] Within a quarter-century, the Edgar Thomson Works and other steel mills in the Monongahela Valley had reduced the cost of producing steel rails from more than $36.50 a ton to $12 a ton. Key to that cost efficiency was managing the flow of raw materials that came together at Pittsburgh.

It was because of Carnegie that Pittsburgh emerged as the first great American steel district instead of Chicago. He realized that it cost more to ship coking coal from Pennsylvania to Lake Michigan by rail than it did to ship iron ore from Michigan and Minnesota to the Lake Erie ports that fed the Monongahela Valley mills. The integration of raw material supplies and manufacturing expertise at the headwaters of the Ohio River in western Pennsylvania was made possible by the inland waterway transportations. That integration would make America the world's greatest steelmaker in the twentieth century.

North–woods loggers in the nineteenth century prided themselves on their ability to stack massive loads of white pine on a single sledge.

CHAPTER SIX

Timber Port

WHILE THE DULUTH-SUPERIOR harbor was emerging as a grain, coal, and iron port during the 1880s and 1890s, the passage of vessels through the two entries from Lake Superior was marked not so much by ship whistles as by the incessant din of hundreds of steam-driven gang saws.

The creation of a modern port infrastructure at the Twin Ports during the last two decades of the nineteenth century required prodigious quantities of wood for ore and coal docks, grain elevators, warehouses, and railroad trestles. Millions of board feet of lumber went into the port facilities during the 1880s and 1890s.[227] At about the same time Duluth-Superior began diversifying from grain and package freight cargoes to include iron and coal, the harbor was also becoming one of the biggest lumber-shipping ports in the world. Carloads of lumber from the pineries of northern Minnesota and Wisconsin arrived by rail almost hourly in the 1890s at the sawmills that crowded the harbor. Gangs of laborers unloaded the railcars and positioned the sawtimber for entry to the mill. Buzz saws and gang saws operating twenty-four hours a day debarked the raw wood and turned it into dimension lumber. Workers on the other end of the mills stacked the finished lumber on nearby docks to await shipment down the Great Lakes to commercial markets.

"Duluth took over the market earlier held by Saginaw, Michigan," wrote Minnesota logging historian J. C. "Buzz" Ryan, "and became the largest lumber shipping port on the lakes. The largest market in the east was Tonawanda, New York, while Chicago was a big market. The Duluth mills built high tramways along the

waterfront and piled their lumber so that it could be loaded directly on to the boats. The railroads built docks along the waterfront at which trainloads of lumber coming from inland mills could be loaded directly on to the boats."[228]

MILLS AT ONEOTA

A sawmill was the first commercial structure of any kind located on the Minnesota side of the St. Louis Bay upstream from Rice's Point.[229] Henry W. Wheeler arrived in the frontier community of Oneota from St. Paul in 1855 and immediately began constructing a sawmill at what is now about Twenty-seventh Avenue West on St. Louis Bay. Wheeler had walked to Duluth carrying a packsack, and soon afterward he ordered a planer, lath-cutter, and associated equipment from a Detroit manufacturer, which were shipped to Oneota through the newly completed Soo.[230]

Other sawmills stood on Minnesota Point at the time, and in 1857, another large sawmill was built on the Minnesota side of St. Louis Bay about a mile up from Wheeler's Oneota mill. In nearby Superior, August Zachau set up a sawmill during the winter of 1854 to cut lumber for construction of the city's Pioneer Hotel.

The sawmills at the head of the lakes had a seemingly inexhaustible supply of timber. The hillsides surrounding Duluth were covered with white and red pine, and the bottomlands of the St. Louis and Nemadji Rivers sported huge stands of tamarack and spruce. Until the Civil War, most of the logging was done locally, and the logs typically were rolled into the waterways and floated to the mills. Local steamboats were employed to tow rafts into the harbor

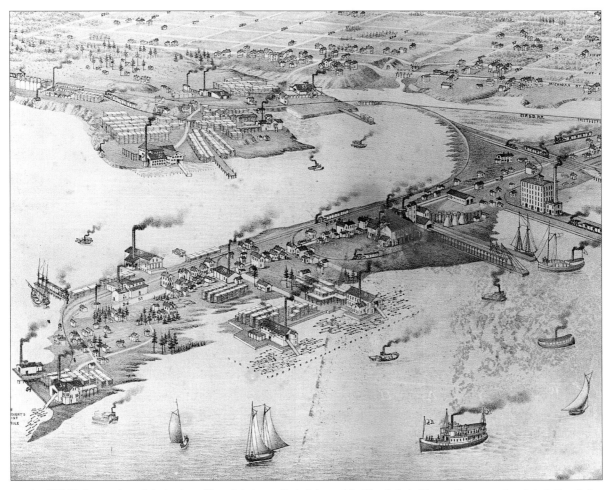

An 1883 bird's–eye view of the lumber mills and docks on Rice's Point and in West Duluth. Many mills are numbered, including Cutler, Gilbert, and Pearson (50), R. A. Gray Company (54), Little, Peck, and Company (55), and Payton, Kimball, and Barber Company (58).

from points many miles up the St. Louis and Nemadji Rivers.

The technology of logging in the mid-nineteenth century was surprisingly sophisticated. Most of the larger mills in the Twin Ports were steam-driven. A boiler fueled by bark and wood scraps ran a whipsaw that sat in a frame and cut lumber lengthwise. By the time of the Civil War, the whipsaws and Muley saws (similar to a whipsaw but held rigid in the frame by a heavy spring) were replaced by rotary saws.[231]

Virtually all of the early production was destined for local consumption, and the collapse of the two communities during the panic of 1857 dealt a fatal blow to many of the pioneer Duluth and Superior sawmills. As early as 1857, sawmills in the two communities were already shipping their sawtimber east along Lake Superior to the small Wisconsin communities along Lake Superior's south shore.[232] Most of

the lumber was transported by the small sailing schooners and scows plying the western end of the lake.

The 1857 panic severely hampered the expansion of the lumber industry at the head of the lakes. The first mill in the Twin Ports to change hands in the wake of the Civil War was the Culver and Nettleton Mill on Minnesota Point. The local Peyton and Engler Company purchased the mill, quickly moved it to Connors Point, and installed the first circular saw in Duluth. The firm of Munger and Gray purchased the Wheeler Mill in Oneota in 1869 and enlarged it in the early 1870s after the arrival of the railroad. Munger and Gray also built a second mill at Fifth Avenue West and the bay front in Duluth.[233]

A second depression in 1873 also slowed the development of the Twin Ports lumber trade, although the Northern Pacific Railway's push west to the prairies in the mid-1870s produced a ready-made market for lumber from Duluth and Superior. It would be another decade before Duluth and Superior began their ascendancy in the transportation of white pine lumber.

KING PINE

In the week before Christmas in 1894, the *Duluth Evening Herald* published its annual lumber outlook. The year had opened on a gloomy note. "Starting the year with fears and misgivings at the close of a period of Great Depression," the headline noted.[234] Faced with a lack of credit because of the panic of 1893, the farmers and farm communities of Minnesota and the Dakotas would not likely be seeking lumber shipped west by rail from Duluth-Superior, the newspaper noted. The reporter continued that "it was clearly seen that whatever sales were made during the year must be to buyers in Buffalo, Tonawanda, Cleveland, Chicago and Lake Michigan and lower lake ports."[235]

What the reporter called the "Eastern market" turned out to be lucrative for the lumber industry at the head of the lakes. Between April and December 1894, Duluth mills and docks placed more than 160 million board feet of lumber aboard lumber hookers (lumber-carrying steamers, also known as steam barges) and their consorts for shipment down the lakes. Mills and docks on the Superior side of the harbor shipped an additional 30 million board feet of lumber to markets on the lower lakes. Local consumption and rail movements to points northwest of the Twin Ports added another 150 million board feet to the total.[236] What had started as a year with limited expectations had solidly cemented the Twin Ports' leading role in the Great Lakes lumber trade. Duluth-Superior would reign supreme as the nation's number-one timber port for the next ten years. Then the lumberjacks, timber cruisers, and bankers who handled investment capital for the industry leapfrogged to the old-growth rain forests west of the Cascade Mountains.

From the 1870s to the early 1890s, Michigan had ruled the white pine timber industry. Mills on the east shore of Lake Michigan and the west shore of Lake Huron had cut and shipped billions of board feet of lumber to the growing cities along the lower rim of the Great Lakes.

The white pine, however, was a finite resource. Lumber camps cut everything within a day's walk of the camp, floated the logs down the Grand, AuSable, Black, Titibawasee, and Saginaw Rivers to the mills, and then moved on farther upriver. Nothing was replanted. White pine took

In 1900, when this photo was taken, the Alger–Smith Company's lumber mill in Duluth was one of the world's largest mills, handling millions of board feet of lumber each month.

Logging camps dotted the north woods of Minnesota and Wisconsin at the turn of the twentieth century. Everything in the camp was built of wood, the most abundant resource available.

150 years to grow to maturity, and aspen was viewed as a weed tree, since paper was still made from rags and not wood pulp. The debris of logging, what the loggers called "slashings," was left to pile up in the woods. In dry years, lightning strikes and sparks from locomotives set the slash afire, shrouding much of the state north of Saginaw Bay in smoke for months at a time.

The destructive cycle would be played out in the Lower Peninsula, and then in Michigan's Upper Peninsula, northern Wisconsin, and northern Minnesota before the industry decamped for the Pacific Northwest in the 1910s. Lower Michigan's pineries began to decline in the 1880s.

The lumber barons of Michigan began moving north and west in the 1880s. The first place they landed was the sparsely populated Upper Peninsula. By the mid-1880s, lumbermen from the Lower Peninsula were swarming up the Indian, Sturgeon, Two Hearted, Manistique, Menominee, and other Upper Peninsula rivers in search of marketable pine. New sawmills sprang up in Escanaba, Munising, St. Ignace, and Menominee,

but the bulk of the mills remained in the old lumber towns of Saginaw Bay and Lake Huron.[237] Instead of cutting the white pine in the forests of the Upper Peninsula, many of the logging companies elected to drive the logs down the rivers of the Upper Peninsula into Lake Michigan or Lake Superior. There they would be assembled into giant rafts and towed by steam tugs south to Muskegon or Saginaw. Some of the log rafts were towed as far east as Buffalo and the Tonawandas in New York.[238]

THE LUMBER BOOM ERA

In the 1880s, a two-pronged invasion assaulted the white pine forests of northeastern Minnesota: Michigan lumbermen cutting west across Wisconsin and lumberjacks cutting north from the St. Croix, Snake, and Kettle Rivers of Wisconsin and Minnesota. The cut in Wisconsin took decades and generally proceeded in a southeast-northwest direction. Green Bay and the Wolf River Valley in the state's northeast were the first established pinery, followed closely by the exploitation of the white pine resources of the Wisconsin, Black, and Chippewa Rivers.[239]

The second prong of the invasion came up the St. Croix River from St. Paul to Duluth and Lake Superior. The rich pinelands of the St. Croix and Rum River valleys began to be exploited in the 1850s, with most of the lumber rafted south to the Mississippi River at Minneapolis.[240] Much of the capital investment of the Minnesota phase of the white pine era was homegrown, with St. Paul and Minneapolis developers predominating in the industry. During the 1870s and 1880s, the cut moved north, following the main line of the St. Paul & Duluth Railroad. Loggers reached the Kettle River watershed in Pine County in the 1870s, and Hinckley, just seventy-five miles south of Duluth, boasted a mammoth sawmill as early at 1875.[241]

One investor who had troops in both invasions of the Minnesota north country was Frederick Weyerhaeuser. A German immigrant, Weyerhaeuser had arrived penniless in the United States in 1852. Five years later, he had saved enough money to buy a sawmill and lumberyard in his new home of Rock Island, Illinois. By the time the Civil War was winding down, Weyerhaeuser was buying vast tracts of pineland in Wisconsin.[242] In 1881, he built the world's largest sawmill under one roof at Chippewa Falls, Wisconsin. For ten years, his Chippewa Falls mill produced 400,000 board feet of lumber, shingles, and lath per day.[243] "Frederick Weyerhaeuser was to lumbering what Carnegie was to steel and Rockefeller was to oil," one local Wisconsin historian wrote.[244]

Weyerhaeuser moved into northern Minnesota in 1883. He lent $25,000 to the Knife Falls Lumber Company, started four years before at Knife Falls on the St. Louis River just west of Duluth. In 1886, the firm was renamed the Cloquet Lumber Company, and Weyerhaeuser, a silent partner until then, was named a vice president. During the next fifteen years, the Weyerhaeuser interests created the Northern Lumber Company in Cloquet and built logging railroads and dams in the Cloquet River watershed to tap the timber potential of the region.[245] In 1891, Weyerhaeuser moved to Summit Avenue in St. Paul, where he became great friends with James J. Hill of the Great Northern Railway.[246]

The Charles H. Bradley *of the O. W. Blodgett Lines steams into the Duluth Ship Canal in 1915, towing the consorts* Mary Woolson *and* Goshawk. *Both of the steam barge consorts are loaded with salt, a common back–haul cargo for lumber hookers in the early twentieth century. The* Bradley *was still hauling pulpwood in 1931 when she was rammed and caught fire in the Keweenaw Waterway.*

Knife River was an important log–loading port on Minnesota's north shore of Lake Superior during the early twentieth century. Here, locomotives of the Duluth & Northern Minnesota Railroad position carloads of logs at the mill yards in 1915.

lake there is standing pine to the amount of NINE BILLION FEET."[248]

Michigan lumbermen flooded into the district, flush with cash and eager to lock up timberlands in St. Louis, Carlton, Lake, Cook, and Koochiching Counties. They competed with Minnesota lumber barons and Frederick Weyerhaeuser. New mills in Duluth and Superior were erected to handle the expected volume increase of sawtimber. In 1889, the Scott and Holston Lumber Company purchased the Graff-Murray Mill in Duluth, described as "one of the speediest in the district."[249] The West Superior Lumber Company announced plans to build a 15-million-board-foot mill on Connors Point by the spring of 1891. The Weyerhaeuser syndicate was rumored to be looking for a site in the Twin Ports for the anticipated construction of a 60-million-board-foot mill.[250]

During the 1890s, Michigan lumbermen built a number of huge mills in Duluth and Superior. In 1891, the Duncan and Brewer Lumber Company built a mill with 40-million-board-feet-a-year capacity at Thirty-ninth Avenue West in Duluth.[251] Merrill and Ring, another Michigan outfit, built its mill on Grassy Point in Duluth the same year; ten years later, the mill was sawing more than 50 million board feet of lumber annually. Mitchell and McClure was another Michigan company with substantial holdings in the Twin Ports. In 1895, the firm, which had been in Duluth since the late 1880s, built a new sawmill on Rice's Point that had a capacity of 30 million board feet a year.[252]

A HUNDRED CARGOES

Before 1890, the vast bulk of lumber from the Duluth district went west by rail to the prairie settlements of Minnesota and the Dakotas rather than east by boat. But the infusion of Michigan lumber interests in the Twin Ports and the depletion of the softwood forest bordering Lake Huron dictated that Duluth and Superior would become a major lumber-shipping port during the decade that followed. Mitchell and McClure had anticipated the trend. In the fall of 1890, the Michigan firm announced that it was building a 3,000-foot-long lumber dock

Weyerhaeuser's growing interest in northern Minnesota in the mid-1880s coincided with the rise of Duluth and Superior as the greatest lumber port on the Great Lakes. In 1885, mills in the Twin Ports were finishing about 10 million board feet of white pine and cedar a year.[247] Five years later, Duluth and Superior would be producing more than 150 million board feet of lumber annually. "The Duluth district cannot but be the ultimate leading seat of the lumber industry of the country east of the Rocky Mountains," the *Duluth Saturday Evening Journal* noted in December 1887, "for tributary to this city and Cloquet are the largest pine forests yet remaining in the United States east of the Pacific slope. It is estimated that in the St. Louis River and its tributaries, on the north and south shores of the lake within towing distance of Duluth, on the Nemadji and adjacent streams, and last, but not least, on the American side of Rainy lake and river and about Vermilion in West Duluth just south of the Minnesota Car Company's shops. The $15,000 dock would involve driving more than 18,000 piles into the soft muck bottom of St. Louis Bay.[253]

Lumber shipments out of the port registered a healthy 40 percent gain in 1892 over the previous season, but nearly quadrupled in the panic year of 1893. They jumped nearly 80 percent in 1894, and would increase every year through the end of the century.[254] The movement by vessel and raft down the lakes was governed by two factors: the Michigan mill owners no longer had access to viable resources in their home state, and lake transportation was far cheaper than shipping lumber east by rail. One longtime Duluth sawmill owner noted at the turn of the twentieth century that, "as far as the rates to Buffalo, there was never any competition as the rail was prohibitory."[255]

The steady expansion of the lakes lumber trade out of Duluth and Superior caused a boom in lumber wharf construction during the 1890s. Most of the wharves were located along a three-mile stretch of St. Louis Bay in West Duluth between the end of Rice's Point and the end of Grassy Point.[256] And the great majority of the wharves were piled high with lumber for much of any given year. The wharves along Rice's Point could handle vessels up to 250 feet in length. Those farther upriver handled shallower draft boats of up to 150 feet in length. The work of loading the steam barges and their lumber hookers was one of the most labor-intensive activities in the port at the time. Every piece of lumber had to be loaded into the hold of the vessels by hand, although steam hoists were used for heavy timbers like railroad ties or mine timber. It typically took three days to load a lumber hooker for its voyage down the lakes to Saginaw, Chicago, or the Tonawandas.[257] Crews of "lumber shovers" made up to seventy cents an hour for loading vessels, which occasioned a local editorial writer to point out that "seven dollars a day beats many a railway president's salary, and for unskilled labor, too."[258]

Already by 1889, lumber ships were busy shuttling their cargoes of timber down the

An era came to an end in 1937 when the last log drive in Minnesota was conducted on the Littlefork River south of International Falls.

Great Lakes. In October of that year, the huge new barge *Wahnapitae* loaded 3 million board feet of lumber for Tonawanda, "by 500,000 feet the largest cargo she has ever had on," one observer noted.[259] Some of the vessels in the trade in the late 1880s and early 1890s were able to make the venture more profitable by hauling coal upbound from Ashtabula or Conneaut and lumber downbound. In late November 1889, the steel steamer *Viking* arrived in the Twin Ports to discharge 1,868 tons of coal. She then proceeded to a Duluth lumber dock to be loaded with 1.3 million board feet of lumber bound for the lower lakes.[260]

The pine lumber shipments from the head of the lakes continued to show a dramatic increase during the 1890s. By mid-decade, literally all of the production was destined for eastern markets by lake vessel rather than western markets by rail. In 1896, the Twin Ports handled 485,000 tons of lumber products. Lumber shipments increased an average of 100,000 tons every year, topping out at just under 684,000 tons in 1898, the year of the Spanish-American War.[261] Lake Superior assumed its ascendancy over the Lake Huron lumber trade in the early 1890s. By 1893, shipments from the Lake Superior ports, including Duluth, Superior, Ashland, and Marquette, were four times the lumber shipments from the Lake Huron ports. Duluth alone, with shipments of 180 million board feet, or slightly more than 140 million tons, exceeded the 178 million board feet shipped from Bay City and Saginaw, Michigan.[262]

As the nation approached the new century, lumber production reached its all-time peak at the head of the lakes. In 1898, the Alger-Smith Company, one of the largest Michigan firms, set up operations in Duluth. Founded by Michigan's General Russel Alger, the company had extensive holdings on the north shore of Lake Superior. It purchased the W. H. Knox Mill on Rice's Point and began constructing a logging railroad from Knife River on the north shore to its timber holdings in northern Lake and Cook Counties.[263] By late 1898, the Alger-Smith Company was marshalling huge rafts of north shore white pine for transport down the lakes

by the firm's steam barge *Gettysburg*.[264] The success of the Alger-Smith experiment led to a tremendous increase in rafting from Duluth during the first decade of the twentieth century.

In 1899, lumber production and shipments at the head of the lakes hit a new high. Nearly 940,000 tons of logs, sawtimber, lath, and shingles went down the lakes from Duluth-Superior in 1899 as lumber companies worked around the clock to meet the insatiable demand. The peak year for production appears to have been 1902, when Duluth mills cut 443 million board feet of lumber, although the lake shipments dropped to 659,000 tons that year.[265] All of the local mills had switched to steam-powered gang and band saws by 1899, making the Duluth mills among the most productive in the world at the time.[266]

Duluth mills began declining in production by mid-decade. In 1908, only 141 million board feet of lumber were cut at the head of the lakes, the lowest annual total since the 1880s.[267] In 1915, the cut in Duluth slipped below 100 million board feet for the first time in more than a quarter-century, and six years later, the cut was only 11 million board feet.[268]

The tremendous quantity of lumber cut by mills in Cloquet, Tower, Skibo, Two Harbors, Greenwood Lake, and elsewhere kept shipments from the Duluth-Superior harbor strong for the first two decades of the twentieth century. Lumber shipments from the Twin Ports averaged above 500,000 tons a year from 1900 to 1920, but by 1915 the trend was consistently downward. Much of the cut lumber in northern Minnesota was shipped down the Great Lakes in 1918 to meet the demands of the World War I economy, and when the guns went silent in November 1918, precious little was left to ship south and east. In 1919, much of the 94,000 tons of lumber that was shipped out of the Twin Ports was salvage from the disastrous forest fire in Carlton County the previous autumn.[269]

Shipments would decline every year after that through the 1920s for the simple reason that the white pine and eastern cedar that had fueled the lumber boom at the head of the lakes was gone. Every watercourse leading up from Lake Superior's north shore had been denuded of its timber all the way to its headwaters by 1920. Like they had in Bay City and Saginaw in the 1880s, owners stripped their mills of workable machinery and loaded it aboard flatcars for transport to new mills in the far-off Pacific Northwest. Alger-Smith closed its last Duluth mill in 1920 and dismantled nearly one hundred miles of its railroad up the north shore. When the Scott-Graff Mill closed for the last time in 1926, it signaled the end of an era.[270]

In a sense, the passing of the ports' heyday as a lumber colossus was a nonevent. By 1920, when lumber shipments had declined to 77,000 tons, shipments of iron and coal through the Twin Ports had risen to nearly 42.5 million tons. Even during the boom years of the 1900s and 1910s, lumber shipments had never been more than a quarter or a third of the annual grain tonnage passing through the head of the lakes. In the war year of 1918, when lumber shipments reached an all-time record of 1.62 million tons, 38.2 million tons of iron ore and 11.4 million tons of coal passed through Duluth-Superior.[271]

But the lumber industry never really went away. New technologies introduced during the first decades of the twentieth century allowed Minnesota and Wisconsin loggers to use previously underused species such as aspen, birch, and poplar for papermaking. Grand Rapids, Cloquet, and International Falls, Minnesota, and Park Falls and Ashland, Wisconsin, gained a new lease on life making newsprint and coated magazine stock. But perilously little of the paper made in Minnesota and Wisconsin mills went to the presses in Chicago, Kansas City, or Indianapolis by boat. As the gang saws fell silent in the Twin Ports in the 1920s, a reality became obvious to watchers of marine commerce. The din of saws had long since been drowned out by the steam whistles of ore carriers clogging the harbor.

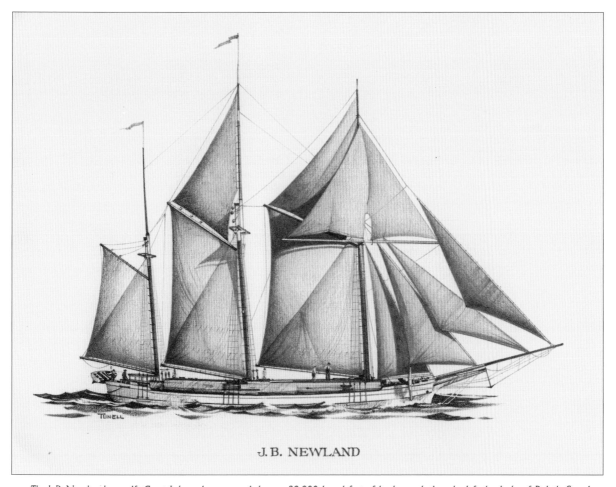

J. B. NEWLAND

The J. B. Newland, a swift Great Lakes schooner, carried some 20,000 board feet of lumber each time she left the docks of Duluth–Superior during the 1880s and 1890s. The 120-footer was in active service until 1937 and was one of the last sailing schooners operating on the Lakes.

THE ERA OF
LUMBER HOOKERS

Lumber shovers load a barge at Grand Marais, Michigan, in 1907. Lumber shovers were the aristocrats of the waterfront, earning 50 cents an hour, with premiums paid for handling oversized boards, hardwood lumber, or other "complications."

GREAT LAKES MARITIME PEOPLE called them "lumber hookers." They were the small steam barges that plied the lakes, their holds filled with sawtimber and their decks piled high with additional cut lumber. From the late 1860s until the end of the Great Lakes lumber trade in the 1920s, the lumber hookers were the vessels that carried the timber from Lake Superior downbound to the lumberyards of Chicago, Cleveland, Toledo, the Tonawandas near Buffalo, New York, and other lower lakes ports. At times in the early 1900s, lumber hookers clogged the lumber wharves and slips of the Duluth-Superior port, as crews of lumber shovers frantically loaded them with white pine and cedar sawtimber, square timber, shingles, posts, and railroad ties for another trip down the lakes.

A typical lumber hooker was just less than 150 feet long and carried an average of 300,000 board feet of lumber.[272] The vessels had one deck and often a raised poop deck. After 1880, most of their pilothouses sat on a raised fore-castle. A tall mast near the bow usually carried a gaff-rigged sail. Later versions often boasted as many as three masts and centerboards, a throwback to the days of sail. Hogging arches resembling bridge trusses often ran along either side of the length of the vessel.[273]

It's not clear where the term "hooker" came from, but the vessels' consort system may provide the answer. The hookers traditionally pulled one or more barges, doubling, tripling, even quadrupling their cargo haulage. When steam propulsion was adopted on the Great Lakes in the 1870s, regional shipyards built as many as 600 lumber hookers between 1870 and 1900.[274]

The smaller steam-powered vessels used in the trade were often called "rabbits." They were well-suited to trading into shallow-draft ports to load or discharge lumber as well as stone, coal, salt, and pig iron.[275] Many rabbits served their niche market of smaller ports into the 1940s.

Lumber hookers were often owned and operated by families. One such family was headed by Charles C. Blodgett of Bay City, Michigan, who bought the *Passaic,* his first lumber hooker, in 1877. Nephew Omer W. Blodgett joined the business; his son, Myron, was born aboard the *Passaic* in 1887.[276] When the lumber industry moved from Michigan to Minnesota in the early 1900s, O. W. Blodgett opened an office in Duluth's Lyceum Building in 1904. Much of the 14.4 million tons of lumber shipped out of the Twin Ports during those years went down the lakes aboard Blodgett vessels.[277]

By 1904, the lumber industry had begun moving to the forests of the Pacific Northwest. The lumber hookers reigned on Lake Superior for another decade, but the local industry was in decline.[278] In the 1930s, when the lakes' last lumber hookers were scrapped, the era had ended.

Lumber shovers load the Langell Boys, *a wooden lumber hooker, on a summer day in 1905. Such hookers carried as much as 400,000 board feet of lumber, stowed both below and on deck, and typically towed a consort of the same capacity.*

Duluth longshoremen load barrels of butter and cheese aboard the Anchor Line steamer Tionesta *in 1915.*

CHAPTER SEVEN

Passengers and Package Freight

WHILE THE DULUTH-SUPERIOR harbor had become one of the nation's preeminent bulk cargo ports during the late nineteenth and early twentieth centuries, it also was the terminal point for the movement of goods and people from the Lower Great Lakes to the rapidly opening frontier to the west. Hundreds of thousands of people, many of them newly arrived immigrants, passed through Duluth-Superior during the period. Most had booked passage from Buffalo, New York, on one of the many passenger steamers that plied the lakes. They arrived at the head of the lakes and transferred to trains headed for homesteads in the Dakotas and Montana. Millions of tons of package freight also passed through the Twin Ports between 1875 and the 1930s. The vast bulk of the package freight—farm implements, groceries, hardware, building materials, and, later, automobiles—were processed at waterfront warehouses and shipped west by rail.

Just as coal arrived at the head of the lakes aboard freighters from the Lake Erie ports and was shipped west to consumers by rail, package goods and people followed the same transportation model. Before the advent of modern paved roads and interstate trucking fleets in the years before World War II, rail and steamship movement of passengers and package goods was common at all the upper lakes ports. Hotels, restaurants, and distribution warehouses were built to cater to the package and passenger trade. The passenger business gradually declined with the settlement of the Northwest frontier in the 1890s and early 1900s, but Duluth-Superior remained a major summer cruise destination for another sixty years.

THE EARLY FLEETS

The movement of passengers and freight across the Great Lakes began with the construction of the Erie Canal in the 1820s. As many as fifty steamboats were built on Lakes Erie and Ontario in the decade following the opening of the Erie Canal in 1825 and the first Welland Canal in 1829 to carry immigrants to the frontier lands of Ohio, Indiana, Michigan, and Ontario. Most of the immigrants had landed in Boston, New York, Philadelphia, or Montreal and were transported west to the Great Lakes aboard canal boats. As early as 1831, a group of steamboats on Lake Erie consolidated to offer daily sailings from one end of the lake to the other. In 1836, a combination of vessel owners operated a fleet of twenty steamboats that carried passengers and cargo from Buffalo to Sandusky, Ohio, and Detroit, Michigan, which were at that time on the edge of America's western frontier.[279]

When the railroads began to push west across Ohio, Michigan, and Indiana in the 1840s, they were quick to recognize the competitive advantage of building and owning their own fleets of passenger and package freight steamboats. Carrying passengers from the immigration ports on the East Coast to the Midwest was a lucrative business, and the railroads were loath to share the profits with existing steamboat lines. In 1848, the Michigan Central Railroad began operating company-owned steamboats from Buffalo westward across Lake Erie to Detroit. Michigan Central's Lake Erie North Shore Line carried passengers on the magnificent 250-foot "palace steamers" *Atlantic* and *Mayflower* that were the talk of the Great Lakes.[280] A contemporary journalist noted that the "fairy palaces of

The wooden propeller Meteor *and the Canadian side-wheeler* Frances Smith *unload passengers and freight at Duluth in the mid-1870s. Thousands of immigrants to Minnesota, the Dakotas, and the prairie provinces came up aboard the two boats from Buffalo, Montreal, and Collingwood, Ontario.*

the imagination were never so gorgeously furnished, nor could the famous barge of Cleopatra, with its silken sails, rival this noblest of steamers."[281] The Michigan Southern & Northern Indiana Railroad followed suit in 1852, placing the three 300-foot steamboats *Southern Michigan, Northern Indiana,* and *Empire State* in the Lake Erie passenger competition. Michigan Central countered the next year with the outlandishly extravagant 350-footers *Western World, Plymouth Rock,* and *Mississippi.* Between 1848 and 1856 twenty-six of the extravagant palace steamers were constructed for the competing passenger lines; every one of them, however, was laid up in the panic year of 1857, and all were either scrapped or cut down to tow barges before the opening guns of the Civil War.[282]

Most of the passenger and package freight steamers built before 1850 were side-wheel steamers. This was true on the lakes as well and the great rivers and the Atlantic coast. The *Great Western,* which came down the ways at Huron, Ohio, in 1838, was something of a landmark craft. She had a spacious upper cabin as well as a main-deck cabin that ran the length of the vessel. Her predecessors were all single-decked

ships, with passenger accommodations and freight together. Although her boilers occupied much of the lower portion of the hull and her holds were crammed with freight and wood for fuel, the *Great Western* was capable of hauling about 300 passengers per trip, in what was then considered pure luxury.[283] Side-wheel steamers were fast, but expensive to build and to operate. Boilers, engines, and auxiliary equipment could add $50,000 to the cost of a hull, an immense amount of money at that time. The steamboats typically carried a crew of forty, more than five times the number of sailors needed to man a sailing vessel, and wood for fuel cost as much as $125 per day.[284]

By the mid-1840s, side-wheel steamers were beginning to be superseded on the Great Lakes by propellers, efficient steam-powered vessels that used a screw propeller instead of paddle wheels. The propellers burned only about a quarter of the fuel consumed by a side-wheel steamer, and they carried about half the engine room crew of the earlier side-wheelers. Consequently, they could undercut the freight and passenger rates charged by the older vessels.[285] Propellers had the added advantage of being narrow enough to navigate the locks of the Welland Canal, which connected Lake Erie with Lake Ontario and the St. Lawrence River, thus offering through connections from Lake Michigan ports to Toronto and Kingston, Ontario, and to Oswego and Rochester, New York, on Lake Ontario. More than 200 propellers were built in Great Lakes shipyards between 1840 and 1870, while the number of side-wheel steamers declined, that class of vessels finding its niche largely in day-excursion lines on Lake Erie and Lake Michigan. Side-wheelers were least suited for the open waters of Lake Superior, where ice and heavy seas often damaged their unprotected paddle wheels. Few side-wheel steamers were to be found on Lake Superior after 1880 as a result. On the lower lakes, a handful survived into the twentieth century.

The earliest steamships that served the head of the lakes were the handful of side-wheelers and propellers that were portaged around the rapids at the Soo before construction of the St. Mary's Falls Ship Canal in 1855. Several of them called at "Superior City" from the time of its first settlement in 1852. The *Manhattan, Napoleon, Swallow,* and *Baltimore* all brought settlers and supplies to the primitive wooden piers built into St. Louis Bay by Superior's first entrepreneurs. Their cargoes were laboriously transshipped from lower lakes ships past the Soo portage, and then loaded on to other boats above the Soo. With completion of the locks, lower lakes vessel owners seized the opportunity to transport copper and iron ore directly from Marquette and the Keweenaw Peninsula and to bring settlers to Lake Superior. Sheldon McKnight and Samuel Ward of Detroit, and the firms of

In this 1883 lithograph, package freight had already become big business at the head of the lakes. Note the long, low freight sheds of the Northern Pacific Railway and Stone-Ordean and C. H. Graves companies lining Commerce Slip to the right-center of the illustration. What is today the Duluth Lakewalk was then platted as St. Croix Avenue.

The propeller City of Fremont *unloads package goods at the Northern Pacific freight sheds in 1885. Note boxcars from at least four different railroads in the foreground.*

A. T. Spencer as well as Leopold and Austrian of Chicago, were some of the first to take advantage of the opportunities afforded by the Soo locks.

Chicago's Albert T. Spencer had served as agent for all of the major Buffalo and Lake Michigan steamship lines during the prosperous 1850s. He organized his own Chicago, Milwaukee, and Lake Superior Line of steamers in 1856, using the propellers *Ontonagon* and *Ogontz* and the side-wheelers *Superior* and *Lady Elgin.* They were among the earliest boats to connect Chicago with Lake Superior ports, organizing just a year after completion of the Soo locks.

The Lake Superior People's Line was organized in 1866 by Aaron Leopold of Hancock, Michigan, and Joseph Austrian of Chicago "at the request of shippers who desired relief from excessive rates." With the propeller *Ontonagon,* and later the *Norman, Peerless, Manistee,* and *Joseph L. Hurd,* the line operated from Chicago to Milwaukee, Manitowoc, Port Washington, Sheboygan, Mackinac, and all ports on Lake Superior. In 1878, the line was consolidated with the smaller A. T. Spencer fleet and incorporated as the Lake Michigan

and Lake Superior Transportation Company. It operated under that name until the turn of the century and faithfully linked the Twin Ports with Lake Michigan's passenger and package freight terminals the whole time.[286]

THE PACKAGE FREIGHTERS AND DULUTH-SUPERIOR

The completion of the first rail line to the head of the lakes in the early 1870s coincided with the introduction of a new kind of vessel to the Great Lakes trade. "Package freighters" differed from conventional passenger and freight propellers in that they had no cabins for passengers. Most were fast, utilitarian craft with little attention given to the beauty of their lines. They carried general cargo both upbound and downbound across the lakes. While the earliest were all wooden vessels, the typical package freighter after 1880 was built of steel and measured upwards of 250 feet in length. Shipyards on the lower lakes built fifty package freighters in the four decades between 1870 and 1910.[287] Many passenger and freight propellers were also converted to exclusively package cargoes during the last quarter of the nineteenth century, so that 116 package freighters were sailing the lakes in 1890, their peak year.[288]

The vast majority of package freight fleets serving the lakes were owned directly or indirectly by railroad companies. In the pre–Civil War years, Buffalo became the lower lakes' terminus for most package freight fleets, since package goods were commonly shipped by rail to Buffalo from East Coast manufacturers and stored in waterfront warehouses. The freighters were loaded at the warehouses and proceeded west across the Great Lakes to other dockside warehouses for unloading. From there, the goods were loaded aboard railcars for shipment to the Midwest and plains states. Package goods—from furniture to dairy products, processed meats, and Christmas trees—came down from the upper lakes to the Buffalo warehouses for distribution to East Coast consumers. Enormous quantities of barreled flour were also brought eastward to the mills at Buffalo.

Typical of the lines operating in Buffalo in the 1870s and 1880s were the Lake Superior Transit Company, which operated combination passenger and freight steamers, and the Lake Erie Transportation and Lackawanna Transportation Companies, which ran exclusively package freight ships. Incorporated in 1878, the Lake Superior Transit Company chartered vessels to run from Buffalo to Duluth, Superior, Ashland, and Marquette. At one time, the firm ran as many as twenty-one vessels between the lower lakes and Lake Superior; for several decades it was the largest fleet serving the head of the lakes. The pride of the Lake Superior Transit Company's flotilla were the "triplets": *India, China,* and *Japan,* all iron flyers constructed by Buffalo's King Iron Works in 1871. The Wabash Railroad, serving Indiana, Ohio, and Illinois, chartered the Lake Erie Transportation Company in 1879 to operate six package freighters between terminals in Buffalo and Toledo. The line extended its routes to Lake Superior in 1889. The Lackawanna Transportation Company began operating package freighters on the Great Lakes in the early 1880s; owned by the Delaware, Lackawanna, & Western Railway, it was known as the Red Star Line, and it operated on the lakes until 1911.[289]

The Lake Superior Transit Company's steamer *Winslow* was a good example of the nineteenth-century vessels that served the passenger and package freight trades. The *Winslow* was a near-weekly caller at Duluth-Superior docks for more than thirty years. Built in 1863, the 220-foot propeller was constructed with the distinctive wooden arches at her sides that made her type so easily recognized. She called at Duluth's Northern Pacific docks from the early 1870s until her career ended abruptly in 1891. She and several near-sisters carried immigrants, baggage, manufactured goods, and foodstuffs on the upbound leg of the journey. Downbound, they usually carried barreled flour back to Buffalo. The vessel could accommodate 80 passengers in cabins and another 250 in steerage. Between decks and in her hold was room for some 1,000 tons of cargo.

The *Winslow* was groping for the Duluth Ship Canal in a fog on October 3, 1891, when she ran aground at Forty-seventh Avenue East, damaging her bottom and flooding her hold. Much of her cargo was lightered, and the ship was subsequently refloated and brought into Duluth's Northern Pacific docks to unload the remainder and to assess the damages. Lying at the dock overnight, the big ship caught fire and burned to the waterline, the result of water seeping into lime in her cargo hold.[290]

Not all of the passenger and package freight lines serving the Duluth-Superior harbor were American. J. and H. Beatty's Northwest Transportation Company of Sarnia, Ontario, began running a small fleet of passenger and package freight vessels from Sarnia to Fort William and Duluth in the early 1870s. Their wooden steamers ferried thousands of immigrant families to the head of the lakes (both the Canadian and U.S. lake heads) during the next thirty years, and hauled beef, flour, and grain down the lakes.

The "lake and rail" route of the package freighters made the Duluth-Superior harbor the western terminus for a large share of the package goods coming up the lakes. Since much of the east side of Rice's Point and St. Louis, Howard, and Superior Bays in the 1880s were already congested with grain elevators and coal docks, and would be the site of lumber wharves and ore docks after 1890, the freight and passenger wharves in the harbor tended to concentrate in the Duluth harbor basin near the heart of the city's business district. The Lake Superior & Mississippi Railroad opened the first freight wharf in the basin in 1870. Its successor, the Northern Pacific Railway, added more warehouses at the site after 1886. A fish-and-merchandise wharf opened at the foot of Morse Street in 1878. The Northern Pacific built another warehouse complex between Sixth and Eighth Avenues West in 1883 and leased the site to the Duluth Storage and Forwarding Company. In 1895, the locally owned White Line Transportation Company built its freight and passenger wharf between Morse and Buchanan Streets, bordering on what is now Canal Park.[291]

Turn-of-the-century cargo statistics for the Twin Ports are elusive, since published annual reports are inconsistent. Tonnage figures were prepared by the local board of trade or by individual journalists. The U.S. Army Corps of Engineers took responsibility for preparation of consistent statistics for the Twin Ports in 1902. Earlier totals sometimes combined the

two ports and at other times listed only one or the other; in some years Two Harbors' commerce was reported with Duluth's, since both were in the same U.S. Customs district. Sometimes commodity statistics combined rail and lake shipments. Another inconsistency involved the measurement of specific commodities such as grain, which was reported in tons one year and bushels the next.

Despite the lapses and inconsistencies, it is clear that Duluth-Superior's commerce in package freight grew steadily following the panic of 1893 as it did in bulk cargoes. General merchandise, carried in passenger and package freight steamers, skyrocketed from 54,199 tons in 1893 to 112,643 tons in 1899 and 219,258 tons in 1905. Fourteen thousand barrels of sugar were offloaded at Duluth's warehouses and merchandise wharves in 1886, while the total climbed to 52,860 barrels in 1893 and 121,128 barrels just two years later. For the next decade the total remained at about 50,000 barrels annually. Twin Ports flour mills provided lucrative cargoes for downbound package boats. Duluth's Imperial Mill began producing in 1888 and several other

Launched in 1893 at Bay City, Michigan, the steel package freighter William H. Gratwick *calls on the Northern Pacific freight sheds on a foggy morning early in the twentieth century. In 1924, the renamed* Glenlyon, *downbound with a load of wheat, went aground off Isle Royale and broke up.*

The steel Anchor Line package freighter Delaware *docks at Superior East End flour mills in 1910.*

mills were constructed soon afterward. Local production went from 85,000 barrels in 1889 to 1.1 million barrels in 1891 and 3.5 million in 1895—a phenomenal forty-fold increase in six years.[292] During the next decade, shipments down the lakes averaged 4 million barrels each year, with an estimated annual valuation of $18 million. For most of the 1890s and the early years of the twentieth century, the package freight trade was dominated by the Northern Pacific and James J. Hill's Great Northern Railway. The Northern Pacific sheds in the Duluth harbor basin handled millions of dollars' worth of package freight every year.[293] "It's only a matter of a few short years when Duluth will rank as one of the leading jobbing centers of the West," a Duluth grocery executive predicted in 1886.[294]

That prediction was borne out two years later when Hill incorporated the Northern Steamship Company in Wisconsin. Hill, who would gain control of the Northern Pacific in the

aftermath of the panic of 1893, had been investing in eastern railroads throughout the 1880s. He reasoned that if he could control terminals in both Buffalo and Duluth, he could in effect ship goods and passengers from the East Coast to Portland and Seattle using his railroads and Great Lakes fleets. His Northern Steamship Company contracted with the Globe Shipbuilding Company of Cleveland in 1888 to build six identical package freighters for $220,000 apiece. They would be the largest package freighters of their time.[295]

Each of Hill's state-of-the-art steel package boats would be 310 feet long and 40 feet wide. With a 24½-foot depth of hold, they carried a respectable 2,800-ton payload, eclipsing the capacities of their wooden contemporaries by almost 100 percent. The ships were built with double bottoms, two decks, and six large gangways. They had 1,200-horsepower triple-expansion steam engines and operated regularly at 13 to 14 knots speed. They were also handsome craft, with black hulls, three raking masts, a visible "sheer" or curvature to their decks, and a distinctive white star on their smokestacks.[296]

The six Northern Steamship vessels—*Northern Light, Northern Wave, Northern King, Northern Queen, North Wind*, and *North Star*—made

season. They hauled general cargo upbound from Buffalo to Duluth, with stops at Cleveland, Fairport, Detroit, the Soo, and Houghton in Michigan's copper country. Upbound, they carried all of the condiments, foodstuffs, and hardware needed for the growing Northwest. Coffee, sugar, and tobacco were staples on nearly every voyage. They carried rolls of barbed wire for the ranchers in the Dakotas and Montana, as well as

The King *steams upbound across Lake Superior on a spring morning in 1930. Lashed to her deck are two dozen new automobiles, which would be unloaded in Duluth and driven to dealerships across the Upper Midwest.*

their debut in the spring of 1889. They were profitable from the beginning. That first year on the lakes, the *Northern Light* reported expenses of less than $100 a day for wages and coal. By 1890, the six boats were averaging an annual profit of around $25,000 apiece.[297]

For nearly fifteen years, the Northern Steamship Company's six package freighters were weekly callers at the warehouses and merchandise docks at the head of the lakes during the navigation

bagged cement for building projects in the Twin Cities, Fargo, and Sioux Falls. The bulk of the material was destined for Hill's warehouses in the Twin Cities, where it was either consumed locally or shipped west in Great Northern boxcars. On the downbound trips, the Northern Steamship Company boats typically carried bulk grain or barrels of flour for the Buffalo elevators that served Hill's eastern railroads, the Erie and the Lehigh Valley. They had no passenger accommodations.[298]

The Northern Steamship Company was just one of about a dozen package freight fleets that traded on the Great Lakes between 1880 and World War I, most of which called regularly on the Twin Ports. The Pennsylvania Railroad's Erie and Western Transportation Company, popularly known as the Anchor Line, was one of the larger fleets on the lakes. Operating both passenger craft and package freighters, it had as many as twenty vessels in service at any given time. The New York Central Railroad's Western Transit Company built nine of the largest package freighters then in operation on the Great Lakes between 1898 and 1913.[299] Vessels of the Lehigh Valley Transit Company were also frequent callers on the Lake Superior ports. Virtually all of the existing package freight lines were reorganized into a single operation as the Great Lakes Transit Corporation in 1915 when the new Panama Canal Act forced the railroad companies to give up their wholly owned steamship subsidiaries. Great Lakes Transit Corporation started its operations with twenty-eight ships, all of large size.

The last of the package freighter fleets to set sail on the lakes, and one of the few fleets founded after the 1915 divestiture by the railroads, was a homegrown Duluth operation. Founded in 1923 by Duluth shipbuilder Alexander McDougall, his son Miller McDougall, local investors Marshall and Royal Alworth, and Duluth banker Stephen E. Kirby, the Minnesota Atlantic Transit Company started operations with two vessels, the *Twin Cities* and *Twin Ports.* The firm quickly purchased four other ships from the federal government that had been built for World War I cargo transportation. The four vessels were distinctive 251-foot "lakers," dozens of which had been built at local shipyards for the government's Emergency Fleet Corporation in 1918, 1919, and 1920. The McDougalls wanted the four vessels named with one-syllable names that could easily be understood over the telephone or Teletype. Kirby, the son of noted Detroit naval architect Frank E. Kirby, was a well-known Duluth poker player. He suggested that the firm name the vessels the *Ace, King, Queen,* and *Jack,* a suggestion the board quickly adopted.[300]

The firm soon became known to lake-watchers as the "Poker Fleet."[301] The Minnesota Atlantic Transit Company owned and operated a massive brick terminal on Railroad Street in Duluth, and the Poker Fleet vessels carried upbound all manner of goods, including coffee, canned goods, bagged peanuts, paints, rubber, general merchandise, and new automobiles.[302] From the Railroad Street terminal, the Minnesota Atlantic boats carried cargo to Port Huron, Michigan, where butter, eggs, bagged flour, linseed, and bagged cement were transferred to railcars of the Grand Trunk Railroad for shipment to Buffalo and points east. The Poker Fleet's distinctive ships were constant visitors in Duluth and Superior between 1923 and 1941, when most of its ships were requisitioned by the U.S. Army Quartermaster Corps for wartime service. What remained of the fleet was sold to the Great Lakes Transit Corporation.

"KNOWN FROM LAKE TO COAST"

The prodigious westward tide of freight naturally spawned a profitable warehousing enterprise in the Twin Ports. The locally owned Chapin-Wells Hardware Company, founded in the early 1890s, operated a massive warehouse complex in the Duluth harbor basin adjacent to downtown Duluth. A. B. Chapin, a Michigan lumber entrepreneur, had moved to the Twin Ports to take over an existing family wholesale business. The company reorganized and changed its name to the Marshall-Wells Hardware Company in 1893 when Albert Morley Marshall joined the firm as a co-owner. Marshall was an Ohio native who had worked in a Saginaw, Michigan, hardware wholesale house for twenty years before arriving in Duluth on the eve of the panic of 1893.[303] He turned Marshall-Wells into one of the largest wholesale distributors in North America. By the early twentieth century, the firm operated branches in Spokane, Washington; Portland, Oregon; Winnipeg, Manitoba; and Edmonton, Alberta. By the 1920s, its business was exceeded by only two other wholesalers, one in Chicago and the second in St. Louis. Five company sales representatives covered a territory from Bismarck, North Dakota, to Eau Claire, Wisconsin.[304] One of his contemporaries noted in 1918 that "no other merchant in the great northwest has been the equal of Mr. Marshall in the vision and optimism which so benefited this great area of expansion ... and no other has accomplished so much as he."[305] Marshall-Wells's neighbors on Lake Avenue and the streets surrounding the Duluth harbor basin included the Kelley-How-Thompson Company, the Stone-Ordean-Wells Company, and the F. A. Patrick Company. Kelley-How-Thompson's line of Hickory brand hardware and tools was advertised as "known from lake to coast." Stone-Ordean-Wells, which was consolidated out of several smaller firms in 1896, was one of the largest wholesale grocery companies in the Northwest. F. A. Patrick, which was founded in 1901, wholesaled woolen goods from the Northern Plains to the East Coast.[306]

The package freight era on the upper lakes reached its zenith during the first decade of the twentieth century but the industry was a major employer in Duluth-Superior through the 1920s. Several factors contributed to the demise of the package freight industry on the lakes, however, in the years just before World War II. The Panama Canal Act of 1912 forced railroads to divest themselves of steamship companies serving the same routes by 1915.[307]

Once the fleets became independent, they actually became competitors to the railroads, which, by the end of World War I, were quicker and more efficient at delivering package goods across the interior of North America. The onset of the Good Roads Movement in the 1920s created a network of all-weather macadam and asphalt roads throughout the Midwest. On the heels of widespread road-building, over-the-road trucking companies began to emerge as major competitors to both the railroads and the Great Lakes package freight lines during the 1930s.

The final blow was struck early in World War II when the U.S. government in effect nationalized and requisitioned the handful of package freight steamers still plying the lakes. The federal Merchant Marine Act of 1936 had empowered the government to requisition vessels for defense purposes. Sixteen package freighters were still on the lakes when the 1942 navigation season opened. Few of them had made money during the preceding Great Depression decade. The Poker Fleet had been absorbed by the Great Lakes Transit Corporation in 1941 after nearly two decades of losses. The sixteen vessels fitted

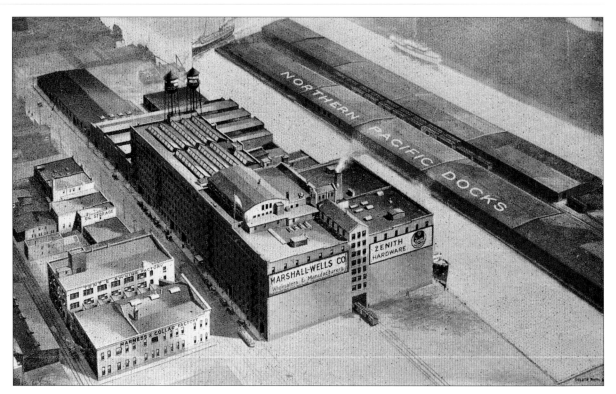

Aerial views of local landmarks were popular postcard subjects in the early years of the twentieth century. Marshall–Wells Company was one of the Upper Midwest's largest, most complete hardware distributors.

out for service in the spring of 1942 were down from twenty-six in 1930; they all sailed under the pennant of the Great Lakes Transit Corporation.[308]

In the summer of 1942, the War Shipping Administration requisitioned fourteen vessels of the Great Lakes Transit Corporation's fleet as replacements for merchant ships lost in the German U-boat offensive along the East Coast.[309] Four of the vessels were returned to Great Lakes Transit in 1943 when no shipyards could be found on the Gulf Coast to convert them for saltwater service.[310] The other ten vessels were successfully converted and saw action in coastal commerce during the war. None of the ten package freighters was lost to enemy action, and in 1947 the War Shipping Administration offered to sell all ten back to Great Lakes Transit. The company, which by then was perilously close to going out of business, couldn't afford the $500,000 repurchase price, and the ten ships were sold instead to the Overlakes Freight Corporation, a firm that operated automobile haulers and bulk freighters on the Great Lakes. Overlakes promptly sold eight of the vessels to European scrap yards, making a tidy profit in the process. The last two package freight vessels were scrapped in Great Lakes shipyards shortly after.

For all intents and purposes, the package freight business died with the outbreak of World War II. Even had the war not intervened, it is unlikely that the package freight trade would have survived into the 1950s. Competitive pressures from railroads and over-the-road trucking firms had all but sounded the death knell for the industry fifteen years earlier. The passing of the industry left the Twin Ports with little but memories of that colorful era and of the massive eight-story brick buildings ringing the Duluth harbor basin that once bustled with wholesale trade.

PASSENGER ERA COMES TO AN END
During the 1890s and early 1900s, the liners and package freighters supplemented their general cargo business with a thriving passenger trade. Thousands of immigrants, newly arrived from Southern and Eastern Europe, booked passage in

Albert M. Marshall built a hardware distribution empire during the first three decades of the twentieth century. His descendants became some of Duluth's best-known philanthropists.

Buffalo, Cleveland, and Collingwood, Ontario, for the Twin Ports, where they would jump off for homesteads in Minnesota, Iowa, Montana, and the Dakotas. Others would disembark at Houghton, Michigan, on the upbound trip, where they would find work as muckers and trammers in the deep-shaft copper mines of the Calumet and Hecla Consolidated Copper Company or the Quincy Mining Company. More established immigrants would sometimes book passage downbound on the package freighters to go back to Europe, returning to the Old World to find and bring back a wife. Others came back to America with parents or siblings. Many young Serbs, Croats, Slovenes, and Montenegrins went back to their ancestral homes to fight the Turks in the innumerable Balkan Wars between 1900 and 1912.

The passenger trade diminished rapidly after 1910 as American xenophobia began discouraging immigration from Southeast Europe. Then, too, by 1915, precious little land was left to homestead out west. By the time World War I ended in the fall of 1918, the immigrant passenger business on the lakes had dried up.

THE
AUTOMOBILE TRADE

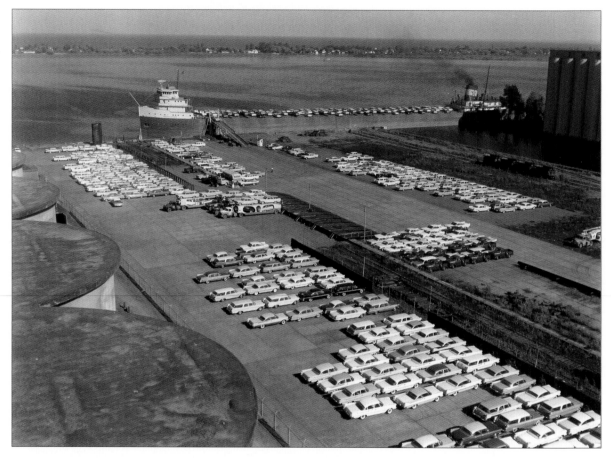

Nicholson Transit Company's Joseph H. Frantz *unloads more than a hundred cars from her decks at the company's dock off Garfield Avenue in September 1957. In 1950 alone, the Duluth auto docks handled nearly 41,000 cars and trucks.*

FROM WORLD WAR I until well into the 1960s, the Duluth-Superior harbor was a key distribution point for many of the vehicles sold in Upper Midwest automobile dealerships. Before rail automobile carrier cars or over-the-road semitrailer automobile carriers became a fixture on the nation's highways, automobiles were lashed to the decks of bulk or package freighters in Detroit and shipped up the Great Lakes. Duluth, Milwaukee, and the Canadian cities of Port Arthur and Fort William were the primary receiving ports for this unique American trade.

The automobile trade became a big business on the lakes just after World War I when Detroit automakers realized that their production capabilities outstripped their transportation abilities. Creating a network of automobile dealerships and distributorships took up the first decade of the modern industry's history. In the early days, Ford, General Motors, Chrysler, and their predecessors hired drivers to shuttle the cars to dealerships. But as the number of automobiles exponentially increased after World War I, automakers began looking for more efficient methods of transportation.

It's unclear when the first automobile went up the Great Lakes on the deck of a freighter, but the trade was well established by the mid-1920s. Duluth was a natural terminus. From the Zenith City, automobiles were either driven or placed aboard railroad flatcars for transport primarily to Minneapolis–St. Paul, but also to Fargo and Grand Forks, North Dakota; Sioux Falls, South Dakota; and as far south as Des Moines, Iowa.

From the 1920s until the 1960s, the Duluth auto terminal was located just inside the Aerial Lift Bridge in the Duluth harbor basin. Freighters would pull into the terminal slip and discharge their cargoes of new Fords, Chryslers, Whippets, Pontiacs, or any of a dozen other name brands. George "Skip" Skuggen, who started sailing with Wilson Marine Transit Company immediately after World War II, recalled that several outside rows of the automobiles on deck would have backed down a ramp to the dock.[311]

The Wilson Marine Transit Company freighters usually back-hauled automobiles to Duluth in the late summer and fall, when the new models came out. The typical freighter could accommodate 100 to 120 automobiles on deck. "They had planks they put between the hatches," Skuggen said. "We drove them all the way up on deck,

and we set them on the planks that way."[312] In late summer, when fair weather was expected, the automobiles were simply driven aboard and had their parking brakes set. During the fall months, the deck cargo was chained down. Still, there were accidents. "There were a few times when we lost them over the side when [the ship] would get into a roll," Skuggen recalled.[313]

The automobile trade generated a unique salvage episode in the annals of Lake Superior's maritime history. On the evening of November 30, 1926, the bulk freighter *City of Bangor* was wallowing in heavy seas off Copper Harbor on Michigan's Keweenaw Peninsula. Aboard her decks were 220 new Chrysler and Whippet automobiles upbound from Detroit to Duluth. Captain W. J. Mackin turned the 446-foot vessel about, hoping to round Keweenaw Point and seek refuge on the lee side of the rocky finger of land. When the thirty-year-old vessel's steering gear failed, the *Bangor* was driven ashore about five miles east of Copper Harbor.[314]

By December, Lake Superior was frozen fast from the *City of Bangor* to the Copper Harbor shore. Salvage crews lowered a ramp, backed the cars on to the ice, and drove them on an ice road into Copper Harbor. When the county plowed out the road in March, the automobiles were driven to nearby Calumet, where they were loaded aboard rail flatcars and returned to Detroit for reconditioning. The salvagers saved 202 of the 220 cars aboard the wrecked vessel.[315]

By the mid-1950s, railroads had designed carriers that could more quickly and efficiently move cars from Detroit to the nation's automobile showrooms. But for more than thirty years, waterborne transportation had been the most efficient and cost-effective way to get cars to market in the Upper Midwest.

The new concrete piers of the Duluth–Superior harbor were completed in 1902, but no aerial bridge yet spanned the Duluth Ship Canal.

CHAPTER EIGHT

A World-Class Port

THE EDITORS OF THE prestigious *Encyclopaedia Britannica* called Duluth and Superior in its 1911 edition "one of the finest natural harbours in the world. . . . The natural entrance to the harbour is the narrow channel between the two points, but there is also a ship-canal across Minnesota Point, spanned by a curious aerial bridge 400 ft. long and 186 ft. above the water. The unusually favourable position for lake transportation, and the extensive tributary region in the N.W., with ample rail connexions, make Duluth-Superior one of the greatest commercial ports in the country."[316]

There was no question that the Duluth-Superior harbor had been endowed by nature with attributes that made it among the finest in the world. But for the harbor to become "one of the greatest commercial ports in the country," it had to be shaped to fit the needs of late nineteenth- and early twentieth-century vessel traffic. That shaping process required a major and almost continual investment of time, effort, and money on behalf of public and private interests. Dredging of navigation channels and turning basins, construction of bridges, erection of navigation aids, and maintenance of slips demanded enormous investments of time and money in the decades bracketing the turn of the twentieth century. Without constant maintenance and improvement, the Duluth-Superior harbor would have remained just a fine natural harbor with little potential for commercial traffic.

BRIDGING THE GAPS

In the early days of Duluth and Superior, residents used boats to travel between the two communities. Pioneer resident George Stuntz operated a state-chartered ferry service between

Minnesota Point and landings on the Wisconsin side of Superior Bay.[317] During much of the 1870s and 1880s, Captain Albert C. Majo was one of Duluth's best-known residents. Majo operated steam-powered ferryboats between the bay front in Duluth and the Tower Avenue slip in Superior.[318]

Since the community of Duluth grew up around settlements on Minnesota Point, the first bridging attempts were designed to cross the Duluth Ship Canal. A rowboat ferry served residents until 1879, when a footbridge was built. The first bridge, however, was used only during the winter because it wasn't high enough to allow vessel clearance underneath. The footbridge lasted until the early 1880s, at which time it was replaced by a five-cent rowboat ferry.[319] When Minnesota Point was incorporated into the city of Duluth in 1890, the city took over operation of the ferry, instituting twenty-four-hour free service.

During the 1890s, the city of Duluth submitted to the War Department's and the U.S. Army Corps of Engineers' numerous plans for drawbridges, lift bridges, and roller bridges to span the Duluth Ship Canal. All were rejected as potential hazards to navigation.[320] In the 1890s, Minnesota Point emerged as a popular summer resort for affluent Duluthians, and the city redoubled its efforts to find a bridge that would satisfy the requirements of the Corps of Engineers. Finally, in 1904, the city submitted plans for a bridge that met the specifications of the corps. Modeled after a bridge that had recently been erected in the French port city of Rouen, the Aerial Ferry Bridge, as it was known at the time, was built of vertical steel towers on either side of the ship canal, connected by a horizontal steel truss across the top of the structure. The lower edge of the truss stood 150 feet above the surface of the water, allowing unimpeded navigation for vessels using the ship canal.[321] Access to Minnesota Point was provided with the addition of a carriage suspended on rails beneath the truss. The carriage had a capacity of just over sixty-two tons and could carry everything from a fully loaded streetcar to several delivery trucks or 350 passengers.[322] Operated by batteries with a hand-winch system as a backup, the carriage could make a round trip in less than five minutes.

The Aerial Ferry Bridge was built in 1905. During the navigation season, it was operated twenty-four hours a day, with two trips an hour scheduled for nighttime and early morning hours.[323] The bridge served Duluth's needs for a quarter-century. In 1929, increasing traffic to Minnesota Point, which had become a year-round residential neighborhood, convinced the city that it needed to rebuild the bridge with a lift span. The carriage was replaced in 1930 by a 900-ton roadway lift that took fifty-five seconds to rise to its height of 135 feet above the water, more than enough clearance seventy-some years later to allow even the largest vessels to slip through beneath the bridge.[324] Duluth's signature landmark was placed on the National Register of Historic Places in 1973.[325]

Bridging the harbor itself proved to be a less daunting task, primarily because the railroads serving the Twin Ports took the lead in addressing the problem. The Northern Pacific Railway built the first bridge across St. Louis Bay in 1885 to connect Connors and Rice's

Swedish immigrants were paid $2 a day to haul gravel to a steam–driven cement mixer for making footing blocks on the Duluth East Pier in 1899. The new range light is in the background.

Points. Known officially as the Minnesota Draw-bridge and Wisconsin Drawbridge (depending on which side of the harbor one lived on), the 290-foot-long structures later became known to residents at the head of the lakes as "the old bridge with the turn in it."[326] The Minnesota Drawbridge had a single track, and the Wisconsin Drawbridge sported a double track. The two bridges carried the ports' growing grain traffic during the late 1880s.[327]

Rail congestion on the approaches to the Minnesota and Wisconsin Drawbridges led to the construction of the Grassy Point Draw-bridge across the St. Louis River in 1887. Built by the St. Paul & Duluth Railroad, which was later acquired by the Northern Pacific, the Grassy Point Drawbridge allowed the St. Paul & Duluth access to the rapidly developing Elevator Row in Superior.[328]

The erection of coal and ore docks on both sides of the harbor created demand for more bridges in the 1890s. In 1892, the Duluth & Winnipeg Railway built its St. Louis River Bridge well upriver at New Duluth. The drawbridge gave the Duluth & Winnipeg access to the new ore docks on Allouez Bay, and on November 11, 1892, a Duluth & Winnipeg train carried the first load of Mesabi Range iron ore across the newly com-pleted bridge.[329] The Duluth & Winnipeg was absorbed into the Great Northern Railway in 1898, and the acquiring railway had a long line between Cloquet and the ore docks in Superior, albeit one with a better grade than the Duluth, Missabe, & Northern Railway trackage downhill from Proctor. Shortly after the turn of the twentieth century, the Great Northern elected to abandon the former Duluth & Winnipeg line. The St. Louis River Bridge served as a vehicle bridge for several years before the Great Northern dismantled the span in 1909.[330]

The growth of Duluth-Superior in the 1880s and early 1890s generated the need for bridges to move people rather than cargo between the two communities. By the early 1890s, most res-idents of the Twin Ports got around by street-car. Electric street railways were incorporated in Superior and Duluth as early as 1882,

although the first systems linking the two cities used horse-drawn streetcars instead of electric-powered trolleys. Shortly after Superior was incorporated as a city in 1889, the Douglas County Street Railway Company was merged into the Superior Rapid Transit Railway Com-pany, which began an aggressive program of electrifying the streetcar lines.[331] The Lamborn Avenue line served the rapidly growing Howard's Pocket area of the city, home to the American Steel Barge Company shipyards. Because of the employment and commercial activity, the streetcar company built its Lamborn Avenue Bridge in 1893.[332]

The Lamborn Avenue Bridge was just a local line. In the 1890s, there was still no reliable way for residents to cross St. Louis Bay between Duluth and Superior without resorting to the dangerous precedent of walking along existing railroad bridges. In 1890, the Minnesota and Wisconsin delegations in Congress introduced legislation that would allow Duluth and Superior to jointly build a toll bridge between the two communities. It took three years for the two cities to even agree on where the toll bridge would cross the harbor, and it wasn't until 1895 that the Duluth-Superior Bridge Company was incorporated to build a streetcar bridge con-necting the Twin Ports.[333] The Minnesota and Wisconsin legislatures passed enabling legislation in their respective 1895 sessions to allow bond-ing for construction of what was designated the Duluth-Superior Bridge.[334] Construction on the 485-foot drawbridge across the harbor between Rice's and Connors Points got under way in 1897. The bridge itself sported a revolving drum forty feet in diameter that opened and closed the center swing span. At the time of construc-tion, it was reputed to be the largest center swing span bridge in existence.[335]

The completion of the Interstate Bridge was one of the final steps in creating the modern bridge infrastructure that served Duluth-Superior and its industries for much of the first three-quar-ters of the twentieth century. The twenty-five-year effort to bridge the harbor culminated in the 1910 completion of the Oliver Bridge. It crossed the river below the older St. Louis River

The wooden steamer W. B. Morley *passes beneath the new Duluth Aerial Bridge in this 1908 postcard view.*

The Duluth–Superior ferry Hattie Lloyd, *a fixture in the harbor for more than two decades, passes beneath the center span of the Interstate Bridge about 1910.*

Bridge. Built by the Duluth, Missabe, &
Northern Railway and named for Henry W.
Oliver, the Pittsburgh executive who headed the
region's major iron ore firm, the Oliver Bridge
served the new Minnesota Steel Company mill
in Gary–New Duluth. With a 300-foot center
span, the nearly 2,200-foot-long double-deck
Oliver Bridge would remain one of the key railroad bridges in the Twin Ports for more than
eighty years.[336]

Bridge construction between 1885 and 1910 tied
the two ports at the head of the lakes into a
single maritime commercial powerhouse. It
remained for the U.S. Army Corps of Engineers
to officially unify the two ports.

UNCLE SAM TAKES A HAND

The virtual explosion of grain, coal, iron ore,
lumber, and package freight tonnages on the
Great Lakes in the 1890s brought with it the
recognition that the maritime transportation
system connecting Duluth-Superior with
Buffalo, New York, was a key driver in the
emerging industrial economy of the United
States. The nation's steel mills, many located on
the shores of the lower lakes, depended upon
the waterborne transport of iron ore, limestone, and coking coal for the prodigious productivity gains that would make America a
world leader in steel production by the first
decade of the twentieth century.[337] The railroads
pushing west from the Great Lakes were fueled
by coal hauled up by water to Duluth-Superior
from the coalfields of Pennsylvania. The growing
cities of the Midwest and Middle Atlantic states
were being built from the ground up by dimension lumber shipped down the lakes from
Michigan, Wisconsin, and Minnesota. More than
35 million people, over half the nation's population in 1900, lived in the states bordering the
Great Lakes.[338]

It had become obvious to the U.S. government
by the early 1870s that shipping on the Great
Lakes was big business. In 1881, Congress
assigned maintenance and oversight of the Soo
Locks to the U.S. Army Corps of Engineers.
When it took over operation in 1881, the corps
immediately enlarged the existing locks by

dredging 16-foot channels through the St. Mary's
River and building a new lock to handle the
200-foot bulk freighters that were becoming
increasingly common on the Great Lakes.[339]
Because the channels in the Duluth-Superior
harbor had been dredged to only 12 feet, some
of the largest freighters on the lakes in the
1880s were unable to fully load at the grain
elevators in the Twin Ports. Commerce grew
rapidly during the decade despite the harbor's
limitations. More than 5.4 million bushels of
wheat a year passed through the Soo Locks
during the first half of the 1880s. By the second half of the decade, wheat traffic through
the Soo had more than tripled, to an average
of 18.4 million bushels a year.[340] Other cargoes
showed similar gains. Coal increased from an
annual average of 463,000 tons in the early
years of the decade to an annual average of
1.4 million tons in the last years of the decade.
Iron ore jumped from an annual average of
868,000 tons in the first half of the decade
to an annual average of 2.5 million tons during
the second half of the 1880s.[341]

With the prospect of even greater cargo movements in the 1890s, the corps began planning a
major expansion of the Soo Locks together
with improvements to the major harbors on the
Great Lakes. Instrumental in the planning phase
was Major Orlando M. Poe of the corps' Detroit
District. An Ohio native, Poe had helped survey
the northern Great Lakes in the 1850s.

Poe, who served as district engineer of the
Detroit District from 1870 to 1873 and again
from 1883 to 1895, was in charge of the Soo
Locks and all of the connecting channels in
the Great Lakes. In early 1891, then Colonel Poe
submitted his recommendations to Congress
for a uniform channel, 20 feet in depth and
300 feet wide, for all of the connecting channels of the Great Lakes from Chicago and
Duluth-Superior to Buffalo.[342] Poe's recommendations were strongly backed by the Duluth-
Superior Harbor Improvement Committee and
its organizer, shipbuilder Alexander McDougall.
In 1892, Congress passed the Rivers and Harbors Act, which authorized $3.35 million to
deepen Great Lakes channels to 20 feet. Four

While contractors for the U.S. Army Corps of Engineers were busy improving harbors the length and breadth of the Great Lakes in the 1890s and early 1900s, other crews were completing the construction of the Poe Lock at Sault Ste. Marie, which opened to commercial traffic in 1895.

years earlier, Congress had appropriated the money to start construction on a new lock at the Soo that would be 800 feet long and 100 feet wide. As it turned out, the new lock was completed by the time Congress actually appropriated the money for the channel-deepening project. The new lock opened for commercial traffic on August 3, 1896. By that time, General Poe had been dead almost a year. The popular officer had slipped and injured himself while inspecting lock construction in the summer of 1895. He died October 2, 1895, and the corps honored his memory by naming the new lock after him.[343]

Money for improvements to the Duluth-Superior harbor started flowing to the Duluth District of the Corps of Engineers in the summer of 1896. The corps knew that Duluth-Superior's needs were as great or greater than any of the other Great Lakes ports slated for harbor improvements. As far back as 1883, the corps had noted that "the harbor of Duluth is in reality an artificial one."[344]

The average natural depth of the harbor was 9 feet, and only work done under the earlier Rivers and Harbors Acts of 1873 and 1881 had resulted in average channel depths of 16 feet.[345] Five years later, in 1886, the federal government created the Duluth District of the Corps of Engineers; in 1888, the district was enlarged to include most of the south shore of Lake Superior.[346]

Major Clinton B. Sears, the Duluth District engineer since 1892, had argued persuasively for more money than Congress had intended spending. In 1895, Sears began collecting harbor statistics and reported that the Duluth-Superior harbor had logged visits from 1,100 ships. The value of the commerce handled by the Twin Ports that year exceeded $100 million, he reported.[347] In the end, Congress agreed with Sears's estimates for Duluth-Superior harbor improvements. On June 3, 1896, Congress appropriated $3 million for the necessary work. The legislation also effectively combined the two harbors into one. Last, the

1896 appropriation established a "continuous contract system" for the harbor improvement work, replacing the old piecemeal contract system that hampered district engineers. Under the terms of the 1896 act, the district engineer was able to assign long-term dredging contracts.[348]

arrived in Duluth to begin excavating the outer end of the ship canal.[349] The dredge began by digging a 24-foot-deep trench on the outside of the South Pier. At the same time, work crews began driving 50-foot Norway pine piles into the lake bottom to support the timber cribs and concrete superstructures that

The concrete piers lining the Duluth Ship Canal have withstood more than a century of ice and thaw cycles. Here, the bulk freighter Home Smith slogs through heavy ice into the harbor in 1910.

The capstone of Sears's audacious plan for improving the harbor was a total reconstruction of the Duluth Ship Canal. His proposal called for widening the canal from 200 to 300 feet and lengthening the piers from 1,200 feet to 1,600 feet, and deepening the entry to at least 20 feet. Before it was complete, the task would require nearly 1,000 men and more than a decade of effort.

Work got under way late in the summer of 1896 when the steam dredge Old Hickory

would make up the piers. The piles were cut off underwater at a depth of 24 feet to provide a uniform surface for the cribs. More than 5,000 pilings were used in the construction of the two piers at Duluth.[350]

By 1900, work continued as the crews poured 9,000 barrels of portland cement for the north pier and finished off the concrete superstructure for both piers. During 1901, 9,000 tons of stone riprap were placed around the base of the two new piers to ensure against erosion and undermining by lake currents, while topside crews erected ninety-eight cast-iron lampposts along the walkways. It was the finishing touch.[351]

While crews were undertaking reconstruction of the Duluth Ship Canal, others had begun work on the breakwaters and piers protecting the Superior entry some six miles to the east. The $2 million project took eight years to complete. It involved replacing the 1875 wooden piers with monolithic concrete piers similar to those used on the ship canal, plus the ambitious task of adding 3,600-foot stone breakwaters to protect the entry and

Between 1900 and 1906, the Corps of Engineers dredged more than seventeen miles of channels in the harbor to the 20-foot depth. The last jewel in the crown of the huge project was the creation of a protected anchorage basin inside the harbor that would shelter dozens of vessels in stormy weather.[354] When the harbor improvement project was finally completed, Duluth-Superior had been turned into one of the finest commercial harbors in the nation.

The work was finished in the nick of time. The flood of ore from the Mesabi Range

A rare view of the Superior entry during the turn-of-the-century harbor modernization. In this photo taken November 9, 1900, crews are dredging the channel and removing the old East Pier. The new West Pier is under construction at left.

to still Lake Superior's stormy waters. The project also widened the entry to 500 feet. It was not completed until 1908.[352]

Colonel Sears's nine-year tour of duty as district engineer ended in 1901, but the project was in capable hands. Throughout his time in Duluth, Sears was assisted by John H. Darling. Another capable assistant on the decade-long harbor improvement project was Captain Charles S. Barker, who served on the district engineer's staff from 1887 to 1903.[353]

began cascading into the ore docks of the Twin Ports after 1895. By 1906, the year that the anchorage basin was completed, the ore docks in the harbor were handling 19.3 million tons of Mesabi ore a year. Nearly 10 million tons of grain, coal, lumber, and package goods swelled the total for Duluth-Superior that year to 29.2 million tons.[355] Almost 5,600 vessels visited the head of the lakes in 1906, down from nearly 8,000 in 1902—and a confirmation of the fact that vessels were getting larger and needed the increased depth in the harbor to maneuver and load properly.[356] At the Soo, the Weitzel and Poe Locks were already reaching their maximum capacity by 1906. The superintendent of the locks logged 22,155 vessel passages during 1906 and registered tonnage of more than 41 million tons. Three-quarters of the tonnage was iron ore.[357] In 1907, the Corps of Engineers began construction of yet another major lock. Named the Davis Lock in honor of Colonel Charles E. L. B. Davis, the Detroit District engineer from 1904 to 1908, the $6.2 million project got under way in the summer of 1907.[358] The 1,350-foot-long Davis Lock opened in 1914, just in time to handle the increased volume of downbound iron ore and grain destined for America's defense effort in World War I.[359]

The lumber hooker Simon Langell (foreground) steams past five dredges excavating the anchorage basin in the inner harbor. The 1906 deepening of the basin marked completion of the turn-of-the-century harbor improvement program.

The 1906 strike by licensed seamen against the Great Lakes fleets idled many vessels in the newly deepened anchorage basin of the Duluth–Superior harbor.

COMMERCIAL FISHING

A Duluth–based Sam Johnson Fish Company crew gathers an April smelt harvest in the late 1950s.

THE U.S. ARMY CORPS OF ENGINEERS' ten-year harbor improvement project neared completion in 1906, making the Duluth-Superior port one of the most modern in the nation. Yet it was still the home port for a commercial fishing fleet that had provided a livelihood for area residents since the Twin Ports were settled a half-century before. Much of that fleet would later disperse up Lake Superior, following the lake trout, herring, whitefish, and siscowet as they were fished out in the 1920s and 1930s.[360]

The heyday of commercial fishing on the west end of the lake lasted from the 1880s to the 1930s. Though the work was dangerous, especially in spring and fall when the best fishing coincided with the lake's worst weather, 195 commercial fishermen lived in Duluth by 1895; dozens more operated collection stations in French River, Knife River, Larsmont, Two Harbors, Grand Marais, and other north shore communities.[361] Most of the barreled fish was sent by rail to Minneapolis, St. Paul, Chicago, Kansas City, and St. Louis.[362] Much of the catch was salt herring, a delicacy for immigrant Scandinavians and Germans of the Midwest.[363]

Some boats were steam-powered craft, often converted tugboats; most were mackinaw sailing boats or open skiffs. Trout fishermen used nets set on reefs and shoals, as well as hand lines with baited hooks set in deep water.[364] Most fishermen were Scandinavian immigrants, predominantly Norwegians, although Swedes and Finns made up the majority in communities such as Larsmont, Minnesota.[365] Norwegian immigrant Sam Sivertson and his brother, Andrew, sailed in 1892 from Duluth to Isle Royale, where they operated a collection station for the Booth Fisheries Corporation.[366] Sam and wife Theodora were aboard the Booth Fisheries packet *America* in June 1928 when it struck a reef and sank off Washington Harbor. They and their fellow passengers were rescued.[367]

For most of the peak years, the A. Booth Packing Company controlled the fisheries on Lake Superior. Founded in Chicago by Alfred Booth, a British immigrant, the company started buying fish off the Lake Michigan docks in the 1850s and distributing them to restaurants. By 1885, A. Booth and Sons controlled commercial fishing from Chicago to Escanaba, Michigan.[368] The Booths established a branch in 1885 at Bayfield, near Wisconsin's Apostle Islands. In 1886, they opened a branch in Duluth when they bought out J. E. Cooley, who had concluded "that the surest way to make money in the fish business is to keep out of it."[369]

By the mid-1890s, the Duluth Booth office handled the distribution for fish collected from the Apostle Islands to the Canadian border. During the 1890s and early 1900s, the Booth offices in Duluth operated a fleet that included the *S. B. Barker, T. H. Camp, A. Booth, Hunter, Hiram R. Dixon, Liberty, C. W. Moore, Bon Ami, Easton,* and *America.*[370] The steamers traditionally offered passenger and freight service to the isolated communities along the north shore.

From 1900 to 1920, the Booth interests employed several hundred people in Duluth and Bayfield, and bought fish from as many as 400 commercial fishermen on Lake Superior.[371] The Duluth Booth branch reached its peak in 1915 when it shipped more than 10,000 tons of fish out of the Twin Ports. But over thirty years, fish stocks had been overharvested. In 1885, 5 million pounds of whitefish were netted; by 1900, the catch dropped to 1.75 million pounds.[372]

Lake trout and herring became the mainstays of commercial fishing. Lake trout production increased from 1.65 million pounds in 1879 to 5.8 million pounds in 1899, mostly to replace the depleted whitefish catch.[373] Similarly, the herring catch, the only commercial production to grow after the 1920s, went from nearly nothing in 1879 to 1.3 million pounds in 1899.[374] As late as WWII, the remaining commercial fishermen netted 5 million pounds of herring a year.[375]

The fall-off of lake trout stocks in Lake Superior after 1920 was compounded by the the Great Depression. In the late 1930s, the penultimate blow was struck when the sea lamprey population exploded in Lakes Superior, Huron, and Michigan. The lamprey, an eel that preyed on game fish such as lake trout, had been in Lake Ontario since at least the 1830s.[376]

With the exception of the herring fishery, the Lake Superior commercial fishing industry had dwindled to near nothing by 1940, another of the once seemingly impregnable port industries that almost vanished with the passage of time.[377]

The whaleback Colgate Hoyt *passes through the Soo Locks in 1896. Named for one of shipbuilder Alexander McDougall's investors, the* Hoyt *was the prototype for subsequent whalebacks and designed to tow several consort whaleback barges.*

CHAPTER NINE

The Shipbuilders

TO BE RANKED AMONG the Great Lakes' foremost ports in the late nineteenth and early twentieth centuries, a city had to claim a viable shipbuilding industry. Cleveland's Globe Shipbuilding yards were known for high-quality workmanship from one end of the lakes to the other, and the Dry Dock Works on Detroit's waterfront designed and built some of the most elegant cruise vessels on the lakes. Shipyards in Buffalo, Toledo, Bay City, Manitowoc, Milwaukee, and Chicago built thousands of vessels, from schooners and barges to fine passenger liners and giant steel bulk freighters.

Shipbuilders in the Duluth-Superior harbor competed with the best in the nation during the thirty years from 1888 to the end of World War I. Duluth- and Superior-built "whalebacks" carried iron, coal, and grain from Lake Superior all over the Great Lakes and back, and several times to European ports as well. With their rounded bows and decks awash with water, the distinctive "pigboats" were a constant advertisement for the shipbuilding prowess of the yards at the head of the lakes. During World War I, Duluth and Superior shipyards would build more than 100 coastal freighters for the U.S. maritime war effort.

Duluth-Superior in the early twentieth century was also a major center for ship repair and provisioning. The Pittsburgh Steamship Company, U.S. Steel Corporation's iron ore fleet, had its headquarters in Duluth. As a result, many of the fleet's 112 vessels found winter berths there.

ORIGINS OF TWIN PORTS SHIPBUILDING

Shipbuilding in Duluth-Superior goes back to the earliest days of the two communities. The first shipyard in the region was built at the mouth of the Nemadji River in east Superior by pioneers R. G. Coburn and Diederich Schutte in 1858. In 1869 the famous Merritt family of Duluth constructed the scow schooner *Chaska* at Oneota, the present site of the Duluth, Missabe, & Iron Range Railway ore docks. Nine years later, in 1878, George Brooks of Superior reportedly built the first steam vessel at the head of the lakes.[378]

Napoleon Grignon, a French-Canadian immigrant, was the most successful of the early shipbuilders in the Twin Ports. He arrived in Duluth sometime in the mid-1870s and established a small shipyard at Buchanan Street on Minnesota Point, near the ship canal. Grignon incorporated his operation in 1880 as the Marine Iron and Shipbuilding Company, and he won contracts for some fifty wooden tugs and dredge scows during the next decades. The yard also did considerable repair and maintenance work on local vessels. Then under the management of Martin Christiansen, Marine Iron Works moved to larger facilities at Eleventh Avenue West in 1918, where the company constructed another fifty-seven vessels before 1940, many of them under contract for the federal government.

The marine contracting firm of Upham, Williams, and Company of Duluth built a handful of tugs and barges for the firm's own use during the 1880s, and sometime in the mid-1880s built a floating dry dock, the first on Lake Superior. Relatively small by most shipyard standards, the dry dock was large enough for tugs and small steamers. In 1889, the firm repaired the propeller shaft of the 200-foot steamer *City of Fremont* in the dry dock. The Upham, Williams, and Company dry dock was acquired by Grignon's Marine

Iron and Shipbuilding Company before the turn of the twentieth century and was still in use by Marine Iron Works in the 1920s.

Duluth and Superior had modest but respectable shipbuilding facilities with the dawning of the Gay Nineties, but the local yards certainly did not enjoy world renown. That distinction would require two things: vision and investment capital. The Twin Ports found both in Alexander McDougall.

McDougall was a native of a small fishing village on the island of Islay off Scotland's windswept west coast. In 1852, when he was seven, his family moved to Glasgow, where his father worked briefly as a police officer.[379] Two years later, the family immigrated to Canada. Their destination

Alexander McDougall, an immigrant from Scotland's Isle of Islay, made Duluth–Superior into a major shipbuilding port in the late nineteenth and early twentieth centuries. He died in 1923, eight years after this photo was taken.

was Nottawa, Ontario, a village two miles from Collingwood, where other residents from Islay had settled. Tragically, patriarch Dugald McDougall died there in a sawmill accident two years later, when Alex was eleven.

In 1860, Alexander McDougall was apprenticed to a blacksmith, a job he hated. The next year, he left home and signed on as a deckhand aboard the propeller *Edith.* He sailed all that summer and fall and returned to Nottawa in November, bearing a new cookstove for his mother.[380] For nineteen years, recalled McDougall in his autobiography, "I followed the Lakes as deckhand, porter, second mate, mate and pilot, and then captain."[381]

When McDougall finally settled ashore in 1880, it was in Duluth. The Scots captain had steamed through the Duluth Ship Canal many times during the 1870s, and he had found the rockbound north coast of Lake Superior similar to the landscape of his native Islay. For much of the early 1870s, he had captained the Anchor Line's *Japan,* hauling passengers and freight between the head of the lakes and Buffalo.[382] Later in the 1870s, he had invested in a commercial fishing venture while he served as captain aboard the *City of Duluth.* He had married Emmeline Ross of Toronto in the summer of 1876, and when their son Ross was born two years later, McDougall began looking for a place to settle down.

In 1880, he purchased a house in Duluth at Fifth Avenue West and First Street, moved his family to the Twin Ports, and started a stevedoring business. His first clients were the Northern Pacific, the Wilson fleet, and Smith-Davis and Company of Buffalo.[383]

McDougall's stevedoring business employed several hundred laborers during the early 1880s; together with a vessel brokerage, it made him a leader in Duluth's maritime community. He was a respected member of the board of trade and a tireless promoter of the Duluth-Superior harbor.[384] Although it was at first known to relatively few people, McDougall also quietly began pursuing more imaginative schemes. On the long voyages

McDougall gathers his American Steel Barge Company staff for a photograph in 1895. The company founder is seated third from the left in the front row, a draftsman's pencil tucked behind his right ear.

across the lakes during the preceding years, he had sketched out all kinds of inventions. One of his ideas was for an unorthodox ship type that he thought might revolutionize the carriage of bulk cargoes. He envisioned a steel hull of unconventional design that might be built more cheaply than contemporary wooden ones, and ultimately prove more efficient as well. What he really wanted to do in Duluth was to build ships.

McDougall's dream was a double-bottomed steel ship that would be roughly tubular in cross-section, with rounded decks and full, square holds to maximize cargo capacity. They would have no regular deckhouses, but instead round turrets enclosing cabins and machinery. Topping off the strange design were a bow and stern that tapered to a point.[385]

In 1885, McDougall opened an office at the corner of Third Avenue West and Superior Street for his ship brokerage. About the same time, he began buying up waterfront land in Duluth for

a potential shipyard.[386] He built his first ship, the *Barge 101,* in 1888 at Fifteenth Avenue West and Railroad Street.[387]

Barge 101 was unlike anything seen on the Great Lakes before or since. From the waterline down, her construction was unremarkable. But above the waterline, the 191-foot vessel differed sharply from the conventional naval architecture of the day. "Instead of a deck like ordinary vessels," a contemporary newspaper account said, "this craft will have a round top, which will be a continuance of the hull."[388] The barge was 22 feet wide and had a capacity of 1,600 tons of bulk cargo, loaded through nine sliding hatches on the rounded deck.[389] McDougall had built the barge with his own money, using crews employed by his stevedoring firm. Like anything new, *Barge 101* was greeted with derision and incredulity by the established Great Lakes industry.

"After demonstrating my ideas by models," McDougall recalled years later, "I could not get

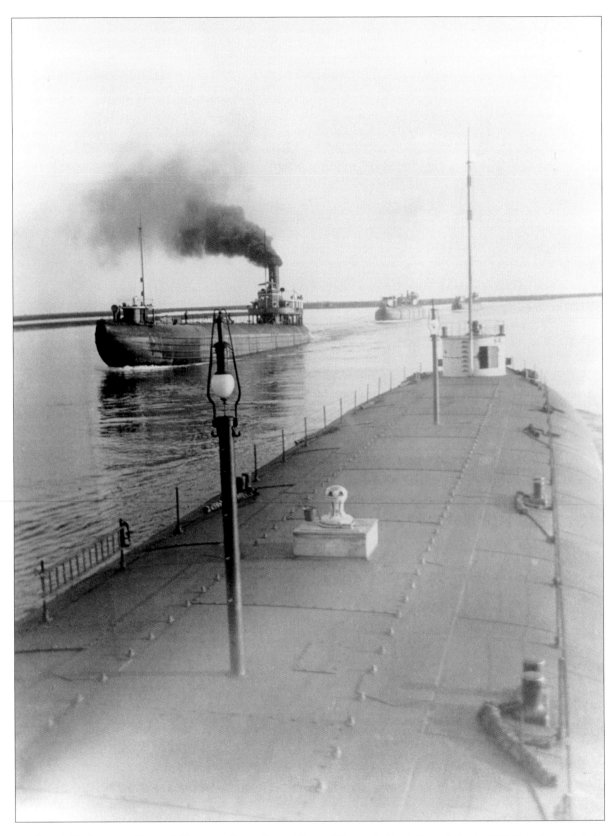

The whaleback steamer Thomas Wilson *tows* Barge 126 *and* Barge 127 *past the* Frank Rockefeller *in 1897. Note the small deck hatches on the* Rockefeller *secured with rubber gaskets, and the arc light standards spaced along the deck. After an illustrious career on the lakes, the* Rockefeller *became the museum ship* Meteor *in Superior. The ill–fated* Wilson *was sheared in half off the Duluth entry in 1902 with a loss of nearly half her crew.*

anything from ship owners and captains except comments such as: 'She will roll over, having no masts to hold her up;' or 'She has no flat deck and bulwarks to keep the waves off;' or 'You call that damn thing a boat,—why it looks more like a pig.'[390] The name "pigboat" stuck, but the shipbuilder didn't care. McDougall preferred to call his creation a "whaleback," the nickname by which the vessels became known on the Great Lakes. He painted *Barge 101* red, white, and blue, and dispatched her to nearby Two Harbors to pick up a load of iron ore.[391] The barge was towed down the lakes by the tug *Record* and discharged her cargo at Cleveland in July 1888.[392] For much of her fifteen-year career on the lakes, the *101* was towed by vessels of the Wilson

intrigued by the whaleback design. He quickly put together a consortium of East Coast and Cleveland investors and formed a company to build whalebacks at the head of the lakes.

THE AMERICAN STEEL BARGE COMPANY

The new company was called the American Steel Barge Company. Directors included Hoyt, Charles L. Wetmore, and brothers Charles L. and James L. Colby, all Rockefeller associates.[396] The firm reserved $25,000 in stock for McDougall in exchange for the patents to the whaleback, and McDougall was promised an additional 20 percent of the capital stock when he could afford to purchase the shares. McDougall immediately telegraphed Duluth to

McDougall's first hull, Barge 101, *shortly before its launching in June 1888. Originally scheduled to be named* Nonsuch, *the hull reverted to a more prosaic barge numbering system.*

Marine Transit fleet, owned by McDougall's old friend Captain Thomas Wilson.[393]

McDougall had invested much of his savings in building *Barge 101*.[394] If the Scotsman were to build more whalebacks, he had to find investment capital to underwrite the venture. He spent the summer and fall of 1888 seeking financing for his shipbuilding business. In early 1889, he appeared at the offices of John D. Rockefeller in New York City.[395] Colgate Hoyt, a longtime associate of the reclusive oil baron, was

start ordering supplies for construction of several more whaleback barges. Between the summer of 1889 and December of 1890, the American Steel Barge Company launched four whaleback barges and the steamer *Colgate Hoyt* at its Duluth shipyards.

With the Rockefeller syndicate's money behind him, McDougall had big plans for building whalebacks. But the Scotsman's biggest problem was finding the space to build several ships at once. The company's property in Duluth had

The anchor chains through the hawse pipes of this turn-of-the-century whaleback steamer (at the American Steel Barge Company docks in 1893) show why Great Lakes mariners called the vessels "pigboats."

room to build only two hulls at a time. In the fall of 1889, McDougall began seeking roomier accommodations for his venture. He investigated a waterfront parcel in West Duluth, but he was being wooed by community interests across St. Louis Bay in West Superior, Wisconsin. R. J. Wemyss, general manager of the Land and River Improvement Company, saw the potential in McDougall's shipyard as a Superior employer. He persuaded the Superior City Council to offer McDougall a plot of vacant waterfront land, along with a subsidy of 10 percent of the firm's payroll costs and dry dock costs. The package was worth $200,000, and McDougall agreed to move the American Steel Barge Company across the state line.[397] The site of the proposed ship-yard was Howard's Pocket, a shallow bay on the west side of Connors Point that separated the point from the mainland.[398]

The subsidy was one of the best deals ever made by the city of Superior. By 1893, more than 1,200 workers were swarming over the shipyards on the Wisconsin side of the harbor.

Superior had a population of just under 12,000 people in 1890. Three years later, its population had more than doubled, and some estimated the Wisconsin port city's population was close to 30,000 in 1893.[399] Millwrights, boilermakers, arc and acetylene torch welders, and other skilled tradesmen employed in the shipyards bought homes in the many new additions springing up in Superior. Hundreds of laborers spent their paychecks in the pharmacies and grocery, dry goods, and hardware stores lining Tower Avenue and Belknap Street.

McDougall's crews descended on Howard's Pocket soon after the ice retreated in the spring of 1890. They dredged five slips to a depth of 13 feet to serve as launching ways for the expected production of the yards. Carloads of 60-foot-long Douglas fir arrived via the Northern Pacific to frame up the ways. McDougall erected barn-like structures with movable walls so that construction of ships could continue through the brutal Wisconsin winters. Sand was brought in by rail to fill the swampy portions of Howard's

Pocket; it served as a stable foundation for the piles supporting the shipyard's 350-foot docks.[400]

On August 16, 1890, whaleback *Barge 107* was launched at the American Steel Barge Company's new, state-of-the-art shipyard. Half of the community turned out for the gala celebration, accompanied by the Superior Military Band. In November, the shipyard launched the steamer *Joseph L. Colby* and *Barge 109.*[401] Launchings came almost weekly during the summer of 1891. The company sent six barges, three steamers, and a conventional oil barge down the ways that year and followed up with six freighters, a passenger steamer, three barges, and the yard tug *Islay* during 1892. Capitalization of the common stock was increased from $2 million to $5 million in the winter of 1890–1891, and the company's annual payroll approached $1 million by the end of 1892.[402] McDougall's shipyard on Howard's Pocket was by far the largest single employer in the Twin Ports at the time.

Of more importance to the long-term financial health of Superior was American Steel Barge Company's 1891 decision to build a dry dock adjacent to its launching ways. Dry docks, which were used to repair ships, were few and far between on the Upper Great Lakes.[403] The dry dock in Howard's Pocket took nine months to build and cost just under $1 million. Crews assembled at the site Christmas week of 1891 and dug the mammoth dry dock with picks, shovels, and horses pulling wagons and drags. When it was completed in September 1892, it was the largest on the Great Lakes.[404]

With the completion of the dry dock, McDougall and Superior seemed to have a bright future. But the panic of 1893—the same economic upheaval that crushed the aspirations of Duluth's Merritt family—had ramifications across the bay. Like the Merritts, McDougall was beholden to the Rockefeller interests for financial backing.[405] In the fall of 1892, Colgate Hoyt, McDougall's patron, went to Europe to rest and recover from a serious bout with typhoid fever. Rockefeller tapped Frederick T.

Gates, his longtime assistant, to replace Hoyt in looking over his iron ore and shipping interests at the head of the lakes.[406] Gates scrutinized the Rockefeller investments with much more skepticism than did Hoyt, his predecessor. In late 1892, McDougall had signed a fifteen-year exclusive contract with the Merritts to carry newly developed Mesabi Range iron ore down the Great Lakes from Duluth. The contract would have been worth millions to McDougall and the shipyard, but Gates cancelled the contract when he removed the Merritts from management of the Mesabi mines and the Duluth & Iron Range Railroad.[407]

When the panic hit with its full fury in the fall of 1893, McDougall found himself overextended. "Still worse was to come," he later wrote of that time. Attorneys for the bondholders claimed that he owed the company $150,000. "I had to sacrifice my stock to redeem the pledge. For most of it I had paid par; I had created a business that doubled in value up to the arrival of Gates; I had to let mine go for fifty cents on the dollar."[408]

McDougall remained the general manager of American Steel Barge Company, but his heart was no longer in the business. The panic depressed shipbuilding across the lakes, and the Superior shipyards built no vessels from June 1893 until the spring of 1895. Even then, the company built only three vessels in 1895, just one of them a whaleback. In 1896, it built another three ships, but only one was a true whaleback. The last of the whalebacks built in Superior came down the ways in 1898. Fittingly named the *Alexander McDougall,* the 413-foot steamer incorporated the hull of a whaleback and the bow of a more conventional steel freighter.[409] From 1895 to 1899, the Superior firm did more repair work in its dry dock than new construction.

For all their uniqueness, the whalebacks did not revolutionize shipping on the Great Lakes. The 1890s were a time of great ferment in Great Lakes shipbuilding, and the whalebacks soon were overshadowed by conventional steel steamers 400 and 500 feet long. After 1900,

Dozens of vessels winter–berthed at Superior Shipbuilding Company yards in West Superior in 1900. Most of the vessels shown became part of U.S. Steel's Pittsburgh Steamship Company fleet the following year.

the whalebacks were hampered by the development of new unloading systems at lower lakes ports. The hatches on the whalebacks were not big enough to handle the clamshell buckets and Hulett unloaders then coming into general use on the lakes.[410] Still, McDougall had built thirty-nine ships in Duluth and Superior between 1888 and 1896 and four more whalebacks were constructed at coastal yards. American Steel Barge had built nineteen whalebacks, twenty-three barges, and the passenger steamer *Christopher Columbus,* plus the tug *Islay.*[411] Nearly sixty years later, four whalebacks were still in service on the Great Lakes. "Of any group of 43 ships built between 1888 and 1896," wrote Great Lakes maritime historian Edward Dowling in 1957, "I doubt if one will find four ships still sailing."[412]

IRON BOTTOMS FOR UNCLE SAM

With the concentration of Great Lakes shipbuilding in Cleveland, Lorain, Detroit, and Chicago after 1900, American Steel Barge Company effectively left the shipbuilding business to its larger, better-financed competitors. The company did a thriving dry dock business during the period from 1900 to 1915, servicing the repair needs of the whaleback steamers and barges of Rockefeller's growing Bessemer Steamship Company fleet.[413] It was obvious to residents at the head of the lakes that the shipyard at Howard's Pocket would unlikely return to the glory days of the 1890s, but the dry dock provided steady work to many of the 400 families that lived in the neighborhood.

The American Steel Barge Company was swept up in a major consolidation of Great Lakes shipyards during 1898 and 1899. In the bold maneuver, it was reorganized as the Superior Shipbuilding Company, a wholly owned subsidiary of the huge American Ship Building Company. The company built an incredible 175 new ships during the first five years of its existence, despite a widespread shortage of steel.[414] The Superior yard alone produced two steel barges and twenty-seven freighters between 1900 and 1911.

The outbreak of World War I in Europe in the summer of 1914 gave new life to the Great Lakes shipbuilding industry, Duluth and Superior included. Although the administration of President Woodrow Wilson followed a policy of strict neutrality, there was strong Anglophile sentiment in Washington, D.C. Between 1914 and

U.S. entry into the war in the spring of 1917, Great Britain suffered horrendous losses to its merchant marine and fishing fleet. During the first three years of World War I, the British lost as many as 675 fishing boats and nearly 2,500 merchant ships to German submarines and surface raiders.[415]

The first orders for ships from overseas started arriving in the Duluth-Superior shipyards early in 1917. Those first tenders were for canal-sized coastal freighters that would be built and delivered to shipping concerns in Scandinavia and France for use in the Baltic and North Seas. Called the "Frederickstad" ships after the Norwegian firm that had designed them, the vessels had a length of just over 261 feet, a width of almost 43 feet, and a draft of just

The Superior Shipbuilding Company turned to the construction of conventional ships after the whaleback era. Here, the steamer Edward Y. Townsend *is launched in August 1906.*

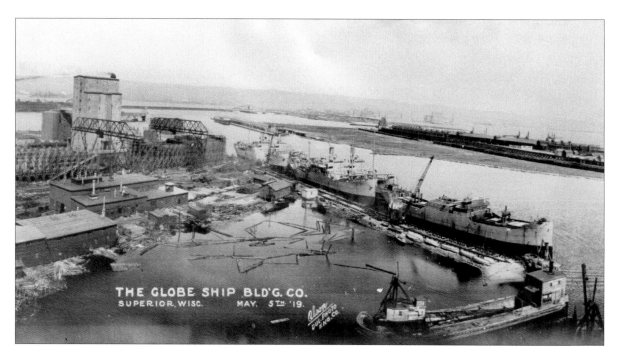

Several Frederickstad lakers are fitted out at the McDougall–Duluth shipyard in Howard's Pocket of Superior Bay in early May 1919. These were the last lakers launched at the shipyard, since World War I had ended nearly six months earlier.

under 20 feet. Their hulls were riveted steel with a raised forecastle, poop, and center island on their single decks. The Frederickstads were powered by triple-expansion steam engines developing 1,250 to 1,550 horsepower.[416] Superior Shipbuilding was the only firm on Lake Superior to secure a contract from the British, which called for the construction of three vessels.[417]

Scarcely before the keels were laid on the first order of Frederickstad ships, the British government's comptroller of shipping placed a mammoth order with American and Canadian yards for similar vessels that were dubbed "lakers." The March 1917 order called for the construction of 112 hulls, 100 of which were to be sailed directly to Great Britain. The newly organized Globe Shipbuilding Company of Superior received tenders for four ships, and the McDougall–Duluth Company of Duluth was awarded tenders for another four. Superior Shipbuilding Company also received orders for an additional four ships under the contract with the British.[418]

Globe Shipbuilding Company had been formed in Superior in early 1917 to build trawlers for the Atlantic seaboard. Its incorporators were

all Superior business executives and investors. The site they picked for the new venture was on Howard's Pocket at the foot of Hughitt Street, just down from the Superior Shipbuilding Company yards.[419] With the award of the British contract in the spring of 1917, the founders rapidly expanded the site. By the end of the year, the Globe facility contained five launching ways and three fully enclosed fitting-out berths, which enabled the firm to work year-round. Overhead, four electric cranes allowed construction crews to easily move rivets and construction materials. The yard also was equipped with steam locomotive cranes. The entire plant occupied four city blocks, and administrative offices were located on three floors of the adjacent Bemis Building.[420] The Globe yard turned out a total of twenty-four ships before the war ended.

The other new entry into the Twin Ports shipbuilding business was organized by veteran shipbuilder Alexander McDougall. Following the death of his wife in 1908, McDougall divided his time between inventions, business ventures, local politics, and consulting; he advised shipyards in Collingwood and Kingston, Ontario, about shipbuilding methods and dry dock construction. The sinking of the *Titanic* in April 1912 seduced McDougall back into shipbuilding. He designed a double-hulled vessel sometime in 1913 for the newly expanded New York State Barge Canal. His new "canaller" would be rectangular in cross-section with a wedge-shaped bow, and could be built in as little as eight feet of water.[421]

McDougall wanted to get back into shipbuilding at the head of the lakes. In the summer of 1915, he approached Chester Congdon and Marshall Alworth, both wealthy Duluth iron ore investors, and tried to interest them in financing a shipyard to build the seagoing canal boats he had designed. Both declined to get involved.[422] McDougall next went to New York to see Julius Barnes. Then forty-two years old, Barnes was probably the largest grain exporter in the United States. A native of Little Rock, Arkansas, he had moved to Duluth with his parents in the early 1880s. Barnes had gone to work for Ward Ames, one of the prominent grain buyers in Duluth, in 1889 at the age of sixteen; five years later, he started his own grain-buying firm and soon was dividing his time between Duluth and an office in New York City.[423]

Duluthian Julius Barnes was a major investor in Alexander McDougall's shipbuilding yards during World War I.

The McDougall–Duluth shipyard at Riverside built dozens of Frederickstad ships during World War I. In this 1919 photo, the Lake Markham *is in the final stages of being fitted out. In the slip behind her is the* Lake Indian. *Several other Frederickstad ships are in various stages of completion in the background.*

Some of the Frederickstad lakers actually did spend much of their careers in the lakes. Minnesota–Atlantic Transit Company's package freighter Jack, *one of the vessels of the firm's famous poker fleet, was a surplus World War I–era Frederickstad ship.*

McDougall returned to Duluth, leased his old shipbuilding yard at Fifteenth Avenue West, and began placing orders for steel. On January 1, 1916, he, Barnes, Ward Ames Jr., and Mc-Dougall's son Miller signed papers at a Duluth attorney's office incorporating the McDougall-Duluth Company.[424] By August, the company had laid the keel for the first canal boat, the *R. L. Barnes.*[425]

For once, Alexander McDougall was in the right place at the right time. Three months after the *R. L. Barnes* was launched in December 1916, the British government placed orders for four Frederickstad ships with the new shipbuilders. The contract was worth $370,000.[426] With the tenders for four ships in hand in the spring of 1917, McDougall began looking for larger quarters. In August, he and Barnes purchased

a large parcel of riverfront land well up the St. Louis River at Ironton. Within weeks, crews were grading the site for the McDougall-Duluth shipyard and for a town site the purchasers called Riverside.[427]

Meanwhile, the United States had entered World War I on the side of Great Britain and France in April 1917. With the declaration of war, Congress passed the Merchant Shipping Act and created the Emergency Fleet Corporation to oversee construction of new bottoms for the U.S. war effort. Within days of its formation, the Emergency Fleet Corporation requisitioned all ninety-nine British "lakers" under construction in American Great Lakes yards. McDougall and Barnes had realized back at their first meeting in New York in 1915 that the U.S. merchant fleet was woefully unprepared to meet the transport demands of a world war. Now, their vision was about to be rewarded.

In May 1917, the Emergency Shipping Board contracted for 346 oceangoing cargo ships to be constructed at thirteen Great Lakes shipyards. A total of fifty-eight hulls were awarded to McDougall-Duluth, Superior Shipbuilding, and Globe Shipbuilding companies. The vessels were variants of the Frederickstad ships, with some burning oil and others burning coal; all were destined for service on the Atlantic. They were popularly referred to as lakers, since virtually all the ships of the type were built at Great Lakes yards and virtually all bore the names of American lakes. All told, Duluth-Superior shipyards would build nearly seventy-five lakers from 1917 to 1920.[428]

The shipbuilding boom was one of the most spectacular economic development initiatives in the Twin Ports since the harbor was opened to maritime commerce in the 1870s. By the end of the war in November 1918, 1,500 people were working at the Globe yard and nearly 2,000 people were employed at the Superior Shipbuilding Company. McDougall-Duluth also employed nearly 4,500 workers at Riverside. Nearly 10,000 people were working in shipbuilding and related industries at the end of World War I, dwarfing the number of workers at the American Steel Barge shipyard during the firm's heyday in the early 1890s.[429]

Duluth and Superior had proven before that they were capable of meeting the shifting challenges of maritime commerce. By 1918, the Twin Ports had become one of North America's most important centers of maritime commerce, exceeded in tonnage only by the ports of New York and Philadelphia. The head of the lakes would maintain that ranking through the Roaring Twenties.

In the spring of 1906, the U.S. Army Corps of Engineers was finishing construction of its Duluth office building. The bow section of the Mataafa *beached at left was a sobering reminder of the big lake's fury.*

STILL A
DANGEROUS LAKE

Waves pound the Mataafa *as she wallows helplessly in the surf off the Duluth Ship Canal. Twin Ports residents keeping watch on shore were powerless to help as nine crew members in the stern section froze to death during the November 1905 tragedy.*

THE 1907 CREATION of the protected anchorage basin inside the Duluth-Superior harbor was tacit recognition by the U.S. Army Corps of Engineers that Lake Superior was still a dangerous place to be. At the turn of the twentieth century, an estimated 50,000 sailors made a living on the boats. Many lived in Duluth and Superior, and their families routinely held their breath when the telegraph wires relayed news of vessels lost to storms on the big lake. Sometimes Twin Ports residents became eyewitnesses to the lakes' dangers, as they did on June 7, 1902, when the Pittsburgh Steamship Company's *Thomas Wilson* sank off Eighth Avenue East. The 308-foot steel whaleback often loaded iron ore at the harbor for the steel mills down the lakes.[430] As the *Wilson* sailed outbound through the Duluth Ship Canal, the *George G. Hadley* of Toledo was inbound. The 308-foot wooden coal freighter sliced into the *Wilson,* cutting her in two.[431] Crewman swam through frigid waters for the *Hadley,* which was less than fifty yards away.[432] But the *Wilson* sank in three minutes, taking nine of its twenty crewmen.

The *Wilson* tragedy had happened inexplicably on a calm day. The next chapter in Duluth-Superior's sometimes tempestuous relationship with Lake Superior came in the teeth of one of the fiercest gales on the Upper Great Lakes in the twentieth century. The "*Mataafa* blow" of November 27–29, 1905, was given its name to commemorate the sinking of the steel bulk freighter *Mataafa* just off the newly constructed piers of the Duluth Ship Canal. Nine crew members froze to death within plain sight of thousands of Duluth residents, all helpless to do anything to avert the tragedy.

Historian Fred Landon once wrote that "of all months in the year, [November] is the most dreaded by lake sailors who can recall many a ship and its men that went out on a late trip—perhaps the expected last trip—and lost out to the wild storms and the treacherous seas that this month can bring."[433] Following a vicious blow during November 23–25, 1905, skippers cautiously edged into Lake Superior to complete what would likely be the last trip of the season. Conventional wisdom held that a November storm would be succeeded by three to seven days of calm weather as a high pressure area drifted east across the lakes.[434] One vessel leaving port on November 27 was the *Mataafa*. Built in Cleveland for the Minnesota Steamship Company, the 430-foot steel bulk freighter had later become one of the 112 modern vessels in U.S. Steel's Pittsburgh Steamship subsidiary. With Captain R. H. Humble in command, the *Mataafa* left port just after 4:00 p.m.

At about 7:00 p.m., a nor'easter slammed across the Twin Ports. By early morning, gusts over eighty miles an hour were recorded at Duluth.[435] In the harbor, several vessels grounded when their anchors wouldn't hold in the howling winds. "The port of Duluth was a shambles," wrote Julius F. Wolff Jr.[436]

When the sun rose November 28, wreckage from vessels caught on the lake in the blow littered the north shore. The Pittsburgh Steamship Company's *Crescent City* was lodged on the rocks northeast of downtown Duluth. The *Lafayette,* another "Pittsburgher," with her barge consort, the *Manila,* was broken up on Encampment Island northeast of Two Harbors.[437]

Navigation was still treacherous as several vessels that had left the Twin Ports the previous afternoon tried to return. The first was the *R. W. England,* a 363-foot steel steamer that ran for the Duluth Ship Canal at full speed but quickly grounded on Minnesota Point just east of the canal.[438] The next to try was the 478-foot steamer *Isaac Ellwood,* which pounded first into the North Pier and then into the South Pier before making it into harbor.[439]

The last vessel to attempt the hazardous passage was the *Mataafa.* Shortly after 2:00 p.m., Captain Humble first ordered the line to his consort barge, the 450-foot *James Nasmyth,* let loose.[440] Canal currents and wind-driven seas held the ship perpendicular to the North Pier, swung the bow around 270 degrees, and pushed the vessel into shallow water 100 feet off the pier. Within an hour, the waves broke the *Mataafa* in two.[441] Temperatures plunged to below zero by nightfall, with the wind chill at minus forty degrees.[442] Thousands of residents kept watch by bonfire through the night, heartened by glimpses of a fire fed by Humble and some of his men. At first light, fifteen frostbitten survivors from *Mataafa*'s bow section were rescued, including the captain. All nine crew members in the stern had drowned or frozen to death.[443]

All told, the November 1905 storms—including the "*Mataafa* blow"—took seventy-eight lives on the Upper Great Lakes and destroyed nineteen vessels. Damage estimates ran as high as $2 million.[444] The stormy season was a reminder that even improvements to the Twin Ports harbor were of little help against the gales of November.

The trading floor of the Duluth board of trade was a pivotal location for world wheat markets when this illustration appeared in Northwest Magazine *in 1887.*

CHAPTER TEN

Zenith City of the Unsalted Seas

IN OCTOBER 1919, the Duluth, Missabe, & Northern Railway completed Dock No. 6 at its West Duluth ore dock complex on St. Louis Bay. Construction had begun on the new concrete and steel ore dock in the spring of 1917, just weeks after President Woodrow Wilson asked Congress to declare war on imperial Germany.[445] Railroad executives had clearly anticipated the flood of iron ore that would cascade down the Great Lakes in case the United States got involved in the European war that had already been raging for nearly three years. The ore docks in West Duluth dated to 1893, and some were built of timber. Even the newer docks at the complex, built in the first decade of the twentieth century, were built of timber and steel.[446] The new dock envisioned by the DM&N would handle whatever tonnage the Mesabi Range could divert its way, and it was designed to last for generations. It was to be the first ore dock at the head of the lakes built of concrete and steel.

Dock No. 6 was an affirmation of the Twin Ports' emergence as North America's bulk port. It was also an icon, a symbol of how important iron and steel had become to U.S. industry—and nowhere more important than at the head of the lakes. The new dock stretched more than 2,300 feet into the harbor. More than 1 million board feet of timber was used in construction of Dock No. 6, as well as 174,000 feet of 12-inch sheet piling, 30,000 tons of steel, and 60,000 cubic yards of concrete. Trains coming down the hill from the DM&N's Proctor yards were positioned on the trestle where they dumped their ore cars into the hoppers some 85 feet above the water. A total of four tracks were laid atop the 76-foot-wide docks.[447] The approach to the docks stretched across a nearly

3,500-foot steel viaduct, giving the dock and the approach a length of more than a mile.

The iron ore hoppers, or pockets, lined the full length of the dock on both sides. There were 768 pockets along the dock, 384 on each side. Each pocket could hold the equivalent of eight standard railcars of ore; Dock No. 6 had a capacity of more than 150,000 long tons of iron ore when full.[448] In 1919, as many as three ore boats could load on each side at the same time. At the time, Dock No. 6 was the largest such structure ever built in North America. It still is.

A FRENZY OF CONSTRUCTION

Dock No. 6 was the last major bulk cargo facility built in the Twin Ports until the 1940s, and it capped a remarkable decade of expansion of the iron ore and coal docks at the head of the lakes. Between 1910 and 1920, the railroads and coal companies serving the Twin Ports rebuilt or expanded most of the original dock facilities that had been erected during the first construction boom in the 1890s. The DM&N was not alone in the ambitious expansion of its West Duluth facilities.

The Great Northern Railway spent more than $1.5 million between 1907 and 1925 upgrading its complex of ore docks on Superior's Allouez Bay. In 1907, Great Northern crews rebuilt the wooden Dock No. 1, first erected in 1892. The 2,244-foot dock was converted from a steam system to an electric propulsion system during the winter of 1925.[449] In 1911, Great Northern built Dock No. 4, its first concrete and steel superstructure on Allouez Bay. Jutting 1,812 feet into the bay, Dock No. 4 towered 75 feet above the water. With 302 pockets, the new dock had a capacity of more than 90,000 tons of iron ore. Great Northern's Dock No. 3 was built in 1902 and expanded in 1904. With the completion of Dock No. 4 in 1911, Great Northern engineers began making plans for rebuilding Dock No. 3 in steel and concrete.

Great Northern wasn't finished with its massive ore dock upgrade project. In 1923, the railway replaced the twenty-four-year-old Dock No. 2, which had been built of wood in 1899. Soaring more than 80 feet above Allouez Bay, the concrete and steel dock extended 2,100 feet into the water, and its 350 ore pockets had a total capacity of 122,500 tons of rich Mesabi iron. Also expanded during the 1923 construction was the nearly 2,900-foot elevated steel approach to the four docks.[450]

The final rebuilding of the Great Northern ore dock complex took place between 1925 and 1928, when construction crews replaced Dock No. 1 in phases.[451] The work took place over three winters and resulted in a concrete and steel dock that was a virtual twin of Dock No. 2.[452] As a result of Great Northern's fifteen-year

modernization project at its Allouez ore dock complex, the head of the lakes boasted a bulk cargo handling facility that was unparalleled in the world. With its 440,000-ton storage capacity, Great Northern's Allouez dock complex was second in capacity only to its neighbor across the harbor in West Duluth. The investment by the DM&N and Great Northern during the 1910s and 1920s would make Duluth-Superior the world's preeminent iron ore port for the remainder of the twentieth century.[453]

Ore docks, however, weren't the only bulk cargo handling facilities in the harbor to be upgraded during the 1910s and 1920s. Coal continued to be a major inbound commodity through the Twin Ports during the period, and the coal companies that controlled the trade on the Upper Great Lakes continued to expand and improve the coal docks that lined both sides of the harbor. The early years of the twentieth century were the high point of America's coal economy. Most of the coal flowing into the Twin Ports was bituminous from Pennsylvania, West Virginia, and Ohio, shipped up from the coal ports on Lake Erie. The bulk of the coal arriving at the head of the lakes was quickly transferred

Following the completion of Dock No. 4, the West Duluth ore docks often handled as many as four steel bulk freighters at a time. The lakers shown are (from left) the Senator, *the* William H. Truesdale, *and the* Francis E. House, *circa 1910.*

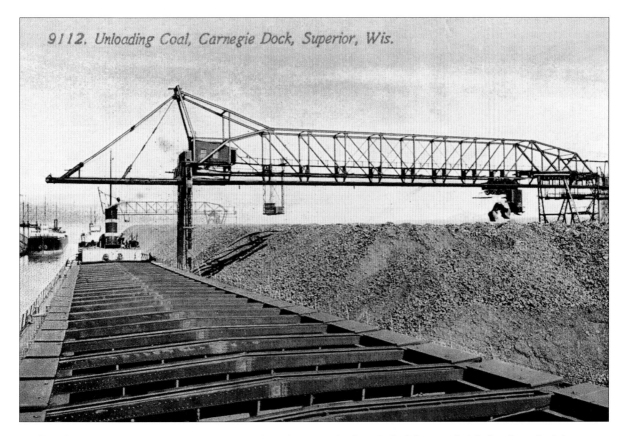

9112. Unloading Coal, Carnegie Dock, Superior, Wis.

This 1911 postcard depicts how the bridge cranes, such as this one at the Carnegie Coal Company dock in Superior, unloaded bulk freighters.

into railcars and shipped to coal dealers handling residential and industrial accounts from Minneapolis to the Rocky Mountains.

The period between 1905 and 1920 witnessed a major expansion of the Twin Ports' coal-handling facilities. In 1906, the Northern Coal and Dock Company built a 600,000-ton-capacity coal dock on Superior Bay. Three years later, the Philadelphia and Reading Coal and Iron Company erected a 400,000-ton-capacity coal dock immediately adjacent to the Northern Coal facility. The DM&N built what was then the largest coal dock in the harbor on the west side of Rice's Point in 1907. With a 625,000-ton capacity, the dock was located at the foot of Twenty-ninth Avenue West in Duluth and was in use until after World War II. The Pittsburgh Coal Company built its Coal Dock No. 7 on the east side of Rice's Point in 1908. The 250,000-ton-capacity dock served the company through the disappearance of the upbound coal trade in the 1950s. Berwind-White Coal Mining Company erected a 700,000-ton-capacity coal dock just to the west of the Northern Pacific Wis-

consin Drawbridge in 1907 and added a second, 500,000-ton-capacity coal dock north of the Grassy Point Bridge Drawbridge in 1913. That same year, the Island Creek Coal Company eclipsed the DM&N's record for largest coal dock in the harbor when it built an 850,000-ton capacity dock at the foot of Fiftieth Avenue West in Duluth. The final coal dock built in the harbor was Northwestern Fuel Company's Dock No. 4. The 430,000-ton-capacity dock was erected in 1920 on the site of an abandoned lumber wharf on the east side of Rice's Point.[454]

The grain and flour milling business at the head of the lakes continued to expand during the period, but not at the rapid pace of the iron ore and coal industries. The Northern Pacific Railway rebuilt its Elevator D complex on the south side of the bay-front slip in 1908, nearly doubling the elevator's capacity to 2.5 million bushels. The Capitol Elevator Company, which had succeeded the Duluth Imperial Milling Company in 1912, added two elevators to its complex on the east side of Rice's Point in 1916. Elevator No. 6 had a capacity of 1.4 million

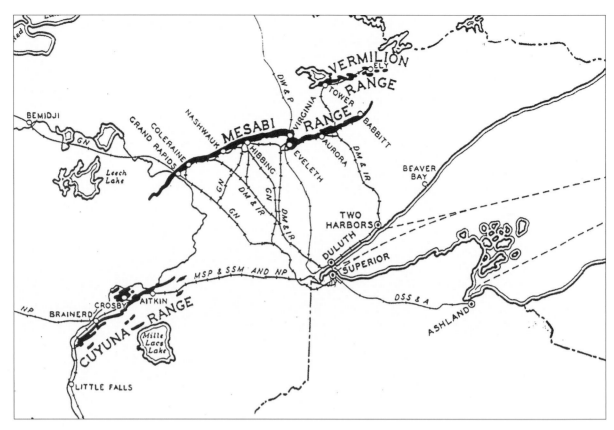

Minnesota's three iron ranges provided the bulk of North American iron ore in the first half of the twentieth century.

bushels, while Elevator No. 7 was slightly smaller. Together, the two new elevators made up 60 percent of Capitol's total capacity of 4 million bushels. Three years later, in 1919, Consolidated Elevator Company built Elevator 1 at its complex off Birch Avenue on the east side of Rice's Point. In 1923, the newly formed Occident Terminal Division of Russell-Miller Milling Company built a 4.5 million-bushel capacity elevator at the foot of Elm Avenue on the elevator row of the east side of Rice's Point, expanding an Elm Avenue pier already occupied by an F. H. Peavey elevator.[455]

Dozens of other wharves and docks were built in the harbor between 1905 and the early 1920s. Freight docks, lumber wharves, public docks, grocery wharves, fish docks, and sand and gravel wharves all contributed to the Twin Ports' maritime ascendancy during the first two decades of the twentieth century.

SUPPLY AND DEMAND

There was one simple reason for the spate of dock and wharf construction in Duluth and Superior during the period: in the thirty years

between 1890 and 1920, the Twin Ports had become an integral part of the industrialization of the United States. In 1920, bulk cargo on the Great Lakes accounted for 13 percent of the total ton-miles of commerce recorded in the United States, and half of the ton-miles carried on the Great Lakes originated on Lake Superior.[456] Minnesota's Mesabi Iron Range spawned the web of railroads and bulk maritime commerce that had propelled the head of the lakes to such a position of prominence in American industrialization. In 1890, the range had been a trackless wilderness. Thirty years later, the region was crisscrossed by rails. In 1920, the railroads of the Mesabi Range and the docks at the head of Lake Superior handled more than 75 percent of the iron ore consumed by the American steel industry—30 percent of the world's iron ore production.[457]

Year in and year out, Duluth and Superior handled a virtual flood of iron ore in the early years of the century. In 1900, the ore docks of the Twin Ports had moved nearly 6 million tons of Mesabi ore. The number exceeded 10 million tons in 1902 and 1903 and rose to more than

19 million tons in 1906. Shipments leveled off at 14 million tons in 1908 in the wake of the panic of 1907 but sharply rebounded to nearly 22.5 million tons in 1909. Shipments through the Twin Ports' ore docks averaged 13.9 million tons during the first decade of the twentieth century, almost seven times the annual 2-million-ton average reported in the 1890s.[458]

The tonnage numbers more than doubled in the next decade. The Twin Ports reported their first 30-million-ton year for iron ore in 1913. The banking panic of October 1913 cut that number by one-third during the 1914 navigation season, but the outbreak of war in Europe in August 1914 set the stage for a massive expansion of iron ore shipments through the port. In 1916, Duluth and Superior set a record for iron ore shipments—38.3 million tons, nearly double the tonnage of two years before. Shipments averaged 38 million tons a year for the next two war years, dropping to just under 31 million tons in

1919. For the decade, iron ore shipments averaged 29.2 million tons a year.[459]

The World War I surge of iron ore through the Twin Ports saw nearly 145 million tons of Minnesota ore go down the Great Lakes in the four years between 1916 and 1919. It illustrated an inescapable reality that would be borne out three more times during the twentieth century: war was good for the local economy. In 1916, before the United States entered WWI, Minnesota had mined 44.5 million tons of iron ore, nearly 60 percent of the U.S. total and more than all the other states combined. Michigan, the next most abundant source of iron ore in 1916, mined just over 18 million tons.[460] In May 1917, six weeks after the U.S. declaration of war, *Skillings Mining Review* commented on prospects for the upcoming navigation season. "It is but a few years ago when shippers of iron ore and students of transportation were looking forward to the time

Around 1900, trainloads of ore recharge the Duluth, Missabe, & Northern's West Duluth ore dock pockets.

when Lake Superior mines would send forth 50 million tons in a single season," *Skillings* noted on May 26. "They have suddenly had their perspective changed to the extent that they may now speculate as to when the Lake Superior iron mines will send down 75 million in a season. The record this year would be above 70 million if there were boats enough to make the delivery at lower lake docks."[461]

CUYLER ADAMS AND HIS DOG, UNA
The prewar years were also the first time that the Twin Ports began handling major tonnages of a new cargo—manganiferous iron ore from the newly opened Cuyuna Iron Range. Located south and west of the Mesabi Range in Crow Wing County, the Cuyuna had been opened in 1913. The range had been discovered and mapped out in the late 1890s and early 1900s by Cuyler Adams, an Illinois-born entrepreneur who had

made a fortune in "bonanza farming" in Dakota Territory in the 1880s. In 1903, Adams and two other investors incorporated the Orelands Mining Company to begin developing claims near Deerwood. Two years later, Adams's wife suggested a name for the new range: Cuyuna. The name combined the first three letters of her husband's name with the name of his St. Bernard, Una.[462]

Between 1905 and 1911, several mines were opened, and the Soo Line completed a spur from the new range to Duluth-Superior to compete with the Northern Pacific. Uncharacteristically, the Oliver Iron Mining Division, the U.S. Steel subsidiary that controlled much of the mining on the Mesabi Range, expressed little interest in development activity on the Cuyuna. Pickands-Mather, the Cleveland-based ore company that was instrumental in developing ranges

One of the toughest, dirtiest jobs during the natural ore era involved using long iron poles during early spring and late fall to loosen frozen ore in the ore cars so it would fall into the dock pockets.

in Minnesota, Michigan, and Wisconsin, was involved in development work on the Cuyuna from the start. The Cuyuna also benefited from a growing pool of homegrown mining investment capital in Duluth.[463]

Ore started moving from the Cuyuna Range to Duluth-Superior during the 1911 navigation season.[464] The first ore came from the Kennedy Mine and was destined for the Soo Line's new dock in Superior. Two years later, the first shipment of ore from the Cuyuna to cross the new Northern Pacific docks in Superior was consigned to the holds of the *E. N. Saunders*.[465] The pace of shipments from the new range picked up dramatically as the United States prepared for the possibility of being drawn into the European war. Cuyuna Range ore was rich in manganese, which was destined for the manufacture of special alloy steels, particularly those used in armaments.

COAL AND GRAIN

Even considering the prodigious flow of iron ore through the port from the Mesabi and Cuyuna Ranges during World War I, ore tonnages still only aggregated but 70 percent of the total tonnage reported at Duluth-Superior. Coal and grain maintained their positions throughout the 1910s as the ports' second and third most important cargoes, thus justifying the capital investment on coal docks and grain elevators since early in the century. Tonnages of both cargoes climbed steadily during the 1900s and 1910s, although coal registered more spectacular gains than the grain trade.

The boom in coal dock construction was driven by a doubling of coal tonnage each decade between 1890 and 1920. In the 1890s, the average annual tonnage received by coal docks at the head of the lakes was 2.15 million tons. Coal tonnages exceeded 4 million tons in 1903, 5 million tons in 1906, and 7 million tons in 1907. For the first decade of the twentieth century, coal shipments through the Twin Ports averaged 4.38 million tons. By 1910, coal tonnages were above 8 million tons, a level that the industry maintained for the next two shipping seasons. In 1913, receipts leaped to nearly 11 million tons

before falling back slightly the next three seasons. During the war years of 1917–1918, tonnages exceeded 11 million tons both years. For the decade, the average annual coal tonnages had doubled once again to 9.5 million tons.[466]

Grain tonnages made slow but steady growth through the 1900s and 1910s. Grain shipments had first topped 2 million tons in 1898, and the average for the 1890s was 1.3 million tons a year. Grain wouldn't top 2 million tons a year again until 1912, although tonnages were remarkably steady during the first decade of the twentieth century, dipping below 1 million tons only once—in 1904, and then just barely—and climbing to 1.97 million tons in 1909. The Twin Ports finished the decade with an average annual grain shipment of 1.45 million tons.[467]

The outbreak of war in Europe in the summer of 1914 and the subsequent disruption of world export patterns proved to be a shot in the arm for Duluth-Superior and U.S. wheat shipments. Grain shipments through the Twin Ports topped 2.7 million tons in 1912 and again in 1913 and shot up to 3.3 million tons in 1915. The price of U.S. wheat spiked to a then record of $3.17 a bushel in the spring of 1917 upon American entry into the war, but difficulty in securing railcars for the Northern Plains reduced the tonnage shipped through Duluth-Superior to just over 2 million tons in 1918. Still, the Twin Ports ended the decade with an average annual throughput of grain of just under 2 million tons.[468]

Because of the fragmented nature of the grain business, which included thousands of small farmers, country elevators, grain terminal elevators in ports and rail centers, and federal and state requirements that grain be graded and cleaned to uniform standards, markets were self-regulated by a network of grain exchanges across the United States.[469] In the Twin Ports, the Duluth board of trade played an integral role in fostering an orderly market for the often chaotic business. Incorporated in 1881 and reorganized in 1902, the board maintained a trading pit atop its imposing headquarters building at 301 West First Street. The seven-story

The Lake Ledan *was one of dozens of oceangoing lakers built at Superior shipyards during WWI. For their voyage across the North Atlantic, they were painted with camouflage patterns to hide them from German U-boat patrols. Many returned to the Great Lakes during the 1920s as package freighters.*

In 1917, during one of the coldest springs on record, ice jams plagued the Twin Ports and western Lake Superior until early June.

steel, stone, brick, and marble structure at the corner of Third Avenue West and First Street was the nerve center for the grain industry in the Upper Midwest.[470] The board of trade owned the building, but in itself transacted no business save for providing a trading floor in the building. But the fact that most of the grain companies, grain commission agents, vessel agents, and the inspectors and weigh masters of the Minnesota Railroad and Warehouse Commission all had offices in the building meant that the board of trade was synonymous in the minds of most people in the Twin Ports with the grain trade.[471]

The grain trade, coupled with iron ore, coal, package freight, and lumber, made up the vast bulk of the cargo movement through the Twin

Ports in the 1900s and 1910s. Since the late 1890s, total tonnage had doubled each decade. The Twin Ports passed the 10-million-ton mark in 1898 and never looked back. The numbers, in fact, continued going up. Nearly 22.7 million tons passed across the docks and wharves in 1905, a record that was shattered the next year when 29.2 million tons came through the port. In 1907, the record was eclipsed again with a 34.8-million-ton year. The average annual tonnage for the 1900s was almost 22 million tons.

Records just kept being broken in the 1910s. The first 40-million-ton year was 1912. The next year, tonnage soared to almost 46.9 million tons, leading many observers of the port scene to predict a 50-million-ton year in the near future. They had to wait only three years. In 1916, more

Weather could sometimes hamper dock operations in the Twin Ports. This collapsed coal bridge crane went down in a windstorm on May 26, 1914, six months after the big blow of November 1913.

than 52 million tons of cargo passed through the Twin Ports, a total that was equaled during each of the next two war years. Duluth and Superior finished the decade with an average annual tonnage total of 43 million tons.[472]

An inescapable reality of maritime commerce on the Upper Great Lakes at the time was that while tonnages were increasing, the number of vessels visiting the port was declining. In 1900, when total tonnage was 11.7 million tons, there were 5,667 vessel visits. By 1918, total tonnage had reached 53.7 million tons, but the number of vessel visits had dropped to 5,454. In essence, tonnage had nearly quintupled in eighteen years, but the number of vessels was actually smaller. One factor that played into the increase in cargo productivity was the decline of the lumber trade. At the beginning of the century, nearly 700,000 tons of lumber were moving out of Duluth-Superior, most of it piled aboard small lumber hookers. By 1919, the lumber tonnage had dropped below 100,000 tons. By far the biggest factor, however, was the increase in size of the vessels in the bulk fleet on the Great Lakes. By 1905, vessels of the newly launched Gary class operated by the Pittsburgh Steamship Company were routinely hauling 10,000 tons of iron ore down the Great Lakes from Duluth's Mesabi Docks.[473] The retirement of many of the smaller steamers that had called at the head of the lakes and their replacement by much larger steel bulk freighters had a marked impact on productivity. In just twenty years, the average amount of cargo per transit in and out of the Twin Ports more than quadrupled. That search for productivity would be a theme in Great Lakes maritime commerce for decades to come.

Great Lakes storms continued to take a toll on the vessels of the fleet. Perhaps the worst of the 1910s was the big blow of 1913. Like the *Mataafa* storm eight years before, the 1913 storm was a potent mixture of cold Canadian air and a warm, moist air mass from the Gulf of Mexico clashing over the Upper Lakes. Unlike the 1905 storm, the full brunt of the weather front of November 8–10, 1913, hit considerably east of the west end of Lake Superior. Still, more than a dozen vessels foundered in the mountainous waves of Lake Huron and Lake Superior during the second week of November 1913.

UNPRECEDENTED PROSPERITY

For Duluth and Superior, the economic upheavals of 1873 and 1893 were dim memories in the first two decades of the twentieth century. Bank panics in 1907 and 1913 caused barely a ripple in the Twin Ports' increasingly important maritime economy. Tonnages dropped by 10 million tons or more in the year following the panic of 1913, but rebounded sharply in the season following the down year. Maritime commerce created thousands of jobs, but the increasingly diversified economy at the head of the lakes protected Duluth and Superior from the economic upheavals of the past.

Much of that diversification was industrial in character. In the spring of 1907, the U.S. Steel Corporation announced plans to spend nearly $6 million on a new steelmaking complex on the St. Louis River at the far west end of Duluth.[474] For civic boosters, the announcement was a confirmation that the "Zenith City" would take her rightful place in the new century as the "Pittsburgh of the West."[475]

The "Steel Trust," as many Duluthians called U.S. Steel, already had a visible presence at the head of the lakes. The Pittsburgh Steamship Company, U.S. Steel's ore fleet, was headquartered in Duluth, as was the Oliver Mining Company, its major iron ore subsidiary. The Duluth, Missabe, & Northern Railway, another Steel Trust subsidiary, employed thousands of residents of Duluth and nearby Proctor. So when U.S. Steel exercised the options to take seventeen hundred acres near Fond du Lac, Minnesota, in August 1907, Duluthians greeted the news with enthusiasm. "Chicago fifty years ago did not have 20,000 population," the *Duluth News-Tribune* pointed out. "It now has more than 2,000,000. Duluth will equal its growth in half the time."[476] The new steel mill was expected to employ more than 2,000 workers, and city planners estimated that the workforce would add 10,000 people to the city's population.

The creation of what was known as the Minnesota Steel Division of U.S. Steel provided another boost to the economy at the head of the lakes. The new steel mill rolled its first billets in December 1915, and U.S. Steel's investment eventually exceeded $10 million. By the early 1920s, the Duluth mill employed more than 1,000 people and was making tin plate, sheet steel, wire, and nails for distribution to customers in the Upper Midwest.[477]

Superior enjoyed a similar burst of prosperity during the period. Thousands of residents found work in traditional maritime industries, including the city's many shipyards, ore and coal docks, grain elevators, and lumber wharves. Thousands of other residents worked on the five railroads that connected the city with much of the Upper Midwest. With a population pushing 50,000 in 1920, Superior had more than tripled in size since 1890. The city was one of the wealthiest in Wisconsin, and nearly half of its 130 miles of streets were paved before World War I.[478] Even without a steel mill, Superiorites could look with boundless optimism on the postwar era.

Twin Ports residents awoke to the news on August 15, 1914, that the first vessel to transit the Panama Canal was expected to make its crossing later in the day.[479] Some readers might have skimmed the item. After all, the front pages that summer were dominated by reports of French and German armies moving toward a rendezvous somewhere on the Marne River west of Paris. But the opening of the canal across the Isthmus of Panama would have a major impact on world trade patterns in the decades ahead. And those effects would be felt all the way to the head of the lakes.

The U.S. Steel plant on the far western end of Duluth was a major employer in the Zenith City from 1914 until the 1970s.

PEAVEY'S
FOLLY

Frank Peavey was a giant of the Upper Midwest grain trade in the late 1800s. His experiment with concrete silos at the port of Duluth revolutionized grain storage.

FRANK H. PEAVEY transformed the grain markets of the Upper Midwest and the world. The concrete silo—one of Peavey's innovations introduced a century ago in Minnesota, first in a Minneapolis suburb and later in Duluth—is still the industry standard. His invention replaced dangerously flammable wooden grain storage facilities, and thus made a case for insurance companies to lower premiums. In the process, Peavey revolutionized the storage of grain not only in the Midwest, but around the world.

Frank Peavey came west from Maine to Chicago and then to Sioux City, Iowa, after the Civil War. He started building and buying country elevators in the mid-1870s, and by 1885 had moved his operations to the Twin Cities. The next year, he built one of the world's largest elevators in Minneapolis for the then astounding sum of $3.5 million. By 1895, his terminal elevators on the Portland, Oregon, waterfront allowed him to control the wheat harvest from Lake Superior to the Pacific Northwest.[480]

Peavey had long felt there was a better way to store grain. For more than fifty years, American grain elevators had been built of wood. Millers and grain industry executives felt that wood had enough give to retain its shape when grain was drawn from the bottom of the elevator. But wood was flammable, and grain dust made wooden elevators explosions waiting to happen. The accident record for grain elevators was horrendous, and by the 1890s grain entrepreneurs paid up to $150,000 a year in insurance premiums on larger terminal elevators.[481]

Peavey began investigating the potential of building concrete elevators in the mid-1890s. Most grain men scoffed at the idea, claiming concrete would crack when grain poured out the bottom. In the late 1890s, Peavey Company hired C. F. Haglin to build an experimental concrete elevator in St. Louis Park, a Minneapolis suburb where the firm already operated its Interior Elevator. Haglin designed and built a circular concrete tank that was 125 feet tall. The structure was poured in one continuous operation in what was one of the first uses of the slip-form technique of concrete construction.[482]

When the reinforced concrete tower reached a height of nearly 70 feet in the fall of 1899, Peavey halted construction to test his theory. Workmen hoisted grain in buckets to the top and dumped the buckets inside. Peavey stored the grain in the silo over the long Minnesota winter, and when spring arrived he arranged a public showing of the tower's ability to store

grain safely and cleanly. Workers had dug a concrete pit next to the silo, and when Haglin pulled the rope to release the grain, the wheat poured down a ramp into the pit. There were no cracks in the concrete, and the wheat was dry and in top grade condition.[483]

Peavey made plans to take the pilot silo into full-scale production. The site he chose was the Port of Duluth-Superior.[484] He had purchased the Belt Line Elevator Company at Superior in 1896, and soon acquired the city's three Globe Elevator Company elevators.[485] In the fall of 1900, workers began pouring concrete on Rice's Point in Duluth for a complex of cylindrical concrete silos. Each would hold 75,000 bushels of wheat. The twenty smaller silos had a capacity of 55,000 bushels each. All told, the terminal could store 3.35 million bushels. Another 1.4 million bushels were stored in a wooden working house next to the site.[486] Just ninety days after the first concrete pour, crews finished the work. The *Minneapolis Journal* called the Peavey-Duluth Terminal "the first concrete elevator in the Western Hemisphere and much the largest in the world."[487]

To show his confidence, Peavey stored 1 million bushels of wheat in the new silos over the winter of 1900–1901 without insuring the contents. When the wheat proved to be in perfect condition in the spring of 1901, property and casualty insurance companies began offering to insure stored grain in concrete silos for one-sixth the rate applied to wooden elevators.[488]

Within a decade, the concrete silo complex at Duluth was duplicated in ports and milling centers around the world. "Peavey's Folly" brought about a transformation in the storage of grain worldwide. Frank Peavey died of pneumonia in December 1901, less than a month after contracting a cold while Christmas shopping in Chicago. He never lived to see his belief in concrete elevators vindicated, but his memory is perpetuated by the concrete monuments the world over.

James J. Hill's Northern Steamship Company epitomized luxury transportation on the Great Lakes at the turn of the twentieth century.

CHAPTER ELEVEN

The Golden Age of Cruise Ships

IN THE 1890s and early 1900s, the package freighters supplemented their general cargo business with a thriving immigrant passenger trade.[489] But after 1910, as restrictions on the number of immigrants to the United States grew and as the opportunities to homestead out west dwindled, the Great Lakes passenger business began to dry up. By the time World War I ended in the fall of 1918, the immigrant passenger business on the Great Lakes had all but evaporated. It was replaced by a new kind of travel market. Leisure travel had come into its own by the turn of the twentieth century. Americans began traveling for the sheer joy of it.

Railroad ownership of the package freight lines on the Great Lakes ensured that the region would share in the trend toward leisure travel. By the 1890s, railroad-owned package freight lines had been carrying immigrant passengers for half a century. It was becoming increasingly obvious that the immigrant passenger business was nearing its end, so the railroads began to investigate the feasibility of offering summer cruises on the lakes. The idea was a natural.

Summer travelers started to arrive in Duluth and Superior during the late 1880s. Many came up from Buffalo on the Anchor Line, aboard the *China, Japan,* and *India.* Put into service in 1871, the year after the railroad arrived in Duluth, the three package-and-passenger freighters made the round-trip from the head of the lakes to Buffalo in fourteen days, with stops in Erie, Cleveland, Detroit, Port Huron, Mackinac Island, the Soo, and Houghton. Each ship was 220 feet in length with a beam of 32 feet and had accommodations for immigrant passengers in steerage and first-class passengers in deckside

cabins. The *China, Japan,* and *India* offered Buffalo-Duluth service for more than forty years.[490]

James J. Hill was perhaps the first to see the potential of leisure travel on the Great Lakes. Hill, the dour Scotsman who built the Great Northern Railway empire and created the Northern Steamship Company to serve the package freight interests of his eastern and western rail networks, believed in doing things well. In the spring of 1892, Hill contracted the Globe Iron Works of Cleveland to design and build two passenger ships that would be the model for cruising on the Great Lakes. Globe laid down the keel of the first ship in the fall of 1892 and the second ship in the spring of 1893. Even the panic of 1893 couldn't stop the two passenger ships from being built. The first, which Hill christened the *North West,* slipped down the ways in January 1894. The second, christened the *North Land,* was launched one day shy of a year later.[491]

The vessels were virtual twins and unlike anything that had been seen on the lakes. Two quadruple expansion engines drove twin screws and gave *North West* and *North Land* a top speed of twenty miles per hour.[492] Painted white with three yellow smokestacks, the 385-foot passenger steamers each had a crew of 147 and could carry more than 400 passengers a trip.[493] At a time when electric lights were considered a luxury item in most homes, the two vessels boasted 1,200 incandescent electric bulbs.[494]

The passenger quarters on the two flyers were unprecedented on the Great Lakes. Staircases between the decks were built of white mahogany, and lounges were furnished with leather and brass. The vessels were outfitted with dining

The gentlemen's smoking lounge on the Northern Steamship Company's North West in 1895 was plushly appointed in red velvet, leather, and mahogany.

In what is believed to be its only visit to the Twin Ports, the North American approaches downtown Duluth in the fall of 1954. The Georgian Bay Line vessel typically cruised between Chicago and Buffalo.

rooms, smoking rooms, and salons. The women's salon featured a grand piano. First-class cabins lined the two upper decks, but most passengers booked passage in one of the 108 double-berth cabins below decks. Passage for a round-trip ticket between Buffalo and Duluth cost as little as $30 during the 1890s, and travelers could book passage aboard for transfer to one of the railroads that served the vessels at either end of the line or anywhere in between.[495]

For more than twenty years, the *North West* and *North Land* set the standard for luxury

China, Japan, and *India* with the *Tionesta, Juniata,* and *Octorara.* Unlike the *North West* and *North Land,* the three new vessels of the Anchor Line were combination package and passenger freighters.[497] Named for rivers in western and central Pennsylvania, the *Tionesta, Juniata,* and *Octorara* were 360 feet in length, had a capacity of 350 passengers, and carried up to 3,500 tons of cargo. The three vessels directly competed with the two ships of the Northern Steamship Company, and they made a round-trip between Buffalo and Duluth in just nine days.[498]

The passenger car crosses the Duluth Ship Canal behind the Northern Navigation Company's Hamonic, outbound on a fall morning in the 1910s to Sarnia, Ontario, and Detroit.

travel on the Great Lakes. For all but one year during that period, both vessels were employed in the Buffalo-Duluth run from May until October.[496] The opulence of the two Northern Steamship passenger liners encouraged other fleets to bring out new passenger liners of their own. Between 1902 and 1910, the Anchor Line replaced its older triplets

In 1913 and 1914, the Chicago, Duluth, and Georgian Bay Transit Company brought out the *North American* and *South American* for the Great Lakes cruise trade.[499] Built by the Great Lakes Engineering Company at Ecorse, Michigan, in the spring of 1913, the *North American* had an overall length of 291 feet. The next year, the *South American* was launched. At 321 feet in length, she had a slightly larger passenger capacity than her older sister—521 passengers versus 450 passengers.[500] The Georgian Bay Line ran the *South American* from Buffalo to Cleveland, Detroit, Mackinac Island, Munising, Houghton, and Duluth, while the *North American* went from Buffalo to Cleveland, Detroit, Mackinac, Georgian Bay, Harbor Springs, and Chicago.[501]

CRUISING NORTH OF THE BORDER

U.S.-flagged boats weren't the only cruise vessels operating on Lake Superior. From the 1870s, Canadian-owned package and passenger freighters had been passing upbound through the Soo Locks for the Canadian lakehead cities of Port Arthur and Fort William. Most operated out of Collingwood on Lake Ontario, a three-hour rail trip from Toronto, or from Sarnia.[502] From 1900 to the 1920s, the Northern Navigation Company's *Majestic* and *City of Collingwood* were weekly visitors to the passenger docks of the Canadian lakehead. The Canadian Pacific Railway Company's steel steamers *Alberta*, *Algoma*, and *Athabasca* were built in Scotland in 1883 for weekly service between Collingwood and the lakehead. When the *Algoma* was wrecked at Isle Royale in 1885, taking some forty-five lives, it was replaced by the larger *Manitoba*. In 1907, the 365-foot *Keewatin* and *Assiniboia* also joined the fleet. Because much of the Canadian West was populated later than the Great Plains states, all of the Canadian vessels handled immigrant passengers during the first two decades of the twentieth century.[503]

In 1912, the Northern Navigation Company commissioned a shipyard at Port Arthur, Ontario, to build a 385-foot passenger vessel that would be the queen of the Canadian lakes. The *Noronic* was launched at the Canadian lakehead in 1913 and immediately began scheduled service between Sarnia, Ontario, and the lakehead. She joined two smaller sisters, the *Huronic* and *Hamonic*, built in 1901 and 1909 respectively.[504]

The heyday of the passenger cruise business on Lake Superior encompassed the years 1895

With its commercial fishing stations dotting the western half of Lake Superior, the Booth Fisheries' United States and Dominion Transportation Company capitalized on that network to carry summer tourists around the lake.

to 1915. Thousands of visitors from the mid-Atlantic and Midwest states disembarked in Duluth during that period and discovered the beauty and many recreational activities of the north and south shores of Lake Superior. But the passage of anti-trust provisions of the Panama Canal Act in 1912 forced the railroads to divest themselves of passenger and package freight lines, and after 1915, the railroads became direct competitors of the Great Lakes cruise lines. The railroads could offer better and faster schedules, and rail passenger accommodations compared favorably with those offered by the cruise ships.

Fire was a constant threat to the passenger boats. With their wood-paneled staterooms, layers of paint, and lacquered cabin berths, the passenger vessels were tinderboxes. Dozens of passenger steamers were lost to fires, particularly before the advent of steel shipbuilding. The *North West* was a total loss when it caught fire at its fit-out berth in Buffalo in early June 1911.[505] In September 1922, the *South American* burned while in a lay-up berth at her home port of Holland, Michigan. Her owners rebuilt her, and she sailed a full schedule during subsequent summer seasons.

Two fires a decade-and-a-half apart spelled the beginning of the end for the Great Lakes passenger trade. The *Morro Castle* blaze off the East Coast in 1934 with its resulting loss of life caused the U.S. government to institute tough new fire regulations for passenger vessels, including those on the Great Lakes.[506] The Anchor

Line had taken *Tionesta* and *Juniata* off the Buffalo-Duluth run in 1933 to serve the Chicago World's Fair.[507] *Tionesta* was retired in 1935, and rather than pay $100,000 per vessel for fire regulation modifications, the owners laid up *Juniata* and *Octorara* at the beginning of the 1936 season.

On a September morning in 1949, the 385-foot *Noronic*, then the flagship of the Canada Steamship Lines fleet, caught fire at her berth in Toronto. Before firefighters got control of the fierce blaze, 119 passengers lost their lives. Canadian and U.S. maritime regulations introduced in response to the conflagration aboard the *Noronic* essentially banned wooden superstructures on passenger vessels.[508]

The *North American* and *South American* lasted on into the 1960s, as did the Canadian sisters *Assiniboia* and *Keewatin*. By then, cruising had become a memory.[509] But Duluth and Superior shared in that memory, a memory of an era when travel on the Great Lakes was truly elegant.

The rebuilt South American *was only five years from her ignominious end when a postcard photographer caught her departing Duluth in the summer of 1960.*

THE PETROLEUM BUSINESS IN THE TWIN PORTS

In 1952, the B.A. Peerless (left) and Imperial Leduc load crude oil for the Lakehead Pipeline Company in Superior's East End before heading to refineries at Sarnia and Clarkson, Ontario. The Lakehead dock loaded out more than 20 million barrels of Alberta crude that year. After extending its pipeline to the Toronto area in 1957, it closed the Superior dock in 1958.

IN THE EARLY 1900s, roads from Duluth-Superior to other Minnesota-Wisconsin communities were poor or nonexistent. The network of paved highways that current generations take for granted were then gravel or dirt. The best way to get to Two Harbors, Grand Marais, and other north shore towns remained the fishing steamers that delivered supplies along the shore and to Isle Royale. To get to Duluth, residents of Virginia, Hibbing, and the Mesabi Range took the train. Rail travel to and from the Twin Cities and Madison, Wisconsin, linked Duluth-Superior to the outside world.

In 1913, Henry Ford opened his moving assembly line in suburban Detroit, and overnight America fell in love with the automobile. Ford made millions of Model T's at his plant in Highland Park, Michigan, and put America on the road.[510] The creation of an automobile culture demanded two absolute necessities: paved roads and gasoline.

A distribution network for gasoline already existed in the Midwest by the time automobiles began to appear on the scene. And it was oil baron John D. Rockefeller, who had dictated so much of the history of the head of the lakes and its tributary regions, who provided the fuel that powered the automotive transformation in the Midwest.

Rockefeller's Standard Oil refineries were located in Cleveland and Lima, Ohio, and he had an instinctive understanding of the cost efficiencies of shipping refined petroleum via the Great Lakes. It was no accident that he built his newest refinery on the Lake Michigan shoreline in Whiting, Indiana, east of Chicago. For most of the 1880s, Rockefeller had chartered upbound bulk freighters to haul barrels of kerosene to Upper Great Lakes ports.[511] In Duluth, his company used a freight dock to unload the vessels, storing barrels of the highly flammable kerosene in a complex of warehouses stretching along the harbor for more than a mile from Twentieth Avenue West. The early operations in the harbor, however, were plagued by fire. In 1888, a Standard Oil warehouse at the foot of First Avenue West had been destroyed in a spectacular blaze.[512]

Before the fire, Standard Oil had been talking to city officials about building a tank farm on the waterfront or across the bay on Rice's Point.[513] Now, however, the hazard had the company embroiled in a controversy with the Duluth City Council, and it wasn't until 1891 that the company built a major dock and tank-farm complex on the

Superior side of the harbor.[514] That same year, Rockefeller directed Russell C. Wetmore and Colgate Hoyt, two of his oldest associates, to begin building a fleet of tankers to haul refined product from the Whiting Refinery across the Great Lakes. Wetmore and Hoyt were already involved as financial angels for Alexander McDougall's American Steel Barge Company, and they engaged him to build a steel-hulled barge for the new company.[515] Dubbed *S.O. Co. No. 55,* the barge was towed down the lakes and entered the coastal trade, and within four years American Steel Barge was busy building two larger barges for Standard Oil, *S.O. Co. No. 75* and *S.O. Co. No. 76.*[516]

From 1891 until early in the twentieth century, the Standard Oil tank farm handled about 100,000 barrels of kerosene and lubricants a year. By 1910, receipts at the Twin Ports had more than tripled to 350,000 barrels.

The arrival of the automobile age in the Upper Midwest was evident when Standard Oil's Superior bulk terminal handled an astonishing 720,000 barrels in 1912, double the total of just two years before. In 1913, shipments topped 1 million barrels, and for the first time the Superior bulk terminal handled more gasoline than kerosene. Shipments doubled again to 2 million barrels in 1920 and climbed gradually during the 1920s. Gasoline dominated the shipments from Whiting to Superior, and when the Great Depression descended upon the Great Lakes in 1930, observers predicted that the Standard Oil fleet would be as devastated by economic conditions as the iron ore and grain fleets. It wasn't. Automobile use just kept increasing during the depression, and gasoline shipments kept pace. By 1939, Standard Oil was shipping nearly 5 million barrels—194 million gallons of gasoline—to the Superior terminal for distribution all across the Upper Midwest.[517]

With mines and logging camps closed and unemployment rates exceeding 25 percent, hundreds of Twin Ports residents got their start in life during the Great Depression with the Civilian Conservation Corps. These CCC enrollees worked at a camp near Brimson, Minnesota, in 1935.

CHAPTER TWELVE

The Lean Depression Years

AT THE BEGINNING of the last week of October 1929, the Duluth-Superior maritime community was looking forward to concluding one of the best seasons in the Twin Ports' long history. With about six weeks to go before ice choked off the harbor and closed another year of shipping on Lake Superior, the 1929 season was shaping up to be a record-breaker in almost every respect.

Indeed, when all of the numbers were tallied in mid-December, Duluth and Superior had surpassed the 60-million-ton mark for the first time. The cargo tonnage record, exceeding total commodities shipped through the ports during World War I, was 7 to 9 million tons more than in any of the previous four years. Iron ore shipments were the backbone of the Twin Ports' bonanza year. A veritable flood of ore—more than 44 million tons—flowed across the docks at the head of the Great Lakes in 1929. The U.S. steel industry—the end user of all that Mesabi, Vermilion, and Cuyuna Range ore—produced a record 63 million tons of finished steel in 1929, and upper lakes iron ore shipments for the year totaled more than 65 million tons.[518] Ports along the lower rim of the Great Lakes all reported record tonnages of iron ore, limestone, and coal in 1929.

The Duluth-Superior port seemed to have a bright future on Monday, October 21, 1929. That future evaporated during the following ten days. What has become known to generations of economic historians as "Black Thursday" and "Bloody Tuesday" ushered in a wave of selling on Wall Street that defined a decade for America and the world. The crash on Wall Street did not cause the Great Depression, but it produced the psychological underpinnings for a loss of confidence in the boom years of the 1920s. Like the panics of 1873 and 1893, the coming decade would bring untold misery to millions of Americans.

THE DEPRESSION ON THE LAKES

In Duluth-Superior, the Wall Street crash of 1929 was a news story, but no more momentous perhaps than President Calvin Coolidge's visit to the Mesabi Iron Range or the 350-pound black bear that wandered into the coffee shop of the Hotel Duluth.[519] For Duluthians, the really big news that fall of 1929 was the progress on the conversion of the Duluth Aerial Bridge. The suspended ferry car that had carried people and vehicles back and forth to Minnesota Point for nearly twenty-five years made its last trip on July 1, 1929. The next day, crews from the Kansas City Bridge Company began installing a 386-foot lift span to carry traffic across the Duluth Ship Canal. Work would go on throughout the winter, and the completely refurbished bridge would open in time for the 1930 navigation season.[520]

The 1930 season on the lakes was an inevitable disappointment, but not unduly alarming. Total shipments through the Twin Ports slid by a quarter, to 45.7 million tons. Iron ore shipments made up the bulk of the lost tonnage, dropping 13 million tons from the 1929 high of 44 million tons.[521] Coal held relatively steady—down 900,000 tons from 10.8 million tons the previous year—and grain shipments of nearly 2 million tons were actually up by 250,000 tons from 1929.[522]

Amid a growing litany of business layoffs and plant shutdowns, the nation entered the new year of 1931. Steel executives put on a brave face, despite existing economic conditions, but those in the know at the head of the lakes braced for tough times. The first clue that the 1931 navigation season was unlikely to match the levels achieved in 1930 came shortly after the first of the year, when Pickands-Mather suspended stripping of overburden at its giant Mahoning pit on the Mesabi Range.[523] The Mahoning pit had never been idle since it first opened at the turn of the twentieth century. It would stay idle for two years.

When the 1931 navigation season opened in April, an eerie stillness fell over the lakes. Most of the fleets didn't fit out until June, and those that did operate sailed on sharply reduced schedules.[524] Steel demand, ore production, and

Great Lakes shipments all plummeted. Only 26.4 million tons of cargo passed across the docks of Duluth-Superior in 1931, down nearly 20 million tons from 1930. Iron ore shipments dropped by half, to 15.5 million tons, the worst year for iron ore since the postwar recession year of 1921.[525] Coal arriving through the Twin Ports dropped more than 2 million tons to 7.7 million tons.[526] Grain, at 1.17 million tons, suffered its worst year since 1926.

The season ended on the same down note that it had begun. On October 31, Pittsburgh Steamship Company's *Thomas W. Lamont* took the final ore cargo of the season from the Duluth, Missabe, & Northern's docks in West Duluth.[527] The ore docks at Two Harbors, Minnesota, and Ashland, Wisconsin, closed the

Marine Iron and Shipbuilding Company's steam tug Fashion *was pressed into service to run a ferry scow across the Duluth Ship Canal during the 1929 aerial bridge conversion.*

Contractors' vehicles line Lake Avenue during the conversion of the Duluth Aerial Bridge.

same day. A week later, Great Northern Railway announced that the last cargo out of its ore docks on Allouez Bay would sail on November 12.[528] The 1931 navigation season essentially closed a month early.

"LIKE A BEAR BLUNDERING INTO A TEST PIT"

Old-timers could console themselves that the Great Lakes had experienced down years before, but this was different from 1873 or 1893 or 1907. This wasn't a panic. It was a depression. In 1930, 1,352 of the nation's nearly 31,000 state and national banks failed. The next year, another 2,300 banks went into insolvency.[529] Nearly 55,000 businesses failed in 1930 and 1931, more than 10 percent of all U.S. businesses. Those businesses that were still operating in 1932 were likely running at a loss. The combined

business deficit early that year was more than $5.4 billion. Unemployment nationwide at the new year of 1932 stood at eight million people. By summer, twelve million Americans would be out of work.[530]

Minnesota and Wisconsin were hit particularly hard by the onset of the Great Depression. One of the more tragic stories of the decade involved the contraction of family farms in the Upper Midwest. By 1932, wheat prices were at a low of 36 cents per bushel, down from as high as $1.20 per bushel in the mid-1920s.[531] A decade of drought, tight credit, and low grain prices at a time when most Americans were enjoying the prosperity of the 1920s pushed many farmers over the edge in 1932 and 1933. By 1933, 60 of every 1,000 Minnesota farmers were in bankruptcy or foreclosure.[532]

The Duluth Aerial Bridge was just weeks from being converted into a lift bridge in the spring of 1930.

But nowhere in America was the jobless toll more sharply outlined than on Minnesota's Mesabi Range. In the early winter months of 1932, more than two of every three workers on the range were unemployed.[533] Walter Havighurst, in his history of the Pickands-Mather Company, wrote that "while the rest of the country slid gradually into depression the iron towns fell in like a bear blundering into a test pit."[534] From 1932 to 1934, most of the iron mines on Lake Superior's six mining ranges ran only intermittently. Because the mines had electrified many of their operations during the 1920s, the unemployment toll was not as bad as it could have been.[535] Still, miners and their families quietly packed belongings and left Minnesota every day during the lean years of the early 1930s.

The reason for the pall hanging over the Mesabi and other ranges of Minnesota and Michigan in the winter of 1932 was the collapse of the nation's steel industry. By March 1932, steel mills were shuttered and blast furnaces were banked in every steelmaking region in the country. It

was an ill omen for the Great Lakes fleet and Duluth-Superior. In January 1932, American Steamship Company announced that three of its largest bulk freighters would spend the season in dry dock at Lorain, Ohio, where shipyard workers would convert the vessels to self-unloaders.[536] It was tacit acknowledgment that the 1932 season was likely to be a loss. In February, the price of copper dropped to 6 cents per pound, the lowest ever recorded.[537] In March, the Duluth, Missabe, & Northern and the Chicago & Northwestern Railways both announced they would do extensive renovation work on their ore docks in Duluth and Ashland.[538] The construction work was further evidence that 1932 was shaping up to be the worst season on the Great Lakes since 1893.

On March 31, Augustus B. Wolvin died at his home in Duluth. Wolvin, seventy-four, had been synonymous with the upper lakes ore trade for more than half a century. Wolvin had started sailing as a cabin boy in the early 1870s and had come ashore in the late 1880s as a Duluth-based vessel agent. During the next decade, Wolvin established himself as one of the most capable vessel agents on the lakes. In the late 1890s, he began managing fleets for Cleveland owners, and when U.S. Steel was formed in 1901, the Steel Trust asked Wolvin to be the first manager of its Pittsburgh Steamship Company subsidiary.[539] Wolvin left the Pittsburgh Steamship Company in early 1904 to oversee the launch of his namesake for the Wolvin-owned Acme Steamship Company. When the *A. B. Wolvin* came down the ways in 1904, she was the largest bulk freighter on the lakes and the model for most of the vessels built during the first half of the twentieth century. *Skillings Mining Review* eulogized the longtime Duluthian by noting that Wolvin "conceived the plan of eliminating stanchions and introducing girders and arches to support the deck and sides."[540] At 560 feet long, the *Wolvin* was nearly twice the size of the 300-footers launched just the decade before. Wolvin's design would dominate the lakes' iron ore trade until after World War II.

"Gus" Wolvin's death on the last day of March was poignant. The ice on Lake Superior was once again retreating, signaling the opening of another shipping season. It was perhaps merciful that death claimed Wolvin when it did, for the old Great Lakes mariner might well have died of a broken heart had he lived to see the 1932 shipping season. Like the year before, the 1932 season started slowly.[541] But unlike the season of 1931, it never recovered. Just over half of the 405 bulk carriers in the Great Lakes fleet left port in 1932, and most sailed only for a trip or two before heading back in for lay-up.[542] When the season ended in October, Duluth-Superior had been dealt a body blow. Only 2 million tons of iron ore moved through the Twin Ports in 1932, the lowest seasonal total since 1895.[543] Coal dropped another 2 million tons from the 1931 totals, and only because farmers were liquidating inventories for cash did the grain total go up 12 percent to 1.33 million tons.[544] Total tonnage for the year was 10.5 million tons—the worst tonnage in thirty-five years.[545]

By the time the 1932 navigation season ground to an ugly close in the fall, America was in the midst of a presidential election. President Herbert Hoover, the Iowa-born engineer who had worked with Duluthian Julius Barnes on the campaign to feed a starving Europe in the wake of World War I, bore the brunt of the blame for the nation's slide into economic chaos. Hoover was as much a victim of the depression as an unemployed iron miner in Hibbing, Minnesota, and his greatest failing was doing too little too late to address America's endemic economic problems. Americans went to the polls in November 1932 and elected Franklin Delano Roosevelt to the White House in a landslide.[546] Roosevelt, the ebullient former governor of New York, had an instinctive understanding of the federal government's role in pulling the nation out of its economic malaise.

Roosevelt's New Deal injected millions into the economy through public works programs and reined in the abuses that had plagued the nation's financial system. The Twin Ports directly benefited from the public works programs as the U.S. Army Corps of Engineers in 1933 accelerated the dredging of major navigation channels in the Duluth-

After a lifetime in maritime commerce at Duluth–Superior, Augustus Wolvin died just before the 1932 shipping season opened. Had he lived, he would have been devastated by the carnage on the Great Lakes caused by the Great Depression.

A Great Lakes bulk freighter takes on iron ore at DM&N's No. 3 dock in West Duluth in 1930. The chutes were lowered and raised by hand, and the leaf-style hatch covers were pulled open by cables from deck-mounted winches.

Superior harbor to twenty-three feet.[547] Several Works Progress Administration programs in the Twin Ports put several hundreds of residents to work building roads, sidewalks, sewage plants, airports, and other civic projects.[548] Thousands of young men from Minnesota and Wisconsin joined the Civilian Conservation Corps and spent the middle and late 1930s improving the forests of the northland.

The head of the lakes and the rest of the country gradually pulled out of the economic doldrums after 1933. Shipments through the Twin Ports rebounded sharply to 22.5 million tons in 1933 as iron ore through the ports climbed more than sixfold to 13 million tons. Shipments made incremental gains in each of the next two years, reaching 29.2 million tons in 1935.[549] A restructured steel industry accelerated the strong comeback in 1936 and 1937, as iron ore movements reached 31 million tons in the former year and a near record 42.9 million tons in 1937. The 57.1

million tons total in 1937 was only 3 million tons less than the record year of 1929.[550] The reality of the long-term nature of the economic upheaval brought totals crashing back to earth in 1938, when iron ore shipments of 11.6 million tons were less than 30 percent of the totals the year before. Total shipments of all commodities for the year—23 million tons—were 40 percent of the totals in 1937. Even after five years of federal priming of the pump under FDR, the nation's economy was far from completely recovered.

TROUBLE ON THE DOCKS

The collapse of maritime employment during the early 1930s put unprecedented pressure on labor-management relations, both at the Twin Ports and lakes-wide. For much of the 1920s, the Great Lakes fleets had entrusted their labor relations to the Lake Carriers' Association, the Cleveland-based trade organization that represented the interests of fleet owners. Wages held steady through much of the 1920s, but the onset of the depression in 1930 and 1931 caused the LCA to institute a 20 percent pay cut across the board for nonlicensed personnel. In 1932, the pay cut was somewhat academic. Fleet sailings were so sporadic that most boats that did fit out for the season sailed with licensed officers only. Captains sailed as mates, and mates sailed as deckhands.[551] Fleet owners attempted to keep a nucleus of trained, licensed personnel for the inevitable rebound of lakes shipping.

On the docks, the situation was much more chaotic. Duluth-Superior had supported a resident population of thousands of longshoremen, grain millers, licensed tug men, shipyard and coal dockworkers, dredge men, and engineers. Many had been organized as far back as the 1890s by the National Longshoremen's Association of the United States, a predecessor of the International Longshoremen's Association, and membership peaked at 3,000 in the Twin Ports during the World War I era.[552]

By 1900, the International Longshoremen's Association had 50,000 members, all on the Great Lakes. There were ILA locals in the Twin Ports as early as the 1900s, but because of the seasonal nature of the work, longshoremen at the time were sometimes difficult to retain from year to year.[553] From 1905 until the early 1920s, the ILA—which was affiliated with the craft unions of the American Federation of Labor—fought an organizing battle with the Industrial Workers of the World.[554] IWW locals in the Twin Ports waged a two-year labor war with the ILA and dock owners during World War I over pay and working conditions. When a 1919 work stoppage ended, the ILA locals at the head of the lakes had been critically wounded by the strife, since fleet owners and dock operators did not distinguish between the ILA and the IWW. The boom economic times on the docks in the 1920s further eroded the ILA's power on the Great Lakes, as wages and working conditions were good enough that many dockworkers saw no need for a union. When the Great Depression descended with a fury during the winter of 1930–1931, the huge mass of unemployed workers in Duluth-Superior ensured that wages would be kept low on the docks.

Edward L. "Buster" Slaughter started to work on the docks in the Twin Ports in the mid-1920s. Born in 1904, the son of an Irish-American dock superintendent, Slaughter would become one of the ILA's most potent voices during the next sixty years. "I got in the picture pretty well back in the 1920s," Slaughter recalled in an interview in the mid-1970s, "and I worked straight through for 10 years on the waterfront as a longshoreman. I handled sacks. I handled cargo, and it was tough. I didn't have too much weight in those days, but I had enough determination to show that I wasn't going to be shown up by anybody."[555]

When the depression arrived in 1930, Slaughter and the longshoremen found themselves working for reduced wages. "We got a 10-cent cut in wages right off the bat," he said. "We went out on strike, but we weren't organized. We just said that we wouldn't work."[556] The dock owners brought in strikebreakers, and Slaughter remembered pitched battles with rocks and brickbats during the tumultuous spring of 1931. Duluth police commissioner Warren Moore led squads of police officers down to the waterfront to confront the strikers.

Confrontations between strikers and police were not all that uncommon during the 1930s. Teamsters clashed with Minneapolis police in a series of running street battles in 1934, and striking journalists were teargassed by Duluth police on the street in front of the *Duluth News-Tribune* in 1936.[557] On the waterfront, Slaughter helped the ILA organize Local 1279 in 1932. Gradually, the new local began signing contracts with waterfront employers. Like many unions in the 1930s, the ILA was helped by the activist labor policies of FDR's New Deal. Congressional passage of the Norris-LaGuardia Act in 1934, which limited the use of injunctions against picketing, and the Wagner Act of 1935, which gave workers the right to vote for union representation, strengthened the hand of labor organizers like Slaughter.

Slaughter was elected vice president of the Duluth Central Labor Body in 1935, but the ILA organizer had one more task to attend to before the 1930s ended.[558] Local 1279 was infiltrated by communists, and Slaughter led the effort to purge the local.[559] Years later, he recalled that "a committee went into the place and messed it up a little bit. They didn't do too much, broke some chairs and tables and what have you, and threw papers around. They got the message because they moved out of there."[560] With the expulsion of the communists, the ILA would become the major labor organization representing waterfront workers in the Twin Ports. Slaughter would go on to organize nineteen ILA locals in Minnesota and Wisconsin representing more than 2,800 longshoremen.[561]

A NEW DAY DAWNS
At the end of the decade, communism was not the major problem facing the world. Armored, mechanized German panzer divisions crossed the Polish border in the early morning hours of September 1, 1939. Within thirty-six hours, France and Great Britain, citing mutual aid treaties with the Polish government, declared war on Nazi Germany. The European war that

diplomats had been dreading since the peace treaty was signed at Versailles twenty years earlier was now an accomplished fact. Two years later, in 1941, those who were able to remember "the world war" would be referring to that earlier conflict as World War I.

Gripping news of tank battles and cavalry charges on the plains of western Poland shared the front pages of Twin Ports newspapers with the passing of a local landmark. On September 3, 1939, the day that Great Britain and France declared war, local residents mourned the demolition of Duluth's incline railway.[562] The funicular climbed the hillside at Seventh Avenue West, and, for forty-eight years, the cars going up and down the steep hill had been one of Duluth's premier tourist attractions and a symbol of the Zenith City to nearly three generations of Great Lakes sailors.

As the wrecking crews swarmed over the incline railway site, the 1939 navigation season was

The steamer Henry Steinbrenner *takes on grain at Cargill's Itasca Elevator in the 1930s. At the time, Cargill controlled more than half of Superior's elevator capacity.*

entering its final stretch. Iron ore shipments had rebounded sharply from the mini-depression year of 1938, and before ice closed the shipping lanes for good in December, ore shipments would total 26 million tons, two-and-a-half times the tonnage handled the year before. A late season grain push would see shipments pass the 2-million-ton mark, the first time that level had been achieved since the 1928 season.[563] The eight big grain elevators on the Superior side of the harbor worked around the clock to meet the demands during October and November. The 38 million tons of cargo handled in 1939 were well above the ten-year average of 32.3 million tons, and it gave the maritime community hope that the last of the depression was finally over.

Although nobody seriously thought that the United States would get involved in a European war in 1940, longtime participants in the maritime economy were realistic enough to know that the belligerents would have an insatiable demand for bread and steel. The United States was officially neutral the winter of 1939–1940, but FDR was making it known—and not subtly—that the Roosevelt administration considered the Nazi regime of Adolf Hitler a real threat to world peace and security.[564] Six weeks after the outbreak of the war in Europe, Roosevelt engineered a key congressional victory for his support of Great Britain with a repeal of the arms embargo provisions of the Neutrality Act. In effect, Great Britain and France could buy U.S. weapons as long as they paid in cash and shipped their purchases across the Atlantic Ocean on their own vessels.

For the nation's steel industry, the repeal of the arms embargo was the final sign that the depression was over. Steel production ramped up to meet the needs of the belligerents, and 1940 proved to be the best year for the domestic steel industry since 1929.[565] The pickup in industrial output quickly rippled back up across the Great Lakes. Much of the fleet fitted out early in the spring of 1940, and when the ice jams retreated in April, the ore docks were a beehive of activity. Before the navigation season ended in early December, Duluth-Superior had sent 42 million tons of Mesabi and Cuyuna ore down the lakes. It was the third best year for iron ore in the Twin Ports' history, exceeded only by 1929 and 1937.

Even given the eager anticipation for a repeat performance on the lakes in 1941, there was a sober reminder late in the 1940 season that Great Lakes shipping was still an inherently hazardous occupation. An Armistice Day blizzard blew across the lakes, hammering Lake Michigan with winds in excess of 100 knots.[566] Like the storm of November 1913, the Armistice Day blizzard wreaked much more havoc on the lower lakes than it did on Lake Superior. Most of the vessels on the big lake were able to find anchorage to ride out the storm, but on northern Lake Michigan the storm took a deadly toll. The *Anna C. Minch* and her crew of twenty-four disappeared off Pentwater, Michigan, as did the *William B. Davock* and her crew of thirty-three.[567] Also lost in the hurricane-like blow were the fishing tugs *Richard H.* and *Indian*.[568]

Storms aside, another omen occurred late that year. On November 3, 140 enlisted men and officers of the 49th and 50th Division of the 10th Battalion of the U.S. Naval Reserve marched down Superior Street to the Union Depot, where they boarded a train for Chicago. The reservists were under the command of Lieutenant Arthur M. Clure, a Duluth admiralty attorney who would play a big part in the port's history the next decade. In Chicago, they were to board the *U.S.S. Paducah* and take her through the Great Lakes and the St. Lawrence River to the Brooklyn Naval Yard, where the *Paducah*, *U.S.S. Dubuque*, and *U.S.S. Sacramento* would be commissioned for active sea duty.[569] The crew of the *Paducah* would be the first of thousands of Twin Port residents to see active duty during the next five years.

DULUTH-SUPERIOR
IN 1939

The Duluth incline railway was perhaps the city's most famous landmark during the years between WWI and WWII. Visible from miles out on Lake Superior, the railway with its funicular cars was scrapped in 1939.

PERHAPS NO METROPOLITAN area of its size in the United States was more uniquely oriented to the water than Duluth-Superior in 1939. The twin towns enjoyed the distinction of being the nation's second-largest port in terms of tonnage. New York was number one, but millions of residents of the five boroughs could live a lifetime without coming into contact with the waterfront along the East River. The same couldn't be said of Duluth-Superior. The Minnesota and Wisconsin cities existed to serve the needs of the Great Lakes maritime community.

In 1939, the combined population of the two communities that bordered Minnesota's St. Louis Bay and Wisconsin's Allouez Bay—140,000 residents in all—were reminded every day during the eight-and-a-half-month navigation season that Duluth and Superior were waterfront towns.

Climb the steep hills above Fourth Street in Duluth and you couldn't miss the lake gleaming deep blue in the summer sunshine or dazzling frosty white in the winter chill. Cross the Arrowhead Bridge to Superior and you wouldn't wait more than a quarter of an hour for an upbound coal boat to pass. Crack your bedroom window on a misty July morning and you would hear the mournful wail of a foghorn. Order a beer in a local bar and the guy sitting on the stool next to you was likely a mate on an ore boat in port for two or three days for repair to his vessel's rudder or propeller. Open the pages of the *Duluth News-Tribune* after supper and you'd read that the United States and Canada were exploring the possibility of opening an international seaway along the St. Lawrence River.[570]

It was almost impossible to live in the Duluth-Superior area in 1939 and not have some connection with the waterfront community. Port industries and services accounted for thousands of jobs, and tributary industries employed thousands more. In that last year of the Great Depression, more than 40 percent of the Twin Ports' employment base could be traced to the nearly fifty miles of harbor frontage that dominated the head of the lakes.

If you didn't work on or for a waterfront business, you lived in Duluth-Superior because someone else in your family did. Perhaps your father was in his last year before retirement from the big coal briquetting plant over in Superior. Maybe your older brother, a vessel agent since returning from Europe in World War I, had gotten his first job as a runner with Alastair Guthrie's grain brokerage at the Duluth board of trade. Or your younger brother might be making his way up the licensed ladder, working as a second mate this season with the Buckeye Transportation Fleet. Perhaps your younger sister married a guy three years ago and moved up over the hill with him to Proctor, where your brother-in-law was now a dispatcher at the town's Duluth, Missabe & Northern Railway's yard. And maybe his four brothers all worked for one or another of the eight railroads that served the Twin Ports.[571]

In 1939, ninety-eight wharves or terminals lined the Duluth-Superior harbor. Seven huge ore docks, some nearly half a mile long, graced both sides of the harbor, and twenty-one coal docks—most equipped with traveling bridge cranes—dotted the waterfront. A total of eleven big elevator complexes stood like sentinels over the Twin Ports, a monument to Frank Peavey's daring experiment with storing grain in concrete silos nearly forty years before. Collectively, the elevators provided storage capacity for an astounding 48 million bushels of wheat. Three big storage warehouses, innumerable sites for bulk freight storage, one floating dry dock, two graving dry docks, and seven marine repair docks rounded out the harbor facilities at the head of the lakes.[572]

Not only was your whole family employed in some aspect of the Twin Ports maritime community, just about everybody you knew was. With generations of experience in every facet of maritime operations, Duluth-Superior was poised to become the most efficient port in the world during the next six years. During World War II the Twin Ports satisfied an ever-increasing demand for iron ore, grain, and battleships to help the Allies win their fight against Nazi Germany and Japan.

An all-woman welding crew poses at Walter Butler Shipbuilders before World War II ended in 1945. One woman likened her welding work to "embroidery . . . but tougher."

CHAPTER THIRTEEN

The Twin Ports at War

THE MARITIME COMMUNITY at Duluth-Superior was in wind-down mode on Sunday, December 7, 1941. The shipping season was in the process of wrapping up. Already, skim ice was forming in the harbor, and bulk freighters of the Pittsburgh Steamship Company were straggling into their winter berths with a last load of Lake Erie coal. The lights had been on Saturday night at Elevator Row as canallers and smaller freighters rushed to stow the last load of downbound wheat for the season. Some of the offices at the Duluth board of trade were occupied this Sunday morning as grain merchants and vessel agents made last-minute phone calls and tidied up paperwork.

The season that would come to an end in less than a week's time had been spectacular. In early 1941, President Franklin D. Roosevelt had pushed through his Lend Lease Program to assist Great Britain in its war with Nazi Germany, and the nation's steel mills had operated at full capacity for most of the year. The 43 million tons of iron ore handled through the Twin Ports had bettered 1940's shipments by nearly 800,000 tons—only a million tons short of the 1929 record. Coal receipts had increased 1.5 million tons over 1940 to finish the 1941 season at 8.67 million tons. The insatiable demand for grain, especially from Canadian mills, pushed wheat and small grain shipments to more than 2.5 million tons, the best single year for grain at the head of the lakes since 1924. Speculation in the board of trade was rife about the future impact of the Farmers Union Grain Terminal Association's just-completed $1.5 million elevator, a 4.5-million bushel facility whose 270-foot head house at the foot of Superior's Tower Avenue punctuated the harbor skyline.[573] The year ended with total tonnage of 57.8 million tons, the second best in the Twin Ports' history after 1929.[574]

With the British hanging on in North Africa and the German panzer armies stalled outside Moscow, it was a sure bet that the war in Europe would continue into its third year.[575] War overseas was literally yanking the United States out of a decade of depression, and few communities in the nation benefited more than the Twin Ports. Planning was already under way for the 1942 season, and fleet agents at Duluth-Superior were breathing a sigh of relief that President Roosevelt's intervention earlier in the week had seemed to avert a threatened nationwide rail strike.[576] Now, if the ice would just stay thin on the upper lakes over the winter, maybe the Great Lakes could get an early start on the 1942 season and squeeze a couple of extra trips in before the season ended again next December.

Those still at their desks at the board of trade that Sunday probably heard the news announcer break in on the radio shortly after 1:30 p.m.: Japanese planes had attacked the American naval base at Pearl Harbor in the Hawaiian Islands.

"War Declared on Jap Nation," the headlines in the *Duluth Herald* and *Superior Evening Telegram* screamed the next day.[577] The newspapers reported on the stirring speech FDR had made to both houses of Congress, and announced the near unanimous congressional approval of a declaration of war.[578] What Roosevelt, in his rolling cadences, termed "an unprovoked and dastardly attack" called America to action as never before. It would be three-and-a-half long years before Duluth-Superior and the rest of the nation were again at peace.

THE GREAT LAKES MOBILIZE FOR WAR

Even before the official declaration of war, the U.S. Coast Guard Station at Duluth had cancelled all leaves and instituted round-the-clock patrols of the harbor.[579] It was an action duplicated up and down the Great Lakes, punctuated by fears of similar attacks in the days immediately following the Japanese bombing of Pearl Harbor. Under terms of an agreement with Japan (the Tripartite Pact), Germany and Italy exercised their obligations to their Far Eastern ally and declared war on the United States within days of the U.S. declaration, and fears switched to a German attack. The Soo Locks, the hub of the Great Lakes transportation system, became perhaps the most vulnerable choke point in North America. If the locks were bombed or sabotaged, America's steel mills would be shut off from their principal source of iron ore.[580] In March 1942, the War Department officially formed the Sault Ste. Marie Military District and began moving in the first of what would become more than 7,000 American troops by the following summer to guard the vital installation.[581]

The fears of axis sabotage seemed justified shortly after the first of the year when a Superior grain elevator was destroyed in a spectacular fire. Blasts ripped through Elevator X on Superior's St. Louis Bay early in the morning of January 10, 1942. Within minutes, the elevator, built in 1888, was consumed by flames. It was apparent to the first crews on the scene that the $2 million elevator and its 1.25 million bushels of grain were likely to be a total loss. Fire lines were set up to keep the blaze from spreading to adjacent Elevator S.[582]

By noon on the day of the fire, FBI special agents had arrived from Minneapolis to investigate the possibilities of sabotage. The fire was eventually determined to have started from machinery sparks, but the FBI presence was indicative of how jittery northland citizens were about the new war they found themselves fighting.[583]

Fears of axis treachery aside, the Twin Ports and the Great Lakes maritime community quickly mobilized to help America win the war. Iron ore would be critical to the nation's defense efforts,

and in mid-January 1942, President Roosevelt appointed Sears, Roebuck, and Company executive Donald Nelson to head the War Production Board, perhaps the most efficient of all of FDR's alphabet agencies. The WPB had wide-ranging powers over the nation's steel mills, manufacturing plants, natural resources, and transportation systems, and by April the board had issued the target for the upcoming navigation season on the Great Lakes. The goal was set at 88 million tons of iron ore.[584] Substantially, all of the ore flowing down from the Lake Superior iron ranges was earmarked for the defense effort. American industry made a rapid conversion from civilian to military production. Twin Ports Boy Scouts spearheaded scrap drives, collecting tin cans, automobile parts, brass, and old bedsprings.[585] The nation needed every ounce of metal it could lay its hands on for the fight ahead.

On the docks of the Twin Ports, the spring of 1942 broke early and mild. Ice was all but non-existent on Lake Superior in late March, and the first vessels began arriving before the month was out.[586] Lake Superior is fickle, however, and falling temperatures in early April created a massive ice jam in Whitefish Bay. After what appeared to be one of the more promising starts in memory, the full complement of more than 290 freighters in the Great Lakes ore fleets didn't get out and running at full capacity until almost May.[587] When the fleet did start moving that 1942 season, however, it was with a purpose and focus rarely seen in Great Lakes history. In May, the fleet handled 12 million tons of iron ore, shattering the previous record by more than 500,000 tons.[588] Records fell every month that season, and in midsummer, the War Production Board upped the iron ore quotas to 91 million tons. The U.S. Coast Guard generally looked the other way when it came to load limits, and many a vessel "kissed bottom" in some of the shallower connecting channels of the Great Lakes. Captains were told by fleet offices in Cleveland, Detroit, and Duluth to defer maintenance until winter lay-up and keep moving. The WPB requisitioned all of the fourteen vessels of the package freight fleet in July and consigned most to coastal routes for merchant marine duty, a commentary on the shipping shortages caused by the U-boat offensive that spring.[589]

Planners in Washington worried that fall storms would disrupt the flow of iron ore down the lakes, and when northern Minnesota registered below-freezing temperatures before Labor Day, those fears seemed prudent. Even though the fall was colder than normal, the iron ore railroads at the head of the lakes moved steaming equipment into position in the yards at Proctor and Two Harbors as early as the third week of October. As a result, they never lost a day's shipping time because of weather.[590] When the final cargo of iron ore headed down the Great Lakes two days after the first anniversary of Pearl Harbor, the fleet had broken every record for cargo movement. Just over 92 million tons of iron ore had flowed out of Lake Superior to the nation's industrial heartland, exceeding the WPB's amended quotas and setting the United States on the road to winning the war of production with the axis.[591]

Two-thirds of the ore shipped during 1942 had come across the docks of the Twin Ports. The 63.2 million tons of Mesabi and Cuyuna ore that poured across the docks of Duluth and

Superior exceeded the previous record by nearly 20 million tons and wouldn't be surpassed until the demands of another war in far-off Korea a decade into the future.[592] Altogether, more than 74.3 million tons of cargo passed through the Twin Ports in 1942, shattering the 1929 record by 12 million tons.[593] Coal and grain tonnages actually dropped slightly from 1941 totals, although part of the decrease for both commodities was due to the WPB's insistence that vessels that traditionally carried grain should haul iron ore instead.

A DISAPPOINTING YEAR

The iron ore shipped during the 1942 season would not again be equaled during WWII. Although the War Production Board considered increasing tonnage quotas to 100 million tons for the 1943 season, some of the most severe ice conditions in half a century on Lake Superior delayed the opening of the season until late April. When the season did open, the quotas had dropped to 91 million tons, the same as the year before. Some vessels were diverted to the grain trade early in the season to meet growing

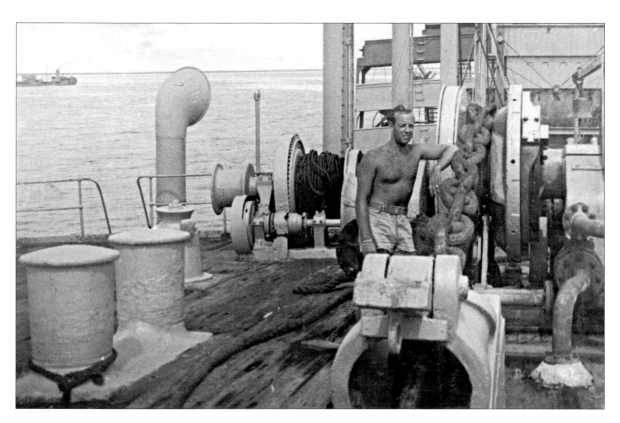

Like many Twin Ports residents, Richard D. Bibby served in the U.S. merchant marine fleet. As second mate aboard the S.S. Bethore Bibby saw extensive service in the Mediterranean, Caribbean, and Red Seas, as well as the perilous North Atlantic. He later gained renown as the M. A. Hanna Company's vessel agent in Duluth–Superior.

wartime demands for wheat and corn at the Buffalo mills, and May and June were much foggier than normal. As the season advanced into summer, the fleet was behind in its iron ore targets and never really caught up. Even though the federal government guaranteed insurance for vessels moving in December, ice on the Upper Lakes halted shipping by the first week of the month.[594]

The 84 million tons of iron ore moved in 1943 was the second best year in history, but still 10 percent below the 1942 record and the quotas set by the government.[595] Most of the drop in ore tonnage occurred in Duluth-Superior, where 1943 shipments totaled 55 million tons. Coal passing through the Twin Ports gained 1 million tons, and grain shipments held nearly steady. Only the expectations raised by the 1942 season dimmed the accomplishments of 1943.

The WPB once again called for the fleets to deliver 90 million tons of iron ore in 1944, but as the new year dawned, it was becoming apparent to some in the Great Lakes maritime community that the demand for iron ore had likely peaked.[596] American manufacturers had converted from building automobiles and refrigerators, and the output during 1942 and 1943 was truly staggering. Even small companies successfully converted. Duluth-based Diamond Tool and Horseshoe Company had converted from manufacturing horseshoes to making automotive tools in the 1920s. When the war broke out, the company converted its Grand Avenue factory to making tank-track adjustors and heavy-duty truck wrenches for the military.[597]

Overseas, 1943 had been the turning point in the war for the allies. All of that equipment surging from America's defense plants accompanied American fighting men and women into battle on the far-flung war fronts of the world. Residents at the Twin Ports avidly followed the exploits of Major Richard Ira Bong, a hometown hero who logged forty kills of Japanese planes in the South Pacific before his death while testing a jet aircraft near the end of the war.[598]

Unlike 1943, the 1944 season fulfilled the promise of fair weather. The navigation season at the Twin Ports opened on Easter Sunday, April 9, when the freighter *Cadillac* of the Cleveland-Cliffs fleet sailed under the Duluth Aerial Bridge, accompanied by "a tumult of whistles by harbor craft."[599] The only ice on Lake Superior at the time was in Whitefish Bay, and that had mostly disappeared by the time the *Cadillac* made her way back down Lake Superior with her load of ore from the Great Northern ore docks in Allouez Bay.[600] By early fall, the steel mills were claiming they had more than enough ore to meet their needs. The War Production Board began diverting vessels to the grain trade, a cargo that had taken a backseat to iron ore in the first two years of the war. A bumper harvest of wheat in 1944, coupled with the need to feed the starving people of Europe and Asia liberated by American armies, galvanized the WPB into encouraging the grain trade on the lakes. The Great Lakes fleet moved just over 81 million tons of iron ore in 1944, slightly less than in 1943. The fleet also moved 16.2 million tons of wheat, the best in any year since 1928.[601]

Duluth-Superior's tonnage in 1944 totaled just over 67 million tons, down slightly from the 1943 totals. Iron ore totaled nearly 52 million tons, off 3 million tons from the 1943 totals, but the slack was partially taken up by grain, which totaled nearly 3.5 million tons. That was the best single-year total since the Twin Ports started shipping grain in the 1870s.[602] Coal receipts were up slightly from 1943 at 9.95 million tons.

By the time the 1945 season opened in March, the war was winding down. Farmers on the Northern Plains recorded their second bumper wheat harvest, and the Great Lakes fleet handled more than 18.7 million tons of grain, most of which was transshipped to feed the nations of occupied Europe.[603] Nearly 76 million tons of iron ore from all of Lake Superior ports went down the lakes in the last year of the war, bringing the four-year total of ore handled by the fleet to more than one-third of a billion tons.[604]

Two-thirds of the nation's ore tonnage had crossed the docks of the Twin Ports. Duluth and Superior handled 50 million tons of ore in

1945, bringing the four-year total to just under 220 million tons.[605] The system of mines, docks, boats, and mills put in place a half-century before proved its worth a hundred times over during World War II. If the Napoleonic wars had been won on the playing fields of Eton, then World War II was won on the docks of the Twin Ports.

"SHIPBUILDING IS IN THE BLOOD"

Furnishing the nation with iron ore and grain wasn't the only contribution Duluth-Superior made to winning the war. Re-creating their role in America's defense efforts in World War I, the Twin Ports became one of mid-America's major centers of shipbuilding between 1941 and 1945. At the peak of activity in 1944, more than 14,000 workers built ships in seven Duluth and Superior yards.[606] David Skillings, the Duluth journalist whose weekly publication provided comprehensive coverage of the Lake Superior mining industry, was a perceptive observer of the maritime community. "Shipbuilding is in the blood of the people of Duluth-Superior," Skillings wrote in August 1942.[607]

John Abernethy worked as mechanical superintendent for many years at the Marine Iron and Shipbuilding Company. Robert Fraser, later owner of Fraser Shipyards, once worked for Abernethy and called him "the cleverest man I ever knew."

The shipyards at the head of the lakes built nearly 200 vessels during the war, far outstripping the number of ships built during World War I. In terms of volume and numbers, Duluth-Superior was a distant third to the mammoth shipyards at Manitowoc, Wisconsin, and Ecorse, Michigan.[608] The contributions of such Duluth-Superior yards as Zenith Dredge, Marine Iron and Shipbuilding, Globe Shipbuilding, Lake Superior Shipbuilding, Barnes Duluth Shipbuilding, and Walter Butler Shipbuilders, however, carried on the proud traditions of shipbuilding at the head of the lakes dating back to the ports' establishment in the early 1870s.

Soon after the declaration of war, the U.S. Maritime Commission created the War Shipping Administration to oversee shipyard contracts.[609] Under provisions of a 1939 amendment to the Merchant Marine Act of 1936, the Maritime Commission was already heavily involved in wartime construction on the Great Lakes. The amendment allowed the Maritime Commission to issue credits to any company that wanted to

trade in old vessels for new construction. Pittsburgh Steamship Company immediately took advantage of the provision, retiring a number of fifty-year-old vessels and committing to construction of five new freighters on the Great Lakes. The 1941 contract awarded three of the vessels to the Great Lakes Engineering Works at Ecorse, Michigan, and two vessels to the American Ship Building Company at Lorain, Ohio.[610] The five vessels—the *A. H. Ferbert, Enders M. Voorhees, Benjamin F. Fairless, Leon Fraser,* and *Irving S. Olds*—were launched in the late winter and early spring of 1942. At 639 feet, the *Fraser* and her four identical sisters were the largest boats ever launched on the Great Lakes.[611] The Maritime Commission authorized construction of another sixteen vessels during the 1943 season, bringing the total of new vessels launched for the Great Lakes fleet during the war to twenty-one.[612]

As in World War I, the federal government looked to the Great Lakes for help in building merchant vessels for the coastal service.

Thousands of Twin Ports residents worked in the shipyards, often taking two jobs, during the war. Here, a shift change at Walter Butler Shipbuilders' Riverside yards lines up to punch in.

Shipyards at the head of the lakes would be brought into the effort early in the war. The British Shipbuilding Mission to the United States visited Great Lakes shipyards in late 1941 to assess capabilities. The British desperately needed dry cargo vessels to replace bottoms lost to U-boat and Luftwaffe actions in 1940 and 1941.[613] In early 1942, the War Shipping Administration placed the first orders for dry bulk freighters similar to the Frederickstad-type vessels built on the lakes twenty-four years before. The first contracts went to Barnes Duluth Shipbuilding Company and Walter Butler Shipbuilders in Duluth and Superior. Barnes Duluth, the old Alexander McDougall firm, was headed by Julius Barnes, the Duluthian whose far-flung interests included shipbuilding, shipping, manufacturing, and grain brokering. Barnes organized the Barnes Duluth Shipbuilding Company in April 1941 with a $280,000 guarantee from the Defense Plant Corporation that allowed the company to reopen its World War I shipyard in Riverside.[614] The company quickly secured a contract from the War Shipping Administration to build eight diesel tankers.

Eventually, Barnes Duluth would win contracts to build a total of nineteen tankers, some of them the largest ever built on the Great Lakes.[615]

The Barnes Duluth Shipbuilding Company merged in 1943 with Walter Butler Shipbuilders in Superior. The Butler firm had been formed in 1942 by a St. Paul contractor who took over the operations of the Lake Superior Shipbuilding Company in Superior. Butler immediately secured contracts to build eighteen dry-bulk freighters for the Maritime Commission. During the next three years, Butler would build nearly seventy cargo ships for the War Shipping Administration.[616]

The newly organized Globe Shipbuilding Company completed the construction of eight of the C1-M-AV1 cargo vessels being churned out by the Walter Butler shipyards.[617] Globe had been formed in the spring of 1941 by a group of Superior businessmen. When they couldn't get options on shipyard property in Howard's Pocket operated by a firm of the same name during World War I, they leased property from the Northwestern Fuel Company at the foot of

Hill Avenue and built a new shipyard. Clarence Skamser, the former head of the Superior Association of Commerce and president of the new Globe company, spent most of the summer and fall of 1941 in Washington trying to secure contracts.[618] Skamser and Globe hit pay dirt in late 1941 when the firm was awarded contracts to build ten seagoing tugboats. In December 1942, the firm won a contract from the navy to build eight frigates.[619]

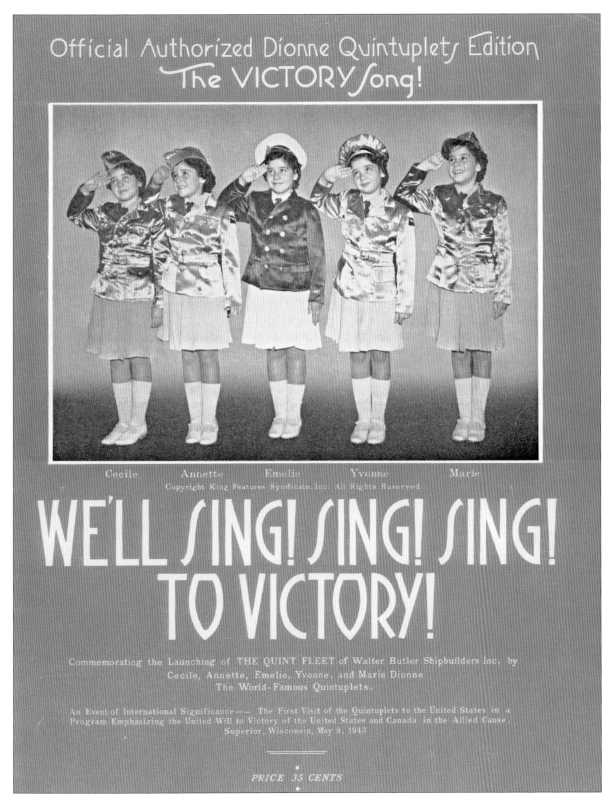

Canada's Dionne Quintuplets journeyed by rail to the Twin Ports on Sunday, May 9, 1943, to dedicate the "Quint Fleet," five ships launched on the same day at Walter Butler Shipbuilders. The girls performed several songs for the huge crowd.

A St. Paul contractor, Walter Butler acquired the former Lake Superior Shipbuilding Company yards in 1942, later absorbed the Barnes Duluth yards, and built nearly seventy ships during WWII.

A. W. Leraan served as president of Marine Iron and Shipbuilding during the company's busiest years in WWII.

Globe's success in building frigates for the U.S. Navy was duplicated by several other Twin Ports' yards. At the same time the frigate contract was let to Globe in December 1942, Walter Butler Shipbuilders was awarded a contract to build thirteen of the British-designed escorts.[620] Two Duluth yards—Marine Iron and Shipbuilding Company and Zenith Dredge Company—spent most of the war building buoy tenders for the U.S. Coast Guard. Marine Iron and Zenith Dredge split an order for thirty-eight of the 180-foot combination buoy tenders and cutters.[621]

Marine Iron and Shipbuilding Company dated back to the shipyard at the foot of Buchanan Street founded by Napoleon Grignon in the early 1880s. Napoleon's son, Peter, took over the business after the turn of the twentieth century and focused on the repair of lakes vessels. The company operated the only dry dock on the Duluth side of the harbor. It weathered the depression by building tugs, derrick barges, and scows for the U.S. Army Corps of Engineers and repairing bulk and package freighters.[622] Marine Iron's next door neighbor on the Duluth waterfront, Zenith Dredge Company, was another old line Duluth firm. Founded in 1905 under the father-son team of Donald B. and Donald C. MacDonald, Zenith Dredge was one of the best-known dredge contractors on the Upper Lakes. Zenith bought waterfront land, dredged slips, filled docks, and sold the developed parcel to grain companies for elevators and utilities for steam electric plants. The company kept a trained crew of workers employed during the 1930s dredging navigation channels on Lakes Superior, Michigan, and Huron.[623]

A BEEHIVE OF ACTIVITY

Shipbuilding activity made the Duluth-Superior harbor a veritable beehive of activity during World War II. In 1944, more than 14,000 workers were employed in the seven shipyards of the Twin Ports. The workforce was almost evenly divided between Duluth and Superior. Work went on around the clock. Manpower shortages were an ever-present problem. Globe and Walter Butler operated buses that picked up and dropped off workers from as far away as Ashland and Phillips, Wisconsin, and Hinckley

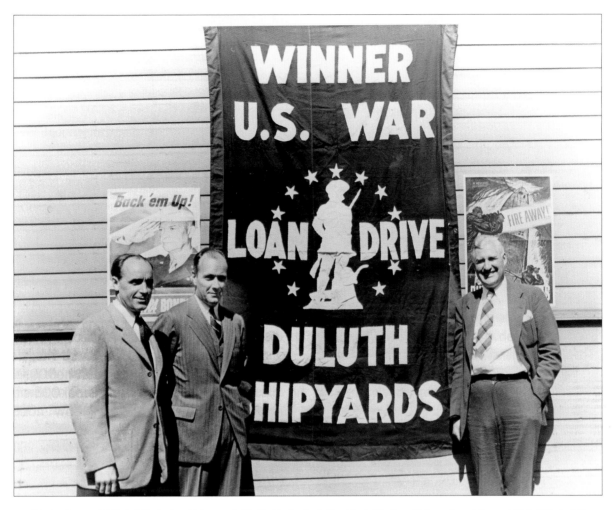

Marine Iron and Shipbuilding's Arnold Leraan (left), Zenith Dredge's Donald C. MacDonald (center), and Barnes Shipbuilding's Julius Barnes celebrate their firms' recognition for achieving goals in a WWII bond drive.

and Aitkin, Minnesota. The Northern Pacific Railway also conveyed shipyard workers on trains between Duluth's Lakeside and Lester Park neighborhoods and the Riverside yards during shift changes. In the Twin Ports' version of "Rosie the riveter," several hundred women worked in the shipyards. Many were employed as welders because the job required a sure eye and a deft touch. One woman welder likened it to "embroidery or petitpoint, but tougher."[624]

Welding was the key to the productivity of the head of the lakes' shipbuilders. Before World War II, most steel ship construction was done with rivets. But advances in arc welding during the 1930s led to a revolution in ship construction during the war. Omer Blodgett, a welding superintendent at Globe's Superior yard, told an interviewer that "early experience quickly revealed that it took a longer time to train a riveter than a welder. Riveters worked in three-

man crews; welders worked independently. Not only that, welding saved up to 30 percent in weight and time."[625] Workers in the Twin Ports' shipyards spent months on end out-of-doors assembling ships in below zero weather. They pioneered cold weather welding techniques that are still in general use sixty years later.[626]

Howard Hagen came to Duluth from the Twin Cities in 1940 to work for Road Machinery Supplies Company selling equipment on the Mesabi Iron Range. Hagen joined Zenith Dredge Company in 1941 and spent the war working with the outfitting superintendent at Zenith's yards at Thirteenth Avenue West. He recalled more than a half-century later how the firm's 1,300 workers swarmed over the yards. "They ended up with three shipways," Hagen said. "They built their hulls with two primary ways, and the third one became more of an outfitting part."[627]

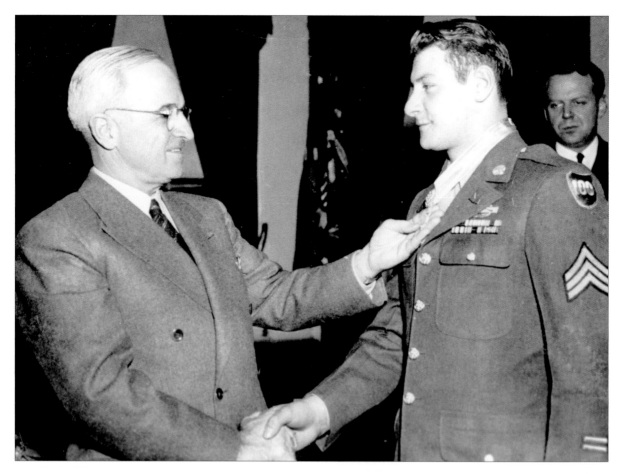

President Harry S. Truman pins the Congressional Medal of Honor on PFC Michael Colalillo in 1945. Colalillo, who grew up in Duluth, later had a long career on the docks, eventually serving as a foreman at the Clure Public Marine Terminal. Truman, a combat veteran from World War I, told Colalillo at the ceremony that "I'd rather have one of these than be president."

The seven shipyards in the Twin Ports launched three and sometimes more ships a week. The second week of August 1942 was typical. On Saturday, August 8, Inland Waterways launched a submarine chaser for the U.S. Navy from its yards on Park Point. The next morning, Globe launched its first seagoing tug, the *Point Sur.* Sunday afternoon, Walter Butler Shipbuilders launched its third coastal freighter, the *William Bursley.*[628] The launchings came on the heels of four launchings the week previous, and were attended by crowds of local residents frequently accompanied by brass bands.[629]

The production of the Twin Ports yards was prodigious. Between May 1943 and August 1945, Walter Butler Shipbuilders launched sixty-six cargo ships, one every twelve-and-a-half days.[630] Zenith Dredge and Marine Iron launched thirty-eight Coast Guard cutters and buoy tenders from October 1942 to September 1944.[631] Globe Shipbuilding launched a total of twenty-seven

cargo vessels, diesel tugs, and U.S. Navy frigates, an average of one per month from the spring of 1942 to the fall of 1944.[632] The shipbuilding industry at the head of the lakes was a vital part of America's defense efforts during World War II.

Two other wartime construction projects would ultimately have more bearing on the future prosperity of the Twin Ports than the bustling shipyards of 1942–1945. Once the war began winding down in the fall of 1944 and winter of 1945, government contracts for new bottoms began to evaporate, and operations at the seven shipyards in Duluth and Superior rapidly ebbed in the summer of 1945. Fears about the vulnerability of the locks at Sault Ste. Marie were exacerbated back in October 1941, when a railroad bridge spanning the Davis and Sabin Locks collapsed. Government planners had long sought to replace the obsolete Weitzel Lock at the Soo, and in 1942, Congress appropriated $8 million to build a new lock on the site of the old.

Construction began in the fall of 1942 and the new MacArthur Lock filled with water in July 1943.[633]

A second wartime construction project stemmed from the memories of ice jams in World War I. In early 1942, the government announced that it would build the world's most modern icebreaker for the Great Lakes. Contracts were let in the summer of 1942, and the Toledo Shipbuilding Company immediately began laying the keel for the new vessel.[634] When she was commissioned as the *Mackinaw* in December 1944, the Battle of the Bulge was raging in Europe and American troops were mopping up Japanese resistance on the Island of Mindoro in the Philippines. Eyebrows were raised about the *Mackinaw*'s price tag of $10 million—$2 million more than for the construction of the MacArthur Lock—but it turned out to be one of the best investments the government ever made on the Great Lakes. The *Mackinaw* proved to be one of the most resilient vessels ever launched on the lakes, and she would spend the next six decades clearing ice for the bulk freighters of the Great Lakes fleet. In 2000, Congress agreed to spend $80 million to build a replacement for the *Mackinaw*.[635]

The Japanese surrender in September 1945 returned the Twin Ports and the Great Lakes to normalcy. Never again would maritime commerce be as critical as it was from 1942 to 1945. Duluth and Superior had demonstrated the ability to meet wartime challenges in the face of material and manpower shortages, and the head of the lakes looked forward with confidence to the conversion to a civilian economy. There was only one major worry. The millions of tons of iron ore that had gone down the lakes from the Lake Superior ranges had mining engineers and mineral economists concerned that the reserves of the vast Mesabi Range were being depleted. Industry insiders took comfort in the fact that scientists at the University of Minnesota were experimenting with a promising substitute for the rich, red ore of the Mesabi.

The Hawser Eye, *one of fifty-one CI–M–AVI coastal freighters built in the Twin Ports during WWII, is launched on June 11, 1945. The diesel-powered ships were the backbone of numerous world merchant marine fleets during the postwar era.*

THE *WOODRUSH*, THE *SUNDEW*, AND THE "180s"

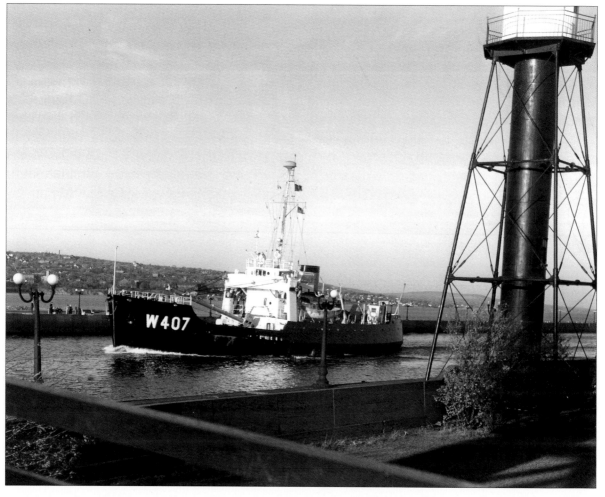

The Woodrush *inbound through the Duluth Ship Canal in 1955. Built by Zenith Dredge Company in 1944, the 180–foot buoy tender was stationed in Duluth until 1978. Her first trip to saltwater came that year when she went through the St. Lawrence River to the East Coast, where she was upgraded for an assignment to Alaska.*

PERHAPS THE MOST ADAPTABLE of all the vessels launched during World War II on the Great Lakes were the 180s. Built at the Zenith Dredge Company and Marine Iron and Shipbuilding Company shipyards in Duluth between September 1942 and September 1944, the thirty-eight multipurpose ships were named for the 180-foot-length of their hulls.

The Duluth-built 180s started life as a design blueprint for the old Lighthouse Service in 1939.[636] Originally slated to exclusively represent lighthouse tenders, the blueprints of the new ships were turned over to a group of talented designers at the Marine Iron and Shipbuilding Company in 1941. After tinkering with the blueprints in the fall of 1941, they recommended a multipurpose vessel to the U.S. Coast Guard that more than stood the test of time.

Marine Iron and Shipbuilding suggested adding search-and-rescue capabilities to the proposed vessels, as well as reshaping and strengthening their hulls for icebreaking duties. The price agreed upon for construction of the vessels was $850,000 to $950,000 each.

Marine Iron quickly determined that it would be unable to build thirty-eight of the 180s in three years' time. The shipbuilder invited its Duluth neighbor, Zenith Dredge Company, to share the contract, and the Coast Guard agreed to the decision. The original ships were of the Cactus class, which included the *Cactus* and twelve identical vessels, all launched between September 1942 and July 1943. Zenith Dredge built seven of the 180s, and Marine Iron launched six. The next group, launched in 1943 between August and November, were in the Mesquite class. The *Mesquite* and four other 180s all were built at Marine Iron.[637]

The final group of 180 vessels built in Duluth were of the Iris class, the largest class built in the Twin Ports. All were launched in 1944, between January and September. The namesake *Iris* and nineteen of her sisters were evenly divided between Zenith Dredge and Marine Iron.

Since World War II, two of the 180s have become synonymous with the head of the lakes. From 1944 to 1978, the *Woodrush*

called Duluth-Superior home. Usually known as "*Woody*" to her crew, the *Woodrush* and the allure of big water enticed several generations of Twin Ports youths into joining the Coast Guard.[638] From 1980 to 2000, the *Woodrush* claimed Sitka, Alaska, as her home port and she was finally decommissioned in 2000.

Retired Coast Guard commander Gil Porter, a longtime Duluth pilot, remembered fondly the time he spent in Duluth between 1959 and 1963 as captain of the *Woodrush*. "Lake Superior is just 340 or so miles long, and I had been many times out in the Pacific, sailing over 2,000 miles, to set my first buoy," Porter said. "So this was just great, and then to be iced in a couple of months during the winter—probably as enjoyable as any job I ever had, actually."[639]

Another of the ships of the Iris class was long near and dear to the hearts of Twin Ports residents: the *Sundew,* launched at Marine Iron and Shipbuilding in August 1944.[640] For nearly a quarter-century, the *Sundew* has broken ice for marine commerce at the west end of the lake, put buoys out in the spring and retrieved them in the fall, and lent a helping hand on innumerable search-and-rescue missions. Scheduled to be decommissioned in 2004, the *Sundew* is expected to become a permanent display in the Duluth harbor.[641]

The *Sundew*'s decommissioning marks the twilight of the useful life of the 180s. In the six decades since the end of World War II, the versatile vessels have seen service on each of the world's five oceans. In 1985, forty years after the last Iris class vessel steamed out of the head of the lakes for the Soo Locks, thirty of the original thirty-eight 180s were still in service with the U.S. Coast Guard. But by 2001, only a dozen of the 180s were still in service—and all are slated to be retired by 2004.

Natural ore flows into the hold of a Great Lakes bulk freighter that was likely more than a half-century old when this photo was taken in 1960. Before the 1960s ended, most of the early twentieth-century fleet of 500-footers would be retired.

CHAPTER FOURTEEN

The Range Resurgent

IN THE FIVE YEARS BETWEEN the end of World War II and the outbreak of the Korean War, it was becoming obvious to the Upper Great Lakes maritime industry that major changes were in store for the bulk cargo trade.

The demand for iron ore during WWII had accelerated the depletion of natural ore resources of Lake Superior's iron ranges. More than 475 million tons of iron ore had gone down the Great Lakes between 1940 and 1945 to feed the insatiable demands of America's armed might—what newspaper columnists called the Arsenal of Democracy.[642] By the end of the war, total reserves in Minnesota and Michigan were estimated at 1.2 billion tons.[643] A whopping two-thirds of the iron ore used in the blast furnaces of the domestic steel industry during WWII had come from the Mesabi Range.[644] Experts warned that another war like the last one would leave no more iron ore on the Lake Superior ranges.

Despite the experts' reservations, the flow of iron ore continued unabated through the Twin Ports of Duluth and Superior during the postwar years. An average of 50 million tons of iron ore per season went downbound on the Great Lakes from the Lake Superior ranges between 1945 and 1950, mostly to fuel the surging demand for consumer durables such as automobiles, refrigerators, and stoves. In August 1950, Inland Steel Mining Company's *Wilfred Sykes* handled the largest cargo of iron ore in the history of the Twin Ports when it loaded just over 19,000 long tons at the Great Northern Dock No. 1 at Allouez Bay on August 9.[645]

Another war came in the first week of summer 1950. The Inmun Gun, or North Korean People's

Army, streamed across Korea's 38th Parallel and routed Republic of Korea and U.S. forces. The Korean War would put the nation back in a wartime posture and increase the already high demand for the rich, red hematite ores of the Mesabi, Vermilion, and Cuyuna Iron Ranges. Wartime demand again shifted the iron ore industry at the head of the lakes into high gear. On September 12, 1950, the Great Northern Railway ore docks at Allouez Bay loaded a record twenty-four boats in twenty-four hours.[646] In 1953, an all-time record of almost 65 million tons of iron ore departed the Twin Ports for the ravenous blast furnaces of the Lower Great Lakes.[647]

The high levels of ore shipments would continue through the remainder of the 1950s, but it was clear to observers of the ferrous mining industry that the natural ores of northern Minnesota were increasingly close to being depleted. "Although the next four years would continue this high level of prosperity," one observer wrote of the record shipments in 1953, "it was the Indian Summer for the transshipment of the old high-grade hematite ore out of the harbor."[648]

Aside from concerns about iron ore supplies, a second troubling development threatened to disrupt the Twin Ports' coal trade from the mines in Ohio and West Virginia through Lake Erie ports to docks at the head of the lakes. A national energy shift from coal to Middle Eastern oil began in the immediate post–WWII years, generating fears of a profoundly negative effect on upbound coal movements through Duluth-Superior. Postwar coal receipts peaked at just over 10 million short tons in 1946 and

One of six big Mallet-type locomotives acts as a temporary steam-generating facility at Great Northern's Allouez ore docks in November 1955, the coldest and snowiest November on the Great Lakes since 1919. In that month, Great Northern steamed nearly 32,000 carloads of iron ore.

began a decades-long decline that would see the trade all but disappear by the 1970s. In 1958, upbound coal movement was only one-third of what it had been twelve years earlier.[649]

Ken Fossum returned to Superior from combat in Europe in 1945 to head the Berwind-White Coal Mining Company's Wisconsin briquetting plant. Berwind and several other coal firms received West Virginia coal at docks in Duluth-Superior and briquetted it into fuel for home-heating customers as far west as the Montana border. Fossum recalled that the high-water mark for the Twin Ports' briquetting industry was the 1947–1948 season. "Then we started to gradually go downhill," he said. "As soon as diesel fuel got in there . . . well, it gradually went down."[650]

The decline in coal receipts accelerated in the mid-1950s when natural gas became widely available to Duluth-Superior and communities in northern Minnesota and the Dakotas, the primary markets for the Twin Ports' coal home-heating business.[651] In November 1951, *Skillings*

Mining Review lamented the end of an era when workers began removing the last of the "wig-wam" coal storage buildings on the Lehigh Valley Coal Sales Company's Tower Bay slip in Superior.[652]

Concerns during the 1950s that the ports' bedrock shipments of natural ore and coal could diminish were offset somewhat by events occurring some distance from Lake Superior. In Minneapolis, Professor E. W. Davis and a team of metallurgists at the University of Minnesota were perfecting a method of beneficiating taconite, a low-grade iron ore that existed in immense quantities in northeastern Minnesota. The existence of taconite had been known since the earliest days of mining on the Minnesota ranges, but the ore was so hard and the iron content so low that the mining companies, with few exceptions, ignored it.

Davis, a Purdue University graduate, had joined the staff of the University of Minnesota School of Mines in 1912 and had made the exploitation of taconite in northeastern Minnesota his life's work. For forty-three years, Davis conducted research on ways to treat the flint-hard iron formation of the Mesabi Range and create a technology that could replace natural ore as the primary feed for America's blast furnaces.[653] What Davis and his staff devised was a method of crushing taconite into the consistency of talcum powder, binding it with special clays, rolling it into marble-sized pellets and heating it at approximately 3,000 degrees Fahrenheit to give the final product the strength to withstand shipping and handling.

Through his dogged persistence, E. W. Davis would inject new life into Minnesota's Mesabi Range. The creation of a year-round taconite industry on the range would transform the domestic bulk carrier fleet on the Great Lakes

between 1955 and 1970. About the same time, in Washington, D.C., and Ottawa, Ontario, momentum was building for the completion of a deep-draft waterway that would connect the Great Lakes and the Atlantic Ocean via the St. Lawrence River. The opening of the St. Lawrence Seaway in 1959 would rejuvenate the port industry in Duluth-Superior for decades to come.

THE EMERGENCE OF TACONITE

A 1945 article in *Fortune* magazine outlined a bleak future for the Lake Superior iron ore industry. Natural ore, the backbone of Great Lakes bulk commerce since 1892, would last no longer than another ten to fifteen years, the authors of the article asserted. Reserves had been depleted by the voracious demand of the Allied defense effort during World War II. The iron and steel industry had begun an accelerated exploration

Great Lakes bulk freighters take on ore at Great Northern's Allouez docks in November 1955. With ice rapidly building up in the bay and slips, vessels were backed up because of subzero weather and the necessity to steam–thaw ore cars.

program late in the war to identify new foreign sources of iron ore.[654]

Vast new deposits of natural ore discovered in Labrador at the end of the war provided the Canadian government with a strong incentive to develop the St. Lawrence Seaway.

Available evidence seemed to corroborate the suspicion that the domestic steel industry was prepared to write off its investments in the Lake Superior iron ore ranges. The postwar discovery of rich iron ore deposits in Brazil and Africa precipitated a diversification of steelmaking to the East Coast. By 1950, Bethlehem Steel Corporation had an exploration and development program in place to exploit newly discovered manganese ore deposits in Brazil near the mouth of the Amazon River—a deposit that could supplant the manganese ore supply from Minnesota's Cuyuna Range.[655]

In the early 1950s, U.S. Steel Corporation built a new blast furnace at its integrated steelmaking complex at Fairless Hills, Pennsylvania, near Philadelphia. Bethlehem Steel erected new blast furnaces at its Sparrows Point, Maryland, mill near Baltimore.[656]

Even while steel industry geologists were traversing the globe looking for new sources of iron ore, the steel companies were quietly ramping up to exploit Davis's taconite-processing discoveries in Minnesota. As early as 1939, Reserve Mining Company was formed by Crispin Oglebay, president and chief executive officer of Oglebay Norton Company, and Charles R. Hook, chair of the board of Armco Steel Corporation. Oglebay and Hook named their taconite partnership "Reserve" to signify, as Davis later wrote, that "they thought of taconite as a long-time future resource that might not be needed for twenty years, but would be there waiting when the

The bumboat Kaner Brothers *docks alongside the* Mariposa *at the Great Northern elevator in Superior in the 1950s. For fifty years Archer–Daniels–Midland operated the elevator, which is now run by General Mills as its Superior annex.*

A fireman stokes the fire box under the boiler of a steam–powered ship in 1949. Most "hand–fired" steamers began to disappear in the 1960s with the advent of diesel propulsion.

right time came."[657] Similarly, the Cleveland-based Pickands-Mather Company had begun buying up leases on state taconite lands on the eastern end of the Mesabi Range in 1941 on behalf of Erie Mining Company, a partnership between Pickands-Mather and four Cleveland steel companies. Erie Mining, which was incorporated in 1940, set up a laboratory at Hibbing two years later to conduct large-scale taconite beneficiation experiments.[658]

World War II had prevented the iron and steel companies from making major taconite investments in Minnesota, but postwar fears about the depletion of natural ore on the Mesabi Range spurred both the Reserve and Erie companies to press forward with plans for commercial development of taconite. Reserve Mining Company won the race to build and operate the first commercial taconite processing plant on the Mesabi. Reserve in 1951 began construction work on a taconite mine at Babbitt near Birch Lake on the far eastern end of the Mesabi Range. The previous year, Oglebay Norton had

sold its interest in Reserve to Cleveland-based Republic Steel, which became a 50 percent joint venture partner with Armco Steel.[659]

Because of the intensive processing nature of taconite concentration, the Reserve partners elected to build a massive taconite mill. Rather than tie into the existing rail network and ship unprocessed ore to a mill near Duluth, the partners elected to build a greenfield mill at a site near Beaver Bay, about sixty miles north and east of Duluth on the north shore of Lake Superior. Reserve also built a fifteen-hundred-home community for the workers who would staff the Davis Works and named the new town Silver Bay.[660]

The Davis Works had an initial production capacity of 3.75 million tons of taconite pellets annually, and it was designed for a maximum capacity of 10 million tons. Construction of Reserve's mine, mill, town site, and harbor was essentially complete at the end of 1955. On a windy April day in 1956, the steamer *C. L. Austin* sidled up to the piers at Silver Bay and loaded 10,800 tons of taconite pellets for the Republic Steel plant in Cleveland.[661]

Erie Mining Company wasn't far behind Reserve. Like Reserve, Erie spent the early years of the 1950s building the expensive infrastructure required to successfully mine and mill taconite. Also like Reserve, Erie elected to mine its ore from a deposit on the eastern end of the Mesabi Range, but Erie chose to build its taconite processing mill in close proximity to the mine. It hacked an entirely new community out of the wilderness northeast of Aurora and named the town Hoyt Lakes in honor of Elton Hoyt II, the president of Pickands-Mather. Erie also built a port from scratch near the tiny North Shore town of Schroeder. The new port, named Taconite Harbor, was connected to the Hoyt Lakes mine and mill by a seventy-three-mile railroad.[662] Erie shipped its first pellets down the Great Lakes from Taconite Harbor in the spring of 1957.

Reserve and Erie planned to provide as much as 20 million tons of taconite pellets for the domestic steel industry by 1960. Blast furnaces were designed specifically to reduce pellets rather than natural ore, and in the process they attained significantly improved productivity; the long, predicted demise of the natural ore industry was finally at hand. And Erie and Reserve were only the outriders of a taconite transformation on the Mesabi Range. By 1954, the Oliver Iron Mining Division of the U.S. Steel Corporation was well along in its experiments with taconite commercialization at pilot plants near Mountain Iron and Virginia, Minnesota.[663]

The resurgence of the Mesabi Range brought about by commercial production of taconite was a mixed blessing for Duluth-Superior. The Twin Ports would retain their preeminent administrative position in the nation's iron ore industry, but the much anticipated 20 million tons of taconite pellets would not initially flow across the ore docks of Duluth-Superior.[664]

During WWII, the Hull–Rust–Mahoning open pit iron mine at Hibbing on the Mesabi Range had shipped as much as 27 million tons of iron ore down the lakes in a single season. Still the largest of the natural ore mines in Minnesota in 1957, the pit would be eclipsed within a decade as taconite came on the market.

The Reiss Steamship Company's Superior *unloads 6,700 tons of coal at the Reiss coal dock on St. Louis Bay in Superior in June 1959. As Upper Midwest homes and businesses converted to oil heat in the 1960s, coal receipts in the Twin Ports plunged. Ironically, the Reiss coal dock became the site of the Superior Midwest Energy Terminal fifteen years later when coal began to move outbound.*

ORIGINS OF THE DULUTH SEAWAY PORT AUTHORITY

For the Twin Ports of Duluth and Superior, the 1950s were a time of construction and new beginnings, but the impetus for new building at the head of the lakes had less to do with the renaissance of the Mesabi Range than with the communities' hopes for a global future. Those hopes literally stretched back decades.

For the Duluth-Superior maritime community, 1954 was the red-letter year that would set the ports' future course. In May of that year, Congress passed the Wiley-Dondero Act, committing the United States to join Canada in dredging and blasting what would become known as the St. Lawrence Seaway from the rapids below Montreal to the upper reaches of the St. Lawrence River.[665] President Dwight D. Eisenhower's signature on the legislation a week after congressional passage set in motion a chain of events that would transform the Duluth harbor during the latter half of the 1950s.

The concept of an independent port authority able to spearhead port development went back

to the 1920s. Bartholomew and Associates, a St. Louis, Missouri, engineering firm, completed a harbor study for the Duluth City Planning Commission in 1927. The study recommended that the U.S. Army Corps of Engineers cut a new, wider entry to the inner harbor through Park Point, about 2.4 miles east of the present Duluth entry. Vehicular and rail traffic down the point would have been expedited by two tunnels bored underneath the proposed new entry.[666]

In the 1920s, the Minnesota and Wisconsin legislatures attempted to come to an agreement on the appointment of a joint harbor commission for Duluth and Superior. The idea of a joint commission would continue to arise over the years, but in 1929 the Minnesota legislature passed a bill creating a port authority in Duluth.[667]

The city of Duluth appointed a three-member commission to oversee the affairs of the harbor. Charter members were J. W. Lyder, Donald S. Holmes, and Leroy M. Pharis.[668]

But during the Great Depression, the Duluth Port Authority went through a period of dormancy until the summer of 1937. At an organizational meeting in his office on August 5, 1937, Mayor C. Rudolph Berghult proposed an ambitious seven-part program for development of the port and its facilities. Heading the mayor's list was construction of a high bridge across St. Louis Bay to neighboring Superior.

The proposed high bridge embroiled the port commissioners in both local and national controversy, principally between Berghult and then 8th District Representative John T. Bernard, who wanted to build a publicly funded toll bridge. There was also fighting over the proposed bridge at home, involving Berghult and Duluth Port Authority president Thomas H. Trelford. In late 1938, the feud culminated with a spate of resignations from the port authority, including that of Trelford.[669]

Pressure for completion of the bridge project still existed sixteen years later when the Duluth Port Authority was once again reorganized. But this time, the spur for city action on harbor development was President Eisenhower's 1954 signing of the Wiley-Dondero Act, creating the St. Lawrence Seaway.

EMERGENCE OF THE MODERN PORT AUTHORITY

The projected opening of the St. Lawrence Seaway in 1959 caused a flurry of development activity on the Great Lakes.[670]

In Duluth, the old port authority was reorganized in November 1954 with the city's appointment of three members: Arthur M. Clure, Samuel Atkins, and Charles S. Hagan. Clure was a natural choice to serve as president of the reorganized board. A native of a small North Dakota farming community, Clure had graduated from the University of Minnesota Law School in 1924 and set up practice in Duluth. During his thirty years in the Twin Ports legal community, Clure had established a reputation as a first-class admiralty attorney and expert on St. Louis County real estate titles. Over the years, he had been active in the U.S. Naval Reserve, and many people credited him with leading the fight to transform the Duluth State Teachers College into the Duluth

campus of the University of Minnesota in the years immediately following World War II.[671]

The task of the reorganized port authority was clear. Clure and his colleagues were responsible for hiring a staff and developing a public marine terminal in advance of the completion of the seaway. That they were more successful in their task than the ill-fated port authority of the 1930s was perhaps due more to the nonpartisan makeup of the group than to any issues involved. The three city members were joined by four more members, two appointed by the St. Louis County board of commissioners and two appointed by Minnesota governor Orville Freeman, later to carry the Democratic Farmer Labor Party banner in Washington as President John F. Kennedy's secretary of agriculture.[672]

The system of port authority representation from city, county, and state has continued into the twenty-first century, its durability the result of the wide range of interests represented and its inherent structure of checks and balances. The four commissioners added to the authority in 1956 reflected this diversity: Seafarers' International Union representative Matt Antilla, St. Louis County commissioners Leonard Theobald and Ernest Luoma, and Minneapolis grain exporter Burton Joseph.

In February 1956, the Duluth Port Authority hired Robert T. Smith, its first executive director. A dapper veteran of the Cunard transoceanic lines and president of a New Orleans stevedoring firm, Smith had the double challenge of assembling a staff and acquainting the maritime community and the public with the organization's mission. From port authority offices on the ninth floor of the Alworth Building in downtown Duluth, Smith began to assemble a staff, including Telford Young, a former Duluthian working in New Orleans who was named assistant port director, and Richard Sielaff, a local educator who was appointed director of research and development.[673]

On April 3, 1956, the Seaway Port Authority of Duluth was rocked when Clure, its activist president, collapsed and died in his Duluth law offices. Clure's death came two days before the opening of another chapter in the history of the Great Lakes–Seaway shipping industry. That first week of April 1956, the *C. L. Austin* left her winter berth at the Knudsen Brothers Shipyard in Superior and steamed up the north shore to the new harbor of Silver Bay to take on the first cargo of taconite pellets shipped by Reserve Mining Company.[674]

Clure's successor was Kenneth Duncan, a 1956 Duluth City Council appointee to the port authority. Duncan, the recently retired manager of Lake Superior ore mines for the Pickands-Mather Company, came to the port authority presidency with nearly fifty years of experience in Minnesota's mining industry. A 1910 graduate of the University of Minnesota School of Mines, Duncan had worked on the Vermilion, Gogebic, and Mesabi Iron Ranges for nearly forty years before moving to Duluth in 1948. Still ahead for Duncan and Executive Director Smith, both relative newcomers to Duluth, were the delicate negotiations leading to the land acquisition, financing, and construction of the Arthur M. Clure Public Marine Terminal.

Time was short. At the end of the 1956 navigation season, the *Duluth News-Tribune* editorialized that "we have then, in all likelihood, only two more navigation seasons coming before the Seaway itself will be in full operation. That thought ought to stimulate quite a little thinking in the next 30 months or so."[675]

BUILDING A PUBLIC MARINE TERMINAL

Legislative approval for funding the Seaway Port Authority of Duluth's ambitious port terminal project in 1957 was only one of a series of steps necessary for the Twin Ports to become an international seaport. With the completion of the St. Lawrence Seaway expected in the spring of 1959, Duluth port commissioners had to work fast to line up funding, acquire land, and build terminal facilities on the Duluth harbor. It was a two-and-a-half year project that consumed $10 million. But the construction of the Arthur M. Clure Public Marine Terminal was completed on time and under budget.

As the first executive director of the Seaway Port Authority of Duluth, Robert T. Smith laid the groundwork for building the Clure Public Marine Terminal and for preparing the Twin Ports to take advantage of the 1959 opening of the St. Lawrence Seaway.

The first task facing the port authority commissioners involved financing the proposed public marine terminal. They had received a commitment of support for the project from Orville Freeman, Minnesota's popular DFL governor. During Christmas week of 1956, Freeman visited Duluth and pledged his full support for development of harbor facilities in the Twin Ports. At the same time, Minnesota's 8th District DFL adopted a resolution calling upon the legislature to support state and county appropriations for the Duluth port.

Robert T. Smith went on a public relations offensive to convince Minnesotans of the necessity of supporting the proposed public terminal. "Basically, the terminal is aimed at recapturing the once lucrative package freight trade," he told the *Duluth News-Tribune* in January 1957.[676]

By March 1957, port authority commissioners had formalized a request for funding. President Duncan called on Governor Freeman in St. Paul and asked for a $5 million appropriation from

the state. "This financing will require appropriations from the city of Duluth, St. Louis County,
and the state of Minnesota," Duncan told
Freeman. "Development of Duluth's port is not a
tax burden on the people of Minnesota."[677]

Not everyone in Minnesota was convinced of
the need for public support of the port terminal. Everett L. Joppa, president of the Lake
Superior Industrial Bureau, the Duluth-based
public relations arm of the iron mining industry, was afraid that the state and county appropriations would come from taxes on Mesabi
Range iron producers. Joppa claimed that the
people of the Iron Range would derive no benefit from the port, and he noted that "iron
mining is not an industry that stands to benefit
from port development."[678]

In St. Paul, the legislators were in basic agreement on the funding package: $5 million from
the state, $4 million from the county, and $1
million from Duluth, but there was squabbling
about who would actually introduce the legislation. Once the initial jockeying for credit was
complete, the bill had surprisingly little opposition in the lower House. "A threatened fight on
the St. Louis County and state fund raising
measures (for the port) failed to materialize," the
News-Tribune editorialized on April 6.[679] Two
weeks later, the $10 million package sailed
through the state Senate. Freeman signed the
appropriations into law on April 29, 1957.[680]

In May, the Duluth City Council agreed to issue
$1 million in bonds to support the port project.
The St. Louis County board of commissioners
turned over eighty acres of tax-forfeited land on
Rice's Point to the port authority. Smith and the
staff had already targeted the Rice's Point area as
the site for the public marine terminal complex.
There were negotiations to undertake with the
property owners on the undeveloped spit of
land; the only activity on the property was a
firing range for a local road and gun club. The
Soo Line Railroad was contacted about selling
twenty-two acres of mostly submerged land, and
Pure Oil Company owned about forty lots in
the area that the port authority was interested
in purchasing.[681]

In July 1957, port authority commissioners
hired the Minneapolis firm of Pfeifer and
Shultz as consulting engineers for the terminal
project. The consulting company was one of
twenty-three firms that submitted bids on the
project; the price agreed upon was $230,000.[682]
The port authority quickly moved on land
acquisition and construction. The Seaway Port
Authority of Duluth, which became known to
several generations of Duluthians as SPAD,
bought twenty-one acres from the Soo Line
Railroad for just over $1,000 an acre. Zenith
Dredge Company was hired for $2.7 million as
low bidder on the land development contract.
The project involved driving 6,000 feet of
steel piles and pumping one million cubic
yards of sand behind bulkheads that would
separate the water of the harbor from the
reclaimed land.

By June 16, the final load of steel piling had left
Pittsburgh bound for the Twin Ports, and the
tug Essayons was somewhere out on the Lower
Great Lakes shepherding the dredge Frank M.
Rogall to Duluth for port terminal construction
work. General contracting work for the warehouse and terminal sheds was awarded to Drake
and Piper of Minneapolis for $1.5 million.
Duluth's own Clyde Iron Works was low bidder
on two gantry cranes at $440,000. McLean-
Astleford Company of Superior was selected
to blacktop two miles of access roads, build a
2,200-foot-long concrete ship apron, and install
9,000 feet of railroad tracks. As the summer of
1958 waned, the Duluth Port Terminal complex
sprang forth from what had been marginal
swampland the year before.[683]

The last winter before the opening of the seaway was a time for introspection and grandiose
plans. Ironically, while the federal government
and the Canadians were spending hundreds of
millions of dollars excavating the St. Lawrence
Seaway, shipping on the Great Lakes was being
hit hard by recession midway through President
Eisenhower's second term. Iron ore tonnage was
down by nearly half from 1957 levels. Only
2,558 ships were loaded and unloaded in the
Twin Ports during the 1958 season, compared
with 2,945 during the 1957 season and 4,281

ships in 1956.[684] Compounding the recessionary woes was the increased tonnage of ore moving in the form of taconite from Lake Superior's north shore ports.

The Northern Pacific Railway was optimistic enough about the future to build eight hundred new boxcars in anticipation of the St. Lawrence Seaway opening. Prominent Duluth banker Willis Wyard was probably most accurate in his predictions when he ventured the opinion in January 1959 that "the Seaway will bring growth, a gradual healthy growth, but nothing as spectacular as an oil boom."[685] A less accurate prognosticator of the seaway's impact upon the Lake Superior region was Alexander E. Freeman. The Winnipeg industrialist put together a consortium of Canadian and American businessmen in the winter of 1959 and announced plans for the International Duluth Seaport Corporation. The company grabbed front-page headlines in Duluth, Minneapolis, and

Winnipeg with its plans to lease 135 acres on the west side of Rice's Point between Twenty-first and Twenty-ninth Avenues West. The $100 million project envisioned the construction of bonded warehouses, grain elevators, a three-deck parking garage, bulk liquid storage facilities, office buildings, and a world trade center with a hundred international tenants.[686]

Freeman's ambitious plans never materialized, and Duluthians were left with the reality of the more modest undertaking accomplished by the Seaway Port Authority of Duluth. The Clure Public Marine Terminal was built without significant cost overruns, and the facility was in operation by the spring of 1959, the target date for the opening of the St. Lawrence Seaway. More important, it gave the port community at the head of the lakes a shot of confidence in its ability to compete in the rapidly changing world of maritime commerce in the postwar era.

American Bureau of Shipping surveyors Don Johnson (left) and Harry Taylor provided classification oversight services during vessel lengthening and renovation projects at Fraser Shipyards in March 1974.

VESSEL REPAIR AND
FRASER SHIPYARDS

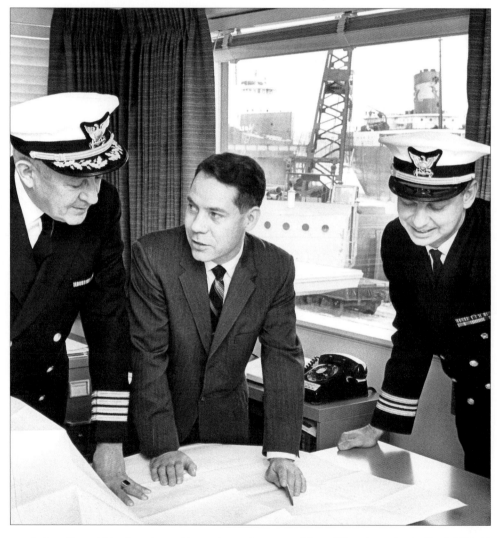

Engineer Trevor White, later vice president and general manager of Fraser Shipyards, confers in March 1965 with the U.S. Coast Guard's Captain Mark Hocking (left) and Lieutenant Commander Edward J. Giesler.

FOR MORE THAN A CENTURY, Superior's Connors Point has been the site of shipbuilding and repair activities. In the early 1890s, the compact piece of waterfront land saw the launching of Alexander McDougall's whalebacks, and subsequent generations built cargo ships in Howard's Pocket during two world wars.

With the end of World War II, contracts to build cargo ships for the U.S. Maritime Commission and fighting ships for the U.S. Navy and Coast Guard disappeared. Most of the seven shipyards that had employed as many as 15,000 Twin Ports residents during the war converted to other uses. Only the American Ship Building Company at Howard's Pocket remained in business, mostly because the company's dry docks lent themselves to ship repair activities for the Great Lakes fleet. In 1946, Knudsen Brothers, a Superior construction firm, purchased the Howard's Pocket site from American Shipbuilding.[687]

Overseeing the yards for Knudsen Brothers was a thirty-year-old superintendent who had already spent half his life in the shipbuilding business. Robert M. Fraser was a Duluthian who, while a student at Denfeld High School, had started working at Marine Iron and Shipbuilding's Duluth yards in 1932. When war broke out, Fraser was named hull superintendent at Globe Shipbuilding Company's Superior yards. From 1942 to 1944, he oversaw the construction of more than thirty merchant marine vessels for Globe.[688]

Fraser spent nearly a decade with Knudsen Brothers, and when the family decided to get out of the business in 1955, Fraser and Byron Nelson purchased the Superior shipyard. The Fraser-Nelson Shipbuilding and Dry Dock Company established itself as the most modern shipyard on Lake Superior. Fraser and Nelson were among the first to see that the Great Lakes fleet would make use of larger, more automated vessels, and in 1961, the company enlarged its dry dock facilities to handle not only the largest vessels then sailing the lakes but the next generation of bulk freighters.[689] Three years later, in 1964, Nelson retired and the business became Fraser Shipyards.[690]

Robert Fraser built Fraser Shipyards into the most modern ship repair facility on Lake Superior. By the time he retired from active management of the company, the firm he headed was known far and wide for its ability to convert straight-deck bulk freighters to self-unloaders, as well as its activities in converting coal-burning vessels to the new diesel-electric propulsion systems.[691]

Fraser sold his shipyards in 1977 to Reuben Johnson and Sons, a construction company based in Superior. Troy Johnson, president of the firm, named Phillip Milroy president and chief executive officer of the shipyard. Milroy, a Superior native, had worked previously as a partner in the public accounting firm of Broeker Hendrickson and Company.[692] Milroy immediately had to weather a strike by Local 117 of the Boilermakers and Iron Shipbuilders Union, but by the fall of 1978, Fraser was reclaiming its place as one of the premier shipyards on the Great Lakes. In the summer of 1979, Fraser secured its first major conversion project when it lengthened the Ford Fleet's *William Clay Ford*.[693] In 1981, Fraser got one of its biggest jobs ever when it won the bid to convert the USS Great Lakes Fleet's *Philip R. Clarke, Arthur M. Anderson,* and *Cason J. Calloway* to self-unloaders.[694] The $30 million job was completed on time and within budget.

With the sale to Reuben Johnson and Sons, Robert Fraser, who had died in 1986, had left his namesake shipyard in good hands. Irish-born Trevor White has served as vice president and general manager since 1990, and for 115 seasons now, a shipyard has been located in the Howard's Pocket area of Superior Bay. "When the present management purchased the shipyard, the name on the door remained the same—Fraser Shipyards, Inc.—because the name stood for quality and tradition," noted Fraser historian Patrick Lapinski in 2003. "As the new century progresses, the small shipyard at Superior continues to do big things for the community and the Great Lakes maritime industry."[695]

On the morning of May 3, 1959, crowds along the north pier of the Duluth Ship Canal salute the arrival of the merchant vessel Ramon de Larrinaga, *the first upbound ship to traverse the newly opened St. Lawrence Seaway. The ship loaded grain at the Peavey and Cargill elevators before departing for Montreal and a voyage across the North Atlantic.*

CHAPTER FIFTEEN

From Tidewater to Bluewater

WHEN THE BRITISH-REGISTERED *Ramon de Larrinaga* passed beneath the Duluth Aerial Lift Bridge on the rainy Sunday afternoon of May 3, 1959, it began a new era for the the head of the lakes. "Twin Ports Linked to Atlantic Ocean," headlines blared the next morning in the *Duluth News-Tribune*. "The 10,000-ton *DeLarrinaga* ploughed into the harbor at 1:15 p.m. to become the first overseas ship to come here via the St. Lawrence Seaway."[696] A crowd of 3,500 people waved and cheered on the north pier of the Duluth Ship Canal as the *de Larrinaga* entered the harbor. Five minutes later, they cheered again as the Liberian-registered *Herald* followed the *de Larrinaga* through the canal. Inside the harbor, members of the Duluth Fire Department saluted the vessel with their fire hoses.[697]

The *de Larrinaga* cautiously made her way to the F. H. Peavey Terminal Elevator through the squalls and scraped the dock as she pulled in. "It was chaos," said Jerry Grandmaison of the S. A. McLennan Agency, which handled the ship's local business. "People were all over the dock and later all over the ship. But the *de Larrinaga* master, Captain Joseph Meade, couldn't have been more gracious."[698]

Meade accepted the keys to the city from Mayor E. Clifford Mork and a plaque from Duluth port director Robert T. Smith. Meade told the dignitaries that the vessel had departed its home port of Liverpool in mid-April and had left Montreal for the head of the lakes the week before. "I didn't know the names of the Great Lakes until a few days ago," he joked.[699]

"NEW GRAIN ROUTE TO THE WORLD"
By the time the Twin Ports officially celebrated the opening of the St. Lawrence Seaway during the second week of July, more than seventy foreign vessels had called upon the two ports at the head of the lakes. Most came into the system light and loaded at the Duluth and Superior elevators with grain for ports in northern Europe.

Port officials were jubilant about the opportunities for shipping the grain of the Upper Midwest to the world. There was a feeling that the seaway would pave the streets of the Twin Ports with gold. But port officials warned that "all these assets of Duluth—the geographical location, modern port equipment and excellent harbor conditions—are enough to make one of the finest seaports in the world. But they cannot assure success. The flow of commerce demands a vital trade area."[700]

That vital trade area—one million square miles containing fifteen million people in ten states—was the richest breadbasket in the world. And because grain was expected to be the cargo most likely to flow overseas from the Twin Ports, Duluth and Superior attracted a host of new grain brokerage and grain stevedoring firms. Since the 1930s, one of the most prominent vessel agents in the Twin Ports was Alastair Guthrie, Inc. Alastair Guthrie, a debonair Scotsman, handled much of the independent grain business at the head of the lakes and was longtime friends with Henry Steinbrenner, the Cleveland shipowner whose Kinsman Line carried a million tons of grain or so each year to Buffalo.[701] In the late 1930s, Guthrie was also an agent for the Hutchinson Fleet, the Buckeye Steamship Company, Columbia Transportation, Cleveland-Cliffs, Inland Steel, Ford, and Canada's Scott Misener Fleet.[702]

When the St. Lawrence Seaway opened, Duluth's Alastair Guthrie was poised to become one of the Twin Ports' most active vessel agents. Guthrie, who had been servicing U.S. grain fleets since the 1920s, had grain contacts around the world.

Alastair Guthrie maintained offices at 600 Board of Trade Building in Duluth, just down the hall from Cargill and one floor below the Peavey offices. When the seaway opened in 1959, Guthrie already had some twenty years' experience in the arcane world of grain exporting. Germaine Guthrie, his widow, recalled in a 2000 interview that her husband began working closely with grain exporters in the late 1930s and early 1940s.[703]

Three other vessel agents with expertise in serving U.S. and Canadian lakers were also adjusting to the seaway trade. Stuart A. McLennan had just hung out his own shingle as the S. A. McLennan Agency after many years with Gordon Noyes, who would soon close his own agency and retire. Jerry Hubbard managed the Duluth office of the Boland and Cornelius Company, a Buffalo-based shipowner. By June, Theodore W. Svensson, primarily a customs broker for nearly a decade, and Robert J. Baker, local office manager for the Occident Terminal Division of the F. H. Peavey Company, established the Svensson and Baker Agency.

Other agents surfaced by the early 1960s, including Captain Ralph Henderson, a tall, articulate Scotsman who in 1959 arrived as master of a British ship, the *LaHacienda*, returned several years later to represent Louis Dreyfus Corporation, and then became president of Lake Superior Shipping Company; George Janos, who left his position with the New York–based Admanthos Shipping Corporation to join local businessman Jack Remington in creating the Duluth-Superior Shipping Agency; and George Head, a transplanted Canadian who ran Sealanes International and represented Federal Commerce and Navigation Company of Montreal.

Since the prewar years, the only grain stevedoring contractor in the Twin Ports had been Duluth-Superior Grain Trimmers, headed in the late 1950s by James C. Sauter, the third generation of the Superior family to run the business.[704] Within short order, Sauter faced a host of competitors. American Grain Trimmers was the first of eight grain stevedoring firms that would locate in the Twin Ports in the late 1950s and early 1960s. An affiliate of Montreal-based Wolfe Stevedoring, American Grain opened offices in Duluth in 1959. Other firms that opened offices soon after American Grain were Rogers Terminal and Shipping Corporation, Cullen Stevedoring, Empire Stevedoring, J. F. McNamara Corporation, Atlantic and Gulf Stevedoring, and Ceres, Inc. Nearly all were managed by ex-oceangoing masters, lured to the head of the lakes by the potential of a brand new grain export market.[705]

Numerous other waterfront businesses were also springing up, especially in specialized services such as pilotage, where a half-dozen former lakes captains and mates established the Duluth-Superior Pilots Association, and the provisioning of goods and supplies. By the end of 1959, several grocery store interests, restaurant owners, and other entrepreneurs began competing with longtime ship chandlers Allouez Marine Supply and Thorp Marine Supplies. The most aggressive of the new chandlers was Norman Camenker, whose family-owned Duluth's Tip Top Market and his Duluth-Superior Ship Chandlery would ultimately monopolize the ocean ship trade for about thirty years before being acquired by Allouez Marine Supply.[706]

The grain export market would certainly develop in the years ahead, and Duluth-Superior would become a true world port. Few people had any idea in that summer of 1959 that the creation of the longest bi-national waterway in the world had been nearly three-quarters of a century in the making.

A PATH TO THE SEA

Like any major engineering achievement, the St. Lawrence Seaway was a combination of political, social, technological, and economic factors that was decades in the planning and execution. As far back as 1892, when Mesabi Range iron ore was just beginning to flow across the docks at Duluth, Congressman John Lind sponsored a resolution on Capitol Hill calling for a joint U.S-Canadian study of the concept to build an

international waterway to connect the Great Lakes with the Atlantic Ocean. Two years later, in 1894, Canadian grain interests established the Deep Waterways Association to promote an all-Canadian route to saltwater.[707] President Grover Cleveland and Prime Minister Mackenzie Borden agreed to form a U.S.-Canadian commission to study the matter. But as the new century dawned, economic interests in Canada began to look at the hydroelectric potential of the St. Lawrence River, the projected main channel from the eastern end of the Great Lakes to the Atlantic Ocean. Suddenly, engineering plans for dams became more prevalent than similar plans for locks.[708]

For their part, the Canadians already had a system of locks that bypassed the Niagara escarpment and allowed small vessels called canallers to pass between the Great Lakes and the St. Lawrence River. The first series of locks to

A WDSM–TV camera operator films the Cleveland–Cliffs steamer Frontenac *at the DM&IR ore docks in West Duluth in 1956 for an NBC "Wide, Wide World" special on construction of the St. Lawrence Seaway.*

bypass the dangerous Lachine Rapids above Montreal had opened in 1779. The success of the Erie Canal, which opened in 1825 in neighboring New York State, led Canadian engineers and politicians to investigate the feasibility of digging a canal of their own. In 1818, representatives from both Upper and Lower Canada agreed upon the necessity of strengthening the existing canal system. By 1821, they began expanding the canal bypassing the Lachine Rapids, finishing the project four years later. While workmen were finishing the Lachine project, other Canadian crews were beginning a second major project to complete the path to the sea. Between 1824 and 1833, the Welland Canal Company employed crews of immigrant laborers to excavate the Welland Canal along the watercourse of Twelve-Mile Creek on the Niagara escarpment.[709] With forty 100-foot locks, the twenty-seven-mile canal bypassed the falls and allowed Canadian vessels safe passage from Port Dalhousie on Lake Ontario to Gravelly Bay on Lake Erie.[710]

In 1841, Parliament combined Upper and Lower Canada into the modern provinces of Ontario and Quebec. The new union government subsequently bought out the interests of the Welland Canal Company. By the time steamships began replacing sailing vessels in the Canadian lakes in the 1850s, the government had enlarged the locks to 150 feet, reduced their number to twenty-six, and increased the depth of the canal to 9 feet; the improved canal was thereafter referred to as the "Second Welland." Work began on the Third Welland Canal in the early 1880s, and it was completed in 1887. By that time, the project had been taken over by the government of Canada, which was confederated in 1867.[711] The Third Welland Canal had a depth of 14 feet, and the locks had a width of 45 feet and length of 270 feet. The expanded canal gave rise to a third generation of canallers, which started calling on the Twin Ports and the Canadian lakehead as early as 1889. The new canallers had a maximum length of 262 feet and could carry as much as 3,000 tons of cargo. Most were designated for the Great Lakes trade, hauling grain from Lake Superior to mills in Montreal.[712] Some of the distinctive canallers actually survived the

opening of the St. Lawrence Seaway and continued sailing into the mid-1960s.[713]

Disheartened by American reluctance to consider joint action in building an international waterway, the Canadian government resolved to once again expand the Welland Canal just after the turn of the twentieth century. In 1913, with war clouds looming in Europe, work got under way on the Fourth Welland Canal.[714] The new canal maintained the original course from Port Colborne on Lake Erie to Thorold, Ontario, but then it struck off in a straight line north along the valley of Ten-Mile Creek to Lake Ontario at Port Weller, about three miles east of the original exit at Port Dalhousie.[715] When the Fourth Welland Canal was finally completed in 1932, the Canadians had what was to become the backbone of the modern St. Lawrence Seaway system a quarter-century in the future. The Fourth Welland Canal boasted seven lift locks and one guard lock. The locks were 850 feet long and 80 feet wide, and had 30 feet of water over the sills. Vessels with a draft of 25 feet could now pass from the Great Lakes to the St. Lawrence River.[716]

The completion of the Third and Fourth Welland Canals spurred action in the United States for a true international waterway. In 1919, Charles P. Craig, a Duluth attorney, filed articles of incorporation for the Great Lakes–St. Lawrence Tidewater Association. The organization was formed with the stated purpose of lobbying Washington, D.C., for a true international waterway that would link the Great Lakes to the Atlantic Ocean in a spirit of bi-national cooperation. The association maintained offices at Duluth and in Washington, D.C., and Craig spent much of his time in the nation's capital. A number of residents of the Twin Ports involved themselves in the activities of the association. One of the most active for more than thirty years was Henry LaLiberte.

A Minneapolis native, LaLiberte graduated from the Lourdes School and the De La Salle Institute before arriving in Superior as an accountant at Superior Manufacturing Company in 1904. Two years later, LaLiberte was named assistant secretary of the company, and in 1913, he joined Cutler-Magner Company in Duluth as assistant manager. At the time, Cutler-Magner operated the largest non-ferrous and non-coal bulk cargo dock in the Twin Ports, handling primarily salt, limestone, and crushed rock. LaLiberte's rise up the corporate ladder at Cutler-Magner was swift and steady. The firm named him general manager in 1916, vice president in 1920, and president in 1931.[717]

LaLiberte joined the Great Lakes–St. Lawrence Tidewater Association shortly after its founding. For the next forty years, he was a tireless advocate of U.S. participation in a seaway that would link his adopted home to the oceans of the world.

The association's lobbying efforts paid off in 1932 when Canada and the United States finally signed the Great Lakes–St. Lawrence Deep Waterways Treaty in Washington, D.C., as one of the final actions of the outgoing Hoover administration. Franklin D. Roosevelt, Hoover's successor in the White House, sent legislation to

Congress in 1941 proposing the construction of a seaway with a 27-foot depth as a national defense measure.[718]

In Congress, matters related to the seaway stalled for nearly a decade. The U.S. Senate narrowly defeated Roosevelt's seaway legislation in 1943, with opposition primarily coming from the East and Gulf Coast delegations, as well as the Mississippi Valley. The railroads lobbied strenuously against the legislation, arguing that creation of a seaway would internationalize the waters of Lake Michigan and would be a public works boondoggle of monumental proportions.[719] Increased postwar trade, however, kept reviving the idea of a bi-national waterway. In 1949, a joint Canadian-U.S. Deep Waterways Commission was once again chartered to look at the possibility of building it. The outbreak of the Korean War in 1950 proved to be the final spur to U.S. participation in construction efforts. Policy planners were growing increasingly concerned about the depletion of Lake Superior's

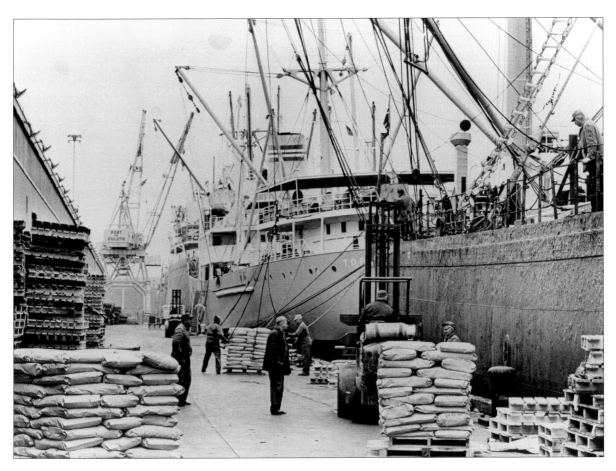

The berths of the Clure Public Marine Terminal form a forest of cranes and deck booms as saltwater vessels take on cargo in the late 1960s, with fortified milk in bags being loaded in the hold of the vessel in foreground.

The $10 million appropriations bill signed by Minnesota governor Orville Freeman in 1957 provided the seed money to construct Duluth's Arthur M. Clure Public Marine Terminal. Surrounding Freeman are, from left, Duluth port director Robert T. Smith; State Representative Willard Munger, Duluth; State Senator Arne Wanvick, Duluth; and State Senator Lawrence Yetka, Cloquet.

iron ore resources, and the development of rich Canadian reserves adjacent to the St. Lawrence River below Quebec City raised the possibility that America's blast furnaces could be fed from Canadian sources should the Mesabi and Marquette Ranges run dry. Besides, the Canadians were going to go through with developing an all-Canada route should the United States once again decline participation in a joint project.

In 1951, the Canadian parliament passed the St. Lawrence Seaway Authority Act and the International Rapids Power Act to finish the seaway and to develop the hydroelectric resources of the International Rapids above Montreal.[720] At that point, a rejuvenated Tidewater Association welded together a coalition of interests that finally persuaded the United States to join the project. Attorney Charles Craig had died, and the association had died with him. Julius Barnes, the Duluthian and New Yorker who had been involved with Great Lakes shipping and grain

commerce since early in the twentieth century, reformed a new Great Lakes–St. Lawrence Tidewater Association to fight the last battles for U.S. participation in the waterway. Joining him in the fray was Duluth physician N. R. Danielian and the son-in-law of Duluth's famous Alexander McDougall, Lewis G. Castle.[721]

Castle was a native of Portage, Wisconsin. He was twenty-eight when he came to Duluth in 1917 to organize the Duluth Creamery and Produce Company and almost immediately left the Twin Ports for service in World War I.[722] He returned to Duluth in 1919 and organized Riverside State Bank. He would spend the next forty years in Twin Ports banking, and for most of the 1930s and 1940s was a tireless advocate of improving transportation in the Upper Midwest.[723]

Castle, Barnes, and Danielian worked overtime during the early 1950s to lobby for American participation in the Canadian seaway project. In

1954, the Canadians forged ahead, establishing the St. Lawrence Seaway Authority to oversee completion of the project. At that point, President Dwight D. Eisenhower's administration finally weighed in with an offer to build a canal bypassing the International Rapids section of the St. Lawrence. The Wiley-Dondero Act, passed in May 1954 by the U.S. Congress, created the St. Lawrence Seaway Development Corporation and obligated the United States to spend nearly $134 million to build two locks near Massena, New York. Minnesota's U.S. senator Edward Thye, a strong proponent of the U.S. seaway legislation, suggested to Eisenhower that Castle be named the first administrator of the Seaway Development Corporation.[724]

SUCCESS AT LAST

With Castle's appointment in place, the Buffalo District of the U.S. Army Corps of Engineers began the arduous task of building the canal and two locks—the Eisenhower and Snell—that would provide the shipping community with the final link in the St. Lawrence Seaway.[725] Excavation on the U.S. portion of the seaway got under way in the late summer of 1955 and continued

Duluth banker Lewis G. Castle, a son-in-law of Alexander McDougall, was appointed by President Eisenhower as the first head of the St. Lawrence Seaway Development Corporation.

almost nonstop for the next three years. Crews rerouted highways and built a tunnel beneath the Eisenhower Lock during 1956 and 1957 and

The Duluth harbor was bustling in 1960. From bottom are the Clure Public Marine Terminal, Peavey elevators, Occident elevators, Nicholson car dock, Capitol 4 and Capitol 6 elevators, Carnegie coal dock, Norris grain elevators E, H, and I, Northwestern Hanna No. 3 coal dock, and General Mills Elevator A.

A grain inspector uses a hollow metal probe to sample grain in a railcar at a Superior elevator in the 1960s.

made improvements to the Long Sault Canal in 1957 and 1958.[726] While construction of the U.S. portion of the seaway was ongoing, a Boston engineering firm oversaw the construction of the Moses-Saunders Power Dam for the Power Authority of the State of New York and Ontario Hydro.[727] The final task in the project was construction of a 3,800-foot International Bridge from Massena, New York, to Cornwall, Ontario. When Corps of Engineers crews turned the bridge over to the state of New York and Province of Ontario in December 1958, the seaway was essentially completed.[728]

When all was said and done, the St. Lawrence Seaway constituted one of the great engineering projects of the twentieth century. It had cost more to build than its proponents had estimated, $470 million, but it had been finished within the five-year window originally envisioned. During those five years, more than 22,000 U.S. and Canadian workers blasted, dug, and quarried some 210 million cubic yards of dirt and rock. "Piled upon a football field," wrote seaway historian

Jacques LesStrang, "it would create a uniformly distributed mountain 22½ miles high. There were 6 million cubic yards of concrete to be poured, enough for a four-lane highway reaching from London to Rome."[729]

The completion of the St. Lawrence Seaway was marked by innumerable celebrations on both sides of the international boundary. One person who wouldn't live to see the completion of the seaway was Duluthian Julius H. Barnes. On the morning of Friday, April 17, 1959, the eighty-six-year-old Barnes was found dead of a ruptured aorta in his room at Duluth's Holland Hotel. In the late 1940s and early 1950s, Barnes's influence and contacts had helped finally convince Congress and the American public that participation in the bi-national waterway was an investment in the nation's future.

"For more than 35 years, he was one of its strongest and most consistent proponents in a long battle being climaxed now by construction crews," the *Duluth Herald* eulogized Barnes's long involvement with the seaway. "His views on the Seaway, which emphasized its value to the nation's economy and national security, as well as to this area, were voiced relentlessly during the fight for congressional action which created the St. Lawrence Seaway Development Corp., headed by former Duluthian Lewis G. Castle."[730]

Had Julius Barnes lived another two-and-a-half weeks, he would have witnessed the fulfillment of the dream that he had nurtured for nearly half his life.

THE BLATNIK LEGACY

One final project remained to be completed before the new seaway could fulfill its promise. In 1957, U.S. Congress passed legislation authorizing the Corps of Engineers to undertake the Great Lakes Connecting Channels Project. One of the sponsors of the legislation was John

Blatnik, Minnesota's 8th District congressman. Blatnik, a DFLer from Chisholm, had enjoyed a colorful career before his election to Congress in 1946.[731] This son of Slovenian immigrants grew up on the Mesabi Range speaking Slovene. A 1935 graduate of the then Winona State Teacher's College, Blatnik taught high school chemistry in Chisholm in 1936 and 1937. He spent 1938 doing graduate work in public administration at the University of Chicago and was named an assistant superintendent of the St. Louis County, Minnesota, school system in 1939. Blatnik's political career got its start with his election to the Minnesota Senate in 1940.[732]

When war broke out, Blatnik volunteered for service with the U.S. Army Air Corps in August 1942. As a native Slovene speaker, he was assigned duty with William "Wild Bill" Donovan's Office of Strategic Services. For more than ten

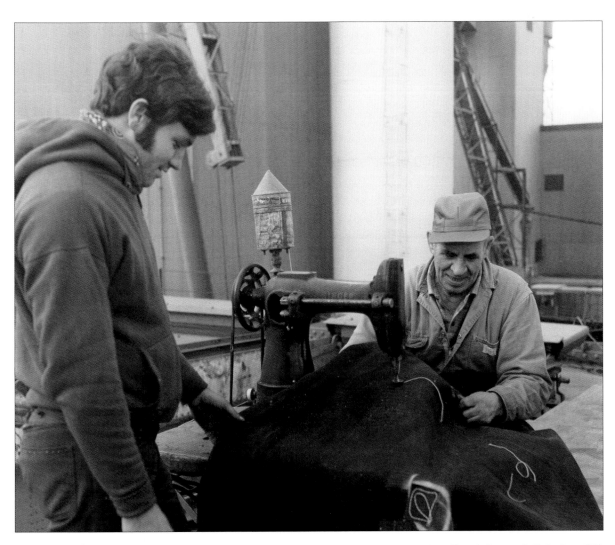

Harvey Anderson of Superior uses a heavy-duty sewing machine to repair a grain hatch tarp on M. A. Hanna's George R. Fink *about 1965.*

Inland Steel's Edward L. Ryerson *sails through the Duluth piers on its maiden voyage in August 1960. The 730-foot vessel boasted 27,000 tons of capacity and 20-foot-wide hatches for quick loading and unloading of iron ore.*

months during 1943 and 1944, Blatnik was chief of mission to Marshall Tito's partisans in Yugoslavia, jumping into German-occupied Croatia and Slovenia several times during that period.[733] When he returned to Chisholm from active duty in 1946, Blatnik immediately began running for the 8th Congressional District seat. He emerged victorious from the DFL primary that summer and went on to win the first of his fourteen terms in Congress in November.

By 1957, Blatnik had been in Congress for ten years and was chair of the House Subcommittee on Rivers and Harbors.[734] The deepening of the Great Lakes Connecting Channels spearheaded by Blatnik and other Great Lakes congressmen was a massive project, budgeted at more than $146 million. During the 1958 to 1964 navigation

seasons, Corps of Engineers crews deepened 150 miles of connecting channels on the Great Lakes from 25 feet to 27 feet. Also on the drawing boards was a similar deepening of all of the channels in the iron ore harbors on Lakes Superior, Erie, and Michigan.

"A MONUMENT TO FREEDOM"

Before the Corps of Engineers' dredges arrived in the Twin Ports to complete the Great Lakes Channel Deepening Project, Duluth and Superior were celebrating the opening of the Blatnik High Bridge, the 7,400-foot-long bridge that towered over the harbor. Its 123-foot clearance allowed for passage of the largest vessels plying the lakes, as well as the next generation of Great Lakes bulk vessels then on the drawing boards. The $21 million concrete and steel bridge was built during 1960 and 1961, with the federal government picking up 90 percent of the cost and Minnesota and Wisconsin splitting the remainder.[735] Designated Interstate 535, the new bridge was the first link in the Interstate 35 system that would link Duluth with the Twin Cities by the 1970s.[736] The new bridge also signaled the death knell for the Interstate Bridge, the Great Northern Railway drawbridge that had been built across the harbor in 1896. Since the 1920s, the span had served as the automobile toll bridge between Duluth and Superior.[737] On the day of the official ribbon-cutting for the new high bridge, the Interstate Bridge closed its gates to automobile traffic for the last time.

More than 4,000 persons attended the official dedication ceremony for the new bridge on a mild December afternoon. John Blatnik,

who had spearheaded the effort to have the federal government pay for 90 percent of the bridge's costs, preferred to pay homage to the American way of life in his brief remarks. "As we find strength in this structure," he told the crowd, "we also find beauty and grace. There is no checkpoint, no Berlin Wall, no barbed wire. It is a living monument to our freedom."[738]

Completion of the St. Lawrence Seaway, the Great Lakes Channel Deepening Project, and the Blatnik High Bridge essentially marked the completion of the outline of the modern port. Two new grain elevators, new terminals for iron ore, coal, and cement, and another cross-harbor bridge would be added in the next twenty-five years. But most of the harbor infrastructure that had been built in the early twentieth century would find itself easily adapted to the Twin Ports' new role as a world port.

The original Duluth–Superior High Bridge, which opened in 1961, was renamed in honor of 8th District DFL Congressman John A. Blatnik in 1971. Attending the ceremonies were, from left: Duluth mayor Ben Boo, Wisconsin governor Patrick Lucey, U.S. Secretary of Transportation John Volpe, Superior mayor Charles Deneweth, John and Evelyn Blatnik, an unidentified man, and Wisconsin congressman Alvin O'Konski.

THE HERITAGE OF MODERN ELEVATORS

Cargill's B1 and B2 terminal elevator complex off Garfield Avenue in Duluth is among the most modern grain-handling facilities in North America.

THE EIGHT MODERN TERMINAL ELEVATORS that call the Duluth-Superior port home share a grain shipping heritage that goes back more than 130 years. AGP, Cargill, CHS, ConAgra/Peavey, and General Mills are the twenty-first-century successors of the 350,000-bushel wooden elevator built in Duluth by the Union Improvement and Elevator Company in 1870.

W. W. "Will" Cargill's brother Sam opened an office in Duluth in 1892 and built the company's first elevator in the Twin Ports.[739] Elevator K held 2.5 million bushels and stood in Superior's East End.[740] Cargill acquired the Belt Line Elevator M in 1915,[741] the Itasca Elevator in Superior in the 1930s, and the Norris Grain Company elevators in 1960. In the 1960s the firm abandoned its Superior properties and in the 1970s purchased the Occident and Peavey elevators from the F. H. Peavey Company, renaming them Cargill Elevators C and D. In 1976, the firm built its state-of-the-art Elevator B1 off Garfield Avenue.[742] When it was unable to interest developers in the adjacent Elevators C and D, Cargill conveyed the site in 1989 to the then Seaway Port Authority of Duluth.[743]

In the 1890s Frank H. Peavey, who had moved his grain trading business north from Sioux City, Iowa, to Minneapolis, became an officer of the Duluth Elevator Company, which had built Elevators 1, 2, and 3 in Superior in 1887. By 1895 Peavey was president of the parent company.[744] By 1896, he controlled two of the largest terminal elevators in the Twin Ports: 5-million-bushel Globe Elevators and 2-million-bushel Belt Line Elevator Company.[745] In 1900, he built the Peavey-Duluth Terminal on Rice's Point. The 3.35-million-bushel complex consisted of fifty tanks, the first major concrete terminal elevator in the world.[746] He soon hired Augustus Wolvin to run the Peavey Steamship Line.[747]

Farmers Union Grain Terminal Association was the next of the modern elevator owners to move into the Twin Ports. The St. Paul–based cooperative built a 4.5-million-bushel elevator in 1942, bought the assets of the Spencer Kellogg Company in 1949, and enlarged its complex by nearly 8 million bushels in the 1950s.[748] When the St. Lawrence Seaway opened in 1959, Farmers Union operated what was reputedly the world's largest grain terminal complex. Farmers Union merged with Northwest Growers Association of Washington State in 1983 to form Harvest States Cooperative, then merged in the 1990s with Cenex and Land O' Lakes Cooperative to form CHS.[749]

The Twin Ports next welcomed General Mills, established in Minneapolis as the Washburn Crosby Company by Cadwallader C. Washburn in 1866. In 1929, Washburn Crosby consolidated its Minnesota, Montana, and Kansas mills and elevators as General Mills, Inc.[750] During WWII, the company produced defense materials and instruments for the navy.[751] In 1943 it also purchased assets of the Twin Ports' Consolidated Elevator Company, including Elevators D, E, G, H, and I. The next year, the firm renamed Elevator D to Elevator A and Annex G to Annex B and sold Elevators E, F, H, and I to Norris Grain Company. In 1977, General Mills completed a major capacity expansion project at Elevator A.[752] In 1989, it leased the old Great Northern Elevators S and X from the Burlington Northern Santa Fe Railroad.[753]

The year 1977 was also a banner one for ConAgra, an Omaha-based food processor that purchased Elevator M in Superior from the Osborne-McMillan Company and acquired the Burdick Grain Company and assigned it to manage Elevator M.[754] ConAgra's next bold move into Twin Ports grain handling came in 1982 when it purchased the Peavey Company. ConAgra designated Peavey as its elevator division and in 1986 bought out Continental Grain Company's lease for an elevator owned by the Chicago & Northwestern Railway.[755]

The last of the current operators to enter the Duluth-Superior grain handling business was also Omaha-based. In 1991, Agricultural Processing purchased International Multifoods Corporation's Capitol Elevator complex.[756] Capitol Elevator Company, founded in Duluth in 1905, built Capitol Elevator 6 in 1917 and expanded it in 1928 and 1978. For much of the 1900s, the Capitol Elevator complex was the flagship grain storage facility on the Great Lakes for International Milling Company and its successor, International Multifoods Corporation.[757]

Early seaway general cargo ships had one and sometimes two "tweendecks" in addition to a lower hold. After the lower holds were loaded, bagged agricultural products—shipped for government agencies and private interests—were stowed first in the wings of the tweendecks and then in the center of the hatches when the covers were replaced.

CHAPTER SIXTEEN

Growth of an International Port

RHODE ISLAND NATIVE Ed Ruisi arrived in the Twin Ports from the New York waterfront in the summer of 1959. The first St. Lawrence Seaway shipping season was just two months old, and Ruisi had been hired by Duluthian Alastair Guthrie to help handle overseas general cargo shipments. Ruisi, a U.S. Navy veteran, had been handling tanker shipments out of Perth Amboy, New Jersey, when opportunity came knocking.

"Matter of fact," Ruisi recalled forty-some years later, "my former boss called me up, and he said, 'I just came back from Duluth, Minnesota. We had a ship up there, and our agent was looking for personnel with a little more experience than they had.' He wanted to know if I knew of anyone, and I said, 'I know just the guy.' He called me up and said, 'Do you want a job in Duluth?' And I said, 'Where is that?' My brother, who happened to be sitting near the phone, heard me say that, and he said, 'Well, that is up where the Mesabi Iron Range is.'"[758]

Ruisi flew to Duluth, interviewed with Guthrie, and accepted the job. It was early July, and the transplanted New Yorker remembered that "everything was green and nice and beautiful and clean, so that cinched it right there."[759] When he arrived back in the Twin Ports ten days later to start work, Ruisi was immediately thrown into the backlog of orders and shipments. The grain business at the head of the lakes was the major benefactor of the opening of the seaway, but it would be a year or two before the Twin Ports grain elevators established efficient procedures for loading saltwater vessels. "Saltwater vessels being a new enterprise up here, there was a lot of confusion in

loading," Ruisi explained. "We were always running into difficulties."[760]

Actually, loading was more of a problem than unloading. Davis Helberg, who was working with Guthrie as a ship-runner that summer, recalled the chaos on the docks in 1959. "Even as an eighteen-year-old boy it was surprising, to say the least, to see how ill-equipped this port was to handle ocean ships," Helberg said. Never mind that there had already been sixty years of major effort by business leaders throughout the community to get the St. Lawrence Seaway constructed. Never mind that there had been five years of advance notice from 1954 to 1959 that the seaway was going to be a reality.

In short order, extensive renovation projects were under way at the port's thirteen grain loading berths.[761] The adoption of new procedures for grain handling fell upon the elevator managers in the Twin Ports. Many of the managers were old school, having run the elevators for twenty years and more. Ray Erickson was typical of the old guard. A native of Duluth, he had started working in elevators in 1923 under Hollis Graves Sr., the dean of Twin Ports elevator operators. Erickson had been named superintendent of the new Farmers Union Terminal Elevator when it was built in 1941, and when Osborne-McMillan bought Elevator M from Cargill in 1952, Erickson was hired as the superintendent. By the time the seaway opened in 1959, Erickson was superintendent of Elevators O & M on the Superior waterfront.[762]

"Ray Erickson was a real gentleman," recalled Jay Van Horn, who worked for Erickson in 1959 and 1960. "All of the superintendents I knew from

Two weeks after the Ramon de Larrinaga *opened the Twin Ports to seaway commerce, the first general cargo ship arrived at Duluth on May 17, 1959. The* TransMichigan *and her near sister, the* TransErie, *were operated by the Poseidon Line of Hamburg, Germany.*

1960 on were the old-timers. These men were all around sixty years old or older, and they were special. They all wore suits to work. This must have been a habit of that generation, because I remember my dad wouldn't go to town unless he put a suit on. Ray Erickson was this way. He came to work in a suit, sometimes a topcoat in the wintertime, and he had a locker in his office and he would take his suit coat off and his top-coat and whatever, and his good hat. He would put on a pair of coveralls and an old hat, and that is the way he went around the elevator and spent the day working at the elevator."[763]

Van Horn was a Superior native, and he had started working as a shoveler at Globe Elevator Company in 1949. He had quit Globe in the late 1950s and had run a grain-trimming crew in Superior in 1959. "The foreign ships that were coming in in 1959," Van Horn explained, "a lot of them were old Liberty ships, and these ships required bulkheading. You had to go on these ships and put feeder boxes in the tweendecks so that the grain would go down to the lower holds, and I ended up on those crews and worked pretty steady through June and July.

We were making pretty good money. It kind of slacked off in August, and I did get out on a few boats trimming grain, but that didn't look so good anymore."[764]

In the fall of 1959, Van Horn was hired on the labor crew at Elevator M in Superior and was eventually offered the job of superintendent of Elevators O & M.[765] He would be the first of a new breed of younger elevator managers in the Twin Ports who would oversee the expansion of the export grain market in the 1960s.

Duluth's F. H. Peavey Company and Superior's Farmers Union Grain Terminal Association were among the first grain firms at the head of the lakes to convert their elevators to load saltwater vessels more efficiently. In the summer of 1960, Peavey built a $4.5 million high-speed grain-loading gallery adjacent to its Duluth elevator. The three spouts on the 114-foot-high gallery allowed crews to load 15,000 bushels of grain per hour from each spout and eliminated much of the expensive and time-consuming shifting of vessels that plagued Twin Ports elevators in the early days of the seaway.[766]

The Farmers Union improvements also involved creation of a loading gallery. The St. Paul–based cooperative, which built a new elevator in 1941, had purchased the adjacent facility from the Spencer Kellogg Company in 1949 to create Farmers Elevators No. 1 and No. 2. Capacity expansions then and through the 1950s swelled the facility's silos to 18 million bushels, making it for many years the world's largest terminal elevator complex. In 1961, loading capability was increased dramatically on the No. 1 side, at the foot of Tower Avenue, when a 450-foot, five-spout gallery was extended along a renovated dock dredged to a depth of 32 feet.[767]

All of the parties to the new trade did learn soon enough that shipping grain in "salties" heading overseas was different than shipping grain in lakers to Buffalo. And the tonnages reflected that evolution in thinking. In 1959, the first full seaway season, grain tonnages through the Twin Ports jumped 1 million tons, to 3.8 million tons. It was the best grain year for the ports in a decade.[768] The next year, grain tonnages increased again, this time to 4.36 million tons. Not only was grain going overseas, it was also flowing down the St. Lawrence River to facilities such as Louis Dreyfus Corporation's new elevator at Port Cartier, Quebec, and the

massive, 12-million-bushel elevator built by Minneapolis-based Cargill, Inc., at Baie Comeau, Quebec.[769] Grain tonnages continued to climb, to 4.41 million tons in 1961, 4.54 million tons in 1962, and 4.73 million tons in 1963.[770] A ten-week grain elevator strike in 1964 dropped tonnages 500,000 tons, but they rebounded in 1965 to almost 5 million tons.[771] The following year, in 1966, more than 5.7 million tons of grain flowed through the port.[772]

Grain exports, mostly to Northern Europe and to Canadian terminals on the St. Lawrence River, accounted for the bulk of the foreign trade handled by the Twin Ports. In 1966, 3.8 million tons of grain went overseas and to Canada, nearly two-thirds of all of the grain handled by the Twin Ports that year.[773] Just over 50,000 tons of general cargo imports flowed across the docks in 1966, well below the import tonnages that seaway proponents had predicted. But the volume of exports more than justified the investment in the seaway, proponents argued, and man-hours for port labor were triple and quadruple what they had been a decade before.

Optimism about the future of the grain business at the head of the lakes was best expressed in February 1966, when Continental Grain

The growth of the Twin Ports' export grain business after the St. Lawrence Seaway opened resulted in elevator construction and expansions. In 1965, the Chicago & Northwestern Railway built the Continental Grain Company elevator on Connors Point. Continental operated the elevator until the F. H. Peavey Company bought it in 1986.

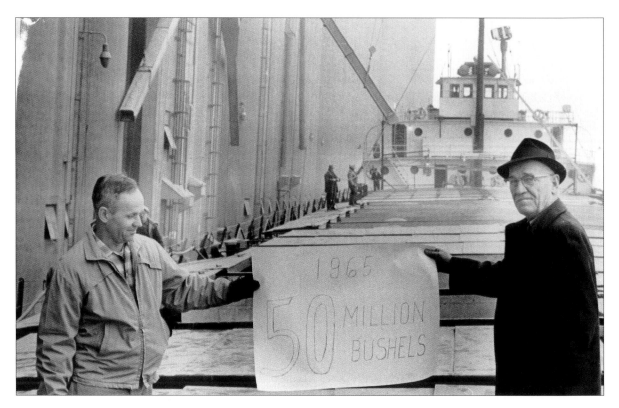

Russell A. Johnson Sr., right, and his son, Russell A. "Noonie" Johnson Jr., celebrate the 50 millionth bushel handled by the Farmers Union Elevator late in the 1965 season. The senior Johnson was Farmers Union's longtime general superintendent in the Twin Ports and was succeeded by his son. The Farmers Union elevators were and, as CHS Elevators No. 1 and No. 2 continue to be, the Twin Ports' largest. From 1941 to 1966, the complex handled in excess of one billion bushels of grain.

Company began operating a new 5-million-bushel elevator on Connors Point. Built by Northwestern Leasing Company in 1965, the new facility was the first elevator built in the Twin Ports in nearly twenty-five years.[774]

THE RISE OF TACONITE

Even with the increase in grain tonnages in the early 1960s, overall tonnages passing through the port dropped significantly during the decade. The 29.2 million tons handled during the 1961 season was the worst overall performance by the ports since the depression year of 1938. Numerous reasons accounted for the drop in tonnage, which saw average annual shipments plummet to 39.6 million tons for the 1960s from the average 58 million tons a year of the 1950s. After the boom years of the Korean War and the post–World War II expansion, steel production in the United States began a decades-long shrinkage. A 116-day steel strike in 1959 opened the doors to imported steel for the first time, and 1961, the first year of John F. Kennedy's presidency, saw the worst recession in America since the late 1930s. Matters weren't helped for

the steel industry in April 1962, when Kennedy used the power of his presidency to persuade steel executives to rescind a price increase.[775] Even gradual U.S. involvement in a new war in Vietnam at mid-decade didn't give the same boost to iron ore shipments that previous wars had.

Iron ore shipments had peaked at 65 million tons in 1953 and had slipped to a third of that six years later. They rebounded to 33 million tons in 1960 and then slid to 22.2 million tons in 1961 and 21 million tons in 1962. For the rest of the decade, iron ore averaged about 30 million tons a year, far below the 46.8 million tons a year averaged in the 1950s. The reason for the decline was simple: For the first time in its history as a port, Duluth-Superior had serious competition as a transshipment port for Mesabi Range iron ore.

Erie Mining Company and Reserve Mining Company, the first two Minnesota firms to embark upon taconite mining and pellet-making in a big way, elected to build rail and dock complexes on the north shore of Lake Superior instead of using the existing infrastructure in the Twin Ports. The reason was primarily geographical. Both of the early taconite pits were in the northeastern stretch of the Mesabi Iron Range at Hoyt Lakes, Aurora, and Babbitt, Minnesota. Company engineers reasoned that it was less expensive to ship the taconite straight downhill to Silver Bay and Taconite Harbor than to use existing railroads to ship all the way to Duluth-Superior.[776]

Old-time vessel agents who had spent a lifetime consigning natural ore from the Mesabi Range to the boats of the Great Lakes fleet derided taconite. Why, they wondered, would the steel industry pay all that money to crush poor rock, bind it into pellets in ball mills, and fire it in kilns at 3,000 degrees?

The truth was that the Mesabi Range's reserves of natural ore were rapidly running out by 1960. The rich, red ore that had been the Twin Ports' bread and butter for nearly seventy years had been largely depleted by the nation's need for steel during World War II and the Korean War. More important, the steel industry's up-front investment in mines, mills, processing facilities, railroads, and new docks for taconite was about to pay huge dividends. Even though the pellets contained a lower iron content than natural ore, their uniformity of size and iron content vastly increased the efficiency of blast furnaces at the integrated steel mills on the lower lakes.

Equally worrisome was the long-term erosion of the coal trade. While natural ore was declining as a commodity passing across the docks of the Twin Ports in the 1960s, so was coal. Average annual receipts of coal back-hauled up the lakes had begun to decline in the 1950s. The Twin Ports had handled an average of 5.2 million tons of coal per year during the 1950s, but in 1958 and 1959 coal cargoes had tailed off to an average of 3.5 million tons annually.[777]

Coal volume just kept declining in the early 1960s, fluctuating between a high of 3.5 million tons in 1965 and a low of 2.7 million tons in 1961.[778] Unlike natural ore, coal reserves weren't declining. Coal, however, was suffering from a

fundamental shift in the way Americans were consuming energy in the postwar world. World War II had spurred the construction of pipelines across much of the Midwest to deliver crude oil and aviation gasoline from the oil fields and refineries on the Gulf Coast to the war industries on the East Coast. The wartime opening of huge new oil reserves in the Middle East flooded the eastern half of the nation with cheap fuel oil and gasoline in the 1950s and 1960s. With the construction of massive refineries at St. Paul and Wrenshall in the postwar years, many homeowners increasingly elected to try the convenience of furnaces fired by number-one and number-two grade fuel oil. By 1955, only 8.2 percent of the households in the United States were heated by coal furnaces.[779]

Natural gas was another competitor to coal. The opening of big new gas fields contributed trillions of cubic feet of natural gas reserves to the nation's supply during the 1950s and 1960s. Pipelines followed the discovery of the new gas fields. Between 1945 and 1982, pipeline and local distribution companies built 172,000 miles of gas pipelines in North America, which represented an investment of $33 billion and provided gas for 40 million homes and businesses. Coal for the home heating market all but disappeared during the period.[780]

There were those in the early 1960s who predicted that the population of Duluth-Superior would double by 1970 because of the rush of business brought about by the opening of the St. Lawrence Seaway. Others in the community feared that the continuing decline in ore and coal shipments would turn the Twin Ports into a shadow of themselves, no matter how much grain went down the lakes to world markets. As it turned out, both sides were wrong. The St. Lawrence Seaway didn't pave the streets of Duluth-Superior and other Great Lakes port communities with gold. The seaway provided a nice boost for grain exporting communities such as the Twin Ports, and Duluth-Superior developed a strong general cargo import market in the 1960s and 1970s. Neither did iron ore and coal shipments dry up altogether. The doomsayers forgot that Duluth-Superior existed because of the interface between the natural

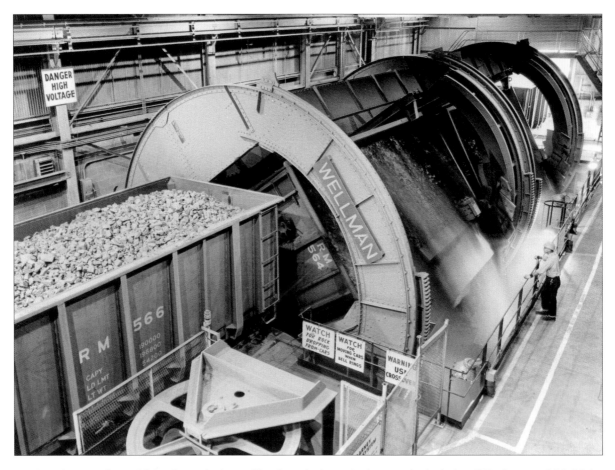

A car dumper at Reserve Mining Company's plant at Silver Bay unloads taconite for processing in the late 1960s. Reserve and Erie Mining Company built Minnesota's first two large-scale taconite plants.

resources of the Upper Midwest and the efficient, inexpensive water transportation system of the Great Lakes. In the early 1960s, the nation's steel industry moved to protect its investment in the waterfront infrastructure of the Twin Ports.

THE TACONITE AMENDMENT

Steel executives worried that a massive investment in the development of Minnesota's almost limitless reserves of taconite could leave the industry vulnerable to the North Star State's somewhat chaotic system of taxing mining properties. Natural ore mines in the early 1960s were subject to a jumble of property, occupation, ad valorem, and production taxes. The steel industry was concerned that the application of property taxes to the major investment required to bring taconite production online would result in a much higher tax rate.

The steel companies wanted to shift to a production tax that would be based on the amount of taconite actually processed and shipped down the lakes. The Minnesota and Michigan legislatures both were amenable to the idea, and, in fact, had given the industry assurances as early as the 1950s that taconite would not be subject to property tax.[781] By 1963, the industry had demonstrated that taconite pellets were more efficient in the blast furnaces than natural ore. But, as Peter J. Kakela has written, "What they wanted first was a guarantee that once built, the state legislators would not raise their taconite taxes inordinately."[782]

The steel industry mounted a high-powered lobbying and public relations campaign in 1963 to persuade the people of Minnesota to amend the state constitution. The lobbyists sought to create a production and occupation taxation system for taconite that would effectively cap taxes at 1964 rates for twenty-five years. The industry used a carrot-and-stick approach. The carrot was the prospect of building several new taconite plants that would employ thousands of Mesabi

Rangers and result in a capital investment of hundreds of millions of dollars in northern Minnesota. The stick was the possibility that the plants wouldn't be built because of the state's antiquated tax system.

Steel executives began dangling carrots in the winter of 1963. In February, Ford Motor Company indicated its interest in joining a consortium of steel companies considering building a taconite facility near Eveleth, Minnesota. In March, the Oliver Iron Mining Division of U.S. Steel announced plans to build a taconite plant near Mountain Iron, Minnesota. Later that month, the Groveland Plant in the Upper Peninsula of Michigan produced its first load of low-iron content pellets. In July, the Eveleth Taconite Company was formally organized.[783] Rumors that other steel companies were investigating taconite projects swept the state in 1963 and 1964. Erie and Reserve produced more than 15 million tons of pellets in 1963, and industry supporters predicted that the total could double by 1970—if the state amended its constitution.[784]

Lobbying for passage of what was becoming known as the Taconite Amendment increased sharply during the 1964 session of the Minnesota General Assembly. Legislators agreed to put the amendment on the November ballot with the important caveat that, as in all constitutional amendments, a scratch vote would be counted as a vote against the proposition. Both political parties were in favor of passage, as were the state's business and labor communities. When the amendment came before the voters on Tuesday, November 3, 1964, it passed by an overwhelming 6-to-1 margin.[785]

The steel industry almost instantly made good on its promise to build and expand taconite facilities in Minnesota. In late 1964 and early 1965, Eveleth Taconite broke ground on its initial 1.6-million-ton facility, while the Hanna Mining Company began building the Butler Taconite plant near Nashwauk and the 2.6-million-ton National Steel Pellet Company facility near Keewatin. U.S. Steel began construction on the first phase of its Minntac plant near Mountain Iron.[786] By 1967, the taconite industry in Minnesota had added 22.7 million tons of pellet capacity on the Mesabi Range.[787]

The expansion of the taconite industry in the mid-1960s did not guarantee that pellets would

The steamer Philip R. Clarke *carries a cargo of taconite pellets at South Chicago in 1977. Reconstruction of ore docks in the Duluth–Superior harbor following the 1964 passage of the Taconite Amendment ensured that the Twin Ports would remain a major force in the U.S. movement of iron ore.*

flow across the ore docks of Duluth-Superior, but it was obvious to industry executives that the Twin Ports would have to be factored into the transportation equation. In 1965, the Duluth, Missabe, & Iron Range Railway Company announced a multimillion-dollar conversion program for its West Duluth ore docks. The project involved the establishment of a thirty-acre taconite stockpile area adjacent to the company's existing ore docks. It also provided for installation of a bucket-wheel reclaimer and conveyor system to move pellets to and from the stockpile area. Last, DM&IR replaced sixty-four chutes and spouts on Dock 6 with specially designed conveyors to speed the loading of vessels. The initial storage area contained room for 2.25 million tons of pellets, and before the stockpile was even half full, DM&IR crews began preparing the ground for a second phase stockpile, which would double the pellet storage area.[788]

In December 1965, Eveleth Taconite Company began shipping pellets for storage to the DM&IR's West Duluth docks. The expansion project constituted recognition by U.S. Steel and the DM&IR that the Twin Ports would continue to play a major role in the Great Lakes iron ore trade. Eighteen months later, the Great Northern Railway bowed to the inevitable and unveiled an $8.1 million conversion plan for its ore docks on Allouez Bay in Superior to handle taconite. The Great Northern built a 2.2-million-ton pellet storage facility—with room to expand the facility to 5.5 million tons—near the Allouez docks. Pellets were transported to the docks along a two-mile-long conveyor belt. At the docks, a pellet stacker and boom system fed the pellets into any of 374 pockets for loading vessels. Great Northern also pioneered a unit-train system at the stockpile, which allowed 75-ton cars to be dumped at the rate of four cars per hour.[789]

By June 1969, the two taconite facilities had already handled nearly 10 million tons of pellets that season, slightly ahead of the collective 8.5 million tons shipped from Two Harbors, Silver Bay, and Taconite Harbor.[790]

Of far greater import to the Twin Ports and the taconite industry that June was the dedication

at Sault Ste. Marie of the largest navigation lock ever built on the Great Lakes. The Poe Lock was built by U.S. Army Corps of Engineers crews between 1966 and 1969. At 1,200 feet long, it dwarfed the MacArthur, Davis, and Sabin Locks. The Poe Lock would accommodate bulk freighters 1,000 feet in length and 105 feet in width. By this time, Bethlehem Steel Corporation and U.S. Steel already had vessels on the drawing boards that would take full advantage of the new, mammoth lock.[791] Those new vessels would bring about a revolution in transportation on the Great Lakes in the decades to come.

PROMOTING THE PORTS

From a public's viewpoint, the biggest change in the Twin Ports during the first decade following the opening of the St. Lawrence Seaway was the existence of new quasi-governmental bodies that promoted the facilities at the ports. The Seaway Port Authority of Duluth and the Superior Harbor Commission both were formed in the mid-1950s to guide the development of public warehouse facilities and to solicit business for the Twin Ports. SPAD consisted of a seven-member board appointed by the governor of Minnesota, the St. Louis County board of commissioners, and the Duluth City Council. The Superior Harbor Commission was essentially a committee of the Superior City Council.

Robert T. Smith guided the fortunes of SPAD for the first dozen years of its existence. By the time he retired in 1968, Smith had more than a half-century of experience in maritime commerce. He started out as a maritime aide to the British consul in Philadelphia in 1916 and then spent twenty years as a vessel agent in the City of Brotherly Love. In 1937, he moved to New Orleans, where he established one of the more successful stevedoring firms on the Lower Mississippi River. During World War II, Smith handled all military stevedoring contracts in New Orleans.[792] SPAD commissioners hired him in 1956 precisely because of his experience in handling ocean cargoes.

During his twelve years at the Duluth Port Authority, Smith put together and trained a staff and began to actively solicit business for the port and its Arthur M. Clure Public Marine Terminal. Smith primarily hired from within the local market, recruiting Howard Wicker, who was to serve as finance director from 1959 until his retirement in 1986; Captain Herman C. Doering, an oceangoing chief mate who would serve as terminal superintendent for nearly ten years until his untimely death at age fifty in 1969; Tony Radosevich, the terminal's chief clerk from 1959 until 1970; and Thomas E. Kennedy, whose career in numerous port authority capacities would span four decades, from 1963 until 2002. Another key hire was Robert H. Smith. A 1937 graduate of the John Marshall School of Law in Chicago, Smith worked for the Chicago, Burlington, & Quincy Railroad before joining the staff of the Duluth Chamber of Commerce in 1939. When he joined SPAD as director of traffic in 1964, he had been traffic commissioner for the Duluth chamber and traffic manager for the Duluth board of trade for a quarter-century.[793]

Under Robert T. Smith, the port authority maintained a relatively high profile for the Twin Ports. SPAD hired stevedores and longshoremen to handle operations at the Clure Public Marine Terminal, sent trade missions to Europe, published a monthly magazine, opened a trade office in Minneapolis, and built a tank farm for edible oils at the Clure Public Marine Terminal.[794] Smith also worked closely with the city of Duluth and the U.S. Army Corps of Engineers to develop the site of the Duluth Arena-Auditorium complex on the waterfront near the Aerial Lift Bridge. The Duluth Arena-Auditorium, the first of numerous waterfront recreational developments, opened in 1966.[795]

A French ship, the Christine, *and two Great Lakes Towing Company tugboats approach Duluth's Cargill elevator in 1971. The* Christine *and other ships with similar "-ine" endings were owned by Union Industrielle Maritime, a Paris–based company, and were regular callers in the port of Duluth–Superior from the 1960s to the 1980s.*

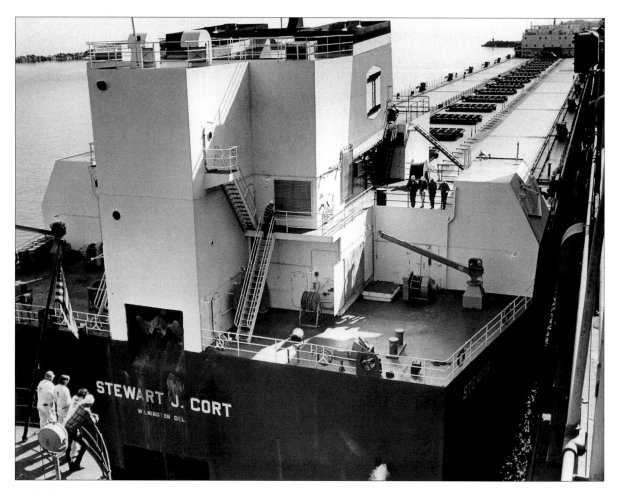

Bethlehem Steel Corporation's Stewart J. Cort *revolutionized Great Lakes maritime commerce when launched in the spring of 1972. The first of the thousand–footers, the* Cort *was designed specifically to haul taconite pellets from Lake Superior to steel mills on the lower end of the Great Lakes.*

The Superior Harbor Commission was much more low-profile than its counterpart across the bay. For one thing, the commission did not own and develop waterfront property. Still, port director Lawrence Sinclear was an effective advocate for the Twin Ports during the eight years he spent in the Superior job, retiring in 1966.[796] Sinclear was succeeded by James C. Sauter, the former operator of Duluth-Superior Grain Trimmers and manager of Empire Stevedoring Company, who served as Superior port director until the mid-1970s.

Robert T. Smith announced his retirement in June 1967, after nearly twelve years as port director in Duluth.[797] The port authority immediately launched a nationwide search for Smith's successor. They found their candidate at another Great Lakes port. In September, SPAD announced the appointment of David W. Oberlin, manager of trade development for the Toledo-Lucas County Port Authority, as the new Duluth port director.[798] Oberlin, a native of Atchison, Kansas, had been around the waterfront for much of his adult life. He had studied chemical engineering at the University of Kansas, sailed submarines during World War II, had worked for Libby-Owens Ford for ten years, and then had gone to the Toledo port when his boss at Libby was named chair of the port board. Along the way, he had made the acquaintance of Duluth port commissioner Conrad "Mac" Fredin, who persuaded Oberlin to apply for the Duluth job in 1967.[799]

Although Oberlin was port director at Duluth for only two years, he had a major impact on the future direction of the port. His biggest decision involved the management of the Clure Marine Terminal. "In those days," Oberlin recalled, "there was a period when the port authority ran the terminal operation. The port authority was

Duluth food broker Marshall Chabot, left, was one of the Seaway Port Authority's first tenants in 1968 when his Mid-Continent Warehouse Company leased Clure Public Marine Terminal property to construct a refrigerated and frozen storage facility. In 1970, Chabot conferred with Duluth vessel agent Sven Hubner, right, and Eric Hallen, general manager of Nordship Agencies, Chicago, which represented a line of refrigerated ships then operating in the Great Lakes. Mid-Continent exported "reefer cargo" in its early years, then focused primarily on domestic and Canadian products.

always in the middle, and I thought that was crazy. So I decided to do it the way they did it in Toledo, which was to lease the facility to a terminal operator and let him handle the stevedoring and the warehousing and management."[800]

The port authority received competitive proposals from eight stevedoring contractors and in early 1969 announced the appointment of Ceres, Inc., as the terminal's managing agent. The company, later to become a worldwide terminal operator, was owned by Christos Kritikos, a former Greek ship officer who founded a stevedoring business in Chicago in 1959 shortly before opening a Duluth office. Kritikos assigned the terminal management in the Zenith City to Kaare Eileraas, a Norwegian and ex–ship's officer who had been running Ceres' local grain stevedoring operation.

Oberlin also moved the port authority in the direction of real estate development. "Then the other thing I wanted to do was to start developing the port land," he said. "So the first thing I was able to do—and when I say I, *the port authority* was able to do—was to get United Parcel Service to take a lease on the property. They are still there. In fact, they just expanded

recently. That was thirty-five years ago. Anyway, that was the first taste we had of getting some income from the land." Oberlin also negotiated a lease on port terminal land for the Mid-Continent Warehouse, which was built by food broker Marshall Chabot. One of Oberlin's final decisions was hiring Davis Helberg away from the *Duluth News-Tribune* in 1968 as SPAD's director of public relations.[801]

David Oberlin's activist administration of SPAD was cut short by President Richard M. Nixon, who named the Duluth port director administrator of the St. Lawrence Seaway Development Corporation in the summer of 1969.[802] Oberlin was the second Duluthian in fifteen years named to head the corporation, and there was little doubt that he would be missed at the head of the lakes. When Oberlin left the Twin Ports, Duluth and Superior were on a decided upswing. The 43.5 million tons of cargo handled at the Twin Ports in 1969 made that the third best year of the decade and almost 4 million tons more than the average year for the 1960s. The 34.4 million tons of iron ore handled at the ore docks of the Twin Ports in 1969 were also nearly 4 million tons more than the average year in the 1960s.[803] More important, taconite seemed to be helping the ports reclaim their primacy in the Lake Superior ore trade. Two-thirds of the ore tonnage shipped through the head of the lakes in 1969 was taconite.

President Richard M. Nixon appointed Robert T. Smith's successor, David W. Oberlin (left), as administrator of the St. Lawrence Seaway Development Corporation in 1969. Congratulating Oberlin are James C. Sauter (right), Superior port director, and A. F. "Tony" Rico, president of Upper Great Lakes Pilots.

THE
ROGER BLOUGH

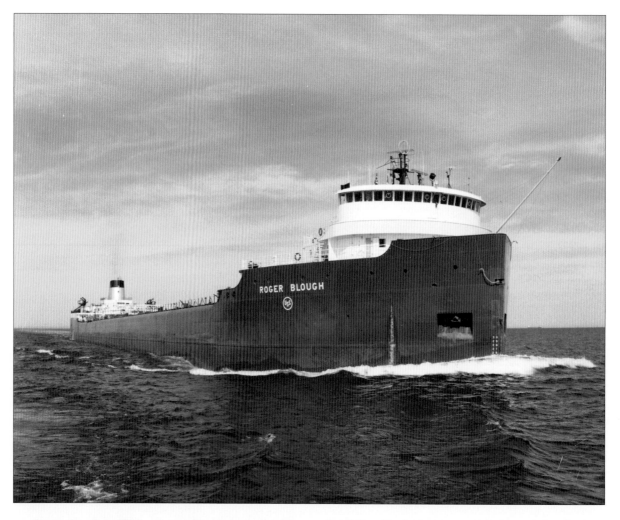

Construction of the 858-foot Rough Blough *heralded a new generation of big self-unloaders that would send scores of smaller bulk carriers to the scrapyards. The* Blough *was scheduled to enter service in 1971, but an onboard fire delayed her delivery until 1972.*

IN JANUARY 1964, John S. Wilbur, senior vice president of the Cleveland-Cliffs Iron Mining Company, told the International Joint Conference of the Lake Carriers' Association and the Dominion Marine Association that taconite development would have a huge impact on the Great Lakes fleet. Transportation of the iron pellets would require bigger and better ships for maximum profitability.

"I have estimated that shipments from presently operating properties and new properties in progress will be about 26 million tons in 1966 and 30 million tons in 1970," Wilbur announced. "You can figure roughly that for every million tons of new taconite, a new freighter will be required. Unfortunately, new taconite developments, if they come, will be too late to save any of the 116 ships of less than 15,000-ton capacity, except a few in the best shape to struggle with ever-rising costs."[804]

Wilbur's speech to the Lake Carriers' Association and the Dominion Marine Association was blunt and to the point: taconite development would not only radically transform the iron and steel industry, it would also change the profile of the Great Lakes fleet. "It may sound strange," he added, "but actually the U.S. lake fleet is suffering far more than the lake mining area."[805]

Wilbur continued by noting that the actual tonnages of ore would invariably drop as more and more iron went down the Great Lakes in the form of taconite pellets rather than natural ore. "For example, 50 million tons of ore at 55 percent iron is roughly equivalent to 42 million tons at 66 percent iron," he said.[806]

His message was simple: the vessels in the fleet would have to get bigger and more efficient to survive.

The iron ore and steel industry paid swift heed to Wilbur's message. By 1966, marine engineers were designing the next generation of Great Lakes bulk freighters. The first to get a design off the drawing board was the U.S. Steel fleet, which contracted with a Cleveland, Ohio, firm to design and oversee construction of an 858-foot self-unloader that would have the capacity to haul 44,500 tons of taconite pellets down the lakes in a single trip. The anticipated 1969 opening of the new 1,200-foot Poe Lock at Sault Ste. Marie suddenly meant that bigger was truly going to be better in the Great Lakes iron trade.[807]

The U.S. Steel Corporation's *Roger Blough* began to take shape at American Ship Building Company's Lorain yards in 1969. Named for the recently retired chair of U.S. Steel's board, the *Roger Blough* would use every new technology to make her the most efficient ore carrier to date on the Great Lakes.[808]

Powered by mammoth diesel engines, the *Roger Blough* would operate at sixteen knots in the open lakes. Because of the uniformity of taconite pellets, the ship was outfitted with a self-unloading shuttle boom and conveyor system that would allow her to offload her cargo of pellets at the lower lakes at the then remarkable rate of 10,000 tons per hour. Although self-unloading ships had been invented in the Great Lakes decades earlier, the *Roger Blough*'s high-speed system elevated the technology to new heights.[809]

When launched in 1971, the *Roger Blough* would be the largest bulk vessel on the lakes by more than 128 feet. Yet the ship never got the opportunity to become the largest member of the Great Lakes fleet. On June 24, 1971, just two weeks before her scheduled launch date, the stern section of the new freighter caught fire and was partially destroyed by a raging blaze that also killed four shipyard workers. By the time the *Roger Blough* was repaired and finally launched in June 1972, she was dwarfed by the *Stewart J. Cort,* the first of the Great Lakes' 1,000-footers.[810]

John Wilbur's forecast held true. The greater efficiencies of the 1,000-footers revived the iron and steel industry. The bonus was that grain and coal also rebounded.

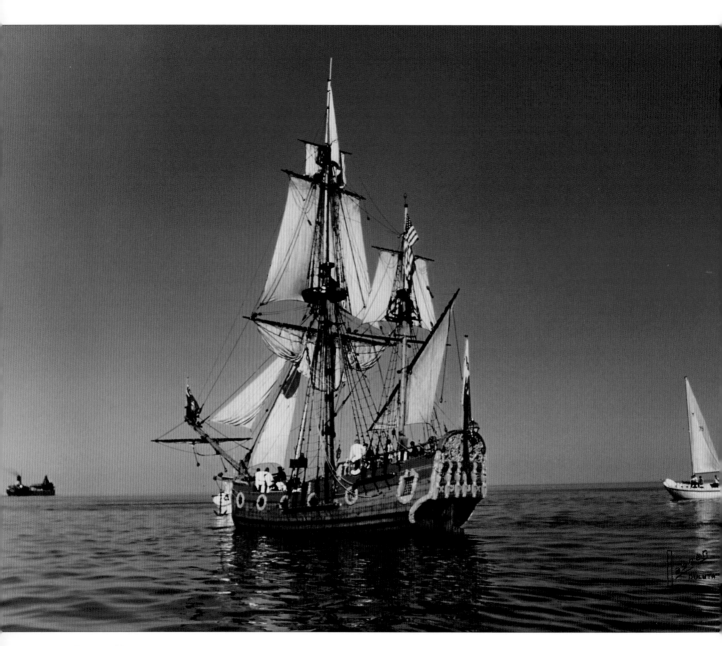

The ketch Nonsuch, *a replica of the vessel that opened western Canadian commerce for the British in 1668, visited Duluth–Superior in 1971 at the end of a three-year tour by the Hudson Bay Company. From Duluth, she was trucked to Winnipeg for permanent display in Manitoba's Museum of Man and Nature.*

CHAPTER SEVENTEEN

Revolutions in Commerce

WHEN THE MOTOR SHIP *Stewart J. Cort* came out in the spring of 1972, the world changed for the Great Lakes fleet, the iron and steel industry, and the Twin Ports.[811] The first of the 1,000-footers, the *Cort* would be followed down the launch ways by a dozen more 1,000-foot lake carriers in the next decade, sparking a revolution in Great Lakes commerce unprecedented in the previous 100 years.[812] Only the 1855 opening of the Soo Locks and the introduction of bulk freight ships in 1870 compared in significance with the advent of the 1,000-footers.

More than three football fields long, the *Cort* had a beam of 105 feet—narrow enough to pass through the 110-foot width of the new Poe Lock at the Soo, but with only 2½ feet to spare on either side. At midsummer draft of 27 feet, the *Cort* could carry 50,000 tons of taconite pellets from the ore docks of the Twin Ports and western Lake Superior to the blast furnaces on Lakes Michigan and Erie.[813] With her sophisticated navigation, radar, and communications gear, the *Cort* could operate in weather conditions that once sent smaller vessels scurrying for shelter in the Lily Pond of Lake Superior's Keweenaw Peninsula or Whitefish Bay. Her self-unloading equipment was capable of discharging 50,000 tons of pellets in hours instead of days. The ship cruised at sixteen knots on the open water of the lakes, making a round-trip between Duluth-Superior and Gary, Indiana, in five days.[814]

The efficiencies of the 1,000-footers were stunning, particularly in regard to crew size and cargo capacity. The early 1,000-footers carried crews of twenty-five to thirty. Most of the 600-footers, which had dominated the lakes' iron ore trade since they were introduced early in the

twentieth century, carried crews of thirty-five or more.[815] For the lake carriers, the 1,000-footers represented a quantum leap in technology and efficiency. A 1,000-footer could easily carry the cargo of four or more 600-footers, and it could carry that cargo faster with less fuel.[816] One result of the introduction of the 1,000-footers was almost a foregone conclusion. Within three years of the launch of the *Cort,* the fleets began consigning their smaller, less efficient vessels to the scrap yards. In 1970, the Great Lakes fleet totaled more than 200 vessels. A decade later, it was just over half that. By the mid-1990s, the American Great Lakes fleet had shrunk to seventy-five ships.[817]

Manpower requirements of the fleet were drastically reduced during the 1970s. More than 3,000 jobs were eliminated during that decade alone. For mariners, the situation was reminiscent of the 1930s, when captains sailed as mates and mates sailed as able-bodied seamen. For licensed personnel, the employment crunch was alleviated slightly by the growth of pilotage services, generated by oceangoing traffic following the opening of the St. Lawrence Seaway in 1959.

Captain Bill Jeffery was typical of the trend. Jeffery, a Duluth native, graduated from high school in 1942 and immediately signed on as a deckhand aboard the Pittsburgh Steamship Company's steamer *Myron C. Taylor.* He worked his way up through the ranks and by 1970 was master of the *Clifford F. Hood,* a crane boat ideally suited for hauling scrap metal downbound and finished steel upbound to the Twin Ports. She was owned and operated by the American Steel and Wire Company, a division of U.S. Steel Corporation.

In 1971, business was slow. "Paper Calmenson was our largest customer up here," Jeffery explained, "and half the steel went to them, and they decided to pull their warehouse out. They had a warehouse over in Superior, so we laid up early and there was a strike besides. Then they decided not to run it the next year. That is when I left."[818]

Like so many of his brethren in the fleet, Jeffery chose piloting as a second career. He piloted on Lakes Superior, Michigan, and Huron for the remainder of the 1971 season and for all of 1972, but at the end of the 1972 season, U.S. Steel called him with a proposition. "I got a call from the fleet office here in Duluth, and Bill Rankin— Captain Rankin was the fleet captain—asked me if I wanted to go to Erie, Pennsylvania, and take a look at the tug-barge that was being launched down there," Jeffery continued. "The tug was being built in New Orleans, so it was just the barge. So, anyway, I looked at it, and they asked me if I wanted the job."[819]

Jeffery took command of the second 1,000-footer on the Great Lakes, the *Presque Isle.* Like the *Cort,* the *Presque Isle* was unique, an integrated tug-barge combination patterned after the system then employed on America's western rivers, with powerful towboats pushing their barges. The 980-foot barge hull had been built in Erie by the Erie Marine Division of Litton Industries, while the tug portion had been built at New Orleans by Halter Marine. In 1973, Jeffery flew to New Orleans, took command of the tug, and sailed it up the East Coast into the Gulf of St. Lawrence and up the St. Lawrence Seaway to Erie.[820] He then conducted sea trials with the integrated tug-barge on Lake Erie and captained the *Presque Isle* on her first voyage to Lake Superior in December 1973.[821]

Jeffery's former command, the 400-foot *Clifford F. Hood,* exemplified what happened with the advent of the 1,000-footers. Built in 1902, the *Hood* was laid up for all of the 1972 and 1973 seasons and was towed overseas for scrapping the next year.[822] The *Hood's* fate was one shared by an increasing number of Great Lakes vessels during the 1970s.[823]

The introduction of the 1,000-footers was a boon to the scrap yards of the Twin Ports and to the Great Lakes in general. The Hyman-Michaels dock was particularly busy during the decade. A fixture on Duluth's downtown waterfront since the 1880s, Duluth Iron and Metal was the descendant of a partnership formed by Max Zalk and Hyman Y. Josephs when they began scrapping old lumber mill machinery on Third Avenue West. From the 1930s to the 1960s, Zalk-Josephs scrapped more than a thousand of the Duluth, Missabe, & Iron Range Railway's obsolete steam locomotives, generating more than 100,000 tons of scrap a year, much of which was carried downbound to the blast furnaces of the lower lakes by the *Clifford F. Hood* and other crane ships.[824] In 1962, Zalk-Josephs sold the business to Chicago-based Hyman-Michaels Company, and the next year the new owners sold the existing scrap yard for development as the Duluth Arena-Auditorium site and relocated Duluth Iron and Metal to the former Northwestern Hanna Coal Dock No. 4 site on Rice's Point. During the 1970s, Hyman-Michaels scrapped an average of more than one vessel per year in its Duluth yards.[825]

NEW CARGOES

For the Twin Ports, the most visible change wrought by the domination of the Great Lakes bulk trade by the 1,000-footers was a rapid decline in the number of vessel transits. The average number of arrivals per year dropped from nearly 5,500 in the 1940s to 4,000 in the 1950s and 2,500 in the 1960s. By the 1970s, the average annual number of vessel transits had declined further to 2,250.[826] But the real impact of the 1,000-footers could be better understood by looking at the statistics for 1973 and 1979, the two best years for tonnage during the decade. In 1973, the Twin Ports handled 48.15 million tons of cargo, with taconite pellets and iron ore accounting for nearly 33.5 million tons of the total. The record cargo year for the decade required 2,600 ship calls.[827] Six years later, in 1979, the Twin Ports handled 47.73 million tons of cargo with 2,164 arrivals.[828] The difference in the number of arrivals was made by the 1,000-footers. In 1973, only the *Stewart J. Cort* was a regular caller at the head of the lakes. By 1979, the *Cort, Presque Isle, James R. Barker, Mesabi Miner, George A. Stinson,* and *Edwin H. Gott* were routinely visiting the ore docks of the Twin Ports.[829]

Cargoes and trade patterns were also changing. The grain trade continued to be dominated by spring wheat, but other grain cargoes were showing surprising strength during the decade. Durum wheat, used mostly for semolina or pasta products, became a staple of Duluth-Superior elevators during the decade. Sunflower seeds first started flowing through the ports in the mid-1960s and reached a peak of more than 1 million tons per year during the early 1980s.[830]

For the grain industry at the head of the lakes, the 1970s were a golden era. Grain shipments through Twin Ports elevators averaged 6.2 million tons per year, well above the 4.5 million tons averaged during the 1960s. In 1973 and again in 1978, Twin Ports elevators handled more than 8.5 million tons of grain, an annual throughput unimaginable even fifteen years

before.[831] At the end of the decade, port officials were eagerly anticipating the first 10-million-ton grain year at the head of the lakes.

Iron ore more than held its own during the 1970s, averaging 28.1 million tons per year, down only slightly from the 30.6 million tons averaged during the 1960s. As the decade progressed, a greater and greater proportion of the iron ore handled on the Duluth-Superior docks was taconite, the outcome both of the decline of natural ore shipments and the construction and expansion of taconite mines and mills on the Mesabi Range. Two new taconite properties started up during the 1970s. Bethlehem Steel Corporation's Hibbing Taconite project went into commercial production in 1976. By decade's end, it was producing 6.25 million tons of pellets per year.[832] In 1977, Inland Steel started its Inland Steel Mining Company project. By 1979, it was producing more than 2.2 million tons of pellets.[833] Existing facilities also underwent significant expansion during the decade. USX, the renamed U.S. Steel Corporation, more than doubled

The Superior Midwest Energy Terminal, then called Ortran or "Orba" after one of the financiers, opened in 1976 to handle western coal shipped through the Twin Ports. In the background are the Interstate Railroad Bridge, the Blatnik High Bridge, and Elevator Row.

the capacity of its Minntac facility near Mountain Iron to 16.5 million tons capacity by 1979, and Eveleth Taconite Company increased its capacity from 2 million tons to more than 5 million tons by decade's end.[834] Total taconite production from Minnesota increased from 35.3 million tons in 1970 to nearly 54.4 million tons in 1979.[835] About 60 percent of that tonnage flowed across the ore docks at the Twin Ports.

Even coal appeared to be on the rebound. In the early 1970s, upbound coal shipments through the Twin Ports continued to decline. The 1.2 million tons handled in 1971 was the worst performance in eighty years. It got worse. In 1972, coal tonnage slipped below 1 million tons, something it hadn't done since 1885.[836] In May 1972, a *Duluth News-Tribune* article about the disappearing coal tonnage was headlined "Docks Doomed."[837] But national environmental policies would soon make Duluth-Superior a coal port once again.

Passage of the national Clean Air Act in 1970 forced electric utilities to seek new sources of low-sulfur coal. In the late 1960s, huge new mines had been brought on line in Montana's Powder River Valley, and the Burlington Northern Santa Fe Railroad began hauling low-sulfur coal in 110-car "unit trains" to utilities in Minnesota and Wisconsin. Burlington Northern Santa Fe resulted from a merger of the Great Northern and the Chicago, Burlington, & Quincy Railroads.

In 1973, Burlington Northern Santa Fe Railroad, the C. Reiss Coal Company, Orba Corporation of New Jersey, and Detroit Edison announced plans for the construction of a $25 million coal-handling facility to be built on 225 acres of land on the Superior side of St. Louis Bay. Under the terms of the agreement, the proposed facility—called Ortran—would be a joint-venture project in which Burlington Northern Santa Fe Railroad would haul the coal to Superior, C. Reiss and Orba would operate the facility, and Detroit Edison would contract for the lion's share of the coal. Detroit Edison contracted with the Boland and Cornelius Company of Buffalo to

ship the coal to power plants on the St. Clair River. With a twenty-five-year coal contract from Detroit Edison, Boland and Cornelius immediately developed plans for two large self-unloading vessels to be built by the Bay Shipbuilding Corporation in Sturgeon Bay, Wisconsin.[838] The Ortran facility began moving coal down the Great Lakes in 1976, and tonnages of one of the Twin Ports' oldest cargoes immediately began to rise from their early 1970s lows, albeit downbound instead of the more traditional upbound flow.[839]

By the time that coal started flowing eastward from Ortran in 1976, the Burlington Northern Santa Fe Railroad was also nearing completion of its $40 million taconite loading facility just east of its existing ore docks on Superior's Allouez Bay. Another longtime Twin Ports tenant also was in the midst of a $33 million expansion of its grain terminal facilities. In the summer of 1973, Cargill, Inc., announced plans to invest in a major upgrading of its Duluth grain handling facilities on Elevator Row. The company signed a letter of intent to operate a new $4.2 million meal-handling facility on the Duluth waterfront and to build a state-of-the-art grain terminal elevator adjacent to its Elevator B.[840] The project, which was partially financed by port authority revenue bonds and an Economic Development Administration grant received a major boost in 1975 when Cargill announced the investment of an additional $5 million to increase storage capacity at the new elevator to 7.2 million bushels, about 50 percent more capacity than had been initially planned.[841]

The Twin Ports also saw a spate of industrial development during the decade of the 1970s. St. Paul's American Hoist and Derrick Company built a 154,000-square-foot manufacturing facility on part of thirty-seven acres of Clure Public Marine Terminal property it leased from the Seaway Port Authority of Duluth in 1975. The facility employed more than 300 people.[842] At the same time, Cargill's North Star Steel announced the construction of a $5 million plant in Duluth to produce grinding balls for the taconite industry on the Mesabi Iron Range.[843]

U.S. Steel Corporation's Philip R. Clarke *proceeds through heavy ice on Lake Superior during the Great Lakes Winter Demonstration Program in 1976.*

NEW CHALLENGES

Even with the resurgence of the coal trade and the capital investment in the Twin Ports, Duluth and Superior still faced several thorny challenges during the 1970s. One that emerged at the beginning of the decade was the growing containerization of world maritime commerce. Before he left to direct the St. Lawrence Seaway Development Corporation in 1969, Duluth port director David Oberlin had moved aggressively to hire a managing agent for the Clure Public Marine Terminal. In April 1969, Duluth port commissioners selected Ceres, Inc., for the job. Ceres, hired on a one-year contract, had operated in the port since the opening of the St. Lawrence Seaway in 1959.[844]

Oberlin's departure for the St. Lawrence Seaway Development Corporation launched a nationwide search for a new Duluth port director. Late in 1969, commissioners announced the

appointment of C. Thomas Burke, who was then the assistant to the director of port commerce for the Port of New York Authority. The thirty-six-year-old Burke, a native of Albany, New York, brought a wealth of experience to the Seaway Port Authority of Duluth.[845] He was a graduate of Albany Business College and Northeastern University's Institute of Transportation, and had a degree from Chicago's Blackstone School of Law. He had worked as sales director and freight agent for East Coast shipping companies and railroads. Commissioners explained that they hired Burke because of his "direct involvement in three basic modes of cargo transportation: ships, motor carriers and rail."[846]

Burke's charge as the new port director was to develop container services for the Twin Ports. A Texas trucking executive, Malcolm McLean, had revolutionized world shipping in the 1950s and

1960s with the introduction of containerization. McLean reasoned that standard-sized containers, suitable for haulage by over-the-road trucks or by flatbed railcars, could be stacked on decks of oceangoing ships. In 1956, he began experimenting with reinforced trailer-truck bodies, lifting the van or container off the truck and on to the ship. When the container reached its destination, another crane lifted it off the deck and placed it on a truck or railcar. In the traditional method of unloading ships, gangs of longshoremen unloaded the cargo from the ships' holds and repackaged it for distribution to terminals inland. It was a laborious and expensive process riddled with theft, pilferage, and damage, and it hadn't improved in centuries. By the early 1960s, McLean's Sea-Land

Ports' most successful business executives. A native of the Iron Range, Paulucci had started Chun King Foods Corporation in Duluth after World War II, providing the nation the only-in-America irony of a poor Italian kid from Hibbing, Minnesota, making his fortune in prepared Chinese food. He sold the company to R. J. Reynolds in 1966 for $63 million.[848]

Paulucci was always a visionary, and even though he has homes in both Duluth and central Florida, his heart—and ideas—were never far from the Twin Ports and the Mesabi Range. In 1963 and 1964, he was a tireless promoter for the Taconite Amendment, which laid the groundwork for the creation of the modern taconite industry.

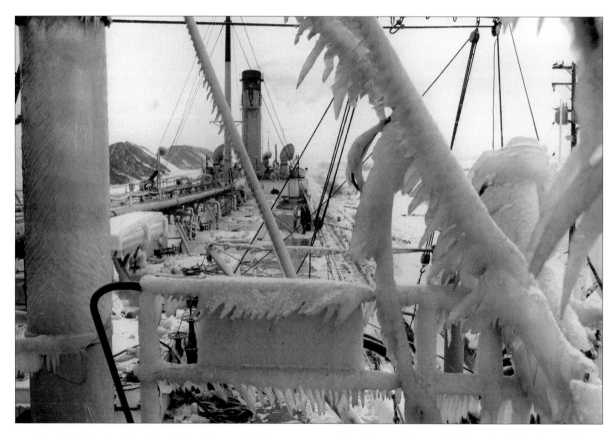

Operating during the Great Lakes Winter Demonstration Program meant coping with tons of ice, as this lake tanker discharging calcium chloride at Hallett Dock No. 7 in the 1970s illustrates.

Company had proved that intermodal container transportation worked. "McLean, the father of containerization, changed forever the way non-bulk cargo moves . . . throughout the world," Davis Helberg of the port authority noted in 1992.[847]

An early proponent of containerization was Jeno Paulucci, who was already one of the Twin

In the 1960s, he proposed building the "missing link" canal, which would connect the Twin Ports with the Mississippi River system via the St. Croix River.[849] Paulucci was also quick to grasp McLean's concept of containerization. In 1959, he persuaded a lake carrier to start a container service between Duluth-Superior, Cleveland, and Buffalo to move Chun King canned goods in

The stern section of Interlake Steamship Company's Charles M. Beeghly *is cut in half as part of a lengthening project at Fraser Shipyards in Superior in the 1970s. Fraser was one of the busiest places in the Twin Ports during the late 1970s and early 1980s as fleets made a major capital investment in lengthening and modernization projects.*

After an uneventful navigation season opening in early April 1972, a nearly month-long siege of easterly winds piled layers of ice into the funnel-shaped western tip of Lake Superior. The ice was so thick that it clogged the cooling-water intake systems for lakers and ocean-going ships as they struggled to reach the ice-free inner harbor. Navigation did not return to normal until nearly mid-June. Here, several vessels slog through ice on the western end of the Lake in mid-May.

containers. Browning Line, a Detroit carrier, committed to the service under the name Detroit Atlantic Lines.[849] The service, carried on by the steamers *W. Wayne Hancock* and *John C. Hay,* operated for only part of the season and disappeared because it was never able to generate enough back-haul freight to the Twin Ports.[851]

In 1974, Burke and the commissioners parlayed a city bond issue and a U.S. Economic Development Agency grant into $2.5 million to create the first full-service container facility in the Great Lakes. The facility, located near the northeast corner of the Clure Public Marine Terminal site, contained eight acres for storage of containers and a Paceco Economy Portainer Crane with a capacity of 30 long tons.[852] The new container facility went into commercial operation during the summer of 1975, but it never fulfilled the potential that Burke and the Duluth port authority had envisioned. To try to jump-start the business, Burke negotiated an agreement with Federal Commerce and

Navigation Company, a big Montreal-based shipowner, whereby FedNav, as it was called, would schedule three ships for container service to Duluth in return for a port authority guarantee of $20,000 in freight revenue per ship. The bold move failed, however, as shippers didn't materialize despite heavy port authority promotion, and the authority absorbed losses on all three ships. In the final analysis, containerization in the Great Lakes was a chimera that was always tantalizingly close but never quite a reality.

The nine-month shipping season on the St. Lawrence Seaway negated the great advantage that containerization gave year-round tidewater shippers and carriers: the "just-in-time" delivery that customers demanded. Moreover, the seaway's limited lock width (ships were limited to a 75-foot beam) and 27-foot depth were not adequate for newer container ships.

In 1975, the feasibility of navigation year-round on the Great Lakes became both an alluring

The new Cargill complex, nearing completion in June 1976, combined a new, high-speed loading facility, B–1 (at right), with a rebuilt old facility, once owned by the Norris Grain Company and renamed B–2 (at left). The facility also featured a flat storage building at center and a loop railway system.

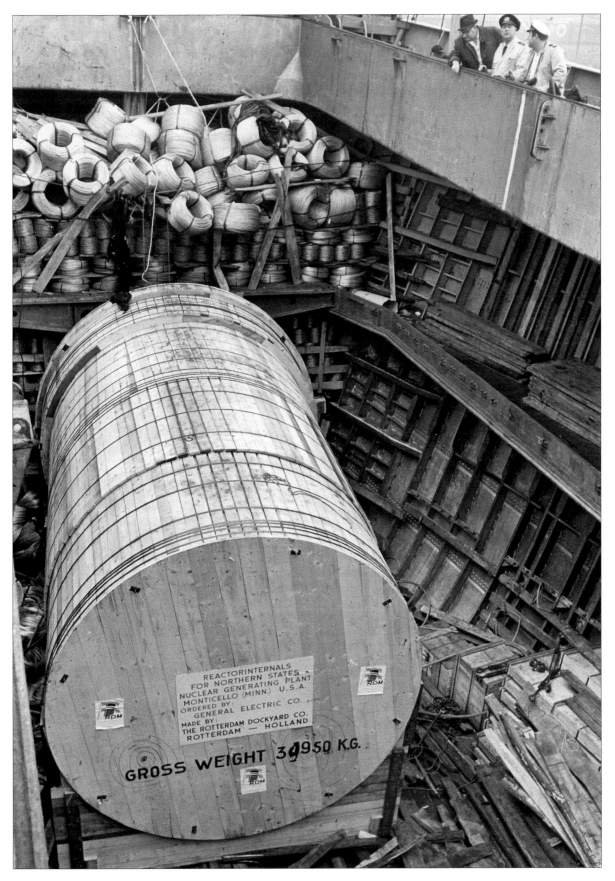

Novel cargoes, such as this huge reactor unit for Northern States Power Company's nuclear generation plant at Monticello, Minnesota, began to arrive with more frequency in the 1970s as regional importers recognized the advantages of St. Lawrence Seaway shipping. At upper right, Theodore Svensson, Duluth customs broker and founder of Svensson Shipping Agency, monitors the unloading of the reactor vessel with two uniformed officers aboard a Hamburg–Chicago Lines ship.

prospect and a difficult challenge. For much of the 1970s, the U.S. Army Corps of Engineers, several other federal agencies, and the U.S. Steel Great Lakes Fleet conducted winter navigation studies to test the potential of operating commercial shipping twelve months on the lakes.

Port director C. Thomas Burke was a strong champion of the winter navigation project. In 1975, he predicted that a twelve-month domestic shipping season would become commonplace by 1980, and that saltwater vessels would operate on the system more than ten months each year. "The combined effect of a mild winter and increased technology have proven this year that a year-round domestic shipping season on the Great Lakes is feasible," he said.[853]

Others in the maritime community weren't convinced that a twelve-month season was either feasible or desirable. Bill Buhrmann arrived in Duluth from Pittsburgh in March 1973 as the potential replacement for the manager of U.S. Steel's Great Lakes Fleet. The fleet had moved its headquarters to Duluth two years before, partly to compensate the city for its loss of the aging U.S. Steel plant in Morgan Park. Buhrmann, who eventually became general manager of the fleet, spearheaded U.S. Steel's participation in the winter navigation experiment for the next six seasons.

"The pier was just full of activity because the corps and the industry were involved in winter navigation and trying to extend the navigation season," Buhrmann explained. "This was because we were now carrying taconite pellets, which didn't know June from January. The whole era lasted about five or six years. It actually started in 1972 or 1973, but it lasted up to about 1980."[854] U.S. Steel and the Great Lakes Fleet in general learned a great deal during the Winter Demonstration Program, especially concerning insulation of the vessels and hull-strengthening for ice operations.[855] Perhaps the greatest lesson was that there are winters on the Great Lakes when it is impossible to operate. The winters of 1977 and 1978 were the worst in North America in nearly a half-century. Rivers froze as far south as Tennessee and Louisiana, and fuel oil and natural gas supplies were near critical shortage lev-

els much of each winter. U.S. Steel didn't run at all in the winter of 1977 or 1978.[856]

Another unexpected obstacle to winter navigation was the opposition of environmentalists. For most of its history, the Great Lakes maritime community had gone about its business of hauling bulk cargo with remarkably little interference from advocacy groups. But the growing strength of the environmental movement in the 1970s found an easy target in the big freighters that hauled iron ore, coal, and grain from the heartland of North America to the lower lakes and the world.

Midway through the winter navigation experiment, the maritime community was reminded of the awesome power of fall storms on Lake Superior. On November 10, 1975, the *Edmund Fitzgerald* of the Columbia Transportation Company fleet disappeared off radar screens during a ferocious blizzard. The 729-foot *Fitzgerald* had loaded 29,000 tons of taconite pellets at Burlington Northern Santa Fe's Allouez docks in Superior on November 9 and set out on her appointment with destiny. The *Fitz* was within an hour of shelter inside Whitefish Bay on the evening of November 10 when she disappeared. Her crew of twenty-nine men was lost, a sober reminder that even in the fall, Lake Superior could give no quarter to the vessels plying her waters.[857]

One final challenge faced by the Twin Ports during the 1970s was the longtime dream of uniting the two ports under a single port authority. In the mid-1970s, Minnesota and Wisconsin appointed a ten-member Interstate Port Authority Commission to "develop a plan for the merger of the port authorities at Duluth, Minnesota, and Superior, Wisconsin."[858] After two years of meetings, the commission issued its report in late 1976. The report found that the issue was hung up on the matter of finances. Duluth had a port authority with more than $10 million in assets on its balance sheet. Superior had a harbor commission that had virtually no assets.[859] Commissioners concluded that "resolving the financial issue at this time would be unworkable."[860] The "complex and controversial financing issue" would torpedo the last and best chance of achieving formal unification of the Twin Ports in the twentieth century.[861]

Unrelated to the Interstate Port Authority Commission's report except for timing, late 1976 was also to bring major changes at the port authority. In short order, the board of commissioners decided not to retain Burke's services and, after major disagreements with Ceres, Inc., the authority was in search of a new terminal operator. The terminal management contract for 1977 was awarded to North Central Terminal Operators, a local firm organized primarily by Captain A. F. "Tony" Rico and Captain Jack P. Lyons, president and vice president respectively of Upper Great Lakes Pilots.[862] Burke was replaced as Duluth port director by Paul D. Pella, the former deputy director of the Chicago Regional Port District. Pella, a graduate of the U.S. Merchant Marine Academy at Kings Point, New York, brought a wealth of maritime experience to his new job, including management and sales of companies involved in Mississippi River transportation.[863]

As the 1970s drew to a close, the Twin Ports could look back on the decade as one of achievement and prosperity. Duluth-Superior had weathered the difficult transition to taconite shipping and the introduction of the 1,000-footers, and the opening of the renamed Midwest Energy facility in Superior held the promise of a resurgence of coal shipments in the years ahead. The grain trade, bolstered by Russian purchases during a post-1976 thaw in the cold war, had the maritime community dreaming of a 10-million-ton year in grain. The disappointments during the decade—the failure to capture a meaningful share of the nation's container business, the collapse of the Interstate Port Authority framework, and the conclusion that winter navigation would not become commonplace—were at least good faith efforts to address some of the problems that had plagued the Great Lakes and Duluth-Superior since the century previous.

If any lesson could be learned from the maritime operations of the Twin Ports over the course of a century, it might be that periods of prosperity and innovation were invariably followed by periods of depression and decline.

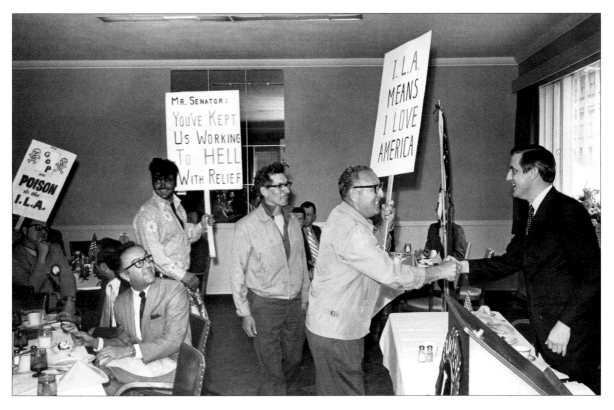

E. L. "Buster" Slaughter (second from right), international vice president of the International Longshoremen's Association, welcomes Senator Walter "Fritz" Mondale (right) to Duluth in 1971 with a carefully staged rally for ILA Local 1366.

THE WRECK OF THE
EDMUND FITZGERALD

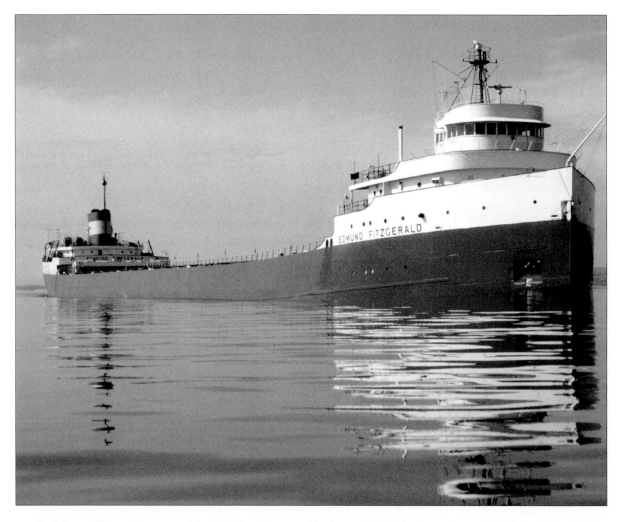

The Edmund Fitzgerald *was named for the CEO of her owner, Northwestern Mutual Insurance Company, Milwaukee, and operated as part of the Oglebay Norton fleet.*

THE FACT THAT THE COLUMBIA Transportation Company's *Edmund Fitzgerald* went down with all twenty-nine hands in a Lake Superior storm on November 10, 1975, was not remarkable, at least not to the Great Lakes maritime community. Man-killing November storms are a fact of life on the lakes, as similar blows in 1905, 1913, 1940, and 1958 had fatally proved.

What was remarkable was that the *Fitz* became a cultural icon after a Canadian folksinger set the tale of the ship's final voyage to the melody of a haunting sea chanty. Gordon Lightfoot's "The Wreck of the *Edmund Fitzgerald*" was released in the summer of 1977, and by fall had become a hit.[864] Those who had never heard of the *Mataafa, Bannockburn,* or *Carl D. Bradley* could instantly identify the *Edmund Fitzgerald.* Lightfoot's lyrics about "ice-water mansions" and "the big Lake they called Gitchigumi" captured the imagination of Americans of all ages.

The story Lightfoot's song told was, like most disasters on the lakes, one of mystery. The *Fitz* had been one of the 730-footers, launched by Great Lakes Engineering Works at River Rouge, Michigan, in 1958.[865] For seventeen years, she had operated in the same relative obscurity of other Great Lakes vessels, hauling iron ore and taconite pellets from the head of the lakes to the blast furnaces in Cleveland and Pittsburgh.

On November 9, 1975, the *Fitz* loaded 26,116 tons of taconite from National Steel Pellet Company at Burlington Northern Santa Fe's Allouez docks in Superior. The vessel departed for Detroit just after 2:00 p.m.[866] Since heavy weather was forecast, Captain Ernest McSorley, a forty-four-year veteran of the Great Lakes, steered northeast to hug the lee shore of Lake Superior. Off Two Harbors, McSorley contacted Captain Jesse Cooper of the nearby *Arthur M. Anderson,* and they agreed to run northeast and then southeast toward Whitefish Bay on the lake's eastern end. Cooper told McSorley he would trail the *Fitz* by ten or twenty miles. By 7:00 p.m., the National Weather Service had issued gale warnings that were upgraded to storm warnings early the next day.

The *Anderson* and the *Fitz* spent the morning running through heavy rain, sixty-mile-per-hour winds, and waves of ten to twenty feet.[867] By afternoon the vessels passed Michipicoten Island and Six-Fathom Shoals, and although the winds maintained a steady speed of fifty miles

per hour, the ships made headway. McSorley radioed Cooper in midafternoon that the *Fitz* was damaged and listing slightly, but he didn't think it was anything the pumps couldn't handle. As snow intensified in the late afternoon, McSorley radioed Cooper to report that his radar was out and to ask the *Anderson* to guide the *Fitz* into the more sheltered Whitefish Bay. At about the same time, the Swedish vessel *Avafors* reported that the light and radio beacon on Whitefish Point were out.[868]

By that time, the *Fitz* was evidently wallowing in thirty-foot waves. At 7:10 p.m., McSorley talked with the first mate on the *Anderson,* Morgan Clark, and confirmed that the ship was taking on water, but added, "We are holding our own." Minutes later, the *Edmund Fitzgerald* slipped off the *Anderson's* radar.[869] The U.S. Coast Guard searched for survivors, but found only scattered debris. Five days later, a U.S. Navy aircraft using magnetic anomaly detection equipment located the *Fitz* in 540 feet of water seventeen miles west of Whitefish Point.

After exhaustive hearings by the Coast Guard's Marine Board of Investigation and the National Transportation Safety Board, reports issued in 1977 and 1978 concluded that the *Fitzgerald's* hatch covers were not watertight and had not been dogged down properly.[870] Most of the Great Lakes maritime community scoffed at the findings. One of the more popular theories was that the *Fitz* holed herself on Six-Fathom Shoals and, because of the buffeting she was taking, McSorley didn't know she was fatally breached until too late. Others speculated that the "three sisters," a wicked series of thirty-foot waves, swamped the *Fitz* and drove her down.

Like many mysteries of the Great Lakes, the demise of the *Edmund Fitzgerald* will likely never be fully explained.[87] But thanks to Gordon Lightfoot, several generations of Americans won't forget that "the iron boats go as the mariners all know, with the gales of November remembered."[872]

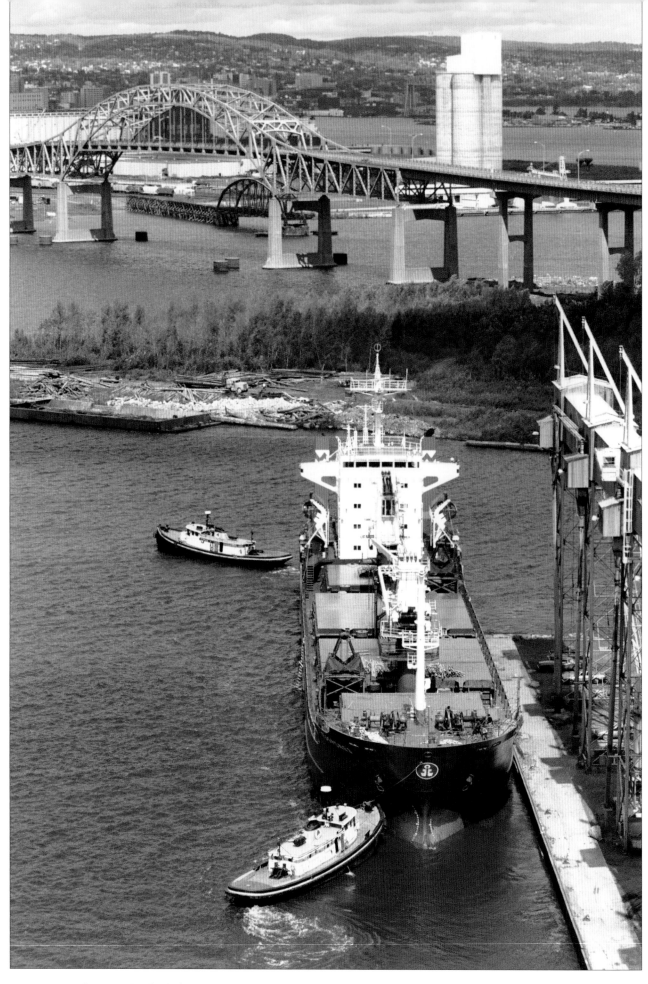

An oceangoing ship backs away from the CHS Elevator No. 1 gallery in the early 1980s. The tugs were owned by North American Towing Company, which tried, unsuccessfully, to compete with the Great Lakes Towing Company.

CHAPTER EIGHTEEN

Retrenchment and Rebirth

DURING THE TAIL END of the 1970s and the early 1980s, the Duluth-Superior port suffered a triple whammy that affected its two principal cargoes for much of the ensuing decade. In some ways, the economic conditions at the head of the lakes during the early to mid-1980s were more difficult to deal with than the Great Depression. At least during the depression, everybody was pretty much in the same boat. Much of the American economy was on a decided upswing during the 1980s, which made the hard times in the Twin Ports all the more problematic. The blows to the local maritime economy came in rapid succession, not unlike the "three sisters," the giant waves of legend that mariners on Lake Superior swear are ship-killers.

The first jolt came in the summer of 1979, when grain millers representing the eight major grain terminal elevators walked off the job.[873] The bitter strike would last for nearly three months and disrupt shipments from one of the largest grain ports in North America. The second setback occurred just five months after the first. In late December 1979, the Soviet Union invaded Afghanistan. Two weeks later, President Jimmy Carter announced a grain embargo against the Soviets, a policy decision that immediately pulled the rug out from under the Twin Ports' growing Russian grain trade.[874] Unnoticed that fall, the opening act in what would become the third harsh blow for the Twin Ports occurred in a Pittsburgh boardroom. In November 1979, U.S. Steel Corporation announced it was shuttering ten obsolete steel mills and processing facilities and laying off more than 13,000 workers.[875] During the next five years, the domestic integrated steel industry would shed millions of tons of obsolete capacity and permanently furlough several hundred thousand employees. The restructuring of the American steel industry and the resulting falloff in taconite tonnage would send shivers through the Twin Ports.

To be fair, 1979 and 1980 weren't the best of years in recent American history. The Carter administration struggled with energy crises, a nuclear accident at Three Mile Island, double-digit inflation, and sky-high interest rates approaching 20 percent.[876] Just before Thanksgiving of 1979, a mob of Iranian students stormed the U.S. Embassy in Teheran and took almost the entire staff hostage.[877] The capstone to a very bad year would come in April 1980, when a rescue mission to free the hostages failed miserably.[878]

America rather quickly recovered from the *anno horribilis* that was 1979–1980, but the effects of the grain strike, the Russian grain embargo, and the restructuring of the nation's steel industry lingered in Duluth-Superior for nearly a decade. The Defense Department's decision to close Duluth's U.S. Air Force base in mid-decade and Jeno Paulucci's announcement less than a year later that he was shifting much of his food manufacturing capacity from Duluth to southeastern Ohio further darkened the communities' economic outlook.

THE STRIKE

As it turned out, the red glow bathing the harbor on the evening of January 21, 1978, was an ominous portent of the travails that lay ahead for the Twin Ports grain business. A spectacular four-alarm fire consumed the Capitol 4 Elevator of the International Multifoods Corporation that cold winter night, burning the ninety-year-old wooden elevator to the ground, destroying more than 200,000 bushels of grain, and gutting the steamer *Harry L. Allen* in her winter berth alongside the elevator. The last wooden elevator at the head of the lakes, Cap 4 burned fiercely for more than six hours. Residents of Ashland, Wisconsin, ninety miles to the east, could see the orange glow in the distance, and utility poles a quarter-mile away caught fire from the intense heat. Waterfront watchers were grateful that virtually no wind fanned the flames that evening. Otherwise, the inferno could have jumped to nearby Cap 6.[879]

The loss of Cap 4 to the fire was fairly insignificant from a grain industry perspective. International Multifoods would likely have written it off for insurance purposes in the not-too-distant future. And Cap 4 would have played only a minor role during the 1978 season, a year in which the Twin Ports registered an all-time record of more than 8.8 million metric tons of grain moved through the elevators in Duluth and Superior.[880]

After his appointment in 1979 as the Seaway Port Authority of Duluth's fifth director, Davis Helberg (left) was often called to Washington, D.C., and to Ottawa, Ontario, to testify before Congress and Parliament regarding the Great Lakes maritime community. Here he huddles with Lewis Gulick, Washington-based representative of American Great Lakes Ports.

Seen in hindsight, the fire at Cap 4 could be construed as the Götterdämmerung of the ports' grain business. Duluth-Superior would register another record grain shipment two years later, when nearly 9.57 million tons of grain flowed through the elevators at the head of the lakes, but after 1980, the tonnages began a precipitous decline that saw shipments drop to

The glow from the blaze that destroyed Capitol Elevator No. 4 on the night of January 21, 1978, was seen from as far as ninety miles away.

one-third of the 1980 levels five years later.[881] Never again would Duluth-Superior approach 10 million tons of grain in a single season.

The 1979 grain millers strike that began two days after July 4 against two of the eight elevators in the Twin Ports had shut down all of the elevators by July 25. "Ripple effects spread almost immediately to all parts of our eight-state trade area," reported Davis Helberg, the newly appointed executive director of the

vessels alongside the docks and anchored out in the lake. The effect of the strike was compounded when Secretary of Agriculture Bob Bergland embargoed all Public Law 480 "Food for Peace" cargo into the Twin Ports. Bergland, a wheat farmer from northwestern Minnesota who had served as Minnesota's Seventh District DFL congressman before being named by President Carter to the agriculture post, made his decision based on incomplete information. Still, Helberg and a delegation of other Duluth-Superior

The grain millers' strike in the fall of 1979 was followed by the Carter administration's embargo of grain shipments to the Soviet Union in the aftermath of the Soviet invasion of Afghanistan. It took nearly a decade for the grain elevators of the Twin Ports to recover from the double blow.

Seaway Port Authority of Duluth, in his second column in *Minnesota's World Port*. "As the strike wore on, our telephone switchboard looked like Broadway at night as the initial concern of our hinterland agribusiness turned to absolute alarm."[882]

The strike, called by Local 118 of the American Federation of Grain Millers, dragged on for twelve long weeks, idling dozens of saltwater

maritime leaders had to travel to Washington, D.C., to convince the U.S. Department of Agriculture that the only workers on strike were those employed by area grain elevators.[883]

Most residents of the Twin Ports understood neither who was striking nor what the strike was about. "A lot of people to this day blame it on the longshoremen," explained Ceres's Chuck Ilenda, a longtime Duluth stevedore. "They say it was the longshoremen that caused it. It had absolutely nothing at all to do with them, so they got a black eye through no doing of their own."[884]

The black eye was the least of the longshoremen's concerns. The 1979 work stoppage was the fourth time since 1964 that the grain elevator employees had gone on strike, and each had hit the longshoremen squarely in their pocketbooks. Most of them earned their living by working in the nine-men gangs that loaded the grain ships, and many "rode the bench" in the hiring halls of the International Longshoremen's Association Local 1366 (Duluth) and Local 1037 (Superior) during the three-month strike. Those with seniority cut their losses by plugging in for jobs handling general cargo with North Central Terminal Operators or with Great Lakes Storage and Contracting Company.[885]

The 1960s and 1970s had been good years for labor in the port. "Oh, yeah, everything was hopping," recalled Russ Wedin, a Duluth native who went to work as a longshoreman in 1960 after graduating from high school. "I raised two children and sent them to college on waterfront business."[886] At the time, it was a relatively simple matter for Twin Ports longshoremen to log the 800 hours in a year necessary to qualify for the union's health, welfare, and pension plan.[887]

The port authority's new managing agent at the Clure Public Marine Terminal was North Central Terminal Operators. NCTO was organized by Captain A. F. "Tony" Rico, a legend in the Twin Ports and Great Lakes maritime communities. Rico had grown up in Duluth's Italian neighborhood on Raleigh Street and gone off to the merchant marine during World War II. Following the war, he worked his way up to first mate in the Midland Steamship Company fleet. When Midland ceased operations in 1958, Rico came ashore as a stevedoring superintendent in the Twin Ports.[888]

On May 8, 1959, Rico was asked to pilot one of the first saltwater vessels to transit the new St. Lawrence Seaway into a grain berth in the Duluth-Superior harbor. Davis Helberg, who was working for Alastair Guthrie at the time, met

Rico when he berthed the *Valiant Nikki* at Cargill's Itasca Elevator in Superior. "Tony remembered from his merchant marine days on the East Coast during World War II that pilots always had a hat and carried a briefcase," Helberg said, "so he wore a hat and took an empty briefcase, rode a small boat with an outboard motor into the lake, climbed aboard the ship, and that is where I first met him in the wee hours of that morning."[889]

The one-time request for his piloting skills opened Rico's eyes to a potential business opportunity. In short order, he and three other master mariners organized the Twin Ports Harbor Pilots Association. By summer, the reorganized Lake Superior Pilots Association had eight pilots on the payroll.[890] In 1960, Rico's testimony before a U.S. Senate committee helped create pilotage rules for the Great Lakes. By 1969, Rico's expanded and renamed Upper Great Lakes Pilots employed about forty pilots and controlled pilotage on Lakes Superior, Huron, and Michigan and on the St. Mary's River.[891]

Rico, fellow pilot Jack P. Lyons, and Minneapolis attorney Jack Chestnut laid the groundwork for North Central Terminal Operators, and made a successful bid for the Clure Public Marine Terminal contract in early 1977. Rico also tapped Davis Helberg to be the new head of NCTO. Helberg, who had served as the Duluth port's public relations director under David Oberlin, had left the port in 1972 to work for Rico at Upper Great Lakes Pilots. Helberg would operate NCTO until 1979, when the Duluth Port Authority hired him to replace Paul Pella as port director.[892]

For Duluth-Superior port labor, the 1979 grain millers strike was a turning point. For much of the 1980s, longshoremen in particular would find it difficult to amass the 800 hours a year needed to qualify for benefits from the International Longshoremen's Association. Many of the younger longshoremen abandoned waterfront work altogether, and an increasing number of Twin Ports young people left the region for economic opportunity elsewhere.

THE EMBARGO

The 1979 navigation season opened with high hopes for increased grain shipments. The grain millers strike cast a pall over what had been hoped would be an excellent year, and the Russian grain embargo instituted by the Carter administration in January, just weeks after the close of the 1979 season, began a downward spiral for the grain business at the head of the lakes that would persist into the 1990s.

Grain shipments from Duluth-Superior had shot upward in 1973, the first full year of the grain pact between the United States and the Soviet Union.[893] The pact had been negotiated in back rooms in Washington, D.C., Moscow, and Europe, and when it was announced in the summer of 1972, the size of the deal was staggering. The Soviets were in the market for 20 million tons of grain for fiscal year 1973 alone, and the U.S. Department of Agriculture estimated that the Soviet Union would purchase $1 billion worth of grain from U.S. private dealers.[894] During the next five years, American grain exports would increase 50 percent, much of that increase designated for the Soviet Union.[895]

The first Russian ships began showing up in the Twin Ports in the spring of 1973. Duluth-Superior was an ideal destination for the Soviet merchant fleet because many of the ships were destined for the Black Sea, where draft and size restrictions were similar to the Great Lakes–St. Lawrence Seaway system. For the remainder of the 1970s, the Russians were frequent visitors to the Twin Ports.

"Rotterdam was a big receiver port, so was Hamburg, and then of course came the big Russian sale," said Sven Hubner, a Danish ship-master who had settled in Duluth in 1963 to join Alastair Guthrie in his vessel agency. "That, of course, was a tremendous boost."[896]

According to Hubner, who would later purchase the Guthrie agency from his mentor, much of the Russian grain in the mid-1970s went to the Black Sea ports or to Latvia, Lithuania, or Estonia. "It was going to not only the Soviet

Duluth mayor Ben Boo greets Captain Vladimir Gomonenko, who brought the Zakarpatye *to Duluth–Superior in April 1973 to load grain for the Soviet Union. The* Zakarpatye's *arrival marked the beginning of a flood of Soviet ships to arrive at the Twin Ports during the mid– and late 1970s to load grain for Soviet Baltic and Black Sea ports as part of the 1972 U.S. wheat sale to the Soviet Union.*

Union, but it was also going to north Europe and then being transshipped," Hubner said. "It was going into the Baltic, different places in the Baltic Sea."[897]

Chuck Hilleren had just finished a tour of duty at the Duluth Air Force Base in 1972. The Benson, Minnesota, native was downtown late one afternoon when he struck up a conversation with Sven Hubner and Bob Baker from the Guthrie-Hubner Agency. They told Hilleren that if he needed a job, he should come by the firm's office the next morning. Hilleren showed up bright and early the following day and began a thirty-year career in the vessel agency business. He couldn't have picked a better time to start.

"That particular year, in 1973, I worked probably sixteen- to eighteen-hour days every day," Hilleren said. "We went from April to December. We had thirteen elevators at that time, and we were running from ship to ship to ship. I would finish up at two o'clock in the morning, come home, get about four hours of sleep, and be back in the office."[898]

And then came the grain embargo. In December 1979, the Soviet Union invaded neighboring Afghanistan to prop up the government of a Marxist ally. More than 40,000 Soviet troops

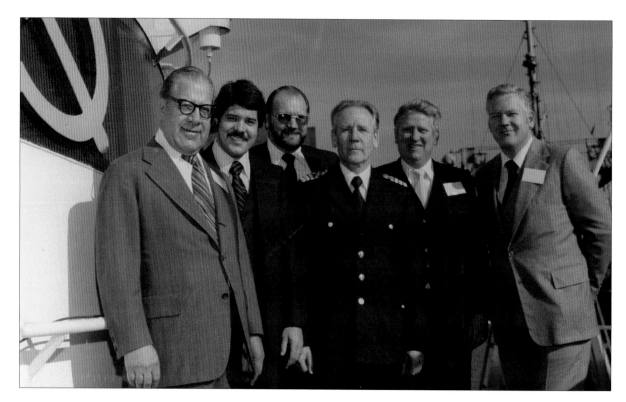

Veteran vessel agent S. A. McLennan (left), whose son Mark (second from left) would succeed him as head of his namesake company, greeted the captain of the Soviet vessel Segeza in 1978. With them are Davis Helberg (third from left), then president of North Central Terminal Operators, Alan T. Johnson (second from right), port authority marketing director, and Sam L. Browman, trade development director and later marketing director when Johnson became port director in Green Bay, Wisconsin.

swarmed into the Afghan highlands during Christmas week.[899] In early January 1980, President Carter announced that the United States would no longer sell grain to the Soviet Union.

Although the embargo immediately sliced about 1 million tons off Duluth-Superior's volume, the true double-impact of the embargo and the strike didn't hit the Twin Ports until a year or so later. The Twin Ports experienced its best grain year ever in 1980, but Duluth and Superior had been fatally wounded by the 1979 strike and the ensuing embargo. One of the ramifications of the strike was an instant surge of new grain barges being built for service on the Mississippi River and new grain hopper cars built for the big railroads. Both had been in short supply during the strike, and shippers would not again take a chance on Duluth-Superior's elevators getting shut down during peak harvest times. Moreover, grain buyers overseas could no longer trust that the United States would honor its commitments, either when it came to the purchase or the delivery of grain. If the United States could place an embargo on the

Soviet Union, why couldn't it do the same to India or France or Turkey?

Grain shipments through the Twin Ports began a sharp decline in 1981, dropping to 7.8 million tons from the 9.56 million tons recorded in 1980. They dropped another million tons in 1982, and by 1984 the 5.63 million tons passing through the ports represented the worst year for grain since 1977. In 1985, grain totals of just over 3 million tons were the worst since 1958, the year before the St. Lawrence Seaway opened.[900] For the remainder of the 1980s, grain shipments averaged 4.2 million tons a year, less than half what they had been at the beginning of the decade and nearly 1.5 million tons less than the decade's average.[901]

Aggravating the grain shift away from the Twin Ports was a major restructuring of railroad routes in the Upper Midwest. The 1978 congressional passage of the Railroad Restructuring and Rehabilitation Act allowed railroads to abandon little-used rail spurs that primarily collected grain from country elevators in the Northern

Plains. Sam Browman joined the Seaway Port Authority of Duluth in 1978 as the port's marketing director. Browman, a soft-spoken Minnesotan, had worked for the railroads for more than twenty years before joining SPAD.[902]

What Browman called the "4-R Act" created a fundamental shift in grain rail transportation patterns. He noted that it gave railroads much greater freedom in abandoning "third level" lines. "And when that happened," he said, "particularly in western Minnesota and North Dakota and South Dakota, there was a wholesale abandonment of branch lines, which forced much greater distances in hauling grain to market by truck. That created large subterminals out in the hinterland for moving grain, and it created a lot of unit-train loading sites. I always felt that that facilitated to a great degree the westward movement of grain, rather than the traditional movement of grain to the Twin Ports."

Sometimes it seemed as though fate was conspiring against Duluth-Superior in the 1980s. Another major transportation shift was to come by the end of the decade, this one political instead of economic. For nearly twenty years, local longshoremen had relied heavily on shipments of bagged agricultural commodities, most of them booked as "Food for Peace" cargo under Public Law 480 of 1954. Administered by the U.S. State Department and operated by the U.S. Department of Agriculture, the program—commonly called P.L. 480—was established to send surplus agricultural products to alleviate hunger and malnutrition in poor nations overseas. By the 1980s, P.L. 480 cargo was the primary source of work for scores of Twin Ports longshoremen who unloaded 50- and 100-pound bags from railcars, transferred them into the warehouses, and loaded them aboard ships.

Nearly all the ocean ships serving the Great Lakes in the early 1980s were foreign-flag because the few remaining American-flag general cargo carriers—assured by law of getting at least 50 percent of the government's monthly P.L. 480 contract awards—forced the cargo though the Gulf ports where the ships were based. But there was plenty of cargo to go

around, and Great Lakes ports usually handled from 250,000 to 400,000 tons per year, with the Twin Ports share averaging 50,000 to 100,000 tons annually.

In 1985, however, U.S. maritime unions began challenging the government's allowance of foreign-flag carriers to handle any and all subsidized agricultural products. Huge volumes of bulk grain had started to move overseas under new programs geared toward stimulating agricultural exports. The U.S. merchant fleet, down to a handful of oceangoing bulk carriers, had neither the bottoms nor the economic ability to compete for the cargoes. Nonetheless, recalled port director Davis Helberg, "The big grain shippers and farm state politicians felt threatened. Out of the blue, they agreed to appease the unions by sacrificing the P.L. 480 program."[903]

The 1985 Farm Bill increased the mandated P.L. 480 percentage of U.S. flag carriage from 50 percent to 75 percent. In return, the unions backed off their demands to force all other subsidized bulk commodities aboard American vessels. It was clear that with only 25 percent of P.L. 480 cargoes nationwide earmarked for foreign carriers, the chance of securing Great Lakes cargoes would be diminished dramatically because overseas shipowners would no longer risk the uncertainties of scheduling service into the lakes.

"Senator Rudy Boschwitz battled valiantly for us," Helberg said, "and, in fact, we held up the entire Farm Bill for several days and finally won a compromise, but it was really only a temporary reprieve. We got a four-year Great Lakes Set-Aside of about 250,000 tons a year, but everyone knew our days in the program were numbered." When the Set-Aside expired after the 1989 season, the Great Lakes were, for all intents and purposes, out of the P.L. 480 business—and hundreds of longshoremen throughout the Great Lakes were out of work.[904]

The confluence of factors—strikes, embargoes, and transportation shifts—conspired to drastically reduce grain shipments from the head of the lakes. "There were two or three years that were very lean, especially going from where it was just absolutely crazy," recalled Chuck Hilleren. "In a normal year, the Port of Duluth–Superior represented 5 percent of the exports in the country in the overall. If there is something that can adversely affect the port like the millers strike or the embargo, it can be quite dramatic too."[905]

It was quite dramatic, but perhaps not as dramatic as the 1980s threat to the Twin Ports' other bread-and-butter commodity: taconite.

RESTRUCTURING AMERICAN STEEL

In the early 1980s, a wag observed that the U.S. steel industry would have been better off if the Japanese had bombed Pittsburgh in 1941 instead of Pearl Harbor. There was more than a little truth to the remark. Most of the steel production capacity of Japan and Germany had been bombed into rubble during World War II. As the nation slipped into a cold war confrontation with the Soviet Union in the postwar years, American policy-makers resolved to build up industrial capacity in Japan and West Germany, which had become U.S. allies in the struggle against communism. The Marshall Plan and other foreign aid programs funneled billions of dollars into rebuilding Japanese and West German heavy industry, including new, greenfield iron and steel capacity.

No similar investment was made in the U.S. integrated steel industry during the postwar period. Most of America's steel mills were old and inefficient. Blast furnaces, coke ovens, and rolling mills mostly dated from the early twentieth century. Some operating facilities in 1980 had been making steel for nearly 100 years. The result was an American steel industry that was no longer able to compete against less expensive imports. Foreign steel had begun coming into the country in 1959, when most of the U.S. steel industry was idled by a steelworkers' strike that stretched on for nearly four months. Steel imports continued to gain market share during the 1960s and 1970s, and by 1980 nearly one-quarter of the steel consumed in the United States was produced in foreign mills.

In 1979, American steel was still at the height of its power. Nearly 60 million tons of taconite

pellets and natural ore went down the lakes that season, leading many observers to conclude that the domestic industry was in as good a shape as it had ever been. For Duluth-Superior, 1979 was confirmation that the Twin Ports was still the logical place to move iron ore down the Great Lakes. More than half the total tonnage carried on the Great Lakes that year—32.16 million tons—originated in the mammoth shiploaders of Duluth and Superior.[906] Only the Thanksgiving Day grounding of the Cleveland-Cliffs Steamship Company's *Frontenac* off Pellet Island near Silver Bay marred what had been an excellent year for the ore trade.[907]

The decline in American steel began in late 1979 when U.S. Steel Corporation announced the first closures of obsolete mills. It picked up steam in 1980 and 1981 as Bethehem, Jones, and Laughlin Steel, Armco, LTV, Youngstown Sheet and Tube, and other giants of the industry followed suit. By late 1981, steel mill employment in the Monongahela Valley up and down river from Pittsburgh—the cradle of the American steel industry for more than a century—was at 35,000, less than half of what it had been in the late 1940s and early 1950s.[908] It would get much worse before the decade was over.

As mills and blast furnaces closed in 1981 and 1982, the industrial din that had been part and parcel of the "Mon" Valley, South Chicago, Gary, Cleveland, and Ohio's Mahoning Valley fell silent. In April 1985, Wheeling-Pittsburgh Steel Company, the nation's seventh largest producer, filed for Chapter 11 protection under U.S. bankruptcy laws.[909] A little over a year later, in July 1986, LTV Steel Corporation followed Wheeling-Pitt into bankruptcy court.[910] U.S. Steel, financially the healthiest of the major integrated steelmakers in the early 1980s, signaled its intention to stay healthy by diversifying out of steel. In the spring of 1982, U.S. Steel spent $6.4 billion to purchase Marathon Oil. Soon after, the Pittsburgh steel giant changed its name to USX Corporation.[911]

As the 1980s approached their midpoint, steel's fortunes continued to sag. In 1970, steel production in American mills accounted for 20 percent

The USS Great Lakes Fleet's Philip R. Clarke *and* Cason J. Calloway *await fit–out at Fraser Shipyards in early 1982 for their first season as self–unloaders. The two ships, plus the* Arthur M. Anderson, *were converted during 1981–1982 at Fraser. The mammoth undertaking involved the rebuilding of all three vessels' cargo holds.*

of the world's total. By 1984, America's share of steel production was less than 12 percent and dropping.[912] Old-timers on the Mesabi Range often made the observation that when the steel industry catches cold, the Range gets pneumonia. By the mid-1980s, the steel industry had full-blown pneumonia, and the Range was on life support.

CONTRACTION ON THE RANGE

In 1979, U.S. Steel's Minntac plant on the Mesabi Range produced more than 16.4 million tons of taconite pellets, just 2 million tons less than the plant's rated capacity. Minntac at the time employed more than 4,200 hourly and salaried workers. Three years later, the bottom dropped out of Minntac's market. In 1982, the big Iron Range plant produced only 3.4 million tons of pellets, a fifth of its rated capacity. Barely more than 1,000 workers manned the mine and mill near Mountain Iron.[913]

It was like that all over the Mesabi Range in 1982. Production plummeted as blast furnaces on the lower lakes no longer called for orders.

Employment in the taconite industry plunged from 16,500 workers in 1979 to one-third of that total in 1982. Plants shut down and unemployment soared to nearly 20 percent in St. Louis County. The situation was similar elsewhere in the Lake Superior iron ore districts. On the Marquette Range in Michigan's Upper Peninsula, Cleveland-Cliffs cut its 1979 workforce of 4,000 people by more than half in the early 1980s.[914] From 1982 to 1987, one of the more thriving businesses on the Mesabi Range involved the rental of moving trucks as thousands of residents packed up and left for good.

For the steel companies, the $3 billion investment it had made in developing the taconite industry during the 1970s seemed to be an extremely bad bet ten years later. The industry had in effect replaced low-cost natural ore with high-cost processed ore. Some industry observers argued that the industry would have been far better off to write off its natural ore investment in Minnesota and Michigan during the 1970s and import high-grade, low-cost natural ore from South America, chiefly Brazil.[915]

Concern about possible competition from Brazilian ore wouldn't manifest itself in the Great Lakes maritime community until late in the decade. What was worrisome to the fleet and port officials in Duluth-Superior was the rapidity of the slide in taconite shipments in the early 1980s. Taconite movements dropped nearly 6 million tons in 1980 to top out at just above 26 million tons. Shipments stayed steady at that level during the 1981 season, and then the bottom dropped out. In 1982, Duluth and Superior handled 15.6 million tons of pellets. Port statisticians had to go back to the depression year of 1932 to find a worse year for iron ore shipments.[916]

"We started that season, 1982, with, I think, twenty-four ships," said Bill Buhrmann, who was then in charge of U.S. Steel's Great Lakes Fleet. "This was our sales projection for the need. That was back in the early part of April, and by June, half of the fleet was laid up. It was really shocking. We couldn't visualize how we could be so far off in our projections of the business level. That was a very traumatic experience."[917]

Coupled with the steady decline in grain shipments, the overall year for the Twin Ports in 1982 was the worst in decades. The 27.4 million tons shipped through the head of the lakes was in a class with 1931, 1934, 1935, and 1938.[918] Things improved gradually from the 1982 low point, but slowly. Only 17 million tons of taconite moved through the ports in 1983, and the 15.7 million tons of taconite handled across the docks at the head of the lakes in 1986 was only marginally better than the nadir of 1982. In 1985, and again in 1986, total tonnage passing through the ports failed to crack the 30-million-ton mark, the first time the Twin Ports had failed to make 30 million tons two years in a row since 1934–1935.[919]

One immediate impact of the ongoing restructuring of the steel industry during the 1980s was a reduction of the size of the American Great Lakes fleet. After 1981, the U.S. Steel Great Lakes Fleet, the Columbia Transportation Division of Oglebay Norton, Interlake Steamship, the Cleveland-Cliffs Steamship Company, American Steamship Company, and

the other major fleets all began retiring their smaller, older vessels. "And, of course, any ships that weren't sailing at that time immediately ended up being candidates for the scrap heap," said Buhrmann. "They were dead. If you didn't have a self-unloader converted by that time, then forget it. You couldn't afford to have one converted; you had to already have it done."[920]

Great Lakes Fleet had foreseen the demand for the more efficient self-unloaders, and in 1981, U.S. Steel contracted with Fraser Shipyards in Superior to lengthen and convert the *Arthur M. Anderson, Cason J. Calloway,* and *Philip R. Clarke* to self-unloaders.[921] The "Triple A's," as local maritime watchers called them, were completed in time for the 1982 season, but because of the collapse of the taconite market, they spent much of 1982 and 1983 in lay-up berths. Still, in the years ahead, the triplets would prove to be one of the wiser investments made by the Great Lakes Fleet.

The other busy facility in the Twin Ports during the early and mid-1980s was the Azcon Scrapyards in Duluth, the former Hyman-Michaels operation. "We had a lot of [ships] scrapped here by a local scrap dealer, Azcon," Buhrmann noted. "He would scrap them as he needed them. He would pull them up and cut a piece off. We tried to sell parts of them, but there really isn't any market for that sort of thing . . . souvenir hunters more than anything else."[922]

From 1980 to 1989, an average of a dozen ships a year were retired and scrapped on the Great Lakes, or towed overseas to the ship-breakers. It was a calamity for the sailors of the fleet, many of whom would move shoreside and never go down the lakes again. It was heartbreaking for the thousands of maritime buffs who could identify stacks and silhouettes of the bulk freighters to bid adieu to old friends. But the carnage was absolutely necessary if a revived Great Lakes fleet was to survive into the 1990s.

RESILIENCE AND RESURGENCE
The restructuring of the American steel industry and the upheavals of the grain millers strike and the Carter grain embargo tested the Twin

Ports unlike any event since the Great Depression. Between 1974 and 1994, the capacity of America's integrated steel industry dropped by half, from 158 million tons to 77 million tons. Capacity at the nation's mini-mills surged from 8 million tons to 37 million tons during the same period.[923] If the steel industry was much smaller than it was at the beginning of the 1980s, it was also much more competitive and productive at the beginning of the 1990s. The surviving mills made the capital investment that would ensure their survival and success in the decade ahead.

U.S. Steel signaled its faith in Duluth-Superior in 1981 when the Duluth, Missabe, & Iron Range Railway began a $26 million project to upgrade its Dock 6 at West Duluth. Built in 1917, Dock 6 went through a three-year modernization project. It was converted to a state-of-the-art shiploader that would allow the railroad, a U.S. Steel subsidiary, to load the 1,000-foot vessels that were then becoming the backbone of the U.S. fleet on the lakes.[924] When the project was completed in the spring of 1984, Dock 6 was capable of loading 100,000 tons of pellets per day.

Another significant change occurred when steel companies began to ship limestone to the Twin Ports rather than to the steel mills. By the early 1990s, most of the taconite mills on the Mesabi Range had converted to a system of fluxing pellets, in which limestone was added to the charge in the taconite kiln rather than in the basic oxygen furnaces at the mills on the Lower Great Lakes. Fluxing pellets added about 2 million tons a year of inbound cargo to the Twin Ports' tonnage mix.

Taconite tonnages though Duluth-Superior rebounded slowly as the decade progressed, but they did come back. Between 1987 and 1993, taconite shipments through the Twin Ports averaged just under 20 million tons per year. It wasn't the 32 million tons that had flowed across the ore docks in 1979, but it was affirmation that the head of the lakes would remain America's iron ore port for the foreseeable future. Grain shipments also recovered by the end of the decade, but not to the levels of

1979 and 1980. From 1988 to 1993, grain shipments averaged 4.5 million tons a year, well below the 9.5 million tons shipped in 1979 but much better than the 3-million-ton low reported in 1985.[925]

The big surprise was coal. The Ortran facility in Superior broke through the 10-million-ton level in 1987, when it handled nearly 11.2 million tons of Montana coal. For the next seven years, shipments averaged more than 11 million tons a year.[926] The congressional passage of Clean Air amendments in 1991 all but ensured that tonnages would increase through the facility as the 1990s wore on. The result was a recovery for the Twin Ports to the 40-million-ton total cargo level that had last been reached in 1980. For the five-year period of 1988–1992, the Twin Ports averaged 39.85 million tons of cargo per year, about 100,000 tons less than the ten-year average during the 1970s boom.[927]

The Twin Ports ended the decade with new waterfront facilities besides ore docks. In 1982, St. Lawrence Cement Company opened its new $18 million cement terminal at the Clure Public Marine Terminal. The 284-foot-high, four-silo complex was partially financed through industrial revenue bonds issued by the Seaway Port Authority of Duluth, and it was built on land leased from the port authority.[928] Late in 1982, the port authority began construction of a 64,800-square-foot general cargo warehouse at the Clure Public Marine Terminal.[929] In October 1984, the Richard I. Bong Bridge between West Duluth and Superior was opened to traffic. The second cross-harbor span in the Twin Ports, the Bong Bridge was a $70 million project shared by Minnesota and Wisconsin with the U.S. Department of Transportation.[930]

The Twin Ports' resilience was never before manifested to the extent that it was during the 1980s. Iron ore and grain, Duluth-Superior's two major cargoes, were under unrelenting pressure for most of the decade, but perseverance has always been a hallmark of the maritime community, and there was reason to believe at the end of the decade that the future held far brighter prospects than the recent past.

THE GREAT LAKES TOWING COMPANY

A fixture in the Twin Ports for nearly a century, the tugboats of the Great Lakes Towing Company are busy every day of the navigation season. Here, the tug Vermont *assists an oceangoing ship into an elevator dock in the 1990s.*

THE GROUNDING OF THE *SOCRATES* off Minnesota Point in November 1985 introduced the nation to the frequently unsung heroes of Duluth-Superior harbor: the tugboats of the Great Lakes Towing Company.

Six tugboats—four owned by the Great Lakes Towing Company—pushed and pulled the *Socrates* for almost a week and finally succeeded in freeing the big saltwater vessel from the sandbar that held her fast.

For almost as long as the Twin Ports had been handling bulk cargoes of iron ore, grain, and coal, the tough little tugboats of the Great Lakes Towing Company had been quietly going about their maritime duties, much as they have in just about every other port on the American side of the Great Lakes. The ubiquitous red and green tugs with the prominent *G* displayed on their stacks have been an essential part of Great Lakes commerce for more than a hundred years now. Almost all named for states, the tugboats of what most people in the maritime community generically called "the towing company" provided an essential link in America's maritime lifelines.

The Great Lakes Towing Company was organized at Cleveland on July 7, 1899, by the most prominent shipowners on Lakes Superior, Michigan, Erie, Huron, and Ontario. Not surprisingly, its list of founding stockholders reads like a "Who's Who" of industrial America at the turn of the twentieth century, and includes John D. Rockefeller, Henry Steinbrenner, Samuel and William Mather, Daniel and Leonard Hanna, Harry Coulby, Alva Chisholm, James Hoyt, James Sinclair, Augustus B. Wolvin—all names intimately familiar to everyone who sails and works on the Great Lakes.[931]

With almost unlimited investment capital behind it, Great Lakes Towing Company began its first navigation season with more than 150 tugboats stationed at every Great Lakes port worth the name. Its fleet has operated in the Duluth-Superior harbor since 1900, for many years under the banner of the subsidiary Union Towing and Wrecking Company. Wolvin, who guided the

fortune of his fleet and that of the Pittsburgh Steamship Company, was the unofficial agent of the Great Lakes Towing Company on the western end of Lake Superior. Wolvin negotiated the purchase of docks and boats for the company in Duluth-Superior and gave it a firm footing in the Twin Ports.

Great Lakes Towing Company is the largest U.S. tugboat company on the lakes. More than thirty-five boats serve more than thirty-five ports throughout Minnesota, Wisconsin, Michigan, Illinois, Indiana, Ohio, Pennsylvania, and New York. The company operates tugboats along the St. Lawrence Seaway as well.

At the beginning of its second century of operations, the Great Lakes Towing Company's tugboats are specially designed with a low profile that allows them ample bridge clearance. Most of the tugs are in the 81-to-85-foot range and have faired hulls that draw 12 to 13 feet of water. The typical company tugboat can provide nearly 57,000 pounds of bollard pull.[932]

Unlike in the old days, when dockside superintendents shouted instructions through bullhorns to crews afloat, the Great Lakes Towing Company keeps track of its widespread fleet through a centralized, state-of-the-art communications and tracking center at its headquarters in Cleveland.[933] In addition to harbor towing, docking, and undocking, the tugboats work as ice-breakers and offer rescue and assistance services as well along 8,300 miles of shoreline on lakes that comprise one half of all the fresh water in the world.

The Great Lakes Towing Company also owns and operates a commercial shipyard, dry dock, and docking facilities specializing in marine repair services for tugboats, ferries, and barges as well as for excursion vessels and large yachts.

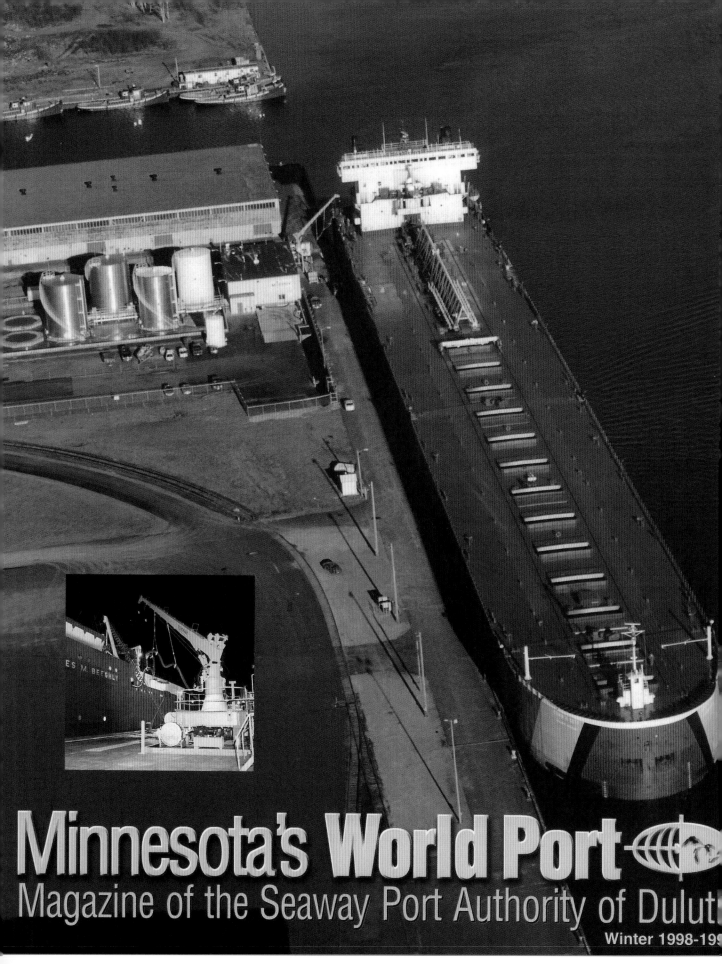

Minnesota's World Port

Magazine of the Seaway Port Authority of Duluth

Winter 1998-1999

The opening of Murphy Oil USA's marine fueling station at the Clure Public Marine Terminal was featured on the cover of the port authority's 1998–1999 winter magazine. The USS Great Lakes Fleet's 1,000–foot Edwin H. Gott was among the first customers after the facility opened in November 1998.

CHAPTER NINETEEN

The Go-Go Nineties

THE TWIN PORTS EMERGED from the wreckage of the 1980s a much leaner Great Lakes maritime colossus. The Duluth-Superior economy lost hundreds of jobs during the decade, and the U.S. and Canadian Great Lakes fleets had come out of the ordeal much smaller than they had been in 1979. But with more than a dozen 1,000-foot vessels in 1990, and nearly every U.S. vessel employed in the iron ore and coal trade converted to a self-unloader, the fleet was more productive by a several-fold magnitude than it had been just a decade before. New shiploaders at taconite docks in Duluth-Superior and nearby Two Harbors meant that the 1,000-foot vessels could be loaded in just hours and back on their way south to the steel mills on the lower rim of Lake Michigan. Fluxed iron ore pellets made taconite mills on the Mesabi Range more competitive, and the reduction of vessel crew sizes meant that the typical crew member sailing the lakes in 1990 had thirty or more years of experience.[934] The number of enrolled vessels in the Lake Carriers' Association, the Cleveland-based trade group that represented U.S. Great Lakes' shipowners, had dropped from 113 in 1982 to 75 in 1990.[935]

But if the Twin Ports maritime economy had survived the 1980s as a smaller, more efficient operation, it was still a major contributor to the economy of its host communities. Economic developers realized that the maritime economy was in many ways the engine that drove the larger economy. In 1990, the Twin Ports produced an economic impact on the region totaling nearly a quarter-billion dollars and supported nearly 3,000 jobs directly and indirectly. Waterfront property in Duluth and Superior generated nearly $3 million in local property taxes, and Superior collected $1.3 million in occupational taxes on cargoes that moved across the city's docks.

Together, taconite and coal accounted for nearly 81 percent of the Twin Ports' cargo in 1991. Taconite shipments had stabilized since the rapid falloff of shipments in the early 1980s, and the Twin Ports would handle an average of nearly 20 million tons of pellets a year throughout the 1990s.[936] But the efficiencies created by fluxed pellets at the mills and the metallurgical composition of the charge at individual basic oxygen furnaces meant that producers were now shipping "designer pellets" down the lakes. "A pellet is not just a pellet anymore," explained Clinton Ferner, general manager of the Duluth, Missabe, & Iron Range Railway, in *Seaway Review* magazine in 1991. "Each pellet is now a customized product, manufactured to each customer's specifications."[937]

Ferner also pointed out that the rapid conversion to fluxed pellets—the Twin Ports handled well over a million tons of fluxing stone in 1991—created new traffic patterns for the rail system at the head of the lakes. "For 100 years," he said, "we simply brought ore downhill from the mine to the ships. Now we've got to handle the limestone going uphill to the plants and then haul it back in the form of pellets. Transportation changes, the flow of material on the Great Lakes changes, and the port use at Duluth changes."[938]

Much of the biggest change in transportation patterns involved the shipment of low-sulfur Montana coal from the Midwest Energy Resources Company facility in Superior. In 1990, the mammoth coal transshipment facility handled

Fred Shusterich (right), president of Midwest Energy Resources Company, visits with Minnesota 8th District Congressman James L. Oberstar in 2001. In 2000, western coal flowing through the MERC terminal exceeded iron ore shipments through the Twin Ports for the first time since the Great Depression.

more than 12.4 million tons of coal. Shipments fluctuated between 10 and 11 million tons for the next several years and then began an upward spiral that saw tonnage records broken every year. A record 13.4 million tons went down the lakes in 1994. By the end of the decade, Ortran, renamed the Superior Midwest Energy Terminal, was handling just under 16.3 million tons of coal, only 1.3 million tons less than the 17.5 million tons of taconite handled in 1999.[939]

"We've added capacity in the sense that we can store, blend, and segregate coal," John Ethen, general manager of the Midwest Energy Resources Company terminal, told a reporter in 1994, adding that MERC had spent more than $8.3 million the previous year on the capacity expansion.[940] The 1994 record of 13.4 million tons of coal shipped from the Twin Ports smashed the seventy-one-year-old record for coal dock volume at the head of the lakes and completed the twenty-year reversal of the Twin Ports from a coal-receipt destination to a coal-shipping port.[941]

SUPERMARKET TO THE WORLD

Grain, the last of the three-legged stool that accounted for the Twin Ports' bulk cargo trade, rebounded sharply during the 1990s. Unlike taconite, which recorded its highest annual

shipments early in the decade and its lowest shipments in 1999, grain did exactly the reverse. In 1991, the Twin Ports moved just over 3.4 million tons of grain. In 1999, Duluth-Superior handled more than 5.8 million tons of grain, the best performance since 1983.[942]

Like their counterparts in the bulk taconite and coal trade, the elevators at the head of the lakes were far more automated and efficient than they had been a decade earlier. Cargill was typical of the modernization initiative that characterized the Twin Ports elevator business in the 1980s. With three elevators and an A-frame bulk commodities building, Cargill's state-of-the-art grain handling capabilities had a combined storage capacity of nearly 10 million bushels. Its newest elevator, opened in 1976, boasted closed-circuit television cameras and a computerized monitoring system capable of giving operators real-time feedback of more than 2,000 points in the elevators' 253 bins and along five miles of enclosed beltways. A truck dump was capable of unloading 150 grain trucks in an eight-hour shift. The elevator's rail yard could handle more than 220 grain hopper cars at a time. Saltwater ships and Great Lakes freighters could be loaded at the rate of more than 100,000 bushels per hour.[943]

Spring wheat and durum remained kings of the export grain business through the 1990s. In many ways, however, the grain business mirrored the transportation shifts that were occurring in the taconite and coal trade. At the beginning of the 1990s, the Twin Ports' seven private elevator systems handled well over 1 million tons of barley each year. "The barley was a mainstay," said Duluth vessel agent Chuck Hilleren. "When we started out every year, the first crop in the growing area was barley. Basically, the slowest months were June and July, where business almost came to a standstill. Then, in the first week of August, the barley crop would be harvested. There was a barley market out there in the Middle East: India, Iraq, Iran, Turkey, and Southwest Asia. There was a heavy demand, even in Northern Europe, for barley."[944]

By the end of the decade, barley had all but disappeared from the Twin Ports' export ledgers. In another reversal of trade, however, barley began arriving from Thunder Bay, Ontario, aboard Canadian self-unloaders that were discharged into hoppers built along the silos at General Mills Elevator A and Cargill Elevator B-2 in Duluth.[945] Barley had become too valuable for domestic brewery production and was no longer likely to be exported overseas for livestock feed.[946] Similarly, in the early 1990s, sunflower seeds were still an occasional export cargo for Duluth-Superior elevators. At the beginning of the decade, explained Chuck Ilenda of the Ceres, Inc., stevedores, "We were what they called a grocery store port. We handled a little bit of everything. We had mustard seed, we had canary seed, we had striped sunflower seeds, the confectionery sunflower seeds, the oil sunflower seeds, beet pulp pellets, green death—which was an alfalfa pellet—and rapeseed."[947]

The oil-seed sunflower trade dropped off dramatically during the early 1990s when European tariffs discouraged the importation of U.S. sunflowers.

Much of the European import trade shifted to the Ukraine and South America, and the flow of sunflowers through Duluth and Superior temporarily dried up within a few years in the early 1990s.[948] Intriguingly, the lost export cargoes were replaced for much of the decade by shipments of corn and soybeans, thanks to hardier varieties that could be planted and harvested much farther north than their traditional ranges. "They have extended the area of growing," Hilleren explained. "They have created hybrids that they can grow in North Dakota. They can grow corn hybrids in North Dakota and realize a decent crop. So now, for most of that area, if they can grow soybeans, they will grow beans over wheat. They will grow beans over barley or even sunflower seeds. It is all a matter of the farmer producing as much as he can or producing as much revenue as he can out of his thousand or two thousand acres."[949]

By the late 1990s, Duluth-Superior was still known as a "supermarket" of the grain industry

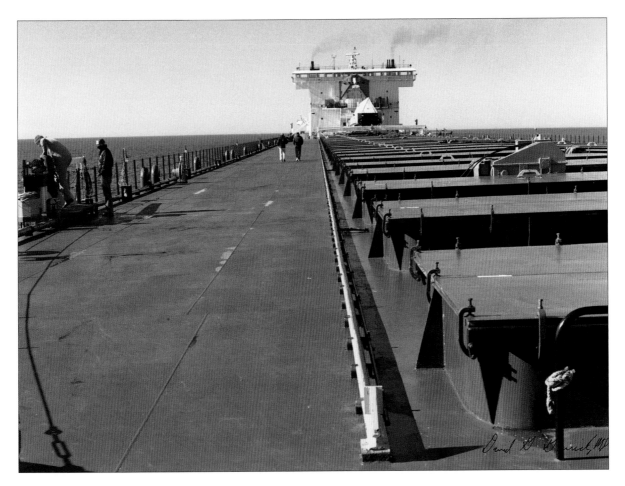

The modern, 1,000-foot lake carriers represented a quantum leap in technology and efficiency, easily carrying the cargo of four or more 600-footers—and carrying that cargo faster with less fuel.

because of the variety of agricultural products that flowed out of the ports' elevators.[950]

SALT, SAND, AND STONE

Although iron ore, coal, and grain get the most attention, they are hardly the only bulk commodities that flow in and out of the Twin Ports. Mountains of minerals move across thirteen docks operated by eight companies serving shippers and receivers through Duluth-Superior's far-flung trade area. Every year, several million tons of limestone, cement, salt, bentonite clay, petroleum coke, fertilizer, and aggregates are in motion or storage at specialized or multi-purpose faciities in the harbor.

Limestone and cement are the port's predominant inbound cargoes. More than 2 million tons of limestone arrive annually at the DM&R ore docks, C. Reiss Terminal, the Hallett Company docks, Cutler-Magner Company's CLM lime plant, Northland Pier, and Minnesota Aggregates. Nearly a half-million tons of cement move through Lafarge Corporation's two docks and the St. Lawrence Cement Company terminal.

GENERAL CARGO AND HEAVY LIFTS

The 1990s would be landmark years for Duluth as it reinvented itself in the world of general cargo, but not until enduring a turbulent shaking out of operators at the Clure Public Marine Terminal. Owned by the Seaway Port Authority since its 1957–1959 construction, the terminal's docks, warehouses, cranes, and forklifts had been operated by Ceres, Inc., from 1969 through 1976 and then were taken over by North Central Terminal Operators. Davis Helberg had been succeeded as North Central's president by Frank

Great Lakes freighters unload bulk cargo at Hallett Dock No. 5 adjacent to the DM&IR ore docks in West Duluth. Acquired by Hallett Dock Company in 1964, the dock handles much of the limestone, bentonite clay, and fertilizer that moves through the Twin Ports.

Puskarich, who in turn was followed by former Superior port director James C. Sauter and then Thomas E. Kennedy, a member of the port authority staff since the early 1960s.

In late May 1987, North Central abruptly terminated its contract, and for the balance of the season, the port authority was forced to operate the facility itself.[951] Kennedy was retained by the port authority to serve as general manager of the terminal. Meanwhile, port director Davis Helberg, finance director John Kubow, and the commissioners analyzed the long-term viability of their public agency running the stevedoring and warehousing operations. They concluded that only a private company could effectively conduct the daily wheeling and dealing with labor, shipowners, and shippers required of a terminal operator. There was strong sentiment among some board and staff members to get out of the terminal business if an established operator could not be found.

Helberg scoured the market and returned with two candidates: a former Great Lakes stevedoring colleague, Daniel E. Meehan of Milwaukee, and Duluth's Thomas Privette, a former grain stevedoring superintendent with American Grain Trimmers and the Clure Marine Terminal's chief clerk since 1968. The latter, although experienced and highly regarded, could not guarantee adequate financial backing, however, and the commissioners turned to Meehan.

An Irishman raised in New York's Hell's Kitchen and a former merchant ship officer, Meehan had an enviable record of success as Milwaukee's terminal operator and was widely recognized in national shipping circles. He had also purchased the former Great Lakes Storage and Contracting Company dock in Superior a few years earlier and expanded his Meehan Seaway Services into Richmond, Virginia, and Cambridge, Maryland. The Duluth port board awarded Meehan a contract in early 1988 and he quickly negotiated a contract with Duluth's International Longshoremen's Association Local 1366.[952] But with the Great Lakes eliminated from handling Public Law 480 (or "Food for Peace") cargo because of the

Since its founding in 1990, Gary Nicholson has served as president of Lake Superior Warehousing Company. Nicholson moved the port authority into handling numerous new niche cargoes.

1985 Farm Bill, and saddled with an archaic ILA contract, Meehan chose not to renew his contract following the 1990 season.

Again, the port authority was concerned about whether it could find another terminal operator and thus stay in the general cargo business. The answer came via a couple of Minnesotans in the winter of 1990–1991. Dennis Hallberg and Tony Phillipi were well known in the regional business community as a result of their ownership of Lakehead Constructors, a successful Superior-based industrial contractor. Hallberg, a native of tiny Cherry, Minnesota, on the Mesabi Iron Range, also owned Kirscher Transport, a Minnesota trucking firm, and Phillipi, of St. Paul, owned a heavy equipment leasing company.[953]

Hallberg and Phillipi named Gary Nicholson as general manager of Lake Superior Warehousing. Nicholson had twenty-five years' experience in intermodal transportation when Hallberg and Phillipi engaged him to manage the Clure Public

Marine Terminal in 1991.[954] Nicholson immediately set about changing the focus for the terminal, which had experienced a sharp drop-off in government-impelled food cargoes after 1989.[955]

Those first several years Nicholson literally pounded the pavement, looking for cargoes that could be stored and transshipped out of the Clure Public Marine Terminal. "Anything I could get my hands on," he said of his marketing and sales effort during the early 1990s. "We had one steel account, and that was our only maritime account. We had to stay within product lines that we could handle. Forest products were a good alternative for us—wood pulp, sometimes lumber, oriented strand board, things that did not require any kind of heat or refrigeration. We have limited heat capabilities for storing cargo, and consequently we wanted to work on the things that we could handle in here without it, so that is what I set about doing."[956]

By the middle of the decade, Nicholson was starting to develop maritime accounts for Lake Superior Warehousing and the port. He was assisted immeasurably by the emergence of new saltwater vessels that could make a profit on handling general cargo between the Twin Ports and Europe.

"The last few years," explained agent Chuck Hilleren, "we have had a lot of new shipbuilding, more than most people realize. A lot of people are getting into the smaller ships and smaller crews now, and we are seeing a tremendous amount of increase in building of ships that can enter the system, but they are smaller ships. The operating expenses on these things are probably half or less than what you would spend on a Handy Size bulk carrier. They are all over the lakes now: Wagenborg, the Green Fleet, others. They are all fitted with bow and stern thrusters. They operate on a crew of eight

Winter 2002–2003 on Rice's Point, and the Arthur M. Clure Public Marine Terminal has a full house of tenants. The Seaway Port Authority of Duluth leased the last parcel of developable property in 2002 to Lake States Lumber Company and Innovative Pine Technology of Aitkin, Minnesota, for a forest products treatment and processing facility, shown under construction at lower center. To the right of the Lake States facility is the East Warehouse Annex, opened in 2002. Combined, the terminal and the port authority's Garfield C & D property (upper center) had five U.S. lakers awaiting spring fit-out.

or nine people, and they do extremely well. Of course, they come into this market and compete with the big boys because instead of 25,000 tons, they are carrying 10,000 tons. And they can do it competitively."[957]

More traditional saltwater vessels have also seen a renaissance since the mid-1990s. "Then we have had the recent new building by FedNav, CanForNav [Canadian Forest Navigation Company] and the Poles," Hilleren said. "They have built a lot of new ships, both big and small."[958]

Lake Superior Warehousing also took a firm hand in resolving labor problems at the Clure Public Marine Terminal that had been festering since Ceres was the stevedore in the 1970s. The company pledged to hire union workers but refused to enter into a contract with Duluth ILA Local 1366. LSW's employees ultimately organized a new local that was chartered by the ILA as Local 2061. Nicholson hired long-time longshoreman Russ Wedin and made him foreman for the permanent crew, which has numbered around fifteen since 1991. "We've got a good group of guys," Wedin said in 2000. "Everybody does their job plus a little bit more. Good people. I tell the guys what to do in the morning, and they do it, and if they get done they go do something else or help each other. It is a whole different ball game."[959]

The result has been a sharp increase in productivity, not unlike that experienced by the ore and coal docks and grain elevators in the harbor. In the late 1970s, unloading a cargo of imported steel coils required a crew of fifteen longshoremen. Now, Wedin said, it's "three men in the hold (two men and a lift truck driver as my foreman), a signalman, crane operator, one man on the dock, one lift truck driver, and one checker. And the productivity went up probably 30 percent. The men running the crane also pay attention to what they are doing and get it done."[960]

Wedin attributed the turnaround at the Clure Public Marine Terminal to his boss. "The biggest change at this port and this facility here happened in 1991 when the Lake Superior Warehousing came in," Wedin said. "Gary Nicholson . . .

if he had been in here from 1959, we would have probably all been wearing mink underwear. I haven't seen that man slow down in ten years. He is constantly out there, constantly getting something. Nothing slides by him. Hard worker. Wonderful person to work for. Treats his men right."[961]

By sheer coincidence, Lake Superior Warehousing's operational success in the 1990s was complemented by major capital improvements at the Clure Public Marine Terminal. Much of the renovation was due directly to a plan developed in 1990 by the late Bill Newstrand, ports and waterways director for the Minnesota Department of Transportation, and port director Davis Helberg. Approved by the Minnesota State Legislature in 1991, the Minnesota Port Development Assistance Program authorized the Department of Transportation to award grants of up to 80 percent of the costs for repairing, rebuilding, or constructing publicly owned, maritime-related facilities. No money came with the legislative endorsement, but in 1995 Helberg and his colleagues at the Mississippi River ports organized the Minnesota Ports Association and engaged the services of Twin Cities lawyer and Duluth native Kevin Walli to spearhead their cause. The first legislative appropriation came in 1996. By 2003, the state had invested about $11 million in the program, and the Seaway Port Authority had been awarded $5.5 million, which it converted into $7.5 million of major port improvements. The largest single project was a $3.7 million, 104,000-square-foot warehouse opened in 2002 adjacent to the public marine terminal's East Warehouse.[962]

One cargo that Duluth-Superior developed into a high art in the 1990s was what the industry calls "project cargoes," usually one-time loads for specific construction projects. Sam Browman, port authority marketing specialist from 1978 to 1998, noted that "probably the most challenging types of cargoes were project cargoes. Overweight, oversized, dimensional pieces of machinery that would be going out to western Minnesota or the Twin Cities or to the Dakotas. In fact, a lot of the stuff we handle is equipment going up into Canada, mostly to Alberta and Saskatchewan."[963]

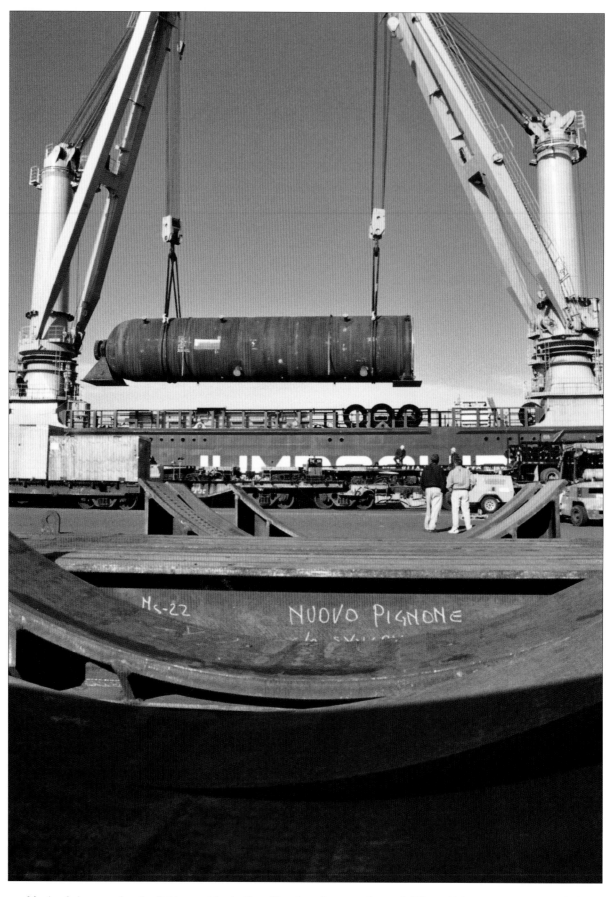

Massive deck cranes aboard a Dutch-owned Jumbo fleet ship swing ashore one of several 400-ton high-pressure reactor vessels destined for an Alberta, Canada, petroleum project in 2002. Unique "heavy-lift" cargoes have become commonplace at Duluth's Clure Public Marine Terminal since Lake Superior Warehousing Company became the port authority's managing agent in 1991.

In the early 1990s, the terminal handled five big reactor vessels that were shipped from Japan and railed by specialty car to Regina, Saskatchewan. The 750-ton reactor vessels were destined for a refinery just outside the provincial capital city and handled flawlessly by longshore and rail crews at the Duluth harbor. At the time, the reactors were the largest shipments ever handled by the Burlington Northern Santa Fe and Canadian Pacific Railways, and each vessel had to be transported by a German-built, specially articulated Schnabel railcar more than 300 feet long.[964]

In the mid-1990s, the Twin Ports handled much of the heavy lift traffic associated with a major expansion of Potlatch Corporation's paper mill in nearby Cloquet. A number of 100-ton cylinders arrived from an Ontario manufacturer and were delivered to construction crews at the Potlatch mill.[965] In the summer of 2001, the head of the lakes got national media exposure when it handled a tunnel-boring machine used to bore a light-rail tunnel beneath the Minneapolis–St. Paul International Airport.[966]

The following year, Lake Superior Warehousing handled an even bigger heavy lift cargo. In the summer and fall of 2002, LSW took delivery of seventeen pressure cylinders on two heavy lift ships owned by a Rotterdam-based company. When the Jumbo *Vision* arrived in port on November 8, it was carrying seven 520-ton pieces of steel cylinders manufactured in Spain and Italy and consigned to the Syncrude UE-1 oil-sands project near Fort McMurray, Alberta.[967] The complicated rail shipment from the Twin Ports to Alberta involved two U.S. and two Canadian railroads, fourteen twelve-axle railcars, and two eight-axle railcars.[968] The shipment went off without a hitch. "Duluth was once again selected as the North American port of entry because of a combination of its facilities for dimensional cargoes, the professional services provided by Lake Superior Warehousing and the excellent rail services and clearances available," Ed Clarke, the senior logistics coordinator for Syncrude UE-1 in Calgary, Alberta, told reporters.[969]

ECONOMICS AND THE ENVIRONMENT

In the summer of 1994, Duluth port director Davis Helberg observed that a European company that had been examining port sites in the United States for a manufacturing plant had been favorably impressed by Duluth-Superior. Company officials had told Helberg that other port locations, particularly those on the East Coast, "no longer have quality shoreside sites that are both affordable and free of suspected ground pollution. It appears that things once intangible—clean air, clean water, scenic beauty, academic excellence, safe streets, good government, distinguishable seasons, an easy drive to work or play—now have taken on identifiable dimensions for folks looking to blend balance and sanity with a good business deal."[970]

Helberg's observation illustrates one of the quieter success stories in the Twin Ports during the 1990s. Economic development on both sides of the harbor, spurred by innovative financing, public investments in land building improvements, and tax increment financing added new companies and plant expansions and hundreds of people to Twin Ports payrolls during the decade.

Following a policy established by port director David Oberlin in 1968, the Seaway Port Authority emphasized industrial development as part of its mission. Economic development in Duluth and Superior was a difficult task in the 1980s when the region's economy was contracting, but after 1990 the local economy began a sustained decade-long record of expansion. By 1995 more than fifty companies were operating on port authority land. Port tenants provided nearly 775 family wage jobs for local residents.[971]

More than half of those jobs were accounted for by businesses in the port authority's Airpark development adjacent to the Duluth International Airport. Started in 1976, Airpark was inadvertently coincidental with the loss of warehouse space in the path of Interstate 35 through Duluth. "Airpark was developed to accommodate the anticipated need for new and relocating businesses," explained port authority economic development director Andy McDonough in 2000.[972] Early sales of lots were slow because of the 1980s recession in the Twin Ports. In late 1989, the port authority launched an incentive program offering

Airpark lots for $100 apiece. Six companies responded, and Airpark finally began to look like a bona fide development park. "We met our goal and returned to selling lots at market rates in 1991," McDonough added.[973]

By the summer of 1999, lots in Airpark were selling for an average of $20,000 an acre. The port authority closed five land sales at the 300-acre Airpark development that summer and began laying plans for a speculative office/warehouse building for the site.[974] By 2002, Airpark reported a total of thirty-six companies and 447 jobs.[975] The tenants were for the most part small businesses, employing an average of ten to fifteen workers, but one-quarter of the thirty-six firms reported employing between twenty and forty people. For a community that had long wrestled with job losses, the success of the Airpark development was a welcome departure from the norm.

On the waterfront, the port authority was filling up the Clure Public Marine Terminal while also redeveloping property across the slip where 100

years earlier Frank H. Peavey had built his revolutionary concrete grain elevator. Cargill, Inc., closed the old C and D elevators in the 1980s and eventually conveyed the property to the port authority. With the help of a $1.2 million state grant, the port demolished the elevators, and by 2002 the twenty-eight-acre site—now called Garfield C & D—had been leveled and prepared for redevelopment. At the Clure Public Marine Terminal itself, the last parcel of undeveloped land was leased in 2002 to Lake States Lumber Company of Aitkin, Minnesota, for construction of a lumber treatment and processing plant. The terminal, once partially under water, part marshland and part rifle range, had become the work address for some 450 people employed by eighteen port authority tenants.

THE 4-T'S
Economists have often identified the nature of the Twin Ports' economy as the 4-T's: taconite, timber, transportation, and tourism. In the 1990s, two of those T's—tourism and transportation— found themselves in an uneasy coexistence. For

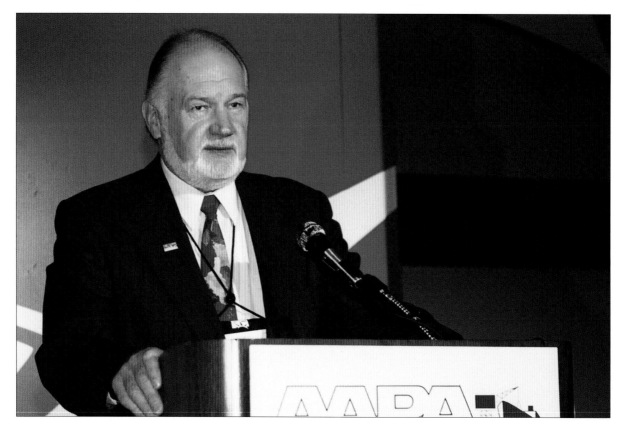

Port authority director Davis Helberg's influence on the maritime community extended far beyond the Twin Ports. He chaired the American Association of Port Authorities in 1994–1995 and simultaneously chaired two powerful AAPA committees in 1995–2003. Founded in 1912, AAPA is the nation's most influential voice for the port and maritime commerce industry.

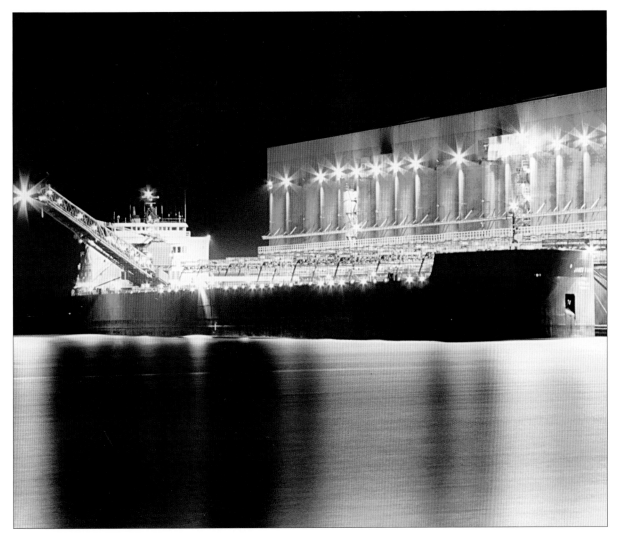

A night shot of Interlake Steamship Company's James R. Barker *loading at the Burlington Northern Santa Fe ore docks in October 1994. The* Barker, *a thousand-footer built in 1976, is the namesake of Interlake's board chair, who was one of the Great Lakes' most highly respected advocates during the past quarter-century.*

much of the decade, tourism became an increasingly driving force for the area's economy. City planners had long realized that Lake Superior was key in turning the Twin Ports into one of the major tourist destinations of the Midwest. Landlocked Minnesotans, Iowans, and Dakotans had been coming to Duluth-Superior for years to ooh and aah over the big boats entering and departing the Duluth-Superior harbor.

In the 1980s, both Duluth and Superior embarked upon economic development projects designed to enhance the Twin Ports' waterfront tourism potential. Superior spent millions of dollars developing Barker's Island, an "artificial" island created decades earlier with materials dredged from the harbor bottom. By 2000, the once brush-covered spit of sand had become

the site of a hotel, restaurant, condominiums, 350-boat marina, and small recreational beach, and was the final resting place for one of Alexander McDougall's whalebacks, the tanker *Meteor,* now a museum ship. In Duluth, city planners spent even more money converting the landward approach to the Duluth Aerial Lift Bridge from a district of seedy warehouses and junkyards into Canal Park, a multi-use development anchored by the U.S. Army Corps of Engineers' Lake Superior Maritime Visitor Center at the foot of the Aerial Lift Bridge. Restaurants, shops, bookstores, hotels, and condominiums catered to the increasing number of visitors to the Twin Ports. With federal interstate highway funds, the city in the 1990s completed an ambitious lakewalk from Canal Park to the end of I-35 at Twenty-sixth Avenue East.

The tourist development in the Twin Ports did not come without a price. City planners no longer necessarily viewed waterfront economic development with the same equanimity as their predecessors. More and more, society demanded to be insulated from the sometimes dirty, sometimes noisy waterfront activity that had provided their parents and grandparents with good-paying jobs. The Twin Ports maritime community found itself in the middle, trying to be encouraging of tourist development while pointing out that Duluth-Superior was, after all, a working harbor.

Duluth port director Davis Helberg called it "creeping glitzism. Cities that turned their backs on our waterfronts now want to exploit them. In the Great Lakes, bridge cranes and bulk cargo facilities that once dominated our skylines have been forced to relocate in some cities and are

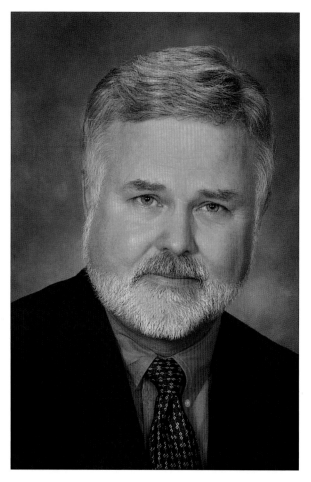

Adolph Ojard was named the Seaway Port Authority of Duluth's sixth director on April 1, 2003. Ojard started his career as a dockworker at the DM&IR Railway and worked his way up to top management ranks at the then USS Great Lakes Fleet in 1997. The Two Harbors native has more than thirty years' experience in maritime and rail commerce.

under heavy pressure in others."[976] At the same time as it was struggling with glitzism, however, the port authority was actively encouraging the development of a Great Lakes cruise industry. In the 1990s, German and French cruise lines began offering Great Lakes cruise packages to European, Canadian, and American passengers. It was the revival of a Great Lakes cruise industry that had been dormant since the 1960s.[977]

Going hand-in-hand with tourism development in the Great Lakes during the 1990s was an increasing societal concern with environmental awareness. The Twin Ports benefited unexpectedly from this new environmental ethic, since the spate of federal Clean Air legislation between 1972 and 1991 led directly to the tremendous growth of ever-increasing low sulfur coal shipments from the head of the lakes to electric power plants on the lower lakes.

Federal Clean Water legislation also had a direct hand in stimulating development of a new maritime facility on the port authority's Clure Public Marine Terminal. The federal Oil Pollution Act of 1990, triggered by the *Exxon Valdez's* massive Alaskan oil spill in March 1989, forced the demise of shipside fueling in Duluth-Superior. Marine Fueling, once an independent company but owned since the early 1980s by Koch Industries of Wichita, Kansas, for decades had delivered bunker and diesel fuel to ships, first with the tanker *William J. Bennett* and then via the *Reiss Marine,* built specifically for Twin Ports service in 1978. The *Reiss Marine* had a virtually spotless record of high performance and spill-safe deliveries, but she wouldn't be able to comply with the stringent new requirements of the 1990 Oil Pollution Act, and she was retired in 1996. Murphy Oil Company, an Eldorado, Arkansas, company, had been the *Reiss Marine's* fuel supplier from its big oil refinery in Superior, and in 1998 Murphy completed a state-of-the-art fueling station on land leased from the Seaway Port Authority. The facility, built at the terminal's Berth No. 3, replaced an animal fats and vegetable oils tank farm that the port authority had earlier dismantled. Within two years, Murphy was servicing more than 200 ships—more traffic in one year than the old tank farm had seen in all of its nearly forty years of existence.

But the maritime community also worried that proposed environmental costs could make traditional waterfront activities noncompetitive, if not eliminate them altogether. As long ago as the 1980s, the environmental community targeted dredging as a polluter. For most of its history, Twin Ports docks and slips have been dredged by private contractors while the federal channels were maintained by the U.S. Army Corps of Engineers and its contractors. Dredging is and always has been an absolutely essential element in the maintenance of efficient and productive maritime transportation systems.

In the 1990s, environmentalists attacked the corps for its dredging policies, charging that dredging stirs up sediments that contain hazardous materials and base metals. As a result of the complaints, maritime interests were plagued during the decade with onerous new regulations that required contractors to dispose of dredged materials on land. The late Keith Yetter, who spent his working career in the Twin Ports dredging business, explained that "today you have to put the material into CDFs—confined disposal facilities—[and] use it for deep storage, or you can dispose of it upland. The states of Wisconsin and Minnesota do not allow in-water disposal."[978]

The dredging issue in the 1980s and 1990s was also made more difficult by two additional factors, one political and one climatic. After five years of heated disagreement by the nation's ports and carriers, an initiative by President Ronald Reagan's administration was adopted by Congress when the 1986 Water Resources Development Act for the first time shifted port and channel dredging costs from the federal government to the "beneficiaries." Besides imposing heavy new taxes on maritime exports, imports, and domestic cargoes, the law also required local communities to pay a significant share for channel improvements.[979] For twenty years, Twin Ports maritime and civic leaders had been trying to get federal money to deepen a three-and-a-half-mile channel from near the DM&IR ore docks to the C. Reiss coal dock

and Hallett Docks 6 and 7 at the upper end of the St. Louis River navigation channel. By the time federal money was appropriated for the $18 million project, the new law required a $6.1 million local share. The Seaway Port Authority mounted a major campaign in 1989 to secure the funds from the Minnesota State Legislature and finally succeeded, only to see the Corps of Engineers increase the local share to $8.5 million. Without any reasonable hope of securing more money, the port authority shifted its attention to widening the St. Louis River Cross Channel between the DM&IR Docks and the Superior Midwest Energy Terminal. The project was completed in 1994 for $1.3 million, and a local share of $700,000.[980]

The second issue that had an impact on dredging involved fluctuating lake levels on Lake Superior. Over time, water levels in the Great Lakes fluctuate dramatically, as much as four feet during the past century.[981] The lake levels are governed by the absence or abundance of precipitation, evaporation, and snowmelt, and typically take decades to change. In 1997 and 1998, the lake levels were high. Two years later, following two consecutive mild winters, they were at the lowest levels experienced in decades.[982] For 1,000-foot vessels, every inch of draft translates to about 240 tons of cargo. With lake levels down seven to ten inches at the end of the decade, the big bulk freighters were hauling 2,000 or more tons cargo less than in the preceding two seasons.[983] And when lake levels get low, as they did in 1999 and 2000, high spots in the connecting channels need to be dredged.

But from an environmental perspective, dredging was a tempest in a teapot compared with the issue of alien invasive species. In the early 1990s, water treatment and electric power plant operators on Lake Erie began experiencing significant restriction of flow in water intake pipes. The problem was soon traced to infestations of zebra mussels, a tiny bivalve that clung to rocks and pipes and bred in the billions. The zebra mussel, however, wasn't native to North America. Its traditional range was from the Black Sea north to the Baltic. Most evidence pointed to the ballast water of saltwater vessels transiting the St.

Lawrence Seaway into the Great Lakes as the likely source of the mussel's hitherto unexplained passage from Europe to North America.

Ballast is indispensable in modern ship-going operations. When traveling without cargo, modern vessels take on millions of gallons of ballast water to help them maintain trim on their voyage. When the vessel reaches a port where it is to load cargo, it discharges the ballast water to make room in its holds for the cargo shipment. Activists soon seized upon ballast water as the culprit in what had become known as the aquatic nuisance species issue and suggested literally throwing out the baby with the ballast water.[984]

In a 2002 speech to an international audience in Rotterdam, Captain Ray Skelton, the Duluth port's environmental and government affairs director, noted that "we face the prospect of eight Great Lakes states and two Canadian provinces proposing separate laws on ballast treatment. There is no possibility of the ten governing bodies of the Great Lakes passing identical legislation."[985]

The last chapter has yet to be written on alien invasive species in the Great Lakes, but the experience with zebra mussels and their kin during the latter half of the 1990s is just one indication of how fast an environmental concern can become a paramount issue.

In an era of global instant communication, the Twin Ports and the Great Lakes will likely face other environmental, economic, and social challenges in the years ahead. Given that Duluth-Superior has been a key component in North America's waterborne transportation equation for three centuries, it's likely that the port will surmount those challenges and, along the way, convert them into opportunities.

The yin and the yang of challenges and opportunities has been part and parcel of the ports' history from the beginning. The challenge of wrestling Montreal canoes across the Dalles of the St. Louis River in the seventeenth and eighteenth centuries gave the region's Native Americans and French Canadian voyageurs the opportunity to wrest the fur resources from the heart of a continent. The challenge of building a canal at the rapids of the St. Mary's River in 1855 gave entrepreneurs the opportunity to build an industrial society on the iron and copper of the Lake Superior hinterlands.

Challenges and opportunities continued apace in the twentieth century. Twin Ports residents and the Upper Great Lakes mining and maritime community took upon an awesome challenge in 1917 and again in 1941 and 1950, providing the industrial sinew of allied war production and giving our nation's soldiers and sailors the opportunity to transform America into a world power.

The challenge of global competition became a reality for Duluth-Superior long before the rest of America woke up to the fact that steel could be made in Yokohama or Lodz as cheaply as in Pittsburgh or Akron. The 1959 opening of the St. Lawrence Seaway created both huge challenges and equally substantial opportunities for the Twin Ports. Some of the high expectations may not have been realized, but nearly a half-century later, Duluth-Superior remains one of North America's preeminent export grain ports.

The challenge of foreign oil in the post–World War II era all but eliminated the movement of upbound coal to the head of the lakes. But when Congress passed sweeping national Clean Air legislation twenty-five years later, Duluth-Superior was quick to capitalize on the opportunity to move environmentally compliant coal from the west down the Great Lakes. Today, Duluth-Superior is one of the nation's great coal ports.

Challenges and opportunities. They have defined the port for three centuries now. And as long as the sparkling freshwater of the St. Louis River flows out through its twin channels into Lake Superior, all who live in Duluth-Superior and all who work to make the Twin Ports the true pride of the inland seas will confront challenges and seek opportunities for centuries to come.

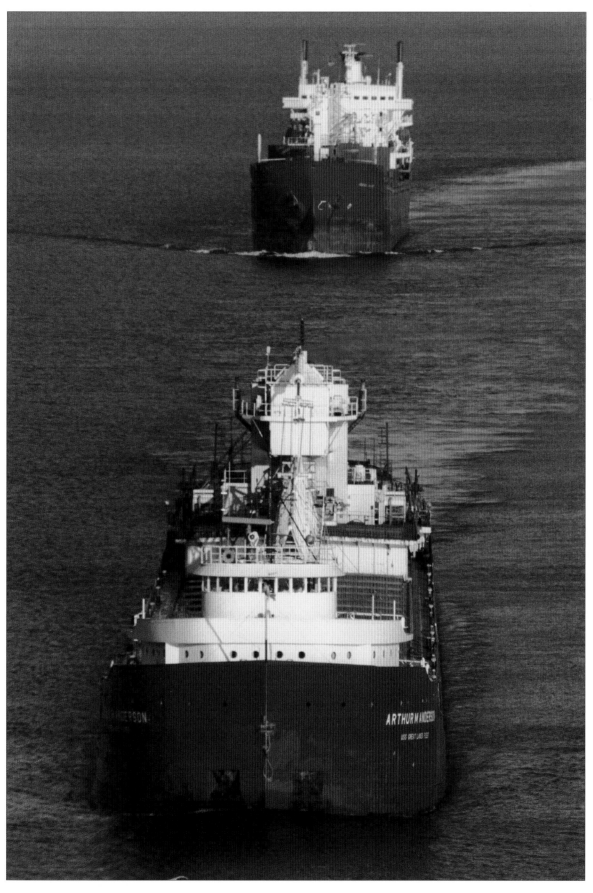

Ships representing two of the major fleets serving the Port of Duluth–Superior at the dawn of the twenty–first century follow one another up Lake Superior bound for the Twin Ports. In the foreground is the Arthur M. Anderson *of the Duluth–based Great Lakes fleet, while just astern is Montreal–based FedNav's* Federal Hudson.

CHAPTER 1: THE VOYAGEURS' HIGHWAY

1. Walter D. Edmonds, *The Musket and the Cross* (Boston: Little, Brown and Company, 1968), p. 9.
2. Thomas B. Costain, *The White and the Gold* (New York: Popular Library, 1954), p. 110.
3. Mark Kurlansky, *Cod: A Biography of the Fish That Changed the World* (New York: Walker and Company, 1997), pp. 24–29.
4. Time Line—"A Brief History of the Fur Trade," www.whiteoak.org/learning/timeline.html.
5. David J. Krause, *The Making of a Mining District: Keweenaw Native Copper, 1500–1870* (Detroit: Wayne State University Press, 1992), pp. 22–23.
6. Peter C. Newman, *Empire of the Bay: The Company of Adventurers That Seized a Continent* (New York: Penguin Books, 1998), p. 39.
7. "Life in the Past—Beaver Hats," www.hbc.com/hbc/e_hi/historic_hbc/Beaver_hats.htm. Hatmakers in Western Europe used a secret formula to soak the beaver pelt for felting. The composition included mercury and lead, and a lifetime of inhaling the fumes led to the onset of senile dementia, hence the term "mad as a hatter." See Johnson, *Dreams of Empire*, p. 42.
8. Krause, *The Making of a Mining District*, p. 26.
9. C. Harry Benedict, *Red Metal: The Calumet and Hecla Story* (Ann Arbor: University of Michigan Press, 1952), p. 12.
10. Walter Van Brunt, *Duluth and St. Louis County, Minnesota: Their Story and People*, vol. 1 (Chicago: American Historical Society, 1921), pp. 5–19.
11. Ibid., pp. 21–23.
12. Ibid., p. 25.
13. Douglas A. Birk, "When Rivers Were Roads: Deciphering the Role of Canoe Portages in the Western Lake Superior Fur Trade," in *The Fur Trade Revisited: Selected Papers of the Sixth North American Fur Trade Conference, Mackinac Island, Michigan, 1991*, ed. Jennifer S. H. Brown, W. J. Eccles, and Donald P. Heldman (East Lansing: Michigan State University Press, 1994), p. 364. Northern Minnesota is unique in that its rivers drain into three of the major watersheds on the North American continent: the Gulf of St. Lawrence to the east, Hudson Bay to the north, and the Gulf of Mexico to the south. The route up the St. Louis River led a paddler west to the Red River of the north through several routes, or south on a wide curve through central Minnesota to the Mississippi River. Paddlers could also leave Lake Superior just east of the head of the lakes and strike south along the Brule and St. Croix Rivers to the Upper Mississippi.
14. William Watts Folwell, *A History of Minnesota in Four Volumes*, vol. 1 (St. Paul: Minnesota Historical Society, 1956), p. 23. Some accounts have Greysolon living in winter quarters to the southwest of Thunder Bay, at the mouth of the Pigeon River, today the boundary between Minnesota and Ontario.
15. Van Brunt, *Duluth and St. Louis County, Minnesota*, vol. 1, pp. 29–31.
16. Folwell, *A History of Minnesota in Four Volumes*, vol. 1, p. 30.
17. Milan Kovacovich, "Daniel Greysolon, Sieur Duluth: An Introduction," in *Duluth: Sketches of the Past—A Bicentennial Collection*, ed. Rick Lydecker and Lawrence J. Sommer (Duluth: American Revolution Bicentennial Commission, 1976), p. 22.
18. Time Line—"A Brief History of the Fur Trade," www.whiteoak.org/learning/timeline.html.
19. Ibid. At the insistence of Benjamin Franklin, the Treaty of Versailles set the border of the new republic along a line northwest from Lake Superior along the Pigeon River, Rainy Lake, the Rainy River, and Lake of the Woods. West of Lake of the Woods, the boundary was to run from the headwaters of the Mississippi River to a point where it crossed the 49th Parallel. But since the headwaters of the Mississippi were well south of the 49th Parallel, the United States was left with the northwest angle of Lake of the Woods, a cartographic anomaly that exists to this day. British negotiators at Versailles wanted a boundary sharply south of the Pigeon River–Rainy Lake–Rainy River line, but Franklin insisted on the more northerly border route, thus preserving the then unknown mineral wealth of northern Minnesota for the young republic.
20. Margaret Beattie Bogue and Virginia A. Palmer, *Around the Shores of Lake Superior: A Guide to Historic Sites* (Madison: University of Wisconsin Press, 1979), p. 37.
21. Ibid., p. 38.
22. Time Line—"A Brief History of the Fur Trade," www.whiteoak.org/learning/timeline.html.
23. Newman, *Empire of the Bay*, p. 45.

The First Ships Appear

24. Grace Lee Nute, *Lake Superior* (Indianapolis: Bobbs-Merrill Company, 1944), pp. 116–17, 161–65.
25. James Davie Butler, "Early Shipping on Lake Superior," in *Proceedings of the State Historical Society of Wisconsin* (1894), p. 92. Nute, *Lake Superior*, pp. 119–20. The second *Recovery* had a brief but colorful history. During the War of 1812 she was dismantled and secreted at McCargo Cove on Isle Royale to avoid capture by the Americans, and she was chartered to the British Navy during 1824 and 1825 for Lieutenant Henry Bayfield's historic surveys of Lake Superior. She ended her days on the lower lakes, having run down the Sault rapids successfully in 1828.
26. David A. Walker and Stephen P. Hall, *Duluth-Superior Harbor Cultural Resources Study* (St. Paul: Department of the Army, St. Paul District, Corps of Engineers, August 1976), p. 51–52. Nute, *Lake Superior*, pp. 173–81.

CHAPTER 2: THE LOCKS AND LA POINTE

27. George Rogers Taylor, *The Economic History of the United States: The Transportation Revolution, 1815–1860*, vol. 4: (New York: Harper Torchbooks, 1968), pp. 32–34.
28. Patrick T. Reardon, "It ain't out of Mark Twain, but Chicagoland's river system is healthy and surging as a recreational asset," *Chicago Tribune*, July 18, 2002. The canal boom from the 1820s to the 1840s was the occasion of a speculative land frenzy that drove prices up across the eastern United States. The panic of 1837 and the coming of the railroads in the 1840s left hundreds of canal projects little more than debt-ridden, water-filled ditches.
29. Taylor, *The Transportation Revolution*, pp. 60–61.
30. Frederick Merk, *History of the Westward Movement* (New York: Alfred A. Knopf, 1978), pp. 169–71.
31. Jared Diamond, *Guns, Germs, and Steel* (New York: W. W. Norton and Company, 1997), pp. 211–12.
32. See Elizabeth A. Fenn, *Pox Americana* (New York: Hill and Wang, 2001), for an excellent discussion of the role that disease plays in military campaigns. Both colonial and British regiments practiced inoculation, which exposed a patient to a milder form of pox and thus created an immunity to the more lethal forms of *Variola*. But the Revolutionary War outbreak of smallpox took a fearsome toll on the Native American allies of the combatants.
33. Diamond, *Guns, Germs, and Steel*, p. 212.
34. Merk, *History of the Westward Movement*, p. 172.
35. Ibid., pp. 4–5.
36. Ibid., pp. xviii–xix.
37. Krause, *The Making of a Mining District*, pp. 113–15. The *Detroit Free Press* called the Upper Peninsula "the *Ultima Thule* of our national domain in the north."
38. Angus Murdoch, *Boom Copper* (New York: MacMillan Company, 1943), pp. 24–25. Houghton's 1841 report was instrumental in the U.S. government's decision to approach the Lake Superior Anishinaabe about adding the Upper Peninsula to the land cessions of the 1837 treaty.
39. William B. Gates Jr., *Michigan Copper and Boston Dollars: An Economic History of the Michigan Copper Mining Industry* (Cambridge: Harvard University Press, 1951), p. 11.
40. Larry Lankton, *Beyond the Boundaries: Life and Landscape at the Lake Superior Copper Mines, 1840–1875* (Oxford: Oxford University Press, 1997), p. 11. A rock monument to Houghton overlooks Lake Superior at Eagle River, one of the more beautiful vistas on the Great Lakes.
41. Burton H. Boyum, *The Saga of Iron Mining in Michigan's Upper Peninsula* (Marquette: John M. Longyear Research Library, 1983), p. 5.
42. T. B. Brooks, "Iron Bearing Rocks," in *Michigan Geological Survey, Upper Peninsula Edition* (New York: 1873), pp. 14–15.
43. Boyum, *The Saga of Iron Mining in Michigan's Upper Peninsula*, pp. 6–7.
44. Ibid., p. 7.
45. Harlan Hatcher, *A Century of Iron and Men* (Indianapolis: Bobbs-Merrill Company, 1950), p. 75.
46. Quoted in Lankton, *Beyond the Boundaries*, p. 33. Senator Clay would likely have looked more kindly upon the project had it been located in the Commonwealth of Kentucky.
47. Lankton, *Beyond the Boundaries*, p. 33. When the federal government began talking seriously about building a second Poe-size lock at the Sault in 2000, the operative word was "cost-sharing" with the states.
48. J. Jay Myers, "The Salesman Who Built a Canal," *American History* (August 2001): 58.

49. Ibid. Erastus Fairbanks was no stranger to state politics. He had been elected governor of Vermont in the fall of 1852.

50. Ibid.

51. Walter Havighurst, *The Long Ships Passing: The Story of the Great Lakes* (New York: MacMillan Company, 1942), p. 203.

52. Myers, "The Salesman Who Built a Canal," p. 60. After one year, Harvey had spent $385,000, and the canal and locks were less than half-finished.

53. Boyum, *The Saga of Iron Mining in Michigan's Upper Peninsula*, p. 14. Five years later, Wilson was at the helm of the schooner *Augusta* when it rammed the steamer *Lady Elgin* in Lake Michigan with the subsequent loss of both vessels and 286 lives. See Havighurst, *The Long Ships Passing*, pp. 204–05.

54. Hatcher, *A Century of Iron and Men*, p. 78.

55. Catherine Calhoun, "Through the Locks," *American Heritage* (September 1992): 26.

56. Myers, "The Salesman Who Built a Canal," p. 60. Harvey outlived all of his contemporaries. He moved to Marquette following the opening of the canal but returned to the East in 1867. He died in New York in 1912.

57. Calhoun, "Through the Locks," p. 27.

58. Ibid., p. 27.

Sails on the Horizon

59. Murdoch, *Boom Copper*, p. 192. It took seven weeks in the summer of 1845 to move the 35-ton *Ocean* overland around the rapids. Crews drew the Detroit-owned sloop across the portage on rollers, winching her forward with a capstan and chains. One observer likened it to moving a house. The rapids consist of a twenty-one-foot drop in the water level in a one-mile section of the river.

60. Nute, *Lake Superior*, p. 121. See also *Detroit Daily Advertiser*, Nov. 14, 1839, and *Oswego* (New York) *Palladium*, November 20, 1839. The *Algonquin* was built at Black River, Ohio, in 1839 and brought to the Sault in November of the same year. She was built to trade between La Pointe and Sault Ste. Marie and survived into the early 1860s, when she was abandoned on the Superior City waterfront and eventually buried in a landfill.

61. The *Independence* was built at Chicago in 1843 by Captain James Averill. In 1845 she was brought to Lake Superior to become the pioneer steam vessel on that body of water. *Independence* was 112 feet long and fitted with two primitive Ericsson screw propellers, one of which is still preserved in the public park at the Soo Locks. The ship was destroyed by a boiler explosion just west of Sault Ste. Marie on November 21, 1853. Other steamers brought to Lake Superior before 1855 are the propellers *Manhattan*, *Monticello*, and *Peninsula* and the side wheel steamboats *Julia Palmer*, *Baltimore*, and *Sam Ward*. See Nute, p. 113 ff.

62. Stonehouse, "The Missing Merchant," p. 3.

63. Mentor L. Williams, "Horace Greeley on Lake Superior in 1848," *Inland Seas* (Spring 1950): 38.

64. Ibid., p. 41. Greeley might never have served to be such an eloquent voice for harbors, lighthouses, locks, and other improvements save for a stroke of luck. On June 12, 1847, he elected to leave the Sault aboard the steamer *Independence* instead of the ill-fated *Merchant*. See Williams, "Horace Greeley Tours the Great Lakes," *Inland Seas* (July 1947): 141.

CHAPTER 3: STEEL RAILS TO THE HEAD OF THE LAKES

65. Hatcher, *A Century of Iron and Men*, p. 82.

66. Ibid., p. 82. The drop in haulage costs from Negaunee to Marquette stemmed from the 1855 construction of the first wooden ore dock at Marquette and the establishment of the first primitive rail lines to serve the mines. See Boyum, *The Saga of Iron Mining in Michigan's Upper Peninsula*, pp. 12–13.

67. Thomas McKenney, *Sketches of a Tour to the Lakes* (Minneapolis: Reprint Editions, 1959), p. 270.

68. Quoted in Van Brunt, *Duluth and St. Louis County, Minnesota*, vol. 1, p. 65.

69. Nute, *Lake Superior*, p. 276. Douglas, who would go down in history for his series of debates with Abraham Lincoln, had pioneered the concept of trading federal land grants as an incentive for railroad construction. His 1850 legislation made land grants available for building the Illinois Central Railroad through his home state and paved the way for the 1855 land grant that encouraged Michigan to build a canal and locks at the Sault.

70. Bill Beck, *From the Foot of Winter Street: The History of Superior Water, Light, and Power Company, 1889–1989* (Superior, Wisconsin: Superior Water, Light, and Power Company, 1989), p. 3.

71. Ann Stultz Bailey, "The Towns That Became Duluth," *Duluth: Sketches of the Past*: 88–89. *Oneota* is an Anishinaabe word meaning "the rock from which people sprang." Reverend Ely's original homesite was at about Forty-second Avenue West.

72. Ibid., p. 89. As a measure of just how difficult land transportation was in 1855, it took Wheeler and his family six weeks to get from St. Paul to Oneota. The family took a river steamer south to La Crosse on the Upper Mississippi and then journeyed by stagecoach across Wisconsin to Green Bay. They crossed Lake Michigan to Harbor Springs, where they took a stagecoach to the Soo. A steamer took them to Madeline Island in the Apostles, where they hired an open mackinaw boat to sail to Superior.

73. Quoted in ibid., p. 89.

74. James MacGregor Burns, *The Vineyard of Liberty* (New York: Vintage Books, 1983), pp. 588–89. The bear market of the summer of 2002 bore some of the earmarks of a nineteenth-century panic. Institutional and individual investors suddenly no longer trusted audited corporate financial reports in the wake of the Enron and WorldCom bookkeeping scandals.

75. Ralph G. Plumb, "The 1857 Depression on the Lakes," *Inland Seas* (Winter 1954): 290–91.

76. Julius F. Wolff Jr., "The Ships and Duluth," *Duluth: Sketches of the Past*: 144.

77. John R. Borchert, *America's Northern Heartland: An Economic and Historical Geography of the Upper Midwest* (Minneapolis: University of Minnesota Press, 1987), p. 31.

78. Merk, *History of the Westward Movement*, pp. 431–35. Southern Minnesota was primarily short-grass prairie, easily cleared for the planting of wheat. The advent of mechanical binders and reapers during the late 1850s and early 1860s, as well as the introduction of the chilled steel plow in 1868, boosted wheat productivity in Minnesota and Iowa exponentially.

79. Folwell, *A History of Minnesota in Four Volumes*, vol. 2, pp. 37–41. Two of the railroads would run north and west to the Red River Valley. The remaining three railroads would blanket the southern third of the state.

80. Ibid., pp. 41–42.

81. Ibid., p. 53.

82. J. L. Harnsberger, "Jay Cooke and Minnesota: The Formative Years of the Northern Pacific Railway, 1868–1873" (Ph.D. diss., University of Minnesota, 1956), p. 19.

83. Ralph S. Knowlton, "The First Century of Your Harbor," presentation made at Duluth, Minnesota, April 23, 1956, p. 2.

84. Walker and Hall, *Duluth-Superior Harbor Cultural Resources Study*, p. 31. That first lighthouse, however, was not equipped with a foghorn. In foggy weather, the lighthouse keeper resorted to shouting through a tin horn to guide mariners into the harbor.

85. "The Army, the 'Essy,' and Her Engine," *The Nor'Easter* (March–April 1979): 1.

86. Ralph S. Knowlton, "A Short History of the Improvements of Duluth-Superior Harbor," presentation to the St. Louis County Historical Society, Duluth, Minnesota, March 24, 1959, p. 4.

87. Quoted in Knowlton, "A Short History of the Improvements of Duluth-Superior Harbor," p. 4.

88. Harnsberger, "Jay Cooke and Minnesota," p. 22. The Wilderness was Grant's first major battle as commander of the Army of the Potomac. The butcher's bill for the two-day battle was 26,000 Union and Confederate casualties. Instead of retreating across the Rapidan River to lick his wounds, as each of his predecessors had done during three years of war, Grant ordered Corps Commander George G. Meade to push southeast toward Richmond, thus sealing the fate of the Confederacy. See William A. Frassanito, *Grant and Lee: The Virginia Campaigns, 1864–1865* (New York: Charles Scribner's Sons, 1983), pp. 46–48.

89. Harnsberger, "Jay Cooke and Minnesota," p. 22. At the time of the land grant, most of what remained of the population of the town sites that became Duluth had pulled up stakes and moved inland to Lake Vermilion to prospect for gold. No gold was ever found in the 1864 rush, but the excitement did give geologists a chance to examine what would become of Minnesota's first iron range.

90. Walker and Hall, *Duluth-Superior Harbor Cultural Resources Study*, p. 27.

91. Brian Trumbore, "Jay Cooke—Part 2," www.buyandhold.com/bh/en/education/history/2000/jay_cooke2.html. Cooke's investment banking house, Jay Cooke and Company, made only $200,000 on the sale of bonds during the war.

92. "Jay Cooke, The Man," www.acs.ohio-state.edu/cookecastle/theman_b.html.

93. Harnsberger, "Jay Cooke and Minnesota," p. 25. Cooke had worked for Clark from 1839 until the firm failed in the panic of 1857. Cooke had then helped his old boss to reorganize the company during the Civil War.

94. Harnsberger, "Jay Cooke and Minnesota," p. 28.

95. Dora MacDonald, *This Is Duluth* (Duluth, Minnesota: Central High School, 1950), p. 67.

96. Franklin A. King, "Railroads at the Head of the Lakes," *Duluth: Sketches of the Past*, p. 182. The trip took sixteen hours, at an average speed of just under ten miles per hour. But before the coming of the railroad, the only way to get from St. Paul to the head of the lakes was to walk—and that might take up to a month—or to come up by horse and wagon.

97. Ibid., p. 182. The newspapers brought up on that first train would have told of the July 24 inauguration of rail service between San Francisco and New York with the successful completion the year before of the first transcontinental railroad.

98. Ibid., p. 182. Most in Minnesota did not know that Banning had already been ousted by the Cooke directors on the board.

99. Quoted in Van Brunt, *Duluth and St. Louis County, Minnesota*, vol. I, p. 234.

Digging the Duluth Ship Canal

100. Walker and Hall, *Duluth-Superior Harbor Cultural Resources Study*, p. 32.

101. Knowlton, "A Short History of the Improvements of Duluth-Superior Harbor," p. 5.

102. Walker and Hall, *Duluth-Superior Harbor Cultural Resources Study*, p. 66. In the spring of 1871, the steamer *St. Paul* inaugurated Duluth's first full navigation season with a load of 11,500 bushels of wheat from Elevator A.

103. The Corps of Engineers spent $110,000 in 1871 and the spring of 1872 lengthening the breakwater by 500 feet. Their efforts were all for naught. The breakwater was heavily damaged in a July 1872 storm and nearly destroyed by a nor'easter in the fall. See Knowlton, "A Short History of the Improvements of Duluth-Superior Harbor," p. 6. One of the victims of the November 12, 1872, storm was the steamer *St. Paul*, which was tied up to the breakwater. The *St. Paul* slipped its moorings in the fierce northeast wind, drifted across the length of Minnesota Point, and crashed into the breakwater guarding the Superior entry before coming to rest about 100 feet off the entry. See Steven J. Wright, "The Forgotten November Storm," *The Nor'Easter* (September–October 1987): 1–3.

104. Quoted in John L. Harnsberger, "Land, Lobbies, Railroads and the Origins of Duluth," *Minnesota History* (Winter 1960): 95.

105. To get construction on the canal under way, Duluth had obligated itself to pay the costs of dredging. The Lake Superior & Mississippi and Northern Pacific railroads, both essentially controlled by Jay Cooke and Company, agreed to jointly assume control of the canal on July 1, 1871, reimbursing Duluth for its expenditures. See Letter, A. B. Neublen, Duluth, to Jay Cooke, Philadelphia, August 11, 1871, quoted in Stuart V. Bradley Jr., "Duluth During the 1870s," in *Duluth: Sketches of the Past*, p. 244.

106. Frank A. Young, *Duluth's Ship Canal and Aerial Bridge: How They Came To Be* (Duluth: Stewart-Taylor Company, 1977), p. 2.

107. Ibid., p. 3. The dock was also known as the Citizens' Dock.

108. Wolff, "The Ships and Duluth," in *Duluth: Sketches of the Past*, p. 145.

109. From August 1863 to November 1864, General Andrew Atkinson Humphreys served as chief of staff to General George Gordon Meade, the U.S. Corps of Topographical Engineers officer who had authorized the first survey of the Duluth-Superior Harbor in June 1861. See *Historical Times Encyclopedia of the Civil War*, pp. 374–75.

110. J. D. Ensign, *History of Duluth Harbor* (Duluth: 1898), p. 8.

111. Ibid., p. 8. Since the water in the bay was several inches higher than in the lake, the water immediately began flowing into Lake Superior once the breach was made.

112. Ibid., p. 8. Most accounts agree that the vessel in question was the *Fero*, although it is variously described as a steamer, a steam yacht, a little ferry boat, and a steam tug. See Letter, Davis Helberg, Duluth Seaway Port Authority, to Ken Hogg, Duluth City Council, April 10, 2001.

113. Ibid., p. 8.

114. Quoted in Ibid., p. 9.

115. Young, *Duluth's Ship Canal and Aerial Bridge: How They Came To Be*, p. 3.

116. Ibid., p. 3. See also Glenn N. Sandvik, *Duluth: An Illustrated History of the Zenith City* (Woodland Hills, California: Windsor Publications, 1983), p. 32 .

117. Ensign, *History of Duluth Harbor*, p. 9.

118. The amount of the bond was eventually reduced to $80,000, and the Northern Pacific Railway evidently spent only $14,000 to construct the dike. See Bradley, "Duluth During the 1870s," p. 244. Belknap served as U.S. Grant's secretary of war from 1869 to 1876, when he was driven from office in a bribery scandal. Belknap Street in Superior commemorates his activities during the ship canal fight. See *Historical Times Encyclopedia of the Civil War*, p. 53.

119. Walker and Hall, *Duluth-Superior Harbor Cultural Resources Study*, p. 35. Major Houston, in the meantime, had changed his earlier opposition to the Minnesota Point canal, noting that the depth of the Superior Entry had not changed since the new canal had been dug. See Ensign, *History of Duluth Harbor*, p. 12.

120. Walker and Hall, *Duluth-Superior Harbor Cultural Resources Study*, p. 35. The increased current also broke up many of the floating islands on the upper reaches of the Wisconsin side of the bay. As late as the mid-1880s, islands of matted vegetation 70 feet long were still floating out into the lake.

121. Ibid., p. 37.

122. Wolff, "The Ships and Duluth," p. 145.

CHAPTER 4: WHEAT TO FEED THE WORLD

123. Walker and Hall, *Duluth-Superior Harbor Cultural Resources Study*, p. 65. Captain Atkins, a resident of Duluth from 1870 to 1876, claimed years later that he had loaded the first cargo of wheat from Duluth on August 2, 1870. Atkins, who was the agent for the Union Steamship Company in 1870, claimed he handled the transfer of 10,000 bushels of wheat from ex-governor Hubbard's mill at Red Wing into the steamer *Arctic*. "The old breakwater dock and elevator were not finished," Atkins recalled in 1902. "So they had to lay down loose boards in order to roll the flour into the boat, and then the wheat was taken in wheelbarrows and wheeled aboard the boat and dumped in, about 10,000 bushels." See News Item, *The Marine Record* 25 (February 27, 1902): 9.

124. Harnsberger, "Jay Cooke and Minnesota," p. 33.

125. Harnsberger, p. 34.

126. Edward B. Nolan, *Northern Pacific Views: The Railroad Photography of F. Jay Haynes, 1876–1905* (Helena: Montana Historical Society Press, 1983), p. 32. Another Civil War commander, then captain George B. McClellan, surveyed the northern route for the transcontinental railroad in 1853–1854.

127. Ibid., p. 34.

128. Ibid., p. 34. Milepost 1 of the Northern Pacific was located at the tiny railroad settlement of Kokomo, just west of Carlton.

129. Ibid., p. 34.

130. Ibid., p. 289. Martin's argument stressed that by the 1870s, railroads no longer needed navigable bodies of water to be profitable.

131. Bradley, "Duluth During the 1870s," *Duluth: Sketches of the Past*, p. 241. Cooke and his brother-in-law made their first purchase of 40,000 acres for the Western Land Association in the summer of 1869. The association's legacy is still reflected in the street names of Duluth's Lakeside neighborhood. Jay Cooke, Pitt, Gladstone, Robinson, and McCulloch Streets all commemorate the Philadelphia and London investors in the association.

132. Nolan, *Northern Pacific Views*, p. 36. It would be two years until construction resumed on a reorganized Northern Pacific.

133. Bradley, "Duluth in the 1870s," p. 244. Weather compounded the financial woes. Ice remained in the lake until July 1874, and a March blizzard in 1876 cut off the village from rail transportation for several weeks and stranded half a dozen vessels in the pack ice, twelve miles from shore.

134. Walker and Hall, *Duluth-Superior Harbor Cultural Resources Study*, p. 37. Even in the depths of the panic, Duluth still reported 290 vessel visits in 1874. None called on Superior.

135. Ibid., p. 37.

136. Elwyn B. Robinson, *History of North Dakota* (Lincoln: University of North Dakota Press, 1966), p. 134. The Dakota Territory was admitted to the union as the states of North and South Dakota in 1889.

137. Harold E. Briggs, "Early Bonanza Farming in the Red River Valley of the North," *Agricultural History* (January 1932): 27–28.

138. Ibid., 135. As its name implies, winter wheat is planted in the late fall or early winter and harvested in the spring. The fierce winters of Minnesota and North Dakota sent frost several feet into the ground and often prevented the seed from germinating.

139. Ibid., 51–52. The suspension of the fine white powdered flour on the compressed air jets created an explosive fuel that is still the bane of the milling industry.

140. Ibid., 52.

141. Henrietta M. Larson, *The Wheat Market and the Farmer in Minnesota, 1858–1900* (New York: Columbia University Studies in History, Economics, and Public Law, 1926), pp. 55–37. Minneapolis, however, took receipt of nearly 33 million bushels of wheat in 1885.

142. Thomas D. Odle, "The American Grain Trade of the Great Lakes, 1825–1873," *Inland Seas,* Part VI (Spring 1953): 53. Oswego, located east of Buffalo on Lake Ontario, handled much of the grain trade on Lake Ontario below or east of Niagara Falls. In 1849, Buffalo and Oswego handled a combined 5 million bushels of wheat and more than 2 million barrels of flour. A bushel of wheat weighs 60 pounds, and a flour barrel when full weighed 216 pounds. See Odle, op. cit., Part III (Summer 1952): 104.

143. Odle, op. cit., Part VIII (Fall 1953): 163. Buffalo merchants established the Buffalo board of trade in 1844 to trade grain futures from the western lakes.

144. Odle, op. cit., Part IV (Fall 1952): 190.

145. "Grain Elevators: A History," http://bhw.buffnet.net/grain/history/history.htm.

146. Joseph Dart, "The Grain Elevators of Buffalo," Buffalo Historical Society, *Publications* 1 (1865): 401.

147. "Grain Elevators: A History."

148. Walker and Hall, *Duluth-Superior Harbor Cultural Resources Study,* pp. 65–66. The typical lakes vessel calling on Elevator A in the 1870s could load approximately 3,000 to 5,000 bushels of grain for the trip down the lakes.

149. Wes Harkins, Listing of Harbor Improvements, Duluth-Superior Harbor, n.d., p. 1.

150. Duluth Seaway Port Authority, Duluth-Superior Harbor Statistics, 1994, p. 1. A good portion of the falloff in 1875 was due to the competition from the southern Minnesota railroads and the Minneapolis milling market rather than to economic conditions. Part of the falloff in 1875 can also be attributed to locust plagues in 1874 and 1875. South central and western Minnesota were particularly affected. See Annette Atkins, *Harvest of Grief: Grasshopper Plagues and Public Assistance in Minnesota, 1873–1878* (St. Paul: Minnesota Historical Society Press, 1984), p. 20.

151. Walker and Hall, *Duluth-Superior Harbor Cultural Resources Study,* p. 66.

152. Duluth-Superior Harbor Statistics, p. 1.

153. Patrick Lapinski, "Superior's Globe Elevator: Monument to the Glory of Grain," *Nor'Easter* (November–December 1996): 2.

154. Harkins, Listing of Harbor Improvements, p. 3. The expansion of Elevator No. 1 in 1880 added another 500,000 bushels of capacity to the harbor's grain-handling facilities.

155. Duluth-Superior Harbor Statistics, pp. 1–2.

156. Harkins, Listing of Harbor Improvements, p. 3.

157. Ibid., p. 3. Naming elevators in alphabetical order is one of those enduring mysteries of the Duluth-Superior Harbor. The practice continued through the construction of Elevator X in 1886.

158. Walker and Hall, *Duluth-Superior Harbor Cultural Resources Survey,* p. 67. By 1886, the original lakefront elevators had passed from the scene. Elevator No. 1 was enlarged to 700,000 bushels in 1880 but was destroyed by fire later that year. The Duluth and Western Elevator Company rebuilt Elevator No. 1 in 1884, but the rebuilt elevator was destroyed in an 1886 conflagration. That was the fate also of Elevator A, which had been enlarged to 560,000 bushels in 1886 before burning down several months later.

159. King, "Railroads at the Head of the Lakes," p. 188. The other nucleus of the Great Northern, which was formed in 1889, was the St. Paul, Minneapolis, & Manitoba. In 1892, the Great Northern extended 1,600 miles from Superior to Spokane, Washington.

160. Harkins, Listing of Harbor Improvements, p. 6.

161. Lapinski, "Superior's Globe Elevator," 1.

162. Ibid., 2–3. Residents of Superior, still chafing over Duluth's extralegal construction of the ship canal in 1871, were not terribly happy with the name "Duluth Elevator Co." towering over the Superior harbor. When Frank Peavey took over control of the elevator in 1894, he wisely changed the name to the Globe Elevator Company.

163. Walker and Hall, *Duluth-Superior Harbor Cultural Resources Study,* p. 68. Duluth-Superior elevators handled more than 25 million bushels of wheat in 1890 and had to divert almost 10 million bushels to elevators in the Twin Cities.

164. Duluth-Superior Harbor Statistics, p. 2.

165. Quoted in Beck, *From the Foot of Winter Street,* p. 3.

In the Eye of the Beholder

166. John W. Larson, *Essayons: A History of the Detroit District, U.S. Army Corps of Engineers* (Washington, U.S. Government Printing Office, 1998), pp. 104–10. The 1.5-mile St. Clair Flats Ship Canal was completed in 1871.

167. Frank E. Kirby, "Shipping on the Great Lakes," in *Transactions,* vol. 53, part 2 (New York: Institute of Naval Architects, 1911).

168. John F. Devendorf, *Great Lakes Bulk Carriers, 1869–1985* (Niles, Michigan: John F. Devendorf, 1985).

169. Dwight True, *Sixty Years of Shipbuilding* (Ann Arbor: Society of Naval Architects and Marine Engineers, 1956), pp. 5–6. See also James P. Barry, *Ships of the Great Lakes* (Holt, Michigan: Thunder Bay Press, 1996), pp. 136, 145 ff.

170. Cf. Devendorf, *Great Lakes Bulk Carriers, 1869–1985,* and Barry, *Ships of the Great Lakes.* For a concise summary see also C. Patrick Labadie and Larry Murphy, "Major Vessel Types on Lake Superior: Sail to Steam," in Daniel J. Lenihan, ed., *Submerged Cultural Resources Study, Isle Royale National Park* (Santa Fe, N.M.: U.S. National Park Service, 1987), pp. 43–61.

CHAPTER 5: IRON PORT, COAL PORT

171. Letter, Alexander McDougall, President, Duluth and Superior Harbor Improvement Commission, Everett, Washington, September 20, 1894, to Colonel O. M. Poe, Senior Member, Commission of Engineers, Sault Ste. Marie, Michigan. The unrelenting slaughter of buffalo by market hunters in the late 1880s led the Lakota to embark upon the disastrous 1890 Ghost Dance War.

172. Frederick Jackson Turner's "The Significance of the Frontier in American History," first given as a presentation to the American Historical Association in Chicago in 1893, suggested that the replacement of buffalo by cattle on the high plains was evidence of the final passing of the frontier. See "Turner, Frederick Jackson," *Webster's American Biographies,* p. 1057.

173. By the time the Duluth Ship Canal was dug in 1871, the United States was producing more than 33 million tons of coal a year. See Louis C. Hunter and Lynwood Bryant, *A History of Industrial Power in the United States, 1780–1930: The Transmission of Power* vol. 3 (Cambridge, Massachusetts: MIT Press, 1991), p. 420.

174. Ibid., p. 415. After the Civil War, the anthracite region of eastern Pennsylvania was connected by rail to Buffalo on Lake Ontario.

175. Wayne G. Broehl Jr., *Cargill: Trading the World's Grain* (Dartmouth College: University Press of New England, 1992), pp. 50–52. Cargill also became an agent for the Union Steamboat Company, which maintained steamer service between Buffalo and Green Bay.

176. Walker and Hall, *Duluth-Superior Harbor Cultural Resources Study,* p. 87. The first coal dock had a capacity of 63,000 tons and was located between Third and Fifth Avenues West. At full capacity, that first coal dock would have been barely sufficient to load one 1,000-foot vessel that regularly calls on the Superior Midwest Energy Terminal for downbound loads of western coal today.

177. Harkins, Listing of Harbor Structures, pp. 1–8.

178. Duluth-Superior Harbor Statistics, p. 2. Major consumers of coal from the end of the Civil War to World War II were the railroads themselves. By 1885, U.S. railroads were burning nearly 30 million tons of coal. Duluth-Superior served as a receiving point for railroad coal that was shipped as far west as Montana and as far east as the Upper Peninsula of Michigan. See Sam H. Schnurr and Bruce C. Netschert, *Energy in the American Economy, 1850–1975: Its History and Prospects* (Baltimore: Johns Hopkins Press, 1960), p. 82.

179. Duluth-Superior Harbor Statistics, p. 2.

180. Harkins, Listing of Harbor Structures, pp. 4–5. Later that summer of 1889, Great Northern built a second coal dock of 500,000-ton capacity adjacent to the first. Until 1909, when it was leased to Carnegie Coal Company, the second dock was reserved for the railroad's use.

181. Ibid., pp. 6–8.

182. Walker and Hall, *Duluth-Superior Harbor Cultural Resources Study,* p. 88.

183. Bill Beck, *Northern Lights: An Illustrated History of Minnesota Power* (Duluth: Minnesota Power, 1985), p. 2. The next year, the

Duluth Electric Light and Power Company, the city's first electric utility, acquired the generator from the sawmill.

184. Walker and Hall, *Duluth-Superior Harbor Cultural Resources Study,* p. 89.

185. Minnesota Historical Society, "History and Development of Great Lakes Water Craft," www.mnhs.org/places/nationalregister/shipwrecks/mpdf/mpdf2.html, p. 7. Interestingly enough, the bulk freighters plying the lakes in the 1890s were only fifty feet longer than the *Hackett.* The deepening of the channels by four feet in 1884 had a major impact on the amount of cargo a bulk freighter could carry.

186. News Item, *Duluth Evening Herald,* May 17, 1888.

187. James R. Marshall, "Back to a Time When Iron Will . . . and Does," *Lake Superior Magazine* (February–March 2002): 11. The iron propeller *Merchant,* built at Buffalo in 1862, was the first iron vessel on the lakes.

188. Minnesota Historical Society, "History and Development of Great Lakes Water Craft," www.mnhs.org/places/nationalregister/shipwrecks/ mpdf/mpdf2.html, p. 7.

189. Marshall, "Back to a Time When Iron Will … and Does," 12–13.

190. David A. Walker, *Iron Frontier: The Discovery and Early Development of Minnesota's Three Ranges* (St. Paul: Minnesota Historical Society Press, 1979), p. 13. Geologists had suspected the existence of a substantial body of ore on the Menominee Range since at least the late 1840s. The range was named for the river forming the boundary between Wisconsin and the Upper Peninsula.

191. Ibid., p. 74. The Gogebic Range was named for the big inland lake north of Ironwood in the western Upper Peninsula.

192. Ibid., p. 74. Ashland's emergence as an iron port affirmed Chequamegon Bay's reputation as one of the finest natural anchorages on Lake Superior's south shore, a fact that French voyageurs and missionaries had known two hundred years before.

193. Hatcher, *A Century of Iron and Men,* p. 147.

194. Walker, *Iron Frontier,* p. 24. Stuntz later gave most of the samples to the Smithsonian Institution.

195. Quoted in ibid., p. 24.

196. Ibid., p. 26. The influence of Harvard University in the development of Lake Superior's mineral resources cannot be overestimated. The Agassiz and Shaw families of Boston, all Harvard graduates or instructors, almost single-handedly developed and controlled the giant Calumet & Hecla copper empire on Michigan's Keweenaw Peninsula in the years following the Civil War. See Gates, *Michigan Copper and Boston Dollars,* pp. 39–63.

197. Hatcher, *A Century of Iron and Men,* p. 148.

198. Franklin A. King, "Two Harbors: Minnesota's First Iron Ore Port," *The Nor'Easter* (September–October 1984): 1. The steel industry in 1880 was busily turning out steel rails and bridge girders. Steel demand would increase almost exponentially during the last two decades of the nineteenth century, as the domestic steel industry began producing the first of millions of structural girders and I-beams for the skyscrapers that would build America's cities up and not out. See Kenneth T. Jackson, *Crabgrass Frontier: The Suburbanization of the United States* (Oxford: Oxford University Press, 1985), p. 113.

199. Walker, *Iron Frontier,* p. 37. The 1881 law called for the payment of a one-cent per ton royalty on iron ore produced, to be shared equally between the state and the county.

200. Ibid., pp. 50–51. Chief among the incorporators of the Duluth & Iron Range Railroad was George Stone.

201. King, "Railroads at the Head of the Lakes," 186.

202. King, "Two Harbors: Minnesota's First Iron Ore Port," 2. Because of soil problems, Ore Dock No. 2 was the first to be finished. It consumed more than two million board feet of lumber.

203. Warren Upham, *Minnesota Geographic Names: Their Origin and Historic Significance* (St. Paul: Minnesota Historical Society Press, reprint edition, 1969), p. 490. In the mid-1880s, Americans avidly followed events in the Soudan, including the siege of Khartoum in 1884 and the death of General Charles "Chinese" Gordon. In 1998, the author flabbergasted a Sudanese cab driver working the Minneapolis airport when he pointed out the existence of Soudan on a Minnesota map. Volunteers at the Tower-Soudan visitors' center were likely equally amazed when carloads of Sudanese began arriving that summer to visit their namesake community.

204. King, "Railroads at the Head of the Lakes," 186.

205. Hatcher, *A Century of Iron and Men,* p. 150. As early as 1886, the Minnesota Iron Company was reporting an annual profit of $300,000. See King, "Two Harbors: Minnesota's First Iron Port," 2.

206. Havighurst, *Vein of Iron,* p. 75. There are reputedly sixteen ways of spelling *Mesabi,* including Mesaba, Missabe, Mesabe, and Missabi.

207. Ibid., p. 153.

208. Ibid., p. 155. Between December 1890 and September 1892, 127 companies were incorporated to develop mines and pits on the Mesabi Range.

209. Walker, *Iron Frontier,* p. 101. The junction was located twenty-six miles west of Duluth and is now the site of the community of Brookston, Minnesota.

210. Walker and Hall, *Duluth-Superior Harbor Cultural Resources Study,* p. 76. That first ore dock stretched 600 feet into the harbor and had a modest capacity of 1,500 tons.

211. Ibid., p. 104. Oliver returned to Pittsburgh and immediately called upon Henry Clay Frick. He persuaded Frick to loan him $500,000 for an interest in his Mesabi Range mining lease, which put Frick's boss, Andrew Carnegie, into the Lake Superior iron ore business.

212. Walker and Hall, *Duluth-Superior Harbor Cultural Resources Study,* p. 76. The first 2,000-ton shipment of Mesabi ore from Superior went down the Great Lakes to Cleveland in November 1892.

213. Stewart Holbrook, *Iron Brew: A Century of American Ore and Steel* (MacMillan: 1939), p. 157. Had the Merritts sold in 1892, it is unlikely that Duluth-Superior would have become the iron port it did. Tower evidently wanted to extend his Duluth & Iron Range Railroad south and west along the Mesabi and then ship the ore to Two Harbors for shipment down the lakes.

214. Ibid., pp. 100–101. Leonidas Merritt was a poet. In the style of Longfellow, he wrote about the family's plans:

> We are going to build a railway,
> With easy grades for transportation,
> From the mines of the Mis-sa-be
> To the smokestacks of the Zenith
> To the furnaces for smelting,
> To the mills where cunning fingers
> Fashion articles for commerce,
> Structural steel and heavy castings,
> Tools and rails and nails and what-not.

215. John Steele Gordon, *The Business of America* (New York: Walker and Company, 2001), p. 175. Overextended railroads were hit especially hard by the panic. Between 1893 and 1897, nearly one-third of the nation's railroad trackage would enter receivership.

216. Ron Chernow, *Titan: The Life of John D. Rockefeller Sr.* (New York: Random House, 1998), pp. 382–85. Rockefeller's interest in iron ore is no mystery. From his office in Cleveland, he could watch the bulk freighters unloading cargoes of Michigan and Minnesota iron ore at the docks of the Cleveland harbor.

217. Ibid., p. 385.

218. Walker and Hall, *Duluth-Superior Harbor Cultural Resources Study,* p. 78. In 1896, more iron ore flowed through Duluth-Superior than through Two Harbors.

219. Duluth-Superior Harbor Statistics, p. 2.

220. Ibid., p. 2. It would be more than one hundred years before the flow of coal through the Twin Ports exceeded the flow of iron ore—but then the coal would be outbound, not inbound.

221. Sandvik, *Duluth: An Illustrated History of the Zenith City,* p. 49. During the 1890s, Duluth had annexed many of the small villages on the eastern and western fringes of the city.

America's Steel District Emerges

222. Holbrook, *Iron Brew,* pp. 189–93. Bessemer's patent was contested in the United States by a Kentuckian who had discovered a similar process in the mid-1850s. The two sides eventually agreed to combine their processes at the U.S. Patent Office in 1866.

223. Ibid., p. 12. In 1879, two English chemists discovered that the phosphorous problem could be all but eliminated by lining the walls of the converter with lime, thus creating a ready market for the immense limestone deposits on Michigan's Lake Huron shores.

224. John P. Hoerr, *And The Wolf Finally Came: The Decline of the American Steel Industry* (Pittsburgh: University of Pittsburgh Press, 1988), p. 87. Because of the impurities burned off the coal in the coke ovens, environmental regulations have all but outlawed most coking operations in the United States. Today, most coking coal used by integrated steelmakers is imported from China.

225. Holbrook, *Iron Brew,* pp. 206–09. Ironically, construction shut down in September 1873 following the failure of Jay Cooke's banking house, an event that provided evidence of the first economic link between Duluth and Pittsburgh.

226. Ibid., p. 209.

CHAPTER 6: TIMBER PORT

227. A board foot is a unit of linear measurement used in the lumber industry equal to a piece of sawn wood one-foot square and one-inch thick.

228. J. C. Ryan, "The Duluth Lumber Industry," *Duluth: Sketches of the Past*. 171.

229. Walker and Hall, *Duluth-Superior Harbor Cultural Resources Study*, p. 57. In mid-nineteenth century America, sawmills were an indispensable part of any community's development. Until locally quarried stone became available late in the century, literally all of the houses and offices in frontier communities in Minnesota and Wisconsin were built of wood.

230. Ibid. Wheeler's mill also produced wooden shingles for roofing and wooden laths for siding. See Ryan, "The Duluth Lumber Industry," 165.

231. Ryan, "The Duluth Lumber Industry," 165–66.

232. Ibid., 166. The Wieland mill on the North Shore of Lake Superior at Beaver Bay owned a small schooner and shipped lumber up and down the North Shore during the 1850s and 1860s.

233. Ibid., 166. Ryan reported several small mills located on Minnesota Point during the 1870s, primarily turning out lumber for the local building trade, as well as doors, window frames, and roofing shingles.

234. "Condition of Lumber Trade," *Duluth Evening Herald*, December 17, 1894.

235. Ibid. Another major concern early in the year had been the tariff bill under discussion in Congress. Lumbermen were concerned that the bill would place lumber on "the free list," which would allow Canadian lumber into the United States duty-free. In 1894, mills in Manitoba and Ontario were prepared to undercut the price for lumber at the head of the lakes by $1 a thousand board feet. Today, nearly 110 years later, the U.S. forest products industry still worries about Canadian lumber winding up on a free list.

236. Ibid. Newspapers at the time referred to railroad freight movements as the "car trade."

237. Theodore J. Karamanski, *Deep Woods Frontier: A History of Logging in Northern Michigan* (Detroit: Wayne State University Press, 1989), pp. 75–76. When the logs began to run out in the Lower Peninsula in the mid-1880s, 112 sawmills operated in the Saginaw area.

238. Ibid., p. 76. Tonawanda and North Tonawanda, both directly across from Buffalo, were major receiving ports for waterborne lumber shipments at the time. Between 1887 and 1890, the Tonawandas, as they were known in the lumber trade, handled an average of 600 million board feet of lumber across their docks each year, more than twice the volume that arrived at nearby Buffalo by boat or raft for the same period. See *History of the Great Lakes, Illustrated* (Chicago: J. H. Beers and Company, 1899), vol. 2, p. 522.

239. Shiela Reaves, *Wisconsin: Pathways to Prosperity* (Northridge, California: Windsor, 1988), p. 89. By the late 1860s and early 1870s, Oshkosh was known as the "Sawdust City."

240. Bertha L. Heilbron, *The Thirty-Second State: A Pictorial History of Minnesota* (St. Paul: Minnesota Historical Society, 1979): p. 175. Stillwater, Bayport, and Winona were also important communities in the story of capital formation for the northern Minnesota logging industry from 1880 to 1910.

241. Lawrence H. Larsen, *Wall of Flames: The Minnesota Forest Fire of 1894* (Fargo: North Dakota Institute for Regional Studies, 1984), pp. 11–14. Originally called Central Station, Hinckley was later named for a director of the Pennsylvania Railroad, a not uncommon practice at the time for towns that grew up along railroad lines.

242. Weyerhaeuser quietly amassed a fortune in the late nineteenth and early twentieth centuries, anonymous to all but the most knowledgeable observers of the forest products industry. He was so low-key that *Who's Who in America* did not include the lumber baron in its annual listings until 1911, three years before his death. See "Weyerhaeuser, Frederick (1834–1914)," www.germanheritage.com/biographies/mtoz/weyerhaeuser.html.

243. Martin Dahlquist, "History of Rusk County, Wisconsin," www.rootsweb.com/~wirusk/history.htm.

244. Ibid. Dahlquist noted that the village of Weyerhaeuser in Rusk County honored the lumber baron, but he is realistic about the legacy. "He left that community with his name, but he left little else but timber slashings."

245. Francis Carroll, *Crossroads in Time: A History of Carlton County, Minnesota* (Cloquet: Carlton County Historical Society, 1987), pp. 145–48. By 1898, the Northern Lumber Company, by

246. Ibid., p. 145. In the late 1890s, Weyerhaeuser built a summer manse on Lake Nebagamon in Douglas County, Wisconsin, just southeast of Superior. See "Logging Gives Birth to a Community," www.lakenebagamonwi.com/newhis/logging.htm.

247. Ryan, "The Duluth Lumber Industry," p. 167. Cedar was primarily used at the time for roofing shingles.

248. "The Lumber Business—Duluth Lumber Statistics for the Past Year," *Duluth Saturday Evening Journal*, December 24, 1887.

249. "Our Lumber District," *Duluth Evening Herald*, December 24, 1889.

250. Ibid. The hills above Duluth were buzzing with activity in 1889. Local logger Morris Thomas was cutting timber along the road that would later bear his name. D. D. McLean was erecting a planing mill at Canosia Lake.

251. Ryan, "The Duluth Lumber Industry," p. 169.

252. Ibid., p. 168. The Mitchell and McClure holdings in Duluth were later sold to another legendary Michigan lumberman, General Russel Alger, who incorporated the holdings into his Alger-Smith Company.

253. "A Dock 3000 Feet Long," *Duluth Evening Herald*, November 6, 1890.

254. Duluth-Superior Harbor Statistics, p. 2. Ironically, Duluth had been a lumber receiving port for much of the late 1880s. Cedar ties cut on the Canadian side of Lake Superior were shipped to Duluth, where they were loaded in railroad cars and shipped west for track construction in Manitoba, Montana, and North Dakota. In 1888, some 400,000 cedar railroad ties flowed across the lumber wharves in Duluth and into waiting boxcars. See News Item, *Duluth Evening Herald*, August 16, 1888.

255. Quoted in Walker and Hall, *Duluth-Superior Harbor Cultural Resources Study*, p. 61. In 1891, it cost $1.40 per thousand feet of board to ship lumber from Duluth down the Great Lakes, about 40 cents more per thousand than it cost to ship lumber from Georgian Bay to Saginaw the decade before.

256. Ibid., p. 61.

257. Ibid., p. 61.

258. News Item, *Duluth Daily Tribune*, October 23, 1889. The lumber shovers were the aristocracy of the docks in the nineteenth century. Crews working on the coal docks in the Twin Ports at the time usually made less than $3 a day, and unskilled miners in the Michigan iron and copper mines rarely made more than $2.50 a day.

259. News Item, *Duluth Evening Herald*, October 7, 1889.

260. News Item, *Duluth Evening Herald*, November 21, 1889.

261. Duluth-Superior Harbor Statistics, p. 1. The Lake Carriers' Association, the trade group representing U.S. flag interests on the Great Lakes, and the U.S. Army Corps of Engineers recorded lumber shipments in net tons rather than board feet. In 1894, the *Marine Record* and the *Mississippi Lumberman* reported that Duluth shipped 180 million board feet of lumber, which translated to just under 258 million tons. See "A Waning Industry," *Duluth News-Tribune*, December 17, 1894.

262. Ibid. Because so much lumber was rafted to Michigan mills from Lake Superior and Georgian Bay, the Wolverine State still led the nation in lumber production in 1890. Second-place Wisconsin's lumber cut was twice that of third-place Pennsylvania. By 1900, Wisconsin, Michigan, and Minnesota secured the top three places nationally, accounting for 25 percent of the national cut. But in a sign of things to come, the South accounted for 32 percent of the nation's lumber production. By 1920, the South produced 42.6 percent of the 34 billion feet of cut lumber in the United States; the West produced 35.7 percent. See Stanley F. Horn, *This Fascinating Lumber Business* (New York: Bobbs-Merrill, 1943), pp. 30–31.

263. Ryan, "The Duluth Lumber Industry," p. 170.

264. Ibid., p. 170. Alger-Smith had been among the first Michigan firms to pioneer log rafting from Georgian Bay to Saginaw and Bay City.

265. Ryan, "The Duluth Lumber Industry," p. 170. Some of the lumber that had gone out of Duluth-Superior in the late 1890s went out of the port of Ashland, Wisconsin, in the early 1900s. Other shipments went by rail south to Chicago and the Twin Cities.

266. Ibid., p. 170.

267. Ibid., p. 171.

268. Ibid., p. 171.

269. Duluth-Superior Harbor Statistics, p. 3.

270. Ryan, "The Duluth Lumber Industry," p. 173. The mill had been idled for several years before World War I.

271. Duluth-Superior Harbor Statistics, p. 3.

The Lumber Hookers

272. Daniel J. Lenihan, ed., *Submerged Cultural Resources Study: Isle Royale National Park* (Santa Fe, N.M.: Southwest Cultural Resources Center Professional Papers, no. 8), p. 56. In the heyday of the Duluth lumber industry, lumber hookers measured anywhere from 80 feet in length to 200 feet. Some of the larger hookers could carry one million board feet a trip.

273. Ibid., p. 57. On some of the older hookers, the hogging arch made loading and stowing lumber an often difficult proposition.

274. Ibid., p. 57. Some older schooners were converted to steam-powered propulsion systems between 1870 and 1880. Several hundred schooners were cut down and refitted as hooker consort barges during the same period.

275. James Cooke Mills, *Our Inland Seas: Their Shipping and Commerce for Three Centuries* (Chicago: 1910), pp. 186–89.

276. C. Patrick Labadie, "Death Brings Memories of Duluth's Lumber Boom," *NorthStar Port* (Summer 2001): 15.

277. Ibid., p. 15.

278. Davis Helberg, "Channels," *Lake Superior Magazine* (February–March 2002): 16.

279. Edward J. Dowling, S.J., "The Reed Fleet of Erie," *Detroit Marine Historian* 29, no. 5 (January 1976): 1–5. One of the more successful early steamboat entrepreneurs was Charles Reed of Erie, Pennsylvania. The Reed fleet was among the more successful Lake Erie passenger vessel combinations from the 1830s until the Civil War.

CHAPTER 7: PASSENGERS AND PACKAGE FREIGHT

280. Gordon P. Bugbee, "The North Shore Line," *Telescope* 21, no. 5 (September–October 1972): 127–35; and 21, no. 6 (November–December 1972): 160–67. The North Shore Line's steamboats were designed by Isaac Newton, a well-known Hudson River shipbuilder.

281. News Item, *Buffalo Morning Express*, July 25, 1857.

282. "Propellers and Canal Boats for Sale," *Chicago Press and Tribune*, March 1, 1860. The panic also decimated the fleets of the competing independent steamboat companies. See "Sale of Vessels of the Lake Navigation Company," *Buffalo Commercial*, April 13, 1858.

283. Minnesota Historical Society, "History and Development of Great Lakes Water Craft," p. 3. The typical side-wheel steamer of the pre–Civil War era carried its propulsion machinery in the hold. The most common arrangement was a vertical or "walking-beam" engine, which consisted of a tall A-frame with a crosshead on top that connected the piston rod on one end with the connecting rod to the crankshaft on the other. In operation, the crosshead rocked back and forth, hence the origin of the name "walking beam."

284. Ibid., p. 4.

285. Ibid., p. 4. The first steam vessel on Lake Superior was the propeller *Independence*, in 1845.

286. News Items, *Chicago Tribune*, May 23, 1866; March 11, 1879; and May 8, 1874. For many years, the 210-foot *Peerless* was the flagship of the fleet. She boasted a main saloon 166 feet long with six beautiful chandeliers and two bronze statues, each holding a lamp, at the head of the main stairway. She had forty-five staterooms, each supplied with water "from the general system of water works." Besides her passengers, she carried about 1,000 tons of freight.

287. Minnesota Historical Society, "History and Development of Great Lakes Water Craft," p. 5.

288. Ibid., p. 6.

289. Edward J. Dowling, S.J., "The Lake Superior Transit Company, 1872–1892," *Detroit Marine Historian* 11, no. 5 (January 1958): 1–4; and "The Lackawanna Fleet," *Detroit Marine Historian* 35, no. 7 (March 1981): 2–3.

290. C. P. Labadie, "Remembering the Winslow," *North Star Port* (Summer 1999): 15. The *Winslow* burned at the present location of the Duluth Entertainment Convention Center, and her smoldering wreck was towed into the harbor and abandoned there. In 1908, her remains were moved upriver and scuttled in shallow water. Her bones rest today just south of the Minnesota Power M. L. Hibbard Plant in West Duluth.

291. Harkins, Listing of Harbor Structures, pp. 2–4. The Northern Pacific also acquired control of DeCosta's Dock, one of the first merchandise wharves in the harbor, on the west side of Rice's Point. After 1889, Warehouse and Builders Supply Company had a merchandise wharf at the foot of the Tower Bay slip in Superior.

292. News Item, "Milling: Production Record Broken by the Flour Mills This Year," *Duluth Evening Herald*, December 17, 1895.

293. Van Brunt, *Duluth and St. Louis County*, p. 323.

294. Ibid., p. 323.

295. Al Miller, "Workhorses and White Flyers: A History of the Northern Steamship Company," *Nor'Easter* 23, no. 2 (March–April 1998): 1–2. Hill always thought big. "A vessel that carries only 1,000 tons cannot compete with a boxcar," he said at the time. "With a steamer carrying 10,000 tons, you have it beaten. The difference in cost between the operation of a boat of 3,000 and one of 12,000 tons is only so much as will cover the employment of two extra firemen, two extra deckhands and the purchase of about 10 tons of coal additional per day; in all, some $28." Hill's philosophy of economies of scale predated the introduction of the 1,000-footer by more than eighty years.

296. News Item, *Duluth Evening Herald*, April 16, 1888.

297. Miller, "Workhorses and White Flyers," p. 2.

298. Ibid., p. 2. In 1890, the six vessels hauled 1.2 million bushels of grain from Duluth and Superior to Buffalo.

299. Edward J. Dowling, S.J., "The Vanishing Fleets: The Story of the Great Lakes Package Freighters," *Inland Seas* (January 1946): 8–9. The 402-foot steamers *Duluth* and *Superior* entered service with the Western Transit Company in 1903 and 1905, respectively.

300. Bill Galinski, "The Minnesota Atlantic Transit Company," *The Nor'Easter* 2, no. 5 (September–October 1977): 1. Kirby's grandfather was President Ulysses Grant's inspector of the navy. A Duluth banker for more than half a century, Kirby was associated for much of that period with Duluth's Northern Minnesota National Bank. Other directors of Northern Minnesota National and its predecessors with ties to the mining and shipping interests of the Lake Superior region included Joseph Sellwood, Richard Griggs, and Lewis Castle. See Bill Beck, *First Bank Duluth: The First 75 Years* (Duluth: First Bank Duluth, 1984), n.p.

301. Galinski, "The Minnesota Atlantic Transit Company," p. 2. The firm later acquired vessels renamed the *Nine* and *Ten*.

302. Ibid., p. 2. Much of the upbound cargo was destined for the Dayton's and Donaldson's department store chains in the Twin Cities. All of the Poker Fleet vessels had refrigerated compartments, which allowed them to serve the emerging dairy industry of northeastern Minnesota and northwestern Wisconsin. The firm's Railroad Street terminal would later become a manufacturing facility for Duluth food manufacturer Jeno Paulucci.

303. Van Brunt, *Duluth and St. Louis County*, vol. 2, pp. 748–49. Marshall's chance to incorporate the Wells-Stone wholesale house came in 1893 when the firm's founders, C. W. Wells and F. C. Stone, died within three months of each other.

304. Ibid., vol. 1, pp. 323–24.

305. Ibid., vol. 2, p. 750. Marshall ceded active control of the company to his son, Seth, in 1918 and served as chair of the board of directors until his death.

306. Ibid., p. 324. Other well-known local wholesalers included the Gowan-Lenning-Brown Company and the Christian-Mendenhall-Graham Company.

307. "Railways Must Abandon Control of Boat Lines on the Great Lakes," *Marine Review* 45, no. 7 (July 1915): 235–40.

308. Daniel O. Fletcher, "Package Freighters: Victims of War," *Inland Seas* (Summer 1961): 131.

309. Ibid., 131–33. From February to June 1942, German submarine wolf packs torpedoed thousands of tons of merchant marine vessels along the U.S. East and Gulf Coasts. The U-boat captains called the action the "Atlantic turkey shoot," and the submarine offensive threatened to cripple the movement of critical petroleum products from Gulf Coast refineries to East Coast war industries. The Great Lakes package freighters were intended to replace the losses from the U-boat sinkings.

310. Ibid., 132–33. Great Lakes Transit operated the four vessels as bulk carriers during the 1943 and 1944 navigation seasons.

311. Tape-recorded telephone oral history interview with George Skuggen, Avon Lake, Ohio, March 5, 2002, p. 3. Skuggen began his career with Wilson Marine Transit Company in 1946. He had just completed his junior year in high school at L'Anse, Michigan.

The Automobile Trade

312. Ibid., p. 4.

313. Ibid., p. 5. Skuggen sailed with Wilson Marine Transit Company as an officer from 1954 to 1964. He came ashore as Wilson's fleet captain in 1964. From 1968 until his retirement in 1990, he was director of the Great Lakes Pilots' staff. In the early 1960s, Skuggen was the skipper of Wilson Marine Transit Company's

B. F. Jones. His father had commanded the vessel when it was the *Charles A. Paul* in the 1940s, and his grandfather had been captain of the 520-foot freighter in 1934 when it sailed as the *General Garretson.*

314. Julius F. Wolff Jr., *The Shipwrecks of Lake Superior* (Au Train, Michigan: Avery Color Studios, 1979), p. 130.

315. Ibid., p. 130. An excellent exhibit at the Eagle Harbor Lighthouse Museum in Eagle Harbor, Michigan, graphically depicts the fascinating story of the *City of Bangor* and its travails.

316. *The Encyclopaedia Britannica: A Dictionary of Arts, Sciences, Literature and General Information* (New York: Encyclopaedia Britannica Company, 1910), 11th edition, volume VIII, Demijohn to Edward, p. 653.

CHAPTER 8: A WORLD-CLASS PORT

317. Walker and Hall, *Duluth-Superior Harbor Cultural Resources Study*, p. 38.

318. "Along the Waterfront," unidentified news clipping, University of Wisconsin Superior Marine Archives, Biographical Files. Majo continued the ferry service until after the turn of the twentieth century when he towed his last boat, the *Hattie Lloyd,* to the boneyard at Duluth's Thirteenth Avenue West.

319. Walker and Hall, *Duluth-Superior Harbor Cultural Resources Study*, p. 39. During the winter when the ship canal iced over, residents found it easier to cross on foot or in horse-drawn sleighs. See also King, "Duluth's Ship Canal and Aerial Bridge: How They Came To Be," p. 4. Minnesota Point residents could buy a family ticket for $1 a month for unlimited crossings. Charles Winters, the ferry operator, charged 25 cents to haul groceries across the canal.

320. Ibid., p. 39. In the mid-1890s, the city actually submitted a proposal for a railway and pedestrian tunnel under the canal.

321. Wesley R. Harkins, "Aerial Lift Bridge, Duluth, Minnesota," undated typescript document, p. 1.

322. King, "Duluth's Ship Canal and Aerial Bridge: How They Came To Be," p. 5.

323. Ibid., p. 5. With 7,000 vessel passages a year to the Duluth-Superior harbor early in the century, the carriage was probably subject to many more delays than the replacement Aerial Lift Bridge is today.

324. Harkins, "Aerial Lift Bridge, Duluth, Minnesota." The lift was powered by electric storage batteries that raised and lowered 450-ton counterweights on each side of the bridge.

325. Larry Oakes, "A Bridge So Near," *Star-Tribune,* July 14, 2002.

326. Walker and Hall, *Duluth-Superior Harbor Cultural Resources Study*, p. 39.

327. Franklin A. King, "Railroad Drawbridges at the Head of the Lakes," *The Nor'Easter* 10, no. 1 (January-February 1985): 2. Replaced and expanded to 482 feet in 1909, the two bridges carried rail traffic for a number of railroads for ninety-nine years. They were taken out of service by the then Burlington Northern Santa Fe Railroad in 1984.

328. Ibid., p. 2. Originally single-track, the Grassy Point span was upgraded to a double-track bridge in 1927.

329. Ibid., p. 4.

330. Ibid., p. 4.

331. Russell L. Olson, *The Electric Railways of Minnesota* (Hopkins, Minnesota: Minnesota Transportation Museum, 1976), pp. 316–17.

332. King, "Railroad Drawbridges at the Head of the Lakes," p. 4. Howard's Pocket is now the site of Fraser Shipyards. The Lamborn Avenue Bridge was dismantled soon after streetcar service in Superior was abandoned in the mid-1930s.

333. Olson, *The Electric Railways of Minnesota*, p. 317. The Bridge Company was a subsidiary of the Great Northern Railway. The Duluth-Superior Traction Company, which had been formed in 1894 to combine the streetcar interests of the two communities, owned a minority share in the Duluth-Superior Bridge Company.

334. Ibid., p. 317. The protracted negotiations for construction of the bridge led the Superior Rapid Transit Railway to build a trestle across the ice in the winter of 1895 to connect the two communities.

335. Walker and Hall, *Duluth-Superior Harbor Cultural Resources Study*, p. 40.

336. King, "Railway Drawbridges at the Head of the Lakes," p. 3. In 1985, seventy-five years after it first opened, the Oliver Bridge still handled ten to sixteen trains a day.

337. "1901—Morgan and Carnegie Forge Big Steel," *American Dreams,* p. 34. In 1904, U.S. Steel, the nation's first billion-dollar company, announced plans to build a major steelmaking complex in the

sand dunes of southern Lake Michigan, twenty-five miles east of Chicago. The Gary Works, named for Elbert Gary, the company's chair, was a recognition that waterborne transportation of raw materials was a critical component of the industry's efficiency.

338. *The Encyclopaedia Britannica: A Dictionary of Arts, Sciences, Literature and General Information,* 11th edition, vol. XII, Gichtel to Harmonium, p. 399.

339. C. Patrick Labadie, "Duluth's Ship Canal," *The Duluthian,* September–October, 1985, p. 39. The new lock was named after Major Godfrey Weitzel, who supervised its construction from 1873 to 1882. See John W. Larson, *Essayons: A History of the Detroit District U.S. Army Corps of Engineers* (Detroit: U.S. Army Corps of Engineers, 1995), pp. 115–19.

340. *The Encyclopaedia Britannica,* 11th edition, vol. XII, p. 399. An average of 682,000 bushels of flour passed through the locks each year during the first half of the 1880s. That increased to an average of 1.8 million barrels each year during the latter half of the decade.

341. Ibid., p. 339.

342. Larson, *Essayons,* p. 133.

343. Ibid., pp. 134–35.

344. *Annual Reports of the War Department for the Fiscal Year Ended June 30, 1883: Report of the Chief of Engineers* (Washington, D.C.: Government Printing Office, 1883), Part 2, p. 1614. Hereinafter cited as *Report of the Chief of Engineers.*

345. Walker and Hall, *Duluth-Superior Harbor Cultural Resources Study*, pp. 42–43. The 1881 act resulted in deepening the channels well up the St. Louis River.

346. Ibid., p. 43.

347. Ibid., p. 44. Sears argued that a federal appropriation of $1 million a year for three years—equivalent to 1 percent of the annual valuation of cargo passing through the port—would turn Duluth-Superior into the finest harbor on the lakes.

348. *Report of the Chief of Engineers,* 1897, Part 1, pp. 386–88.

349. Labadie, "Duluth's Ship Canal," p. 39. The wreckage of the 200-foot wooden sailing craft *Guido Pfister* had to be dynamited and removed from the site before *Old Hickory* could begin dredging.

350. Labadie, "Duluth's Ship Canal," p. 39.

351. P. C. Bullard, "History-Duluth Ship Canal," U.S. Army Corps of Engineers, Duluth District Engineer, 1928, n.p. The crews who worked on the Duluth Ship Canal reconstruction project were typically paid $2 a day for their labor. Many of the hundreds of laborers came to the Twin Ports from the East Coast and remained in Duluth when the job was done.

352. *Report of the Chief of Engineers,* 1902, Part 1, pp. 430–32.

353. Letter, Thom Holden, Duluth District, Corps of Engineers, to Bill Elowson, Superior, Wisconsin, February 13, 1986, UWS Marine Archives. Barker's Island in Superior is named for the longtime Corps of Engineers assistant.

354. Labadie, "Duluth's Ship Canal," p. 40.

355. Duluth-Superior Harbor Statistics, p. 4. The 19.3 million tons of iron ore in 1906 was more than the total tonnage of 16.6 million tons handled in 1904.

356. Ibid., p. 3. The 7,933 vessel visits in 1902 racked up the all-time record for the Twin Ports. Amazingly, 1902 was the height of the corps' harbor improvement project, a testimony to the skill exhibited by contractors in working while avoiding disrupting shipping.

357. *The Encyclopaedia Britannica,* 11th edition, vol. XII, p. 399.

358. Larson, *Essayons,* p. 147. Between 1889 and 1908, the volume of traffic passing through the Soo had doubled every six years. In 1907, the Poe Lock, which had been built to accommodate the passage of four boats at a time, was able to accommodate the passage of only two vessels at a time, and the large 500-foot and 600-foot freighters then being launched were capable of going through the Poe only one boat at a time.

359. Ibid., p. 154. A fourth lock of similar size to the Davis Lock was constructed between 1913 and 1919. The lock was named for Louis Sabin, the longtime corps civilian assistant engineer at the Soo who had helped design and build the Davis Lock.

Commercial Fishing

360. Phil Moy, "The State of Lake Superior's Fishes," Wisconsin Sea Grant Institute, www.lakesuperior.com/online/232/232supplement.html. The siscowet is a subspecies of lake trout that typically inhabits deeper portions of Lake Superior. Because of the much higher fat content of siscowet, they were most commonly smoked or salted.

361. "Settlement and Fishing on Lake Superior, 1854–1930,"

www.mnhs.org/places/nationalregister/shipwreck/mpdf/mpdfl.html. Cooley and Lavaque and the Duluth Fish Company operated collection steamers that ran back and forth up the north shore, dropping off supplies to the isolated fishing communities and returning to Duluth with barrels of salted whitefish and trout. In the 1890s, there was a fish collection station along the North Shore every half-mile from Duluth to Grand Marais. See "Catch and Release Stories: The New Aquarium and Commercial Fishing," Minnesota Public Radio news release, August 8, 2000, p. 1.

362. Ibid.

363. "Ragnvald's Fish Boxes," www.boreal.org/nshistory/journal8.html. The small, silvery fish were split down the back, cleaned, washed, and packed into layers in kegs, with a handful of salt separating each layer of fish. A keg of salt herring weighed approximately 100 pounds.

364. Ibid., pp. 82–83. A favorite place for trout fishing was the reefs surrounding Isle Royale. Baited lines were commonly used to catch siscowet and were often set in water as deep as 800 feet.

365. Mike Roinila, "Finnish Fishermen of Lake Superior," http://sydaby.eget.net/swe/roin2.html. Larsmont, which was settled in 1909, was named for the town of Larsmo in Finland. Prominent Swede-Finn commercial fishing families in Larsmont were the Sjoblöms and Hendricksons.

366. "The Background of the Sivertson Family Business," Isle Royale National Park news release, n.d., p. 1. Stanley and Arthur Sivertson, Sam Sivertson's sons, continued the family commercial fishing business until the early 1990s.

367. Ibid., p. 1.

368. Margaret Beattie Bogue, Fishing the Great Lakes: An Environmental History, 1783–1933 (Madison, Wisconsin: University of Wisconsin Press, 2000), pp. 60–61. Booth and his sons used the latest European technology to collect and pack fish for distribution in the Midwest. A millionaire, Booth was also strongly backed by British capital.

369. Quoted in ibid., p. 67.

370. "Settlement and Fishing on Lake Superior."

371. Ibid. The commercial fishermen associated with Booth worked on account, purchasing supplies on credit from the company at the beginning of the season and having the charges deducted from their catch at the end of the season. One Norwegian fisherman on Isle Royale complained that all he had ever gotten out of fishing for Booth was "an empty belly and a wet ass." See Ingeborg Holte, Ingeborg's Isle Royale (Grand Marais, Minnesota: Women's Times Publishing, 1984), p. 47.

372. Bogue, Fishing the Great Lakes, p. 151. The whitefish catch on Lake Michigan declined from 12 million pounds in 1879 to 1.77 million pounds in 1899.

373. Ibid., p. 155.

374. Ibid., p. 157. The Lake Superior catch, however, was dwarfed by the 40 million pounds taken from Lake Erie in 1899 and the nearly 25 million pounds taken from Lake Michigan.

375. Scott, "Fishing in Lake Superior," p. 81.

376. Bogue, Fishing the Great Lakes, p. 163.

377. Sivertson Fisheries remains one of the commercial fishing firms still setting its nets in western Lake Superior.

CHAPTER 9: THE SHIPBUILDERS

378. Wesley R. Harkins, "Shipyards," March 26, 1974, p. 1. Unpublished, typescript copy located in UWS Marine Archives.

379. "The Autobiography of Captain Alexander McDougall," part 1, Inland Seas (Summer 1967): 92–93.

380. Ibid., 97. McDougall's life might have turned out far differently had not a recruiter rejected him on account of age when McDougall attempted to enlist in the Union Army on his first visit to Chicago in the summer of 1861.

381. Ibid., 98.

382. "The Autobiography of Captain Alexander McDougall," part 2, Inland Seas (Fall 1967): 201. McDougall bought a lot, built a home on First Avenue West, and moved his mother and three sisters to Duluth in the fall of 1871.

383. Ibid., 215–16. The venture began with McDougall's unloading the steamer Hiawatha and consort barge Minnehaha of railroad iron at Duluth in the summer of 1880. It was a rarity for a captain to act as his own stevedore.

384. Robert Clark, "The Advent of the Whalebacks on the Great Lakes," The Nor'Easter 23, no. 5 (September–October 1998): 2. During the 1880s, McDougall made most of his money insuring vessels and cargoes trading out of Duluth-Superior.

385. "Whale of a Tale: McDougall's Designs Set the Pace," North Star Port (Summer 2001): 5. The official term for the bow and stern design is "conoidal."

386. "The Autobiography of Captain Alexander McDougall," part 3, Inland Seas (Fall 1967): 282–84.

387. "The Day in the City," Duluth Evening Herald, June 20, 1888. McDougall nicknamed the barge the Nonsuch in recognition of its unique hull construction. It was officially christened Barge 101. The site of that first shipyard later became the location of the Superwood Corporation's Duluth plant and the Georgia-Pacific hardboard plant.

388. "A Curious Craft," Duluth Democratic Paragraph, February 4, 1888.

389. Edward J. Dowling, S.J., "The Story of the Whaleback Vessels and of Their Inventor, Alexander McDougall," Inland Seas (Fall 1957): 172–75. The ends of the barge were fabricated in a Wilmington, Delaware, shipyard and shipped to Duluth via the Hudson River, Erie Canal, and Great Lakes. See Thomas Wilson, www.mnhs.org/places/nationalregister/shipwrecks/wilson/wilwf.html.

390. "The Autobiography of Captain Alexander McDougall," part 3, 282. The ship's bow and stern were equipped with distinctive iron fairleads for towropes that resembled the nose of a pig, hence the derisive term "pigboat."

391. "West Duluth," Duluth Evening Herald, June 7, 1888.

392. "The Day in the City," June 20, 1888.

393. Dowling, "The Story of the Whaleback Vessels and of Their Inventor, Alexander McDougall," 172–75. Barge 101 was towed to the Atlantic Coast in 1903 and foundered off Maine in December 1908 with a cargo of coal tar in barrels.

394. "The Autobiography of Captain Alexander McDougall," part 3, 283. When the hull of the prototype whaleback splashed into the water in Duluth on June 23, 1888, McDougall's wife turned to her sister-in-law and noted, "There goes our last dollar."

395. Richard J. Wright, Freshwater Whales: A History of the American Ship Building Company and Its Predecessors (Kent, Ohio: Kent State University Press, 1969), p. 44. McDougall paved the way for the Merritt family's approach to Rockefeller four years later.

396. Ibid., p. 44.

397. Ibid., p. 45. Economic development subsidies are nothing new. In the early 1890s, the Muncie, Indiana, City Council offered the Ball brothers free natural gas to fire their kilns to move the glass-making business from New York State to northeastern Indiana.

398. Howard's Pocket is currently the site of Fraser Shipyards. After more than 110 years, it is still fulfilling the purpose that Alexander McDougall first spied in 1889.

399. Encyclopaedia Britannica, 1911 ed., vol. 26, Sub to Tom, p. 113.

400. Wright, Freshwater Whales, p. 47.

401. Ibid., p. 47. The Colby, named for another American Steel Barge director, was eleven feet shorter than the Colgate Hoyt. Otherwise, the two vessels were identical.

402. Ibid., pp. 47–48.

403. Ibid., p. 49. At the time, the largest dry dock on the lakes was in Cleveland, three to four days sailing time from the head of the lakes.

404. Ibid., p. 49. The wooden freighter Neshoto was the dry dock's first customer on September 20, 1892.

405. Al Miller, Tin Stackers: The History of the Pittsburgh Steamship Company (Detroit: Wayne State University, 1999), p. 20. By 1893, Rockefeller had invested $1 million in the American Steel Barge Company.

406. Chernow, Titan, pp. 361–74. Gates was a thirty-nine-year-old former Baptist minister when McDougall met him in 1892. The boyish-looking Gates had been serving a congregation in Minnesota when George Pillsbury, the Minneapolis milling baron, asked Gates to advise him about philanthropy. From the Twin Cities, Gates went to Chicago as the executive secretary of the American Baptist Education Society, where he soon came to the attention of Rockefeller, a devout Baptist.

407. Wright, Freshwater Whales, pp. 48–50. "Rev. Mr. Gates no doubt had ability, but he lacked a broad vision," McDougall recalled in his autobiography. "He did not know how to judge investments whose value depended on future conditions." "The Autobiography of Captain Alexander McDougall," part 3, 297–98.

408. "The Autobiography of Captain Alexander McDougall," part 3, 299.

409. Wright, Freshwater Whales, p. 52. The McDougall sailed for the Pittsburgh Steamship Company until 1936, when she was sold to the Buckeye Steamship Company. She sailed the lakes until after World War II, when she was scrapped at Hamilton, Ontario. See Miller, Tin Stackers, p. 297.

410. Wright, *Freshwater Whales*, p. 52.
411. Dowling, "The Story of the Whaleback Vessels and of Their Inventor, Alexander McDougall," p. 174. McDougal built forty-three whalebacks. Two were built at Brooklyn, New York, one at Everett, Washington, and one in England.
412. Ibid., p. 174.
413. Miller, *Tin Stackers*, p. 23. In the 1900 season, Bessemer Steamship Company operated ten whaleback steamers, twenty whaleback barges, and thirty-seven other conventional bulk freighters. Rockefeller paid $5 million for the whalebacks in the fall of 1899.
414. Wright, *Freshwater Whales*, p. 135 ff.
415. John H. Wilterding Jr., "Duluth-Superior Shipbuilding, 1917–1918: The Pre-War Frederickstad Ships," *The Nor'Easter* 6, no. 2 (March–April 1981): 1.
416. Ibid., 1. The Frederickstad ships had to be built small enough to fit through the locks of the Welland Canal into the St. Lawrence River for passage overseas. Canals and locks on the St. Lawrence River above Montreal dated from French colonial times and allowed the passage of small saltwater vessels into the Great Lakes and vice-versa.
417. Ibid., 1. The first order for Frederickstad ships totaled twenty-five hulls. The Detroit Shipbuilding Company at Wyandotte, Michigan, received a contract to build nine vessels.
418. Ibid., 1. The Great Lakes Engineering Works received orders for a total of twenty-two hulls at its yards in Ashtabula, Ohio, and Ecorse, Michigan.
419. News Item, *Superior Evening Telegram*, January 26, 1917. The original officers were B. C. Cooke, president; Captain Chester A. Massey, vice president; M. McMahon, secretary-treasurer; and James McKellar, superintendent. See also News Item, *Superior Evening Telegram*, March 7, 1917.
420. "Globe Shipbuilding/World War I," unidentified transcript of newspaper article, UWS Marine Archives.
421. "The Autobiography of Captain Alexander McDougall," part 4, *Inland Seas* (Spring 1968): 27. The proposed ship would have a detachable superstructure, which would allow it to pass beneath bridges on the canal.
422. Ibid., 28. McDougall hoped that Congdon and Alworth would want "to help introduce my type of ship as a Duluth enterprise, but these men were so occupied with their iron ore interests that they were not interested."
423. Biography, Julius H. Barnes Papers, Northeastern Minnesota Historical Center, Duluth, Minnesota, Collection S3025.
424. Ibid., p. 29. Ward Ames Jr. was the son of Barnes's original patron.
425. Ibid., p. 29. The boat was named for Julius Barnes's son.
426. Ibid., p. 30.
427. Ibid., p. 31.
428. Wilterding, "Duluth-Superior Shipbuilding, 1918–1920: The American 'Lakers,'" *The Nor'Easter* 6, no. 6 (November–December 1981): 1–4.
429. Ibid., 1. See also Van Brunt, *Duluth and St. Louis County*, vol. 1, p. 292.

Still a Dangerous Lake

430. Minnesota Historical Society, "Lake Superior Shipwrecks," *Thomas Wilson*, www.mnhs.org/places/nationalregister/shipwrecks/wilson/wilson.html.
431. Elmer Engman, "Sounding of a Whale," *The Nor'Easter* 2, no. 3 (May–June 1977): 1. The two vessels were passing port-to-port at the time Fitzgerald gave his orders to turn.
432. Ibid., p. 1. The water temperature off Duluth in early June would likely have been forty degrees Fahrenheit or lower, cold enough to induce hypothermia within minutes.
433. Fred Landon, "November Shipping Disasters," *Inland Seas* (Fall 1955): 221. The Upper Great Lakes are a giant heat sink. It takes Lakes Superior and Huron much longer in the spring to warm up and longer in the fall to cool down. In November, when Arctic air masses bear down on the upper lakes from Canada, the colder Canadian air clashes with the warmer water of the lakes and produces memorable storms. "Invariably the big storms occur in November, which has always been a stormy month on the Great Lakes," wrote climatologist Val Eichenlaub. "At this time of year the atmospheric circulation quickens and large temperature contrasts exist between the vast northern expanse of Canada, already snowcovered, and the lingering warmth of the Gulf States." See Val Eichenlaub, *Weather and Climate of the Great Lakes Region* (South Bend: University of Notre Dame Press, 1979), pp. 288–89.

434. Eichenlaub, *Weather and Climate of the Great Lakes Region*, p. 287. The U.S. Weather Bureau was in its infancy at the time, and mariners preferred to rely on their own experience rather than on Weather Bureau forecasts.
435. Julius F. Wolff, "1905—Lake Superior at Its Worst," part 2, *Inland Seas* (Winter 1962): 273.
436. Ibid., 273.
437. Ibid., p. 274.
438. Frederick, "The Story of the 'Mataafa Blow.'"
439. Ibid.
440. C. P. Labadie, The Port's Past, "Famous for All the Wrong Reasons," *North Star Port* (Fall 1999): 15. Ironically, the *Nasmyth* dropped anchor about two miles off the entry and rode out the remainder of the storm unscathed.
441. Ibid., 15. See also Wolff, "1905—Lake Superior at Its Worst," part 2, p. 275.
442. Labadie, "Famous for All the Wrong reasons," p. 15. Wind chill is the effect that temperature and wind have on exposed flesh.
443. Ibid., p. 15.
444. Ibid., p. 279.

CHAPTER 10: ZENITH CITY OF THE UNSALTED SEAS

445. William D. Middleton, *Landmarks on the Iron Road* (Bloomington: Indiana University Press, 1999), p. 155.
446. Ibid., p. 155. Dock No. 1, the oldest at the railroad's West Duluth facility, had been dismantled in 1913. When Dock No. 6 opened in 1919, Docks No. 2 and 3 were abandoned.
447. Ibid., p. 155.
448. Ibid., p. 156.
449. Douglass D. Addison Sr., *Great Northern Railway: Ore Docks of Lake Superior Photo Archive* (Hudson, Wisconsin: Iconografix. 2002), p. 6.
450. Ibid., pp. 6, 18. The approach construction project was partially the result of necessity. On the evening of January 31, 1922, more than 600 feet of the wooden approach to Dock No. 2 was destroyed in a fire. For visitors arriving in the Twin Ports from the east, the steel dock approach trestle over Highway 53 east of Superior is the first indication of the communities' roots in iron and steel.
451. Ibid., p. 12.
452. Ibid., p. 10.
453. Although the DM&N and the Great Northern were the two major railroads in the Twin Ports ore trade, there were attempts to break the two railroads' monopoly on ore shipments. In 1911, the Minneapolis, St. Paul, & Sault Ste. Marie Railway, better known as the Soo Line, built an 1,800-foot ore dock near the Northern Pacific's Grassy Point Bridge. The 90,000-ton-capacity ore dock was expanded to 2,400 feet in 1917 but abandoned in 1929. The wooden dock was destroyed by fire on August 19, 1930. The Northern Pacific also built an ore dock at the foot of Thirty-first Avenue East in Superior in 1913 and expanded the new dock in 1917 and again in 1926. Both docks were built to handle the ore arriving in the Twin Ports from the newly opened Cuyuna Range. See Harkins, Chronology, pp. 5, 8.
454. Harkins, Chronology, pp. 1–8.
455. Ibid., pp. 3–4.
456. Borchert, *America's Northern Heartland*, p. 53. Lake Superior, by itself, accounted for more ton miles in 1920 than the nation's entire inland river system.
457. Ibid., p. 53.
458. Duluth-Superior Harbor Statistics, p. 3.
459. Ibid., p. 3. The 30.8 million tons of iron ore handled in 1919 was only 1.6 million tons less than the 32.5 million ton of iron ore, coal, grain, and lumber handled in 1909.
460. "Premiere Iron Ore State," *Skillings Mining Review*, September 28, 1918. Wisconsin was in fifth place with 1.3 million tons mined, a comment on the depletion of the reserves of the Gogebic and Menominee Ranges.
461. "Handicap of 5 Million Ton First Few Weeks Season of Navigation in Iron Ore Movement," *Skillings Mining Review*, May 26, 1917. It wouldn't be until the World War II years that the 50-million-ton mark was regularly eclipsed. The all-time record of nearly 65 million tons shipped came in 1953, the last year of the Korean War.
462. Walker, *Iron Frontier*, pp. 247–51.
463. Ibid., p. 252. The Hartley and Congdon interests were both heavily involved in developing mines on the Cuyuna Range. Perhaps more typical of the Duluth investment were companies such as the Cuyuna-Duluth Iron Company, incorporated in 1911 to sink

development shafts near the community of Cuyuna. The company's secretary was E. J. W. Donahue, a former railroad stenographer who began exploring the Cuyuna Range in 1909. For most of the next twenty years, Donahue, who maintained offices in the Alworth Building in Duluth, was associated with mining ventures in Minnesota and oil exploration in Kentucky. See "Cuyuna-Duluth Iron Co.," *Skillings Mining Review* (December 28, 1912): 1; see also "E. J. W. Donahue," Van Brunt, *Duluth and St. Louis County*, vol. 2, p. 817.

464. Walker, *Iron Frontier*, p. 255.

465. "Loading First Cargo of Cuyuna-Mille Lacs Manganese Ore from New Northern Pacific Dock," *Skillings Mining Review* (August 30, 1913): 1.

466. Duluth-Superior Harbor Statistics, p. 3.

467. Duluth-Superior Harbor Statistics, p. 3. One reason for the slow growth in grain shipments through the Twin Ports during the early 1900s was the simple fact that the United States was not yet a dominant force in world grain export markets. Until 1914, Czarist Russia was the world's largest wheat producer. Britain imported huge volumes of grain from its Indian colony. In 1910, the United States trailed Russia, Argentina, and Canada as a wheat exporter. Romania actually exported more barley than the United States did. See Dan Morgan, *Merchants of Grain*, p. 65.

468. Duluth-Superior Harbor Statistics, p. 3.

469. Morgan, *Merchants of Grain*, p. 59. The most important such exchange in the United States in the early years of the twentieth century was the Chicago Grain Exchange. An important function of the exchanges was to provide a futures market, in which grain companies and millers could buy the crop in advance of its harvest—and guarantee farmers a price for their grain at season's end.

470. James Allen Scott, *Duluth's Legacy*, vol. 1, *Architecture* (Duluth: Duluth Department of Research and Planning, 1974), p. 86. Completed in 1895 at a cost of $300,000, the building was the last collaboration of architects Francis W. Fitzpatrick and Oliver G. Trapghagen, who designed much of downtown and residential Duluth in the 1880s and 1890s.

471. *The State of Minnesota v. Duluth Board of Trade, a Corporation, et al.*, State of Minnesota District Court, County of St. Louis, 11th Judicial District, 1906. Copy located in Duluth Board of Trade Files, Northeastern Minnesota Historical Center, University of Minnesota–Duluth, NEMHC S2209 B1F16. In a 1906 anti-trust litigation, the Duluth board of trade argued that it provided "an exchange room in which members of the Board meet daily to conduct their transactions. The Board has caused this room to be properly furnished with blackboard and other facilities for keeping quotations constantly before the members. It has arranged telegraphic facilities so that members can instantly get into communications with other exchanges and with businessmen generally throughout the world."

472. Duluth-Superior Harbor Statistics, p. 3.

473. Miller, *Tin Stackers*, p. 60. At 560 feet long each, the four ships of the Gary class could carry more than three times the ore tonnage of vessels built just fifteen years before—and consume no more fuel in a season than their older sisters.

474. "U.S. Steel Corporation Will Build Monster Plant in Duluth," *Duluth News-Tribune*, April 2, 1907, p. 1.

475. Arnold Alanen, "Morgan Park: U.S. Steel and a Planned Company Town," in Lydecker, *Duluth: Sketches of the Past*, p. 111.

476. "What the Proposed Steel Plant Means to Duluth," *Duluth News-Tribune*, April 2, 1907, p. 1. "Duluth at once becomes one of the great centers of the steel industry, as one of the chief points of the United States Steel corporation for the manufacture of its products," the newspaper told readers.

477. Alanen, "Morgan Park: U.S. Steel and a Planned Company Town," p. 113. By 1917, Minnesota Steel and Zenith Furnace Company, which made pig iron at a mill on the Duluth waterfront, were consuming more than 850,000 tons of Mesabi and Vermilion ore. See "Duluth Iron and Steel Plants Receive 855,000 Tons of Ore During 1917; Industry Will Expand," *Skillings Mining Review* (February 16, 1918): 1.

478. Beck, *From the Foot of Winter Street*, pp. 41–43.

479. "Panama Canal opens today," *Duluth News-Tribune*, August 15, 1914. The first vessel to transit the newly completed canal was the *Ancon* under the command of Captain G. E. Sukeforth.

Peavey's Folly

480. Morgan, *Merchants of Grain*, pp. 54–55. Peavey, who had grown up on the coast of Maine, had an instinctive understanding of

waterborne commerce movements. As early as 1895, he was shipping wheat from Portland to Liverpool across the Isthmus of Panama, unloading the 100-pound sacks on the Pacific side, and reloading them into another ship on the Atlantic side.

481. Ibid., p. 55. The insurance rate was predicated on the value of grain stored in the terminal elevator. In the 1890s, fire insurance rates were typically 1.5 to 1.75 percent. An elevator with a 10-million-bushel capacity of $1 per bushel wheat paid $150,000 to $175,000 a year in premiums, depending on the rates. See Kenneth D. Ruble, *The Peavey Story* (Minneapolis: The Peavey Company, 1963), p. 33.

482. Ruble, *The Peavey Story*, p. 35.

483. Ebeling, "The First Fruit of a New Age," p. 61.

484. Ruble, *The Peavey Story*, pp. 29–30. Peavey's plans for the Twin Ports coincided with the grain entrepreneur's entry into the Great Lakes bulk shipping business. In the late 1890s, he joined Captain A. B. Wolvin of Duluth to incorporate the Peavey Steamship Company. Peavey and Wolvin commissioned four bulk freighters to haul grain from the head of the lakes to Buffalo. The first vessel, the *Frank H. Peavey*, was launched at Lorain, Ohio, in May 1901. The other Peavey boats—the *Frank Heffelfinger, F. B. Wells*, and *George W. Peavey*—came down the ways later the same year. The Peavey Company operated the fleet until 1915 when it sold the four boats to the C. Reiss Coal Company. One mariner who sailed with the fleet said the Peavey boats "rode like an old shoe, and they never failed to come through."

485. Ibid., p. 41. At the time he purchased Globe Elevator, Peavey also acquired Brooks Elevator Company, which operated thirty-five country elevators throughout the Red River Valley of Minnesota and North Dakota. From the time of the company's move to Minneapolis in 1885 until its acquisition nearly 100 years later by Con Agra Foods, Peavey was a significant player in the domestic and international grain industry.

486. Ibid., p. 42.

487. Ibid., p. 42.

488. Ibid., p. 42.

CHAPTER 11: THE GOLDEN AGE OF CRUISE SHIPS

489. Walker and Hall, *Duluth-Superior Harbor Cultural Resources Study*, p. 98. Most newly arrived immigrants got their first view of the Twin Ports from the White Line Transportation Company's terminal wharf in the Duluth harbor basin.

490. William F. Rapprich, "The Anchor Line: *Tionesta, Juniata*, and *Octarora*," *Inland Seas* (Spring 1974): 7–8.

491. William F. Rapprich, "The *North West* and *North Land*," *Inland Seas*: 3–4. John H. Smith, the Globe Iron Works' noted naval architect, designed the two vessels but died before the *North West* was launched.

492. Ibid., p. 5. At full speed, the vessels consumed eight tons of coal per hour.

493. Miller, "Workhorses and White Flyers," p. 3. More than half the crew were stewards and pursers catering to the whims of the passengers.

494. Ibid., p. 3. Henry Villard, the German immigrant who helped organize the Northern Pacific Railway, had pioneered the use of electric lights aboard vessels when he installed a generator aboard one of his Oregon-based railroad ferries in the late 1880s.

495. Ibid., p. 4. Food was extra, but a complete steak and lobster dinner was $2.90.

496. Ibid., p. 8. In 1901, the Northern Steamship Company employed both vessels on a Buffalo-Chicago run to take advantage of the thousands of Americans who wanted to attend the Pan-American Exposition in Buffalo. Northern Steamship brought in a smaller, oceangoing vessel, the *Miami*, to shuttle passengers from Duluth to Mackinac Island, where they could meet the *North Land* or *North West* for passage to Buffalo or Chicago. After one season, the *Miami* returned to its regular Florida-Cuba run.

497. Rapprich, "The Anchor Line," pp. 7–9. On the downbound leg of their voyages, the three new Anchor Line vessels usually stopped in Houghton to load copper ingots for fabricating firms in Buffalo.

498. Ibid., p. 11. During the passenger season, one of the vessels left the Anchor Line's passenger terminal in Buffalo every third day.

499. "Builders Information: S.S. South American, S.S. North American," http://170.211.225.100/georgian_bay/pg2_builders_info.htm.

500. "Last on the Lakes: A Brief History of the Georgian Bay Lines," *Holland Historical Trust Review* 1 (Spring 1988): 1–3.

501. The *North American* rarely made it to the Twin Ports during her career. Wes Harkins, who has forgotten more about the Great Lakes in the twentieth century than most other experts on the lakes know, claimed to Davis Helberg that the *North American* visited Duluth-Superior only once, in the mid-1950s. And he has the photograph to prove it. See e-mail, Davis Helberg to the author, February 1, 2003.

502. W. R. Williams, "The Northwest Transportation Company," *Inland Seas* (Summer 1962): 112–13.

503. Lorenzo Marcolin, "Canadian Pacific Railway Company Steamship Lines—Last of an Era," *Inland Seas* (Spring 1966): 8–12. During the 1912 shipping season, more than fifty passenger vessels regularly called on the Canadian lakehead.

504. William Sullivan, "*Noronic* Burned Forty Years Ago," *Nor'Easter* 14 (September–October 1989): 1–4. Northern Navigation Company was a subsidiary of the Canada Steamship Lines. In 1931, the *Noronic* successfully navigated the new Welland Canal, which opened up Lake Ontario cruises for the popular passenger vessel.

505. Miller, "Workhorses and White Flyers," p. 7. The Northern Steamship Company accepted a $295,000 insurance settlement on the loss and later sold the hulk for $200,000. During World War I, the *North West*'s hull was cut in half and towed through the Welland Canal. One-half of the hull sunk in a Lake Ontario storm, but the stern half was joined with a new bow and renamed *Maplecourt*.

506. *Chronicle of America*, p. 662. When the *Morro Castle* caught fire off New Jersey on Labor Day Weekend 1934, 120 passengers and crew lost their lives.

507. Rapprich, "The Anchor Line," p. 15. *Octorara* maintained the Buffalo-Duluth service in 1933 and 1934.

508. Sullivan, "*Noronic* Burned Forty Years Ago," pp. 1–4.

509. "Last on the Lakes," pp. 1–3. The *North American* stopped sailing in the early 1960s. The *South American* continued Lake Michigan cruises until 1967, when the U.S. Coast Guard banned vessels with a wooden superstructure from carrying overnight passengers. Her last voyage was down the St. Lawrence River to the Montreal World's Fair in 1967. Following the voyage to Canada, the *South American* was purchased by the Seafarer's International Union for use as a floating dormitory at SIU's Lundeberg School of Seamanship at Piney Point, Maryland. She eventually ended her days rotting at a Camden, New Jersey, dock and was finally scrapped in 1992.

The Petroleum Business in the Twin Ports

510. Kenneth Morris et.al., *American Dreams* (Lightbulb Press, 1990), p. 52. Before the advent of the assembly line, automobile production was basically handcrafted. In 1912, Ford made 82,000 Model T's, which sold for $850 apiece. In 1916, Ford made 585,000 Model T's, which retailed for $350 apiece.

511. Al Miller, "Oil on the Water: The Standard Oil Company of Indiana and Its Great Lakes Fleet," part 1, *The Nor'Easter* 24, no. 2 (March–April 1999): 1–2.

512. "A Scorcher Sure," *Duluth Evening Herald,* October 16, 1888.

513. "The Standard's Intentions," *Duluth Evening Herald,* September 20, 1888. The initial plan called for building barrel and cooperage factories in West Duluth and steel tanks on Rice's Point. Standard Oil had recently taken options on 3,000 acres of timberlands seventy-five miles south of Duluth to provide wood for the proposed barrel factory.

514. Walker and Hall, *Duluth-Superior Harbor Cultural Resources Study,* p. 92.

515. "The New Oil Boat," *Duluth Weekly Herald,* August 6, 1891.

516. Miller, "Oil on the Water," part 1, p. 2.

517. Walker and Hall, *Duluth-Superior Harbor Cultural Resources Study,* p. 93.

CHAPTER 12: THE LEAN DEPRESSION YEARS

518. George J. Joachim, *Iron Fleet: The Great Lakes in World War II* (Detroit: Wayne State University Press, 1994), pp. 10–11. U.S. Steel and the steel industry enjoyed the "best second quarter earnings since the war," said *Time Magazine* in July. "Still Strong Steel," *Time,* July 29, 1929.

519. "Camera Tours Iron Range with President Coolidge," *Duluth News-Tribune,* August 3, 1928. See also "Bear Shot in Hotel," *Duluth News-Tribune,* August 19, 1929.

520. "Bridge Rises 25 Feet on First Attempt," *Duluth News-Tribune,* March 21, 1930. Another bridge familiar to Great Lakes mariners opened in 1929. The Ambassador Bridge across the Detroit River connected Detroit and Windsor, Ontario. See Miller, *Tin Stackers,* p. 125.

521. Duluth-Superior Harbor Statistics, p. 3. Steel output at U.S. Steel dropped by a quarter in 1930, and the corporation's profits were nearly halved to $104 million.

522. Duluth-Superior Harbor Statistics, p. 3.

523. Havighurst, *Vein of Iron,* p. 166.

524. Miller, *Tin Stackers,* p. 127. U.S. Steel's Pittsburgh Steamship Company was operating only fifty-nine vessels in 1931. A total of twenty-seven vessels, including all of the fleet's whaleback barges, were never fit out for the season. See "It Was News 40 Years Ago," *Skillings Mining Review,* August 7, 1971. Another major fleet, Interlake, laid up a dozen of its smaller vessels during the year. See Havighurst, *Vein of Iron,* p. 169.

525. Duluth-Superior Harbor Statistics, p. 3.

526. Ibid., p. 3.

527. "It Was News 40 Years Ago," *Skillings Mining Review,* November 6, 1971. The *Lamont* was the newest bulk freighter on the Great Lakes. She was built for the Pittsburgh Steamship Company and launched with the *Eugene P. Thomas* in the spring of 1930. The *Lamont* and the *Thomas* would be the last bulk freighters launched until 1938. See Miller, *Tin Stackers,* p. 126.

528. "It Was News 40 Years Ago," *Skillings Mining Review,* November 13, 1971.

529. T. H. Watkins, *The Great Depression: America in the 1930s* (Boston: Little, Brown and Company, 1993), p. 55. Before President Franklin Roosevelt gained control of the nation's banking system in the mid-1930s, more than 9,000 banks in the United States failed, nearly one-third of the nation's total in 1929. See Morris et al., *American Dreams,* p. 83.

530. Watkins, *The Great Depression,* p. 55.

531. D. Jerome Tweton, *Depression: Minnesota in the Thirties* (Fargo: North Dakota Institute for Regional Studies, 1981), p. 9. Wheat prices fluctuated between 97 cents and $1.20 per bushel for much of the 1920s.

532. Ibid., p. 9. Even diversified farmers felt the lash of the Great Depression. In 1932, hogs in St. Paul and Chicago sold for 3 cents per pound. Minnesota and Wisconsin dairy farmers were selling milk for 2 cents per quart.

533. Tweton, *Depression: Minnesota in the Thirties,* p. 7.

534. Havighurst, *Vein of Iron,* p. 166. Because many of the homes on the range were owner-occupied, the homelessness that afflicted the big cities wasn't particularly evident in Hibbing, Virginia, Mountain Iron, and other range mining locations. A number of people rented homes from the mining companies, particularly in the more isolated locations, but most of the mining companies instituted a moratorium on evictions during the 1930s.

535. Beck, *Northern Lights,* pp. 235–37. Oliver Mining Company increased its electric power consumption sevenfold between 1923 and 1930. Because of electrification and automation, the mining workforce gradually decreased during the 1920s.

536. "It Was News 40 Years Ago," *Skillings Mining Review,* January 22, 1972. The three boats were employed in the limestone trade, which began employing self-unloaders decades before the iron ore fleets did. The predecessor of U.S. Steel's Bradley Transportation Company, which served the limestone quarries of Lake Huron, had begun using self-unloaders in 1908. See Miller, *Tin Stackers,* pp. 115–16.

537. "It Was News 40 Years Ago," *Skillings Mining Review,* February 18, 1972. Unemployment in the iron mining regions of Lake Superior was equaled only by the economic devastation visited on the Copper Range of Michigan's Keweenaw Peninsula. The author's mother, who grew up in a smelting community on Torch Lake, was eleven years old in the spring of 1932. She often talked about walking the tracks of the Duluth, South Shore, & Atlantic Railway with her brothers and sisters, searching for lump coal that had dropped out of gondola cars. They brought the coal home with them and burned it in the parlor stove. One of her funnier stories involved getting hit by a car on the main street of Hubbell, Michigan, one day early in the depression. The car was driven by two Chicago bootleggers who had just unloaded a number of cases of Canadian liquor landed from a ketch near Eagle Harbor. They didn't want to stick around to talk to the police about the accident involving the little girl, so they gave my grandfather cash to get their victim's leg set. It was the most money my grandfather saw that year, and my mother remembered the traumatic incident fondly because every Christmas for several years thereafter, she received a large plush toy in the mail from Marshall Field's Department Store in Chicago.

538. "It Was News 40 Years Ago," *Skillings Mining Review,* March 11, 1972.

539. Miller, *Tin Stackers,* pp. 31–39. Wolvin at first refused the offer, but when U.S. Steel agreed to allow him to run the fleet from Duluth, he accepted.

540. "It Was News 40 Years Ago," *Skillings Mining Review,* April 15, 1972.

541. "It Was News 40 Years Ago," *Skillings Mining Review,* July 8, 1972. There was some activity at the Northern Pacific ore dock in Duluth for manganese ore from the Cuyuna Range in April, but the DM&N and Great Northern docks struggled throughout the 1932 season. The ore docks at Two Harbors didn't see their first boat until July.

542. Joachim, *Iron Fleet,* p. 11. The Pittsburgh Steamship Company didn't fit out its first boat until June. By that time, the nation's blast furnaces were operating at 16 percent of capacity. See "It Was News 40 Years Ago," *Skillings Mining Review,* July 22, 1972.

543. Duluth-Superior Harbor Statistics, pp. 1–3.

544. Ibid., p. 3.

545. Ibid., pp. 1–3. Conditions were dismal in 1932 everywhere on the lakes. The total iron ore tonnage of 3.5 million tons was equivalent to the tonnage shipped in ten days of August 1929. Bituminous coal was at the lowest levels since the mid-1920s and more anthracite coal had been shipped in the 1880s. See Joachim, *Iron Fleet,* p. 11.

546. Nathan Miller, *FDR: An Intimate History* (New York: New American Library, 1983), pp. 12–15. Although he had never been in the Twin Ports before his election to the presidency, FDR had financial roots at the head of the lakes. His father, James Roosevelt, had amassed large land holdings in Superior in the early 1890s and was an early shareholder in Superior's First National Bank. FDR and his half-brother, James Roosevelt "Rosy" Roosevelt, were minority investors in a Superior apartment block at the turn of the twentieth century. See Beck, *At the Foot of Winter Street,* p. 13.

547. Corps of Engineers, United States Army, *The Port of Duluth Superior, Minn. and Wis.,* Lake Series No. 6 (Washington, D.C.: Government Printing Office, 1940), p. 13.

548. Beck, *From the Foot of Winter Street,* pp. 70–74.

549. Duluth-Superior Harbor Statistics, p. 4. The 1935 totals, however, only approximated the ports' average during the 1910s.

550. Ibid., p. 4. Coal averaged 9.5 million tons in both 1936 and 1937, and grain shipments doubled in 1937 to 1.25 million tons. The 679,000 tons of grain shipped in 1936 was a forty-six-year low for the Twin Ports, illustrative of the drought and record heat that scorched the Upper Midwest in the summer of 1936.

551. Joachim, *Iron Fleet,* p. 11.

552. Curtis S. Miller, "Organized Labor: A Look Back," in Lydecker, *Duluth: Sketches of the Past,* p. 212. Delegates from eleven Great Lakes ports met in Detroit in 1892 to form the predecessor union. Three years later, the organization changed its name to the International Longshoremen's Association. See "Our History," www.ilaunion.org/history_creation.asp.

553. There was an ILA local organized in Superior, Wisconsin, in the 1910s. See International Longshoremen's Association, "Constitution and By-Laws," Superior, Wisconsin, revised July 2, 1916, p. 1.

554. "Our History," www.ilaunion.org/history_membership.asp. The Industrial Workers of the World was formed in Chicago in 1905. Its syndicalist, "One Big Union" philosophy contrasted sharply with the craft union philosophy of Samuel Gompers and the American Federation of Labor. The "Wobblies," as IWW members were known at the time, were particularly strong among the immigrant miners and lumberjacks of the Lake Superior country. In 1916, the Wobblies orchestrated a bitter strike against the Oliver Mining Company on Minnesota's Mesabi Range.

555. Barb Sommers interview with Edward L. "Buster" Slaughter, Duluth, Minnesota, n.d., p. 7. The origin of Slaughter's nickname has always been somewhat of a mystery. During the 1980s, the aging labor leader hinted that it came from his prowess with a baseball bat during organizing battles on Great Lakes docks in the 1930s. He also told reporters earlier in his career that he got the nickname from a Duluth doctor, who got tired of setting Slaughter's broken nose. See "Buster Slaughter," *Minnesota's World Port* (June 1975): 19.

556. Ibid., 9.

557. Miller, "Organized Labor: A Look Back," p. 212. The newspaper recognized the American Newspaper Guild a short time later.

558. Ibid., p. 14. Slaughter served as president of ILA Local 1279 from 1932 to 1937. In 1934, he organized a second ILA local, Local 1366, and was its trustee from its inception to 1945. In 1934, he was named president of ILA's Central District. The next year, Slaughter was named an ILA international vice president, a position he would hold for fifty-five years. See "Longtime waterfront leader E. L. 'Buster' Slaughter, 87," *Duluth News-Tribune,* December 21, 1991.

559. Ibid., p. 21. Minnesota and Wisconsin were hotbeds of domestic communism during the 1930s. Gus Hall, longtime general secretary of the Communist Party USA, was a native of Cherry on the Mesabi Iron Range. Communism was particularly strong in the region's Finnish community, and Finnish communists were the shock troops of the Timberworkers Union, which battled logging companies across Minnesota, Wisconsin, and the Upper Peninsula of Michigan in a series of strikes during the late 1930s.

560. Ibid., p. 22.

561. Ibid. Slaughter's gruff exterior and tough guy image masked the inner man. A devout Catholic, Slaughter was a daily Mass communicant when the author served with him on the Seaway Port Authority board of commissioners from 1983 to 1988. He was devoted to his beloved Ann, who preceded him in death by a year. At home in Duluth's Woodland neighborhood, he loved puttering around in the garden. But to this day, the best way to start a lively discussion in a Duluth waterfront bar is to start swapping Buster Slaughter stories.

562. Nathan Cohen, "Junk Heap Claims The Incline," *Duluth News-Tribune,* September 3, 1939.

563. Duluth-Superior Harbor Statistics, p. 4.

564. Miller, *FDR: An Intimate History,* pp. 439–41.

565. Kenneth Warren, *Big Steel* (Pittsburgh Press: 2001), pp. 193, 363. U.S. Steel's 1940 production of 22.9 million tons was 5.3 million tons higher than 1939, more than double the production of 1938, and the best year enjoyed by the steel trust since 1929. U.S. Steel profits of $102.2 million were two-and-a-half times the profit of the year before.

566. Captain R. W. Parsons, "The Storm of 1940," *Inland Seas* (Fall 1961): 202–06.

567. David Swayze, *Shipwreck!* (Boyne City, Michigan: Harbor House, 1992), pp. 67, 155. The canaller *Novadoc* was pushed ashore and broke up on a reef paralleling the harbor at Pentwater. Two men were washed overboard and drowned. The rest of the crew clung to the wreckage and were rescued on the November 13. See "15 Saved, 65 Lost on Lakes," *Duluth Herald,* November 13, 1940.

568. "15 Saved, 65 Lost on Lakes," *Duluth Herald,* November 13, 1940.

569. "140 Duluth Reservists Called Aboard *Paducah,*" *Duluth News-Tribune,* November 2, 1940. The three vessels were all assigned to the Naval Reserve and stationed in the Great Lakes: the *Paducah* at Duluth, the *Dubuque* at Detroit, and the *Sacramento* at Michigan City, Indiana.

Duluth-Superior in 1939

570. "U.S., Canada Nearing Agreement for Seaway," *Duluth News-Tribune,* December 6, 1939.

571. Beck, *From the Foot of Winter Street,* pp. 70–75.

572. *The Port of Duluth-Superior, Minnesota, and Wisconsin,* pp. 33–35, 74, 84, 86.

CHAPTER 13: THE TWIN PORTS AT WAR

573. "City Boasts Tallest Elevator in World" crowed the *Superior Evening Telegram* in an undated 1941 story in historian Patrick Lapinski's files. "Rising abruptly out of Superior's waterfront skyline is a mammoth new structure of shining concrete, which, when completed, will become the tallest terminal grain elevator in the world." The story also reports: "A unique, yet very practical device, entirely new at the Head of the Lakes, will be installed for unloading freight cars. Automatic throughout, it will dump a carload of grain into the 'pit' in six minutes. From there, it will be whisked to the top of the bins at the rate of 25,000 bushels per minute."

574. Duluth-Superior Harbor Statistics, p. 5.

575. *Chronicle of America,* p. 694. President Roosevelt had extended the promise of Lend Lease to the Soviet Union on June 24, 1941, two days after the Nazis unleashed their blitzkrieg on the USSR.

576. "Rail Strike Averted by New Accord," *Duluth News-Tribune,* December 2, 1941.

577. "War Declared on Jap Nation," *Duluth Herald,* December 8, 1941.

578. Ibid. The lone vote against the war came from Congresswoman Jeannette Rankin, a Republican from Montana. A longtime friend of Upper Midwest wheat farmers, Rankin voted the courage of

her pacifist convictions. During her only other term in Congress, she had voted against America's declaration of war against Germany in April 1917.

579. "Area Acts Fast in War Effort," *Duluth Herald,* December 8, 1941.

580. Joachim, *Iron Fleet,* p. 64. Some military planners were concerned early in the war that the *Kriegsmarine,* the German Navy, would steam undetected into Hudson Bay and launch torpedo and dive bombers against the Soo.

581. Ibid., pp. 64–65.

582. "$2,000,000 Blaze Destroys Superior Elevator; Injures 7," *Duluth Herald,* January 10, 1942. The flames were visible twenty-five miles away from the Twin Ports.

583. Ibid. The same night, fire destroyed the Calumet Armory in Michigan's Copper Country, immolating the equipment of several Michigan Army National Guard units. Local residents could have been forgiven for wondering if the two blazes were coincidental. See, "Flames Destroy Calumet Armory," *Duluth Herald,* January 10, 1942.

584. Joachim, *Iron Fleet,* pp. 37–38. In May, the first rationing coupon books were issued to the population, severely limiting the civilian consumption of food, gasoline, tires, and anything made of chemicals. See "Registration to Begin for War Ration Book 1," *Duluth News-Tribune,* May 4, 1942.

585. "Nuggets of News from the *Skillings* Archives—August 15, 1942," *Skillings Mining Review* (August 17, 2002). As is the case with national emergencies, sometimes the best intentions of drive organizers went astray. In August 1942, Secretary of the Interior Harold L. Ickes had to remind scrap drive participants that one classification of scrap the government did not want to see scrapped was old mining equipment. "Every piece of usable or repairable mining equipment is absolutely vital because it cannot be replaced," Ickes wrote.

586. Mariners were blessed by generally good sailing weather for most of the war. See "First Boats May Arrive about April 1," *Skillings Mining Review* (March 25, 1944).

587. "American Boats in Ore Traffic, May 15, Number 291," *Skillings Mining Review* (May 30, 1942). Literally every bottom on the American side of the Great Lakes was consigned to the ore trade.

588. "12,000,000 Tons L.S. Iron Ore in May Is One Estimate," *Skillings Mining Review* (May 23, 1942): 1. The previous record had been achieved in August 1941.

589. Joachim, *Iron Fleet,* pp. 40–41. One of the vessels leaving the lakes in the summer of 1942 was the Minnesota port's namesake. The 402-foot *Duluth* spent her war years hauling cargo out of Seattle. She had spent forty years in the Great Lakes package freight trade. See Edward J. Dowling, S.J., "Three Great Lakes Freighters Now on the Pacific," *Inland Seas* (Spring 1948): 64.

590. Ibid., p. 40. Because ore was washed at the mines, it often arrived at the docks frozen in the railroad cars. In the early days of shipping, crews with long iron poles knocked the ore loose from the cars into the dock pockets. After World War I, most of the docks installed steam sheds on the docks to thaw cars of frozen ore. Crews, some of them local high school students released from class, steamed 4.5 million tons of ore at Duluth-Superior in October and November 1942.

591. Ibid., p. 41.

592. Duluth-Superior Harbor Statistics, p. 5.

593. Ibid., p. 5. Never again would more total cargo pass across the docks in a single season.

594. Joachim, *Iron Fleet,* p. 49.

595. Duluth-Superior Harbor Statistics, p. 5.

596. "90 Million Tons Iron Ore in 1944," *Skillings Mining Review* (February 5, 1944): 1.

597. Sandvik, *Duluth: An Illustrated History of the Zenith City,* p. 118. After the war, the firm became the nation's major manufacturer of pitching horseshoes.

598. "Bong Dies in Plane Explosion," *Duluth News-Tribune,* August 7, 1945. Bong, of Poplar, Wisconsin, joined the U.S. Army Air Force in May 1941 after attending Superior State Teachers College. In 1944, he received the Medal of Honor on Leyte Island from General Douglas MacArthur. In 1945, he returned to the United States and helped sell war bonds when not serving as a test pilot in California. On June 6, 2003, the Richard I. Bong World War II Heritage Center was dedicated near Barker's Island on the Superior waterfront.

599. "Interlake Navigation Opens at Duluth on Easter, April 9," *Skillings Mining Review* (April 15, 1944): 1.

600. "N.W. Holds Boats in Whitefish Bay," *Skillings Mining Review* (April 8, 1944): 7.

601. Joachim, *Iron Fleet,* pp. 50–51.

602. Duluth-Superior Harbor Statistics, pp. 1–5.

603. Joachim, *Iron Fleet,* p. 51. The elevators in Duluth-Superior handled 4.8 million tons of grain, 1.4 million tons more than in 1944 and a record that would stand until 1965.

604. Ibid., p. 51.

605. Duluth-Superior Harbor Statistics, p. 5.

606. Noam Levey, "Ships of Dreams," *Duluth News-Tribune,* April 5, 1998.

607. "Nuggets of News from the *Skillings* Archives—August 15, 1942," *Skillings Mining Review* (August 3, 2002): 16.

608. The Manitowoc Company yards launched twenty-eight submarines for the U.S. Navy during the war. See Dennis McCann, "Manitowoc company built first submarine on Great Lakes," Online *Milwaukee Journal-Sentinel* News, April 19, 1998, www.jsonline.com/news/state/wisl50/stories/0419sesqui.stm. See also "Manitowoc Celebrates 100 Years," www.appliance.com/news/6_27_02.html.

609. John H. Wilterding Jr., "Shipbuilding at Duluth-Superior: World War II's Type N3 Ocean Cargo Craft," *The Nor'Easter* (November–December 1986): 1. Contracts were also let during the war by the U.S. Army, Navy, and Coast Guard.

610. Joachim, *Iron Fleet,* pp. 100–101.

611. "New Chapter in Great Lakes Shipbuilding Industry," *Skillings Mining Review,* March 7, 1942, p. 1. The five new ships had a combined per-trip capacity of 93,000 tons. The six vessels traded to the U.S. Maritime Commission had a per-trip capacity of less than half that of the new vessels. The new bottoms made a major contribution to the iron ore float during World War II.

612. Joachim, *Iron Fleet,* p. 103–05.

613. John H. Wilterding Jr., "Shipbuilding at Duluth-Superior: World War II's Type N3 Ocean Cargo Craft," p. 1.

614. Skip Gilham, "*Liquilassie:* The Homegrown Tanker That Came Back to the Lakes," *The Nor'Easter* (September–October 1982): 2.

615. Ibid., p. 2. The completed tankers were sailed down the Great Lakes to Chicago, where they entered the series of canals that led to the Illinois River and then to the Mississippi River.

616. Walter Butler Shipbuilders, Superior, Wisconsin, Record of WWII Shipbuilding, pp. 1–2.

617. John H. Wilterding Jr., "Shipbuilding in the Twin Ports: Walter Butler Company's C1-M-AV1 Cargo Ships," *The Nor'Easter* (May–June 1994): 1. A total of 208 of the coastal freighters were built at five Great Lakes yards during the war.

618. Barry Singer, "Remembering the Globe: A History of Superior's Famous Globe Shipbuilding Company," part 1, *The Nor'Easter* (May–June 1988): 1. Other organizers were Victor Nelson, chair of Northern Brewery, Roy McMill, Snyder Clemens, and Scott Williamson.

619. Ibid., p. 1. Globe didn't get a contract to build cargo ships until 1943, about a year after Barnes Duluth and Butler started building the coastal freighters.

620. John H. Wilterding Jr., "The Tacoma-Class Patrol Frigates," *The Nor'Easter* (July–August 1982): 1–3. Most of the Twin Ports–built frigates saw escort, weather, and air rescue duty in the North Atlantic between 1943 and 1945. Several Butler-built frigates saw duty during the war with the Russian navy in the Northwest Pacific.

621. Ray Wiemer and Tom Bourne, "Workhorses of the Fleet: The 180s from Duluth," *The Nor'Easter* (March–April 1995): 1. The original contract called for the construction of thirty-nine "180s." The cutter *Ironwood* was built by the Coast Guard at its yards in Curtiss Bay, Maryland.

622. Sandvik, *Duluth: An Illustrated History of the Zenith City,* p. 110. The firm maintained a workforce of about 100 skilled employees during the 1930s, which allowed it to gear up quickly for defense work during World War II.

623. Ibid., p. 106.

624. Quoted in Levey, "Ships of Dreams." Zenith Dredge was the first Twin Ports shipbuilder to train women as welders.

625. John R. Ward, "The Little Ships That Could," *Invention and Technology* (Fall 1999): 37. Blodgett described an all-welded ship as similar to putting together a three-dimensional jigsaw puzzle.

626. Levey, "Ships of Dreams." Defoe Shipbuilding Company of Bay City, Michigan, actually welded vessels upside down. The technique virtually eliminated overhead welding. The hulls were righted for launching by a cast iron cradle that encircled the hull. See Ward, "The Little Ships That Could," pp. 38–39. Defoe delivered more

than 160 vessels to the U.S. Navy during the war. See www.concentric.net/~djdefoe/TheDeFoeStory.htm.

627. Tape-recorded oral history interview with Howard Hagen, Duluth, Minnesota, February 24, 2000, p. 7.

628. "Nuggets of News from the *Skillings* Archives—August 15, 1942," *Skillings Mining Review* (August 3, 2002): 16. The *Bursley* sailed for twenty-one years under various names and owners. In 1952 and 1953, she visited the Great Lakes under Italian ownership as the *Pietro Canale*. She came to grief on the reefs surrounding the Cayman Islands in 1964 and was written off as a total loss. See E. B. "Skip" Gilham, "Travels of the *William Bursley*," *The Nor'Easter* (March–April 1996): 6–7.

629. "Reflect Great Credit on Lake Shipbuilding," *Skillings Mining Review*, August 7, 1943, p. 4. The four vessels were launched on July 30–31 at Barnes Duluth, Butler, Zenith Dredge, and Globe shipyards.

630. Walter Butler Shipbuilders, Superior, Wisconsin, Record of WWII Shipbuilding, pp. 1–2.

631. Roger Losey, "Pride of the Coast Guard—The 180s from Duluth," *The Nor'Easter* (July–August 1985): 1–4.

632. Leathem D. Smith, "War Shipbuilding on the Great Lakes," *Inland Seas* (July 1946): p. 148.

633. Joachim, *Iron Fleet*, pp. 92–94. The lock was named for America's newest hero, General Douglas MacArthur.

634. "The Icebreaker *Mackinaw*," *Inland Seas* (April 1945): 38–40. Ironically, the 1945 season was one of the mildest on the Great Lakes, and the *Mackinaw* saw limited duty that last year of the war.

635. "Oberstar, "Obey Wins Final Approval of Funding for the *Mackinaw* Replacement," Congressman James Oberstar news release, June 30, 2000, p. 1. The replacement will also be named the *Mackinaw*, and her home port will be Cheboygan, Michigan. The new *Mackinaw* is expected to be launched in 2005, a year before her predecessor's decommissioning.

The Woodrush, the Sundew, and the 180s

636. Wiemer and Bourne, "Workhorses of the Fleet," p. 1. The Lighthouse Service was merged into the U.S. Coast Guard in 1939.

637. Ibid., p. 3. The *Mesquite* was stationed in Duluth in 1979 and was a frequent visitor to the Twin Ports in the years following the war. She holed herself on rocks and sunk off the Keweenaw Peninsula's Bete Gris Bay in the spring of 1989.

638. www.uscg.mil/nicknames. Other nicknames for the 180 were *Woody the Warship*, *Wood-rust*, *Wierdrush*, and *Scrub Brush*. Some even called her *Wee Little Battleship 407*, a pun on the cutter's designation, WLB-407.

639. Tape-recorded oral history interview with Gil Porter, Duluth, Minnesota, February 21, 2000, p. 4.

640. C. P. Labadie, "The *Sundew* Looks Right at Home," *NorthStar Port* (Winter 2000–2001): 15. The *Woodrush*, another member of the Iris class, was stationed at Duluth from 1944 to 1978 before being modernized and sent to Sitka, Alaska. The *Woodrush* was retired from active duty in 2001 and sold to Ghana.

641. Ibid. Current plans call for the *Sundew* to be berthed near the museum-ship *William A. Irvin*, which has been on display in Duluth since the late 1970s.

CHAPTER 14: THE RANGE RESURGENT

642. Joachim, *Iron Fleet*, p. 114.

643. Ibid., p. 108.

644. Walker and Hall, *Duluth-Superior Harbor Cultural Resources Study*, p. 84.

645. *Skillings Mining Review* (August 12, 1950).

646. *Skillings Mining Review* (September 16, 1950). The Korean War put unprecedented demand on the Great Lakes fleet. In 1951, the steel industry supplemented lakes shipments of iron ore with all-rail haulage of ore from Minnesota to the steel mills. The industry had tested rail shipments in 1943 and 1944, and most of the 4 million tons of ore that left the Mesabi Range by rail in 1951 went to National Steel's Granite City mill near St. Louis. See "The Week That Was: Nuggets of News from the *Skillings* Archives— August 4, 1951," *Skillings Mining Review* (August 5, 2001): 10.

647. Walker and Hall, *Duluth-Superior Harbor Cultural Resources Study*, p. 84. The 77.2 million tons that went down the lakes the last year of the Korean War is the all-time total tonnage record for the Twin Ports. See Duluth-Superior Harbor Statistics, p. 5.

648. Ibid., p. 84.

649. Duluth-Superior Harbor Statistics, Seaway Port Authority of Duluth, 1999, p. 5. Coal receipts peaked at 8.4 million tons in 1950, dropped by nearly half by 1954, recovered in 1955 and 1956, and slipped to 3.7 million tons in 1959. The 1959 receipts were the worst in fifty-four years and were indicative of the growing use of fuel oil and natural gas for industrial and residential heating applications.

650. Tape-recorded interview with Ken Fossum, Superior, Wisconsin, February 22, 2000, pp. 12–13. Coal briquetting began in the early twentieth century when Pennsylvania coal producers began looking for a by-product use for culm, the coal dust waste produced by anthracite mines. See Guy Elliott Mitchell, "An Ideal Fuel Manufactured Out of Waste Products—The American Coal Briquetting Industry," *National Geographic* (December 1910): 1067–74.

651. Fossum interview, p. 13.

652. "Nuggets of News from the *Skillings* Archives—November 17, 1951," *Skillings Mining Review* (November 2001): 10. The editor noted that "at one time it was anticipated that the shipments of coal to the head of the lakes docks would reach 17 million tons per year. This goal was never reached." Ironically, the 17-million ton goal *was* reached a half-century later, but the coal movement was outbound and not inbound.

653. E. W. Davis, *Pioneering with Taconite* (St. Paul: Minnesota Historical Society Press, 1964), pp. v–vii.

654. "The Iron Ore Dilemma," *Fortune* (November 1945): 128–39, 259–64. See also Warren Olivier, "The Coming Crisis in Iron," *The Saturday Evening Post* (November 14, 1942): 22, 121; and "Can Research Save Mesabi?" *Business Week* (May 11, 1945): 19–21.

655. *Skillings Mining Review* (August 26, 1950). The three things an emerging society needed to possess in the postwar world were a standing army, a national airline, and a steel industry. By the early 1950s, both Brazil and Venezuela were building steel mills with the help of Export-Import Bank financing. See "46 Years Ago in Steel: The Iron Age, July 22, 1954," *New Steel* (July 2000): 9.

656. Beck, *Northern Lights*, p. 386.

657. Davis, *Pioneering with Taconite*, pp. 109–10.

658. Ibid., p. 108.

659. Robert V. Bartlett, *The Reserve Mining Controversy: Science, Technology, and Environmental Quality* (Bloomington: Indiana University Press, 1980), p. 23.

660. Ibid., p. 23. Reserve built its own railroad to connect the mine near Babbitt with the new taconite processing facility, which was named the E. W. Davis Works.

661. Davis, *Pioneering with Taconite*, pp. 168–69.

662. Ibid., pp. 143–44.

663. Ibid., pp. 142–43.

664. Walker and Hall, *Duluth-Superior Harbor Cultural Resources Study*, p. 85. Much of the early flow of taconite pellets would go down the lakes from ore docks at Two Harbors, Silver Bay, and Taconite Harbor, a new facility on the north shore of Lake Superior, which was completed in 1957.

665. Jacques LesStrang, *Seaway: The Story of the Great Lakes and the St. Lawrence Seaway* (Seattle: A Salisbury Press Book, 1976), p. 47. The legislation was named for its cosponsors, Senator Alexander Wiley of Wisconsin and Representative George Dondero, Michigan.

666. Bill Beck, "The Duluth Port Authority: A Look Back to the Early Years, Part I," *The Nor'Easter* 9, no. 2 (March–April 1984): 1.

667. The dream of a unified port authority for both Duluth and Superior is an idea that goes back 140 years and has never come to pass. The first attempt to combine the two communities came in the midst of the Civil War in 1863, when the Minnesota legislature asked the Wisconsin legislature to cede Douglas County, Wisconsin, to the Gopher State. The Minnesota legislators argued that since Douglas County had been settled by Minnesotans, the area rightly belonged to Minnesota. "Whereas, while it may possibly be true, that Douglass County was settled by citizens of Minnesota," the Wisconsin legislators frostily replied, "it is undoubtedly also true that a considerable portion of the state of Minnesota was settled by citizens of the state of Wisconsin." Even then, the downstate legislators in Madison were well aware of Superior's potential, citing the community as possessing "one of the finest harbors on Lake Superior." See Wisconsin Laws of 1863, Resolution Number 3, March 18, 1863.

668. Beck, *Northern Lights*, pp. 261–62.

669. Ibid., pp. 2–3.

670. Ibid., p. 3.

671. "Great Duluthians: Arthur M. Clure," *Duluth Budgeteer* (December 22, 1999).

672. Beck, "The Duluth Port Authority, Part I," 3. Freeman served three terms as Democratic Farmer Labor governor of Minnesota. He was defeated in his bid for a fourth term in 1960. See Dan Cohen, *Undefeated: The Life of Hubert H. Humphrey* (Minneapolis: Lerner Publications Company, 1978), pp. 230–31.

673. Ibid., p. 3.

674. Ibid., p. 4.

675. Ibid., p. 4.

676. Beck, "The Duluth Port Authority: A Look Back to the Early Years, Part II," *The Nor'Easter* 9, no. 3 (May–June 1984): 1.

677. Ibid., 1.

678. Ibid., 2.

679. Ibid., 2.

680. "$10 Million Marine Terminal Approved," *Duluth News-Tribune,* April 24, 1957.

681. "City Starts Action to Acquire Rice's Point Shipping Terminal," *The Duluth Herald,* November 20, 1956.

682. Einar W. Karlstrand, "Mill City Firm to Draft Terminal Plans," *Duluth News-Tribune,* July 16, 1957.

683. Beck, "The Duluth Port Authority, Part II," 4.

684. Duluth-Superior Harbor Statistics, 1999, p. 5. With 2.75 million tons of grain handled during 1958, it would be the last time that the Twin Ports moved less than 3 million tons of grain in a season.

685. Beck, "The Duluth Port Authority, Part II," 4.

686. Ibid., 4.

Vessel Repair and Fraser Shipyards

687. "Fraser Harbor Man of Year," *Superior Evening Telegram,* March 9, 1974, p. 1.

688. "Propeller Club Honors Fraser, Knowlton," *Minnesota's World Port* (October 1974): 22.

689. "Fraser Harbor Man of Year," p. 1. At the time of the expansion of the dry docks, the Great Lakes fleet was undergoing a major transformation. For twenty-two years, from 1927 to 1949, the *Carl D. Bradley* was the largest vessel in the fleet, at 640 feet. The June 1958 launching of the *Edmund Fitzgerald* ushered in a class of vessels 730 feet long. The "730s" would dominate the trade until another exponential leap to 1,000-foot vessels in the early 1970s. See Mark L. Thompson, *Queen of the Lakes* (Detroit: Wayne State University Press, 1994), pp. 136–65.

690. "Fraser, Harbor Man of Year," p. 1.

691. "Fraser Completes Triple Conversion," *The Nor'Easter* (May–June 1982): 1. Fraser's most ambitious conversion project came in the winter of 1981–1982, when it completed the conversion of the *Cason J. Callaway, Philip R. Clarke,* and *Arthur M. Anderson* for the U.S. Steel fleet.

692. Patrick Lapinski, "In the Yard: The History of Fraser Shipyards, 1945–2000," unpublished manuscript, 2001, p. 173.

693. Ibid., p. 179.

694. Ibid., p. 185. See also Patrick Lapinski, "Fraser Shipyards," *North Star Port* (Winter 2002–2003): 9.

695. Lapinski, "Fraser Shipyards," 9.

CHAPTER 15: FROM TIDEWATER TO BLUEWATER

696. Jim Myhers, "Twin Ports Linked to Atlantic Ocean," *Duluth News-Tribune,* May 4, 1959, p. 1.

697. Ibid., p. 1. The *Herald* proceeded to Superior, where a similar-sized crowd greeted her arrival.

698. Davis Helberg, "Channels," *Lake Superior Magazine* (August–September 1997): 16. Grandmaison had joined the S. A. McLennan Agency two days earlier after graduating from the University of Minnesota–Duluth. "By the ship's third day in port," he said, "and the third consecutive day of parties, I remember saying, 'Gee, I really like this job.' Reality set in shortly after that." Grandmaison would stay with the McLennan firm until in retirement in 1997.

699. "Skipper Lauds Seaway," *Duluth News-Tribune,* May 4, 1959, p. 1.

700. Ibid., p. 9.

701. Untranscribed notes from oral history interview with Germaine Guthrie, Duluth, Minnesota, February 24, 2000, p. 1. Guthrie's wife, Germaine, recalled in a 2000 interview how she would keep George Steinbrenner busy while her father met with her husband. The younger Steinbrenner went on to own the New York Yankees, and his family's involvement with Great Lakes shipping and shipbuilding is the genesis of Hall of Famer Reggie Jackson's immortal comment about his boss: "Tell the big kid to go play with his boats."

702. Ibid., pp. 1–2.

703. Ibid., p. 1.

704. Tape-recorded oral history interview with Davis Helberg, Duluth, Minnesota, May 25, 2000, p. 9. As the name implies, grain trimmers shoveled, trimmed, and ensured that grain was stowed properly in the holds of the lakers so it would be safely loaded, with no grain shifting and thus threatening a vessel's stability during the voyage.

705. Davis Helberg, "The Harbor Line—And Now There Are Two," *North Star Port* (Fall 2002): 2.

706. Among those who tried to capitalize on the new ship chandlery business, four prominent local businessmen invested $10,000 each and hired a young Dutch immigrant as manager of Twin Ports Ship Chandlery. One of the four investors, insurance executive Sid Mason, recalled it as "the best $10,000 education I ever had." His partners were grain merchant Lewis Remele, investment broker George Barnum Jr., and lawyer Conrad M. "Mac" Fredin. The company, and the money, were gone within two years. Father and son George and John Regas, who operated the Duluth Coney Island Restaurant, started a company catering exclusively to Greek ships, while a foreign car dealer, Bruce Rapp, and and insurance broker, A. Brookings Brown, also joined the competition. There were occasional reports of skirmishes on the docks as chandlers tried to be the first to get up the gangways of newly arrived ocean ships. See e-mail, Davis Helberg to the author, March 5, 2003.

707. LesStrang, *Seaway,* p. 19. U.S. and Canadian railroads opposed the concept. So also did many owners of Great Lakes vessels, who were concerned that a seaway would create competition from foreign shipowners. It was a theme that would be expressed frequently during the next sixty-five years.

708. Ibid., p. 21. The 1906 formation of Ontario Hydro reflected the new interest in the potential of St. Lawrence River hydroelectric power.

709. William H. Becker, *From the Atlantic to the Great Lakes: A History of the U.S. Army Corps of Engineers and the St. Lawrence Seaway* (Washington, D.C.: U.S. Government Printing Office, n.d.), pp. 2–3. The idea for a canal along the escarpment was first advanced by ex–New Yorker William Hamilton Merritt in 1818. See Joseph Halow, "The Seaway: Your Wheat and Your Customers," *Wheat Farming* (January 1981), p. 3.

710. "History—The First Welland Canal, 1829–1844," http://seaway.co/english/features/Welland/history.html. Gravelly Bay is now known as Port Colbourne, Ontario.

711. Becker, *From the Atlantic to the Great Lakes,* p. 3. New Brunswick and Nova Scotia joined Ontario and Quebec in the Confederation.

712. "History—The Third Welland Canal, 1887–1931." The canallers did frequently backhaul foreign goods offloaded at Montreal to the Twin Ports and the Canadian lakehead.

713. E. B. Gillham, "An Ordinary Canaller," *The Nor'Easter* (November–December 1984): 1–4. As late as 1984, a dozen or so canallers were still in service on the lakes and St. Lawrence River, most as dredges, lighters, or storage barges.

714. "The Fourth Welland Ship Canal," www.welland.library.on.ca/digital/history.htm. Since the turn of the century, Canadian nationalists had been floating the idea of an all-Canadian canal to connect the Great Lakes with the St. Lawrence River. The route most frequently mentioned would have followed the Ottawa River from its confluence with the St. Lawrence to Georgian Bay of Lake Huron, essentially the route of the Jesuits, Recollets, and voyageurs three centuries before.

715. Ibid. As part of the expansion, the Canadian government built piers, breakwaters, and artificial harbor at Port Weller.

716. Ibid.

717. "Personality: Duluth Terminal, Seaway Climax 30 Years of Work," *Duluth Port* (July 1959): 26.

718. "St. Lawrence Seaway Sponsored by National Defense," *Skillings Mining Review* (June 21, 1941): 1. The U.S. cost of building a wartime seaway was estimated at $285 million.

719. LesStrang, *Seaway,* pp. 30–31. One railroad lobbyist described construction of the seaway as "fraught with injurious consequences to the public welfare."

720. Becker, *From the Atlantic to the Great Lakes,* p. 17. In 1948, the state of New York and the Province of Ontario had agreed to jointly develop the power resources of the International Rapids section of the St. Lawrence.

721. LesStrang, *Seaway,* pp. 32–33.

722. Abstract summary of collection, Lewis G. Castle Papers, Northeast Minnesota Historical Center, Duluth, Minnesota. Castle

was a 1913 graduate of the University of Wisconsin, where he quarterbacked the Badgers' undefeated 1912 football team. See Beck, "First Bank Duluth—The First 75 Years," n.p.

723. Ibid.
724. Ibid. Castle died in upstate New York in 1960, the year after the seaway opened.
725. LesStrang, *Seaway,* p. 22. Bertrand Snell, for whom the second seaway lock is named, was a New York congressman instrumental in developing the hydroelectric potential of the International Rapids for the Power Authority of the State of New York.
726. Becker, *From the Atlantic to the Great Lakes,* pp. 80–91.
727. LesStrang, *Seaway,* pp. 56–57. PASNY also built three other power dams along the forty-four-mile stretch of the International Rapids section of the seaway. See "St. Lawrence Seaway," *New York Times,* June 29, 1958.
728. "High Bridge," *New York Times,* June 29, 1958.
729. LesStrang, *Seaway,* p. 64.
730. "Julius Barnes, Duluth Industrialist, Dies at 86," *Duluth Herald,* April 17, 1959, p. 1.
731. "Glossary of Slovene-American Relations: John Blatnik (1911–1991)," http://clinton.hal.si/eng/cl_gl_ol.html. In 1946, Hubert Humphrey, then the mayor of Minneapolis, formed the Democrat-Farmer Labor Party, expelling the communists from the old Farmer Labor Party in the process.
732. "Former U.S. representative John Blatnik," http://minnesotapolitics.net/USCongress/Representatives/Blatnik.htm. At thirty years of age, Blatnik was the youngest member of the Minnesota Senate.
733. "Glossary of Slovene-American Relations: John Blatnik (1911–1991)." While on active duty, Blatnik was reelected to the Minnesota Senate in 1944. See "Former U.S. representative John Blatnik."
734. Blatnik would serve as chair of the House Committee on Public Works during the 92nd and 93rd Congresses. See "Biographical Directory of the United States Congress, Blatnik, John Anton, 1911–1991," http://bioguide.congress.gov/scripts/biodisplay.pl/index=B000550.
735. King, "Railway Drawbridges at the Head of the Lakes," p. 4.
736. "Route of 535," *Superior Evening Telegram,* December 2, 1961, p. 1. In June 1956, President Eisenhower signed legislation that created the $33 billion system of Interstate and Defense Highways. See *American Dreams,* p. 140.
737. "Victim of Progress," *Duluth Sunday News-Tribune,* December 3, 1961. For much of the 1950s, automobiles paid a toll of fifteen cents per passage, plus five cents for each passenger. As many as 3,000 cars per eight-hour shift crossed the bridge in 1961.
738. "Spirited Salute Greets High Span," *Superior Evening Telegram,* December 2, 1961, p. 1.
739. Broehl, *Cargill: Trading the World's Grain,* pp.78–80.

The Heritage of the Modern Elevators
740. Patrick Lapinski, "Once in a Lifetime: An Overview of the Terminal Grain Elevators at Duluth-Superior, 1870–1940," unpublished manuscript, fifth draft, May 12, 1994, p. 32.
741. Broehl, *Cargill: Trading the World's Grain,* p. 79.
742. Lapinski, "Once in a Lifetime," tables 2, 3.
743. Ibid., p. 114.
744. Ibid., pp. 37–38.
745. Ruble, *The Peavey Story,* p. 41.
746. Ibid., p. 41.
747. Ibid., pp. 29–30.
748. Lapinski, "Once in a Lifetime," table 2.
749. Ibid., p. 116.
750. "Pioneer Firms," *Greater Minneapolis* (November–December 1980): 64–68.
751. Ibid., p. 68.
752. Lapinski, "Once in a Lifetime," tables 2, 3.
753. Ibid., pp. 119–20.
754. Ibid., p. 108. In 1979, Superior bought the adjacent Elevator O, one of the oldest such structures in the Twin Ports. During demolition in the summer of 1984, it caught fire and was a total loss.
755. Ibid., pp. 117–18.
756. Ibid., pp. 120–21.
757. Ibid., table 2.

CHAPTER 16: GROWTH OF AN INTERNATIONAL PORT
758. Tape-recorded oral history interview with Edward A. Ruisi, Duluth, Minnesota, May 24, 2000, p. 2. Ruisi's brother was a schoolteacher at the time and had just finished teaching a classroom unit on the steel industry.

759. Ibid., p. 3. Guthrie closed the deal by taking Ruisi for a drive along Skyline Parkway. It wouldn't be the last time that magnificent view of the harbor and the lake stretching east beyond the horizon convinced a potential hire to take the job.
760. Ibid., pp. 3–4. Ruisi, however, handled the general cargo side of Guthrie's business. One of the first imported items he recalled handling was the bell for the new St. Michael's Catholic Church in Lakeside. The bronze bell was cast in France and shipped aboard a German-owned Poseidon Lines vessel to Duluth.
761. When the St. Lawrence Seaway opened in 1959, the port's elevators were operated by General Mills (Elevator A), Norris Grain Company (Elevators E, H and I), International Milling Company (Capitol Elevators 4 and 6), the Russell-Miller Milling Division of Occident Flour Company (Occident), the F. H. Peavey Company (Peavey in Duluth, Globe in Superior), Archer-Daniels-Midland Company (Great Northern Elevator S), the Farmers Union Grain Terminal Association (Farmers Elevator 1 and 2), the Osborne-McMillan Company (Elevators O and M) and Cargill, Inc. (Itasca). By 2003, only one elevator had the same operator and the same name: General Mills Elevator A. Five of the 1959 elevators (Occident, Peavey, Globe, O, and Itasca) have since been demolished by contractors, and Capitol 4 was consumed by a 1977 fire. Elevators E, H, and I were replaced by Cargill's Elevators B-1 and B-2 in 1975. Capitol Elevator 6 is operated by AGP Grain. Great Northern S is General Mills' Superior Annex. Farmers No. 1 and 2 are operated by Cenex Harvest States. Elevator M, owned by ConAgra Grain, is used only for storage. The PV-Connors Point Elevator, operated by ConAgra Grain, opened in 1966 and was operated until 1986 by Continental Grain Company.
762. Jay Van Horn interview, p. 14. In 1959, the O & M Elevator was operated by the Osborne-McMillan Company of Minneapolis. Osborne-McMillan had been started in the 1887 by John D. McMillan and Edward Osborne. John D. McMillan's branch of the Cargill MacMillans to this day spells the family name without the a." Between 1952 and 1954, Osborne-McMillan purchased Elevator M and Elevator K on the Superior waterfront. By 1959, the company operated 200 country elevators in the Upper Midwest and the giant Shoreham Elevator in Minneapolis. Osborne-McMillan renamed Elevator K to Elevator O in 1960 so that the company could paint Elevator O & M on the side of the elevators. See W. Duncan MacMillan with Patricia Condon Johnston, *MacMillan: The American Grain Family—An Illustrated Biography* (Afton, Minnesota: Afton Historical Society Press, 1998), pp. 71–72.
763. Ibid., pp. 10–11.
764. Ibid., p. 11.
765. Ibid., p. 10. Van Horn started as assistant superintendent on June 1, 1960, and took over the elevator complex when Erickson retired the next year.
766. "High Speed Grain Loading Gallery," *SPAD* (October–November 1960): 6.
767. Patrick Lapinski, unpublished histories of Duluth-Superior Grain Elevators.
768. Duluth-Superior Harbor Statistics, p. 5.
769. Ibid., p. 5. Cargill had spent 10 percent of the company's net worth to build the Baie Comeau elevator. John H. MacMillan Jr., the president of Cargill, complained in the fall of 1959 that "the only trouble with the new plant is that it simply is not big enough. The eleven or twelve million bushels of space is only about one-third what we need right now." See MacMillan and Johnston, *MacMillan: The American Grain Family—An Illustrated Biography,* p. 301.
770. Duluth-Superior Harbor Statistics, p. 6.
771. Ibid., p. 6. Labor problems would plague the grain business in the Twin Ports for much of the 1960s and 1970s. A twenty-six-day strike by the grain millers crippled the port again in the fall of 1967. See also "Grain Moves Again: It's Time to Grow, *SPAD* (August 1964): 1, and "Duluth Moves Grain Again," *SPAD* (October 1967): 1.
772. Ibid., p. 6. Grain tonnages would average just under 4 million tons per year for the rest of the decade before beginning a strong, steady climb again in the 1970s.
773. "Tonnages Show Port Growth," *SPAD* (February 1967): 5. Another 370,000 tons of general cargo, scrap iron, animal fats, vegetable oils, and grain by-products for export markets were handled in 1966, bringing the export total to nearly 4.2 million tons.
774. "New Continental Elevator Receives Its First Grain," *SPAD* (March 1966): 6. The new elevator unloaded its first trucks on February 25, 1966.

775. *Chronicle of America*, p. 795. Kennedy lambasted steel industry executives for their "pursuit of private power and profit" at a time when he was jawboning union supporters to hold the line on wages in an attempt to rein in inflation. Inflationary pressures would bedevil the American economy for the next twenty years.

776. Beck, *Northern Lights*, p. 389. The reasons for direct shipping to Lake Superior hadn't changed since the 1880s, when Charlemagne Tower elected to build his own railroad to Two Harbors instead of using existing lines to the head of the lakes.

777. Duluth-Superior Harbor Statistics, p. 5. The 3.5 million tons of coal received at the docks of the Twin Ports in 1958 made it the worst year for coal at the head of the lakes since 1902—and that was the year President Theodore Roosevelt had to finally step in to negotiate the end to the five-month nationwide anthracite strike, the longest labor stoppage in the industry's history.

778. Ibid., p. 6. Average annual receipts of coal in the Twin Ports in the 1960s were slightly less than 3 million tons.

779. Schnurr and Netschert, *Energy in the American Economy, 1850–1975: Its History and Prospects*, p. 245. Number-one and number-two fuel oil are essentially diesel distillates. The only difference is the addition of chemical additives for oil that is stored outside.

780. Bill Beck, *The North American Natural Gas Industry: A Short History* (Privately printed: 1996), pp. 3, 4. Northern Minnesota and North Dakota got most of their gas from Alberta, delivered south and east by Canadian pipelines. The Twin Cities, southern Minnesota, and South Dakota were served by the pipelines of the Northern Natural Gas Company, which brought gas north from the Gulf Coast of Texas. See Beck, *The Energy to Make Things Better: NSP—An Illustrated History of Northern States Power Company*, p. 126.

781. Kakela, "Iron Will," pp. 58–60. Minnesota actually enacted a taconite production tax in 1941.

782. Ibid., p. 61.

783. *Skillings Minnesota Mining Directory, 2001* (Duluth, Minnesota: Skillings Mining Review, 2002), p. 121. EvTac, as it came to be known, was originally a partnership of Ford Motor Company's Rouge Steel Company, Armco Steel, and Oglebay Norton Company.

784. Ibid., p. 100.

785. Ibid., p. 393. In 1964, America was girding itself for a new war. Just two months before passage of the Taconite Amendment, Congress had passed the Tonkin Gulf Resolution, giving President Lyndon Johnson a free hand in beefing up America's military presence in Vietnam.

786. Ibid., p. 395.

787. Kakela, "Iron Will," p. 70.

788. "DM&IR Taconite Storage Facility Adds New Activity to a Busy Harbor," *SPAD* (August 1966): 4–5. At the same time, DM & IR crews were making similar improvements to the company's ore docks in Two Harbors.

789. "Great Northern Opens New Taconite Storage," *SPAD* (July 1967): 6.

790. "Ore Pellets: Port Impact," *SPAD* (June–July 1969): 10.

791. "New Lock Dedicated," *SPAD* (June–July 1969): 3. The Poe Lock was dedicated on the tenth anniversary of the official opening of the St. Lawrence Seaway. Unfortunately, the locks on the seaway were not lengthened to the specification of the Poe Lock. This led to two realities in the decades ahead: the Great Lakes fleet remained landlocked to the Great Lakes; and the increasing size of vessels in the world ocean fleet meant that more and more ships could not pass into the Great Lakes through the seaway.

792. "Port Salutes 10 Year Service of Director," *SPAD* (March 1966): 4.

793. "Robert H. Smith Is New SPAD Director of Traffic," *SPAD* (September 1964): 1. Smith, no relation to his boss, was an expert at deciphering rail and ocean freight rates and had practiced before the Interstate Commerce Commission for nearly thirty years when he joined SPAD.

794. The Twin Ports got its biggest shot of national publicity in the 1960s when a visitor from India took up residence in Duluth. In the fall of 1962, the crew of an Indian vessel docked at Duluth donated its pet mongoose to the Duluth Zoo when they discovered that it was illegal to own the animal. A 1900 law banned the importation of mongooses, a mammal native to Southwest Asia that is legendary for its ability to kill cobras. The federal government argued that mongooses were destructive to the environment and bred so rapidly that they could quickly become pests. When Duluth customs agents learned about the zoo's acceptance of the mongoose, they demanded it be turned over to them for destruction. Outraged Minnesotans rallied to the mongoose's cause. By then named "Mr. Magoo," after a popular cartoon figure of the time, the mongoose was the subject of letters, telephone calls, and telegrams between supporters and various government officials, all the way up to Secretary of the Interior Stewart Udall. At the Minnesota-Purdue football game that fall, Golden Gophers gridiron fans held up signs asking America to "save our mongoose," bringing Mr. Magoo's plight to a national television audience. When the story went national, Udall relented and granted Mr. Magoo a visitor's visa, conceding that one male mongoose at a zoo could not possibly reproduce. President John F. Kennedy, in Duluth in the fall of 1963 shortly before his assassination, agreed that Mr. Magoo had become a symbol. "Let this story of the saving of Mr. Magoo stand as the classic example of government by the people," Kennedy told reporters. Mr. Magoo died at the Duluth Zoo in 1968, was stuffed and mounted, and is still one of the more popular exhibits at the zoo. See Chuck Frederick, "Memories of Mr. Magoo," *Duluth News-Tribune*, December 25, 2002.

795. "Duluth Auditorium Site Prepared at Waterfront," *SPAD* (September 1964): 7. Corps of Engineers contractors spent much of the summer and fall of 1964 filling the old merchandise dock slip near the harbor entry for the Arena-Auditorium building site.

796. "Leader in Growth of Twin Ports Trade, Superior Port Director Sinclear Retires," *SPAD* (July 1966): 5.

797. "Port Director R. T. Smith Resigns," *SPAD* (May 1967): 1. Smith agreed to stay on as port director until the conclusion of the 1967 navigation season.

798. "David W. Oberlin Appointed New Duluth Port Director," *SPAD* (September 1967): 1.

799. Tape-recorded telephone oral history interview with David Oberlin, Palm Desert, California, April 2, 2002, pp. 1–4.

800. Ibid., p. 6.

801. Ibid., p. 6. Oberlin called Helberg's hiring one of the best decisions he made as port director.

802. "Oberlin Nominated for Seaway Post," *SPAD* (June–July 1969): 2. Robert H. Smith was appointed acting port director in Oberlin's stead.

803. Duluth-Superior Harbor Statistics, p. 6.

The Roger Blough

804. John S. Wilbur, "Future Taconite Development in the Lake Superior Area," *Inland Seas* (Winter 1964): 277–81.

805. Ibid., p. 282.

806. Ibid., p. 283.

807. Thompson, *Queen of the Lakes*, pp. 188–89.

808. "U.S. Steel's Super Ore Carrier to be Named After Roger Blough," *Skillings Mining Review* (March 13, 1971): 26. Blough, a Yale Law School graduate, had been head of the corporation's legal department before being named president and CEO in 1955.

809. Miller, *Tin Stackers*, p. 214. The *Blough* was also built 105 feet wide to take maximum advantage of the width of the new Poe Lock. The existing Hulett unloaders at the Lake Erie delivery ports could not work on a vessel more than 75 feet wide.

810. Thompson, *Queen of the Lakes*, p. 188.

CHAPTER 17: REVOLUTIONS IN COMMERCE

811. T. A. Sykora, "1972—A New Era in Great Lakes Transportation," *Inland Seas* (Summer 1972): 131. The *Cort*, which was owned by Bethlehem Steel Corporation and operated by its Great Lakes Steamship Division, was launched at the Erie Marine Division shipyards of Litton Industries in Erie, Pennsylvania, on the afternoon of May 1, 1972. She took on her first load of nearly 50,000 tons of taconite pellets at Taconite Harbor three days later.

812. Although thirteen U.S. lakers are categorized as 1,000-footers, none are considered sister ships. In the strictest of technical terms, "sister ships" are identical in all respects—dimensions, cargo capacities, propulsion systems, crew accommodations, etcetera. Nonetheless, two pairs are nearly identical and are often considered sisters. The Great Lakes Fleet's *Edwin H. Gott* and *Edgar B. Speer* both are 1,004 feet long, 105 feet wide, 56 feet deep (from the main deck to an imaginary line extended perpendicularly from the keel), and carrying capacity at midsummer draft (the *Gott* is 74,100 long tons, the *Speer* 73,700), while Interlake Steamship Company's *James R. Barker* and *Mesabi Miner* are 1,004 feet long and 105 feet deep and have capacities of 63,600 long tons.

813. Thompson, *Queen of the Lakes*, pp. 189–93. The *Cort*, which was partially built at shipyards on the Mississippi River, had a slightly different design than the majority of the 1,000-footers

that would follow her. Consequently, her per-trip cargo capacity was about 10,000 tons less than the second-generation 1,000-footers.

814. Sykora, "1972—A New Era in Great Lakes Transportation," 133. The *Cort's* four General Motors Electro-Motive Division diesel engines developed 14,000-shaft horsepower. Her two 18-foot-diameter variable pitch propellers gave her precision maneuverability.

815. Skelton interview, p. 3. Six-hundred-foot vessels that had been converted to burning oil carried a crew of twenty-six. By the late 1980s, 1,000-footers typically carried a crew of twenty-one or twenty-two, including a captain, three mates, three qualified members of the engine department, eleven deckhands, and three galley mates.

816. Ibid., p. 4. A 600-footer was capable of carrying 15,000 tons of pellets. It had about a five- or six-day rotation between the Twin Ports and Gary, Indiana, and back.

817. Lake Carriers' Association, 1998 annual report, p. 31. In 2002, there were fifty-two U.S. flag hulls operating on the Great Lakes.

818. Tape-recorded oral history interview with Captain Bill Jeffery, Duluth, Minnesota, February 22, 2002, p. 7.

819. Ibid., pp. 8–9.

820. Ibid., pp. 9–10.

821. Ibid., p. 9. Jeffery loaded the first cargo of taconite pellets in the *Presque Isle* at Two Harbors on December 23, 1973. He then took the vessel to U.S. Steel's Gary Works.

822. Miller, *Tin Stackers,* pp. 285–86.

823. Ibid., p. 240. Between 1978 and 1980, the *Edwin H. Gott* and the *Edgar Speer* joined the U.S. Steel Great Lakes Fleet as their first true 1,000-footers. During those two years, U.S. Steel sold or scrapped fourteen smaller vessels.

824. "Export Scrap Cargoes Approach 1967 Total," *SPAD* (October 1968): 4. During the 1960s, much of the scrap generated by Duluth Iron and Metals went overseas via the St. Lawrence Seaway.

825. "Duluth Firm Is Last Port of Call for Veteran Lakers," p. 3. U.S. Steel consigned four of its 600-footers to Duluth Iron and Metals from 1975 to 1977. Hyman-Michaels eventually sold its interests to Azcon Corporation of Chicago, and the old Zalk-Josephs property was renamed the Azcon dock.

826. Duluth-Superior Harbor Statistics, pp. 5–6.

827. Ibid., p. 6.

828. Ibid., p. 6.

829. Thompson, *Queen of the Lakes,* pp. 195–99. The 1979 carrying capacity of the six 1,000-footers in service was nearly 12 million tons of pellets.

830. "Cargo Worth Chirping About," *SPAD* (October 1968): 3. In 1968, the Duluth-Superior Port handled about 3,000 tons of sunflower seeds for European processing plants and for bird seed and confectionery sales.

831. Duluth-Superior Harbor Statistics, p. 6.

832. *2001 Skillings Minnesota Mining Directory,* p. 100. The "Hibtac" property would eventually be expanded to an 8-million-ton annual capacity.

833. Ibid., p. 100.

834. Ibid., p. 100. The production capacity at Reserve Mining Company, one of Minnesota's oldest taconite plants, was reduced from 10 million tons to an average of 7 million tons per year during the late 1970s because of a decade-long litigation over the plant's practice of disposing taconite tailings in Lake Superior's Silver Bay.

835. Ibid., p. 100. The year 1979 was the high-water mark for Minnesota's taconite industry.

836. Duluth-Superior Harbor Statistics, pp. 1, 6. In the 1950s, 1960s, and 1970s, coal's share of commercial and residential energy market had plummeted. But by the mid-1970s, coal-fired electric power plants accounted for nearly three-fourths of America's electricity production.

837. "The Resurgence of Black Gold," *Minnesota's World Port* (Fall 1973): 5.

838. Ibid., p. 5. Boland and Cornelius of Buffalo, New York, then one of the largest operators of self-unloaders on the Great Lakes, subsequently built the 770-foot motor ship *St. Clair* and the 1,000-foot *Belle River* exclusively for the Detroit Edison contract.

839. "Superior Loads Record Coal Cargo," *Minnesota's World Port* 12, no. 3 (1976): 12. The first cargo of coal from the Ortran facility was loaded into the *St. Clair* in June 1976. The 43,000 tons of coal was the largest single cargo of coal ever carried on the Great Lakes.

840. "Duluth Port Gains $15 Million Elevator Complex," *Minnesota's World Port,* no. 2 (Summer 1973): 4.

841. "Cargill Adds to Building Plans in Port," *Minnesota's World Port* (Winter 1975): 20.

842. "New Construction on the Twin Ports Waterfront," *Minnesota's World Port* II, no. 3 (Fall 1975): 12–13. By late 1975, the new facility was already shipping cranes through the Twin Ports to customers in Poland and India. See "American Hoist Ships Giant Cranes," *Minnesota's World Port* (Winter 1975): 21.

843. "New Steel Plant," *Minnesota's World Port* (Winter 1975): 20.

844. "Ceres Appointed Managing Agent," *SPAD* (April–May 1969): 2.

845. "Meet the Youngest Port Director in the Nation," *SPAD* (January 1970): 3. Burke was reportedly the youngest port director in the nation when he accepted the Duluth position in December 1969.

846. Ibid., p. 2.

847. Davis Helberg, "Channels," *Lake Superior Magazine* (February–March 1992): 4. McLean died in 2002 at the age of eighty-seven. By the time of his death, 90 percent of world general, or "break bulk," cargo moved in containers.

848. Jeno F. Paulucci with Les Rich, *How It Was to Make $100,000,000 in a Hurry* (New York: Grossett and Dunlap, 1969), pp. 213–24. Paulucci went on to parlay his stake from Chun King into the foundation of Jeno's, Inc., one of the more successful frozen pizza manufacturers in the United States. He later sold Jeno's and is as of this writing the president of Michaelina's, another successful Italian frozen food manufacturer based in Duluth.

849. E-mail, Davis Helberg to the author, January 21, 2003, p. 1. The idea of a canal dated to the 1890s, when engineers first examined the feasibility of building hydroelectric facilities in northeastern Minnesota and northwestern Wisconsin. One proposal of the time envisioned building a canal from the Mesabi Range to Duluth that would carry 5 million tons of iron ore a year in barges to the Twin Ports. See Beck, *Northern Lights,* p. 42.

850. Helberg, "Channels," *Lake Superior Magazine* (February–March 1992): 4.

851. Ibid., 4. Jeno's, however, continued to use the Twin Ports for handling cargo. In the 1960s, Jeno's regularly shipped tomato paste from Portugal and Parmesan cheese from Argentina to Duluth aboard vessels of the Manchester and Moore-McCormack Lines. See "The Duluth Pizza: City-Size," *SPAD* (January 1969): 3.

852. "Meeting the Container Challenge," *Minnesota's World Port* (Summer 1974): 4–5.

853. "Growing with Minnesota's World Port," *The Duluthian* (June 1975): 10.

854. Buhrmann interview, p. 3. Burhmann had no experience in vessel operations when he was assigned to the fleet. When Buhrmann left for Duluth in 1973, his coworkers in Pittsburgh gave him a sign for his office that read, "The Front End Is the Pointy End."

855. Ibid., p. 4. The steel-hulled vessels were so poorly insulated that sailors' clothes frequently froze to the walls of cabins.

856. Ibid., p. 9. Buhrmann recalled one instance during the winter navigation era when a freighter was stuck in the ice off Conneaut, Ohio, for nearly ten days, prompting some rather novel solutions to getting food to the icebound vessel.

857. Richard L. Pomeroy, "Oil, debris only trace of laker," *Duluth News-Tribune,* November 12, 1975.

858. Interstate Port Authority Commission, *Final Report to the Legislatures of the States of Minnesota and Wisconsin,* December 1976, p. 4. The two states had exchanged resolutions to consider a bistate port authority as early as 1863.

859. "Days Gone By—*News-Tribune* of Dec. 3, 1976," *Duluth News-Tribune,* December 3, 1996.

860. Interstate Port Authority Commission, *Final Report to the Legislatures of the States of Minnesota and Wisconsin,* December 1976, p. 3.

861. Ibid., p. 3. See also memo, Davis Helberg to Commissioners, Bi-State Port Authority, November 28, 2001, p. 1.

862. "SPAD Appoints New Terminal Managers," *Minnesota's World Port* 13, no. 1 (1977): 18.

863. "New Port Director Begins Duties," *Minnesota's World Port* 13, no. 1 (1977): 3.

The Wreck of the *Edmund Fitzgerald*

864. When the author traveled to Charlotte, North Carolina, to interview with Knight-Ridder Newspaper's *Charlotte News* in October 1976, the young staffers in the newsroom all wanted to know if he had been in Minnesota when the *Fitz* sailed.

865. Philip N. Cristal, "The *Edmund Fitzgerald,*" *Inland Seas* (Summer 1958): 120–22. In the summer of 1957, Northwestern Mutual purchased three other bulk freighters for the firm's investment portfolio, the *Joseph S. Wood,* *J. H. Hillman Jr.,* and the *J. Burton*

Ayers. The latter three vessels were operated for Northwestern Mutual by the Wilson Marine Transit Company of Cleveland, while the *Fitzgerald* was operated by Columbia.

866. The Hanna Mining Company, Agents, "Lake Bill of Lading for Bulk Cargoes Other Than Grain and Seed," November 9, 1975.

867. Katie Beck, "We Are Holding Our Own: The Tragedy of the *Edmund Fitzgerald*," unpublished manuscript in the author's possession, March 28, 2001, pp. 1–5.

868. Ibid., p. 5.

869. In 1984, the author rode the U.S. Steel Great Lakes Fleet's *Edwin H. Gott* from Two Harbors to Gary Works. As the 1,000-footer was heading into Whitefish Bay on a beautiful August evening, her captain struck up a conversation with the wheelsman. Nine years before, the wheelsman had held a similar position on the *Anderson.* He told the author and the captain a riveting tale of how the *Fitzgerald* disappeared off the *Anderson's* radar screen.

870. Frederick Stonehouse, *The Wreck of the* Edmund Fitzgerald (Gwinn, Michigan: Avery Color Studios, 1999), p. 196.

871. Controversy over the cause of the tragedy continues to this day. The most recent book on the subject, *The Night the* Fitz *Went Down,* by Captain Dudley Paquette and Hugh Bishop, was published in 2002 by Lake Superior Port Cities, Duluth.

872. Gordon Lightfoot, "The Wreck of the *Edmund Fitzgerald*," Warner Brothers, 1976. "The Gales of November" has also become the name of an annual maritime exposition in Duluth sponsored by the Lake Superior Marine Museum Association. The November 9, 2002, dinner speaker was Dennis Hale, who survived for thirty-eight hours aboard a life raft in late November 1966 when a Lake Huron storm claimed the Cambria Steamship Company's *Daniel Morrell.* All twenty-eight of Hale's shipmates perished.

CHAPTER 18: RETRENCHMENT AND REBIRTH

873. Davis Helberg, From the Director's Desk, "Performance Will Rebuild Confidence," *Minnesota's World Port* 14, no. 2 (1979): 2. One of the more ubiquitous images of the Twin Ports during the past twenty-five years is a sunrise photograph of an armada of saltwater vessels anchored in the outer harbor in the summer of 1979, sitting out the grain millers strike. In 1980, the Minnesota legislature, largely through the influence of Seaway Port Authority commissioner Russel J. Schwandt, Sanborn, Minnesota, and lobbying work done by Helberg and port public relations director Bill Cortes, appropriated $250,000 to the Seaway Port Authority to help restore the Port of Duluth-Superior's image and reputation.

874. "Carter bans grain sales to Soviet Union after Afghan invasion," *Chronicle of America,* p. 866.

875. "Ailing U.S. Steel shuts 10 factories," *Chronicle of America,* p. 865.

876. "Inflation soaring; interest rates fluctuate," *Chronicle of America,* p. 864. In the spring of 1979, the author was a financial reporter with Knight-Ridder's *Charlotte News* in North Carolina. While covering the Chapter 11 bankruptcy of a local real estate investment trust, he had the opportunity to interview the REIT's president. What happened? the author asked. "Well, put it this way," the Tar Heel executive replied. "One morning, I woke up and discovered I had $30 million out there on a MasterCard."

877. "Iranian militants seize U.S. Embassy," *Chronicle of America,* p. 865.

878. "Disaster in Iran's desert," *Chronicle of America,* p. 867.

879. Arvid Morken, "Harry L. Allen—A Soliloquy," *The Nor'Easter* (January–February 1978): 1–3. When the first alarm came in at midafternoon, Duluth fire department personnel thought they had the blaze under control within a half-hour of arrival. But an explosion of grain dust turned the wooden elevator into a chimney, and firefighters spent the next several hours manning a fire line to keep the blaze from the more modern Cap 6, 100 yards or so distant from the fire. Burning rubble from the head house blaze rained down on the *Allen's* wood-lined pilothouse, causing a blaze that quickly gutted the 545-foot (bulk) freighter's forward cabins; the ship's hull also suffered irreparable heat damage.

880. Duluth-Superior Harbor Statistics, p. 6. Retaining Cap 4 could have been important to International Multifoods for more options in blending grades of grain and as an overflow for Cap 6. It would also have given the port one more loading berth.

881. Ibid, p. 6

882. Helberg, "Performance Will Rebuild Confidence," p. 2.

883. Davis Helberg e-mail to author, March 13, 2003. Helberg was accompanied to Washington, D.C., by E. L. "Buster" Slaughter of the ILA and Angus MacLeod, general manager of American

Grain Trimmers. They were joined by James Scala, the Washington representative of Western Great Lakes Terminals Association. Although Agriculture Department officials refused to immediately rescind the embargo decision, they did promise to send an investigative team to the Twin Ports to confirm that nobody was on strike outside the elevator employees. When the team arrived in Duluth-Superior several weeks later, it quickly determined that was the case and lifted the embargo. Still, Helberg said, "we lost a month of potential business because of the embargo."

884. Tape-recorded oral history interview with Chuck Ilenda, Duluth, Minnesota, February 23, 2000, p. 8. Like so many of the labor stoppages at the time, the strike was mostly concerned with wages, which weren't keeping pace with the 10 to 12 percent inflation then rampant in the U.S. economy.

885. "General Cargo: Port's Lifeblood in '79," *Minnesota's World Port* 14, no. 2 (1979): 7. Great Lakes Storage and Contracting owned a Superior dock near the Continental Grain Company elevator, and a Duluth facility, NP Dock No. 2, just off Railroad Street and the foot of Garfield Avenue. Even though they weren't able to work loading grain ships during the strike, longshoremen did log 20,000 hours at the Clure Public Marine Terminal between July and September.

886. Tape-recorded oral history interview with Russ Wedin, Duluth, Minnesota, May 24, 2000, p. 6.

887. Ibid., p. 3.

888. "Mister Great Lakes Pilot," *Minnesota's World Port* 8, no. 1 (1972): 10–11.

889. Helberg interview, pp. 7–8.

890. Ibid., p. 11. The captains and mates aboard U.S. and Canadian lakers hold first-class pilot's licenses and thus do not require outside pilotage services. Oceangoing ships, whose masters and mates typically have little if any Great Lakes navigational experience, require Coast Guard–certified pilots. Until 1990, ocean ship officers with qualified lakes experience could technically get a Canadian endorsement to traverse the lakes' open waters without a pilot, but the option was seldom exercised after the mid-1970s when such ships invariably encountered delays because of alleged pilot shortages or port labor problems. The Oil Pollution Act of 1990 resolved the issue once and for all, establishing mandatory pilotage for all ocean ships anywhere within the Great Lakes–St. Lawrence Seaway system.

891. Ibid., p. 11. Through a memorandum of arrangements with the Canadian government in the 1960s, the United States agreed to divide pilotage responsibilities equally between three geographical districts between the upper end of the St. Lawrence River and Duluth-Superior. Although the number of full-time pilots in District 3 was then set at twenty-four, the Duluth headquarters also dispatched eight Canadian pilots and had about a dozen ex-lakes captains and mates under contract to work when traffic was especially heavy. Upper Great Lakes Pilots was decertified by the Coast Guard in 1991 on grounds that it had exceeded its charter by owning and operating several subsidiary companies representing conflicts of interest. A new organization, Western Great Lakes Pilots Association, succeeded Upper Great Lakes and today serves District 3 through a headquarters in downtown Superior. Captain Rico died April 16, 1996, at the age of seventy-four. See William Gains, "Lake pilots group's connection to supply firm being examined," *Chicago Tribune,* November 23, 1985, and Davis Helberg, "Legacy of a Great Lakes Pilot," *Minnesota's World Port* (Summer 1996): 2.

892. Helberg, From the Director's Desk, "Getting the Great Lakes Together," *Minnesota's World Port* 14, no. 1: 2. Helberg was the first native Minnesotan to be named port director.

893. Duluth-Superior Harbor Statistics, p. 6. Shipments increased from 6 million tons in 1972 to 8.5 million tons in 1973.

894. Morgan, *Merchants of Grain,* p. 153. At the time, the price of a ton of American wheat on export markets was about $60 per ton.

895. Ibid., p. 156. Secretary of Agriculture Earl Butz noted in the summer of 1972 that "this is by all odds the greatest grain transaction in the history of the world. And it certainly is the greatest for us." Quoted in ibid., p. 120.

896. Tape-recorded telephone oral history interview with Sven Hubner, New Bern, North Carolina, February 11, 2002, pp. 5–6.

897. Ibid., p. 7.

898. Tape-recorded oral history interview with Chuck Hilleren, May 24, 2000, p. 3. In those first years of the Russian grain deal, as much as 50 percent of the grain leaving the Twin Ports was

stowed in Russian bottoms. Hilleren was a wet nurse to the Russian ships and crews, handling the ship chandlers, tugs, line-handlers, and the pilots; shifting the ship from elevator to elevator; and loading operations. "You were the liaison for the ship as far as the port went," Hilleren said.

899. "Russians in Afghanistan," *Chronicle of the Twentieth Century*, p. 1164. Afghanistan would be the Soviet Union's Vietnam. Mujahideen, guerrilla warriors financed by the CIA, tied down numerous Soviet divisions during the next decade and installed a radical Islamic government after the Russians left in 1989. Ironically, the Islamic fundamentalism of the mujahideen provided the philosophical underpinnings of Al-Qaeda, the terror organization that orchestrated the 9/11 attacks on the United States in 2001.

900. Duluth-Superior Harbor Statistics, p. 6.

901. Ibid., p. 6.

902. Tape-recorded oral history interview with Sam Browman, Duluth, Minnesota, May 26, 2000, p. 1. Browman had the unenviable task during his first year of work at the port of trying to assure North Dakota farmers that the grain millers strike would end. Browman tells the story of being pulled over in a port car in downtown Grand Forks, North Dakota, and being berated by a farmer about the strike. Meanwhile, a North Dakota gubernatorial candidate proposed mobilizing the state's National Guard to come to Duluth-Superior to operate the elevators.

903. Davis Helberg, fax to author, March 13, 2003.

904. Ibid. Helberg noted that he and Western Great Lakes Ports Washington representative Lew Gulick spent days in the Senate cloakroom during the 1985 Farm Bill debate on the Public Law 480 issue, often in stare-downs with Gulf Coast representatives of the International Longshoremen's Association who were on the opposite side of the issue. "Senator Boschwitz would come out and give us an update, and then race back in to argue some more," Helberg recalled. "One time, the senator came out to report some disturbing news and asked, 'What should I tell them?' Frustrated, I said, 'Tell 'em to go to hell,' to which the good senator immediately said, 'Fine, but give me something I can use.'"

905. Hilleren interview, p. 5.

906. Duluth-Superior Harbor Statistics, p. 5.

907. Thom Holden, "The Fate of the Frontenac," *Minnesota's World Port* (Spring 1980): 6–8. Towed into Fraser Shipyards in Superior, the *Frontenac* was declared a total loss and scrapped several years later. She'd not be the last 600-footer to meet her end in a scrap yard in the 1980s.

908. John P. Hoerr, *And the Wolf Finally Came*, p. 11. Six years later, mill employment in the Mon Valley would be 4,000, just over 10 percent of what it had been in 1981.

909. Ibid., p. 456.

910. Ibid., p. 523.

911. Ibid., p. 132. Soon after purchasing Marathon, oil prices began a decade-long slide. To finance the purchase, USX sold off more than $1 billion in assets, including its Pittsburgh headquarters building, coal mines in Pennsylvania, and several steel district railroad properties. USX continues to sell steel assets to this day.

912. Ibid., p. 94. In 1945, American steel accounted for 54 percent of global production.

913. Mike Hughlett, "USS extends Minntac closure; 400 lose jobs," *Duluth News-Tribune and Herald*, March 6, 1987.

914. Tim Bovee, "Cliffs leading way in race for survival for UP iron mining," *Duluth News-Tribune and Herald*, February 16, 1987.

915. Hoerr, *And the Wolf Finally Came*, p. 94.

916. Duluth-Superior Harbor Statistics, pp. 4, 7.

917. Buhrmann interview, p. 14.

918. Duluth-Superior Harbor Statistics, pp. 4, 7.

919. Ibid., pp. 4, 7. The mid-1980s were a time of economic malaise in the Twin Ports. There was almost no new housing construction, and houses for sale sometimes sat on the market for years. More than one homeowner packed a U-Haul in the dead of night, left the key in the front door, and turned the house over to the bank for foreclosure. A rueful joke making the rounds noted that the only difference between a Duluth house and herpes is that "sometimes you can get rid of herpes."

920. Buhrmann interview, p. 16.

921. "Straight Deckers Get a Face-Lift," *Minnesota's World Port* 17, no. 1 (1982): 18–19. The conversion project provided work for more than 400 Twin Ports residents during a thirteen-month period.

922. Buhrmann interview, p. 16. One factor that prevented more ships from being scrapped on the Great Lakes was the environmental concern. "Now, one of the difficulties of scrapping a ship is the environmental problems associated with it," Buhrmann explained. "As you recall, before asbestos was bad, all the ships had on them was asbestos this and asbestos that. Up until the 1970s, asbestos was the most effective insulator there was for anything that had to have heat retained, so you just couldn't give the ship to anybody that wasn't prepared to handle that problem. So we sold them overseas."

923. Roger S. Ahlbrandt, Richard J. Fruehan, and Frank Giarratani, *The Renaissance of American Steel: Lessons for Managers in Competitive Industries* (Oxford: Oxford University Press, 1996), p. 25. Although the mini-mills use no taconite pellets to charge their electric arc furnaces, the legacy of the Lake Superior iron ore ranges did help contribute to the surge in mini-mill capacity. The hundreds of obsolete Great Lakes bulk carriers scrapped after 1981 provided immense amounts of plate and structural scrap, a grade that is especially attractive for melting in electric arc furnaces.

924. "New DM&IR Shiploader," *Minnesota's World Port* 19, no. 1 (1984): p. 17. The DM&IR financed the project with $7.3 million in internal funds and $11 million in industrial revenue bonds issued by the city of Proctor.

925. Duluth-Superior Harbor Statistics, p. 7. Part of the drop-off in wheat shipments from the late 1970s had more to do with agronomy than politics or economics. The "green revolution" pioneered by Dr. Norman Borlaug of the University of Minnesota produced new wheat strains that were tolerant of growing conditions unheard of ten or twenty years before. As a result, countries like Saudi Arabia and India could grow enough wheat to feed their populations and export to neighboring countries. Then too, Minnesota and North Dakota farmers during the late 1980s were getting less than $2 for a bushel of wheat. See Bud Leuthold, "Fighting Extinction," *The Wheat Grower* (October 1986): 3.

926. Ibid., p. 7.

927. Ibid., pp. 6–7.

928. News release, Seaway Port Authority of Duluth, May 4, 1982, p. 1. St. Lawrence Cement shipped dry bulk cement from its production plant in Mississauga, Ontario, to Duluth for distribution to customers located in the Upper Midwest and northwestern Ontario.

929. News release, Seaway Port Authority of Duluth, November 17, 1982, p. 1.

930. "New Bong Bridge Opens," *Minnesota's World Port* 19, no. 3 (1984): 15. Like the Blatnik High Bridge, the Bong Bridge had a height of 120 feet, which allowed the passage underneath of the largest vessels transiting the lakes.

Great Lakes Towing Company

931. Alexander C. Meakin, *The Story of the Great Lakes Towing Company* (Vermilion, Ohio: Great Lakes Historical Society, 1984), pp. 6–20.

932. "The Great Lakes Towing Company," *NorthStar Port* (Summer 1999): 9.

933. Ibid., p. 9.

CHAPTER 19: THE GO-GO NINETIES

934. Bill Beck, "Duluth to Gary with the *Gott*," *Minnesota's World Port* 19, no. 1 (1984): 18–19.

935. Bill Beck, "They Still Go Down to the Sea in Ships . . . but the Great Lakes Fleet Is Smaller Now," *Minnesota's World Port* 20, no. 2 (1986): 5–7.

936. Duluth-Superior Harbor Statistics, 1990–1999, p. 1. The high for the decade would be 20.6 million tons in 1990; the low, 17.5 million tons in 1999.

937. "The Largest Loading Port in the Great Lakes," *Seaway Review* (October–December 1991): 35.

938. Ibid., p. 36. Maritime observers pointed out that every ton of fluxing stone shipped into the Twin Ports meant two tons of cargo, since the fluxed pellets containing the limestone went back down the lakes several weeks to months later.

939. Duluth-Superior Harbor Statistics, 1990–1999, p. 1.

940. Beck, "Redefining the Movement of Coal," *Seaway Review* (July–September 1994): 6. Much of the surge in the movement of coal from the Twin Ports was due to the passage of federal Clean Air Act Amendments in 1991, which mandated tough new restrictions on noxious air emissions by electric power plants. At well under 1 percent sulphur, Montana's Powder River coal was some of the cleanest-burning coal on earth.

941. Bill Beck, "MERC Record Brings Duluth/Superior Full Circle from Coal Receiver to Coal Shipper," *Seaway Review* (July–September

1994]: 9. The previous record for coal moving through the Twin Ports was the 12.3 million tons received by area coal docks in 1923.

942. Duluth-Superior Harbor Statistics, 1990–1999, p. 1.

943. "Cargill Well-Equipped for Second Century in Port," *Minnesota's World Port* (Fall 1991): 4–5. The automation of Twin Ports elevators reduced workforce needs dramatically in the 1990s. In 1999, Cenex Harvest States Cooperative, the biggest elevator in the Duluth-Superior harbor, with an 18-million-bushel capacity, operated the elevator with twenty-six people. The Farmers Union Grain Terminal Association had opened the elevator in 1941, and after Farmers Union acquired the adjacent Spencer Kellogg Elevator in 1949 and constructed additional storage capacity, it was billed as the world's largest elevator complex. Through a series of mergers, the elevator complex has been operated by Farmers Union Grain Terminal Association, Harvest States Cooperative, and, since 1999, Cenex Harvest States. See Davis Helberg, "The Harbor Line—May You Reach Your Wellness Potential," *Minnesota's World Port* 29, no. 3 (1997): 2. See also e-mail, Davis Helberg to the author, February 18, 2003.

944. Hilleren interview, p. 13.

945. Davis Helberg e-mail to the author, March 5, 2003. Several Twin Ports elevators were originally equipped with unloading legs, mechanized belt conveyors fitted with horizontal belt-width "cups" for discharging grain from straight-deck lakers. By the 1970s, all of the legs had been dismantled or were beyond repair. In the late 1980s, General Mills built a wide-mouth hopper on a silo at Elevator A and began receiving oats from Canadian self-unloaders. Members of Duluth ILA Local 1366 picketed both the facility and the port authority offices, arguing that they should be hired to help unload the Canadian ships. But given that the vessels were self-unloaders and required no stevedoring services, coupled with the fact that neither General Mills nor the shipowners had a contractual commitment with the ILA, the protestors eventually faded away. When Cargill later added a hopper to receive Canadian barley at its B-2 Elevator in the same manner, there were no disturbances.

946. Hilleren interview, p. 17. "We bring in a lot of barley from Canada now for the breweries," Hilleren explained. "It comes into Duluth and is distributed to some of the breweries in the area. Anheuser Busch leases a lot of space in the port, and they have an export program. They grow their own barley out in the Dakotas and Minnesota and export it overseas to where they make Budweiser. They set up their own plants."

947. Ilenda interview, p. 6. Rapeseed, which is grown primarily in northern North Dakota and neighboring Saskatchewan, had its name changed for semantic purposes to canola seed.

948. Hilleren interview, p. 13. Sunflowers were also overly susceptible to disease, requiring North Dakota and Minnesota farmers to rotate crops every few years.

949. Hilleren interview, p. 14.

950. Seaway Port Authority of Duluth, "North America's Interior Seaport," 1993, p. 3.

951. Seaway Port Authority of Duluth, news release, March 31, 1988, p. 1. The parting with North Central Terminal Operators was by mutual consent after contractual changes in early 1987 imposed, for the first time, an element of financial risk on the company. Before that, all operating expenses were underwritten by the port authority, which also paid North Central an annual management fee. On a Friday in May that year, North Central exercised an option to terminate, effective immediately.

952. Ibid., p. 1.

953. "Beyond the Cargo," p. 39.

954. Tape-recorded oral history interview with Gary Nicholson, Duluth, Minnesota, May 23, 2000, p. 1.

955. Ibid., p. 2.

956. Ibid., p. 3.

957. Hilleren interview, p. 9. Handy-size vessels are typically 700 feet long by 75 feet wide. At a mean summer draft of 26 feet, they can carry about 25,000 tons of bulk cargo.

958. Ibid., p. 9.

959. Wedin interview, p. 13.

960. Ibid., p. 14.

961. Ibid., p. 13.

962. Helberg fax to author, March 14, 2003. The Minnesota Ports Association membership is composed of the port authorities in Duluth, Minneapolis, St. Paul, Red Wing, and Winona. Although the Duluth port annually received strong support from its local legislators, led by Senator Sam Solon and Representative Tom Huntley, a former Seaway Port Authority chair, the association's expanded

geo-political base was the key to securing legislative appropriations for the Port Development Assistance Program.

963. Browman interview, p. 8.

964. "Heavy Lift Deja-Vu," *Minnesota's World Port* (July 1990): 4–5. Schnabel cars are unique in the world for the carriage of over-sized, overweight cargoes. The car used in the Duluth shipment was built in 1982 for Combustion Engineering by Germany's Krupp Industries and is said to be the largest ever made. Capable of handling 1.8 million pounds, the thirty-six-axle car has two interlocking units that can be separated for loading and then locked back into place to form one body. After the big Duluth/Alberta project, the car was in storage at the Clure Public Marine Terminal for most of the 1990s. It is now owned by ABB (Asea Brown Boveri) and was eventually dispatched in 2002 for a project in Charleston, South Carolina. "Schnabel" in English means "beak" or "bill."

965. "Give you a lift?" *Minnesota's World Port* (Winter 1995): 7.

966. Rachel E. Stassen-Berger, "One Mighty Big Shovel," *St. Paul Pioneer-Press*, August 17, 2001.

967. Duluth Seaway Port Authority, news release, November 7, 2002, p. 1.

968. Ibid., p. 1. For the November 20, 2002, rail shipment to Alberta, half of the twenty-eight twelve-axle railcars in North America were employed.

969. Ibid., p. 2. A third vessel with heavy lift cylinders for the Alberta project was expected to arrive at the Port of Duluth early in the 2003 navigation season.

970. Davis Helberg, "The Harbor Line—All of a Sudden, Duluth Is the Place to Be," *Minnesota's World Port* (Spring 1994): 2.

971. "Three new tenants swell the number of companies, jobs on Port properties," *Minnesota's World Port* (Winter 1995): 5.

972. Quoted in Judith Munson, "Over the Hill, but Up and Coming," *Duluthian* (January/February 2000): 17.

973. Ibid., 17.

974. Paul Adams, "In search of more room to expand," *Duluth News-Tribune*, August 27, 1999. In just five years, the existing warehouse and office space in Duluth had been all but absorbed.

975. Duluth Seaway Port Authority, Airpark Company/Employment Roster, December 2002, p. 1.

976. Davis Helberg, "On the Waterfront—Gobies and Creeping Glitzism," *Journal of Commerce*, March 3, 1999. The trend of reclaiming waterfront industrial property for multi-use tourism development has included Cleveland, where the Rock and Roll Hall of Fame and the new Cleveland Browns football stadium were both built on port authority land, and Chicago, which built a thirty-six-hole golf course on reclaimed land.

977. Davis Helberg, "Channels," *Lake Superior Magazine* (April–May 1997): 14. Complicating the renaissance of cruise line business in the Great Lakes was the U.S. Passenger Services Act of 1886, which forbids any passenger traffic between U.S. ports that is not carried by vessels other than those built in the United States and owned, registered, and crewed by U.S. citizens.

978. Yetter interview, p. 3.

979. Davis Helberg, "The Dredging Tax Lives," *Journal of Commerce*, February 5, 1999.

980. Davis Helberg, "Channels," *Lake Superior Magazine* (October–November 1990): 16.

981. Davis Helberg, "Channels," *Lake Superior Magazine* (February–March 1999): 14. The lake levels have fluctuated far more dramatically in geological time. The escarpment that rises 600 feet above Duluth and continues up the North Shore of Lake Superior is actually the remnant of an ancient beach.

982. Ibid., 14. The highest water level averages on Lake Superior in the twentieth century occurred in 1985 and 1986. At the time, waterfront property owners complained vociferously about high water damaging docks.

983. Ibid., 14. At 2,000 tons a trip, the lower lake levels mean one less shipload every thirty trips.

984. Captain Ray Skelton, "The View from 600 Feet Up," presentation to Dry Cargo International Bulk Terminal Operations, Rotterdam, March 27, 2002, p. 4. When environmentalists began examining the alien invasive species issue, they discovered that zebra mussels were not the only European hitchhiker to have made their way into the Great Lakes aboard ships. A number of alien species in the lakes—including the European ruffe, a perchlike fish; the round goby, another fish; and the spiny water flea—were branded alien aquatic nuisances.

985. Ibid., p. 4.

ILLUSTRATION CREDITS

Richard D. Bibby Collection, Duluth, Minnesota: p. 29, wooden freighter in locks; p. 116, whaleback's appearance as "pig boat"; p. 135, collapsed bridge crane; p. 163, Richard D. Bibby, second mate; p. 179, laker fireman at work; p. 185, ABS surveyors at Fraser Shipyards, photo by Basgen Photography; p. 186, Fraser Shipyards' Trevor White and Coast Guard officers; p. 197, tarp repair aboard *George R. Fink*; p. 205, Continental Grain Company elevator; p. 230, ocean ship departs Cenex Harvest States Elevator No. 1 gallery, photo by Jerry Bielicki; p. 236, vessel agents S. A. and Mark McLennan aboard Soviet ship, photo by Basgen Photography; p. 247, deck of a 1,000-footer, photo by David G. Merrick, M.D.; p. 259, *Arthur M. Anderson* and *Federal Hudson*, photo by Jerry Bielicki.

Michael Colalillo, Duluth, Minnesota: p. 170, President Truman presents Medal of Honor to PFC Michael Colalillo.

Fred Cummings, Duluth, Minnesota: p. 214, *Roger Blough*.

Duluth Public Library, Duluth, Minnesota: p. 15, fur traders at breakfast, photo of painting by Cornelius Krieghoff (1815–1872), title and year unknown, possibly detail of larger work; p. 32, *View of Duluth from the Heights*, oil on canvas by Gilbert Munger, 1871; p. 63, Charlemagne Tower Jr.; p. 95, Albert M. Marshall; p. 121, Julius Barnes.

Duluth Seaway Port Authority Collection, Duluth, Minnesota: p. 81, schooner *J. B. Newland*, pen and ink by Ken Tunnell; p. 134, camouflaged *Lake Ledan*, pen and ink by Arvid Morken; p. 183, Robert T. Smith, photo by Basgen Photography; p. 191, camera operator at DM&IR Ore Docks, photo by NBC Television; p. 194, Governor Orville Freeman signs $10 million port appropriations bill, photo by Walter H. Wettschreck; p. 199, opening of John A. Blatnik Bridge; p. 202, loading of bagged agricultural products; p. 204, first general cargo ship, photo by Dick Magnuson; p. 206, Russell A. Johnson Sr. and Jr. at Farmers Union Elevators; p. 211, French ship *Christine*, photo by Basgen Photography; p. 213, Mid-Continent Warehouse's Marshall Chabot with Sven Hubner and Eric Hallen, photo by Basgen Photography; David W. Oberlin receives congratulations, photo by Charles Curtis, *Duluth News-Tribune*; p. 216, *Nonsuch*, photo by Basgen Photography; p. 222, icy lake tanker discharging calcium chloride, photo by Basgen Photography; p. 223, lengthening of *Charles M. Beeghly* at Fraser Shipyards; ships caught in ice, photo by Basgen Photography; p. 225, imported nuclear reactor cargo in ship's hold; p. 227, E. L. Slaughter and Senator Walter Mondale; p. 232, Davis Helberg and Lewis Gulick; p. 233, ships idled by grain millers' strike, photo by Basgen Photography; p. 235, Duluth mayor Ben Boo greets Soviet captain, photo by Basgen Photography; p. 242, Great Lakes Towing Company's *Vermont*, photo by John LaFontaine; p. 244, *Edwin H. Gott* arrives at Murphy Oil USA fuel dock, photo by Grandmaison; p. 246, Fred Shusterich and Congressman James L. Oberstar; p. 248, Hallett Dock No. 5, photo by Grandmaison; p. 249, Gary Nicholson, photo by Grandmaison; p. 250, winter on Rice's Point and Clure Public Marine Terminal, photo by Grandmaison; p. 252, Dutch Jumbo ship unloading heavy-lift cargo; p. 254, Davis Helberg at podium, photo by American Association of Port Authorities; p. 255, *James R. Barker* loads at night at Burlington Northern Santa Fe Ore Docks; p. 256, Adolph Ojard, photo by Grandmaison.

Steve Gordon Collection, Two Harbors, Minnesota: p. 121, Riverside shipyard.

Guthrie-Hubner, Inc., Duluth, Minnesota: p. 190, oil portrait of Alastair Guthrie, artist unknown, 1977.

Wesley R. Harkins Collection, Duluth, Minnesota: p. 146, *B. A. Peerless* and *Imperial Leduc* loading crude oil, photo by Lakehead Pipeline Company; p. 165, John Abernethy.

Wesley R. Harkins Photo, Duluth, Minnesota: p. 96, *Joseph H. Frantz* unloading automobiles at Nicholson Transit Dock; p. 142, Great Lakes cruise ship *North American*; p. 172, cutter *Woodrush* inbound; p. 176, Mallet locomotive helps steam ore; p. 177, lakers loading iron ore in Allouez; p. 180, Hibbing's Hull-Rust-Mahoning mine; p. 181, Reiss Steamship's *Superior* unloading coal; p. 188, first St. Lawrence Seaway arrival; p. 198, *Edward L. Ryerson* on maiden voyage; p. 239, USS Great Lakes Fleet vessels awaiting fit-out.

Hibbing Daily Tribune, Hibbing, Minnesota: p. 69, Frank Hibbing.

Bill Kron Collection, Duluth, Minnesota: p. 167, sheet music cover featuring Dionne Quintuplets.

C. Patrick Labadie Collection, Alpena, Michigan: p. 33, newspaper advertisement; p. 41, newspaper advertisement; p. 44, freighter *D. M. Wilson*, photo of painting, artist and year unknown; p. 48, Minnesota Point with hillside in background; p. 53, "Elevator Row"; p. 59, coal dock operations; p. 69, 1910 postcard, DM&N Ore Docks; p. 75, Alger-Smith Lumber Company mill; p. 82, lumber shovers in Grand Marais, Michigan; p. 83, loading lumber aboard *Langell Boys*; p. 88, *City of Fremont* unloading at Northern Pacific freight sheds; p. 94, postcard of Marshall-Wells Company; p. 129, postcard of Carnegie Coal bridge cranes; p. 140, Northern Steamship Company poster; p. 145, postcard of *South American*; p. 209, steamer *Philip R. Clarke* in South Chicago.

Lake Superior Marine Museum Association Archives, Lake Superior Maritime Collection at University of Wisconsin-Superior, Superior, Wisconsin: p. 27, wooden propeller *Cuyahoga* in original Soo lock; p. 30, schooner *Algonquin*, oil painting by Tim Olsen, 1931, said to be based on photograph by vessel owner, a Mr. Bardon, prior to *Algonquin*'s sinking in 1857 at Quebec Dock, Superior, and 1865 abandonment; p. 37, 1870 Duluth and Superior map; barkentine loading at LS&M wharf, photo by Gaylord Photo; p. 39, Lake Avenue from Duluth hillside, photo by Gaylord Photo; p. 40, workers dig LS&M railroad foundation, photo by Gaylord Photo; p. 41, schooner *Chaska* at Oneota, 1871; p. 42, dredge digging ship canal, 1871; p. 46, ice-covered lighthouse, photo by Gaylord Photo; p. 47, children with skiff; p. 50, Elevator A and Branch's Hall, 1872; p. 51, dredge at Great Northern elevator, photo by D. F. Barry; p. 53, Duluth harbor, partial view of larger lithograph *View of Duluth, Minn., 1883*, by J. J. Stoner; p. 54, freighter *Superior* and consort *Sandusky* at Elevator A, photo by Gaylord Photo; p. 58, outbound freighter and Northwestern Fuel docks, photo by McKenzie Photo, Ken Thro Collection; p. 60, harbor activity; p. 74, Rice's Point, partial view of larger lithograph *View of Duluth, Minn., 1883*, by J. J. Stoner; p. 77, *Charles H. Bradley* with consorts, photo by McKenzie Photo, Ken Thro Collection; p. 84, longshoremen load butter and cheese, Ken Thro Collection; p. 86, wooden propeller *Meteor* and side-wheeler *Frances Smith* unload passengers and freight, photo by Gaylord Photo; p. 87, ship canal and vessel activity, partial view of larger lithograph *View of Duluth, Minn., 1883*, by J. J. Stoner; p. 90, package freighter *William H. Gratwick* at Northern Pacific freight sheds, photo by McKenzie Photo, Ken Thro Collection; p. 91, package freighter *Delaware* at Superior flour mills, photo by McKenzie Photo, Ken Thro Collection; p. 92, steamer *King* carrying automobiles, Ken Thro Collection; p. 98, Duluth hillside and, in distance, ship canal with new concrete piers, photo by Crandall and Fletcher, Ken Thro Collection; p. 100, Swedish immigrants building ship canal, Gerard Lawson Collection; p. 102, ferry *Hattie Lloyd* passing under Interstate Bridge; p. 105, freighter *Home Smith* in ice-filled ship canal; p. 106, Superior entry modernization, photo by U.S. Army Corps of Engineers; p. 107, lumber hooker steaming past harbor dredges; strike-idled ships; p. 110, whaleback *Colgate Hoyt* at Soo Locks; p. 112, Alexander McDougall; p. 113, Alexander McDougall and staff, Ken Thro Collection; p. 114, whalebacks *Thomas Wilson* and *Frank Rockefeller*, Ken Thro Collection; p. 115, Alexander McDougall's first hull; p. 118, wintering ships, photo by D. F. Barry, Ken Thro Collection; p. 119, launching of *Edward Y. Townsend* at Superior Ship Building; p. 120, Frederickstad lakers fitting out at Globe Shipyard; p. 122, package freighter *Jack* of the "poker fleet," photo by W. J. Taylor; p. 123, Corps of Engineers building, photo by U.S. Army Corps of Engineers; p. 124, *Mataafa* wallowing in storm; p. 128, West Duluth ore docks; p. 131, ore dock operations, photo by Gallagher Photo; p. 132, breaking up frozen ore, photo by McKenzie Photo, Ken Thro Collection; p. 134, major ice jam, photo by McKenzie Photo, Ken Thro Collection; p. 137, Duluth's U.S. Steel plant; p. 142, gentlemen's smoking lounge on cruise ship *North West*, Ken Thro Collection; p. 143, Aerial Bridge ferry behind outbound *Hamonic*; p. 144, United States and Dominion Transportation poster; p. 150, ferry scow at ship canal; p. 151, Aerial Bridge reconstruction work; p. 152, Aerial Bridge center span nearly completed; p. 154, laker loading ore in West Duluth, photo by McKenzie Photo, Ken Thro Collection; p. 160, woman welding crew at Butler Shipyards; p. 166, shift change at Riverside Shipyards; p. 168, shipbuilder Walter Butler; p. 169, Duluth shipbuilders celebrate successful bond drive; p. 171, launching of *Hawser Eye*, Harold Andresen Collection; p. 174, iron ore flowing into cargo hold, Ken Thro Collection; p. 178, bumboat *Kaner Brothers* and *Mariposa* at Great Northern Elevator, photo by

282

Gallagher Photo; **p. 193**, Clure Public Marine Terminal dock activity, photo by Basgen Photography; **p. 195**, Lewis G. Castle portrait, artist unknown, photograph in *Minnesota's World Port*, vol. 20, issue 2, 1985; busy harbor; **p. 196**, inspector probing grain; **p. 202**, loading of bagged agricultural products; **p. 208**, car dump at Reserve Mining Company, photo by Basgen Photography; **p. 219**, Midwest Energy Resources Company terminal, photo by U.S. Army Corps of Engineers, St. Paul District; **p. 221**, *Philip R. Clarke* in heavy ice, photo by H. G. Weis, Erie, Pennsylvania; **p. 224**, construction of Cargill elevator complex, photo by U.S. Army Corps of Engineers, St. Paul District; **p. 228**, the *Edmund Fitzgerald*, photo by Robert "Bob" Campbell, Grand Ledge, Michigan; **p. 232**, fire at Capitol Elevator No. 4, photo by Mary George.

Marian Lansky, Clarity, Duluth, Minnesota: **p. 62**, western Lake Superior iron ore ranges; **p. 130**, Minnesota's iron ore ranges.

National Portrait Gallery, Smithsonian Institution / Art Resource, New York: **p. 19**, John Jacob Astor portrait by John Wesley Jarvis, ca. 1825.

Patrick Lapinski Collection, Inland Mariners, Robbinsdale, Minnesota: **p. 52**, World's Fair grain car, Negative 0382-3; **p. 156**, *Henry Steinbrenner* loading at Itasca Elevator, Negative 35-17 (30).

Library of Congress, Washington, D.C.: **p. 29**, Soo Locks' fiftieth anniversary.

Shirley A. Martin, Duluth, Minnesota: **p. 108**, smelt harvesting.

Minnesota Historical Society, St. Paul, Minnesota: **p. 12**, *Lake Superior*, Charles Mottram engraving of Frances Ann Hopkins painting, 1873; **p. 17**, *Daniel Greysolon Sieur Du Lhut at the Head of the Lakes, 1679*, by Francis Lee Jacques, 1922, oil on canvas; **p. 19**, Fond du Lac fur trading post, photo from *Sketches of a Tour to the Lakes* by Thomas L. McKenney, ca. 1827.

Minnesota Timber Producers Association, Duluth, Minnesota: **p. 72**, large load of white pine on sledge; **p. 76**, turn-of-century logging camp; **p. 78**, Knife River locomotives and log yards; **p. 79**, last log drive.

T. Truxtun Morrison, Wayzata, Minnesota: **p. 138**, photo of Frank Peavey portrait by unknown artist in *The Peavey Story*, published by F. H. Peavey Company, 1960s.

New York Public Library, New York, N.Y., General Research Division; Astor, Lenox and Tilden Foundatons: **p. 20**, portaging a canoe up rapids from *Canadian Scenery*, London: Virtue and Company (1840–1842?).

Northeast Minnesota Historical Center, Duluth, Minnesota: **p. 38**, Jay Cooke; **p. 51**, James J. Hill; **p. 56**, Hull-Rust-Mahoning Pit, photo by Louis P. Gallagher(?); **p. 63**, Charlemagne Tower Sr.; **p. 67**, Mountain Iron pit, photo by Louis P. Gallagher; **p. 68**, first carload of Mountain Iron ore; **p. 70**, Andrew Carnegie; **p. 148**, Civilian Conservation Corps camp near Brimson, Minnesota; **p. 153**, Augustus Wolvin; **p. 158**, Duluth's incline railway.

Pilgrim Congregational Church Library, Duluth, Minnesota: **p. 36**, Fourth Avenue East docks and breakwater.

St. Louis County Historical Society, Duluth, Minnesota: **p. 22**, *Landscape of Superior, Wisconsin*, by Eastman Johnson, charcoal and crayon on paper, 1857, permanent collection; **p. 65**, Lewis Merritt family.

John Salminen, Duluth, Minnesota: **p. 2**, *Lake Superior* by John Salminen, transparent watercolor, 1999.

Sky View Aerial Photography, Jeff Mohr, Detroit Lakes, Minnesota: **p. 200**, Cargill Elevators B-1 and B-2.

Tim Slattery, Harbor Reflections, Duluth, Minnesota: **cover**, *Charles M. Beeghly*; **p. 6**, cutter *Sundew* at dock; **p. 8**, Duluth-Superior Harbor activity.

Superior Views Studio, Jack Deo, Marquette, Michigan: **p. 34**, Marquette's first gravity ore dock.

U.S. Army Corps of Engineers, Detroit District, Detroit, Michigan: **p. 104**, first Poe Lock under construction.

Wisconsin Historical Society, Madison, Wisconsin: **p. 25**, *Lake Superior Area* (LaPointe on Madeline Island), artist and year unknown.

A. B. Wolvin, 153
A. Booth, 109
A. Booth and Sons, 109
A. Booth Packing Company, 109
A. H. Ferbert, 165
A. T. Spencer, 88
Abernethy, John, *165*
Ace, 93
Acme Steamship Company, 153
Adams, Cuyler, 132
Admanthos Shipping Corporation, 190
Agricultural Processing, 200–01
Airpark, 253–54
Alastair Guthrie, Inc., 189, 235. *See also* Guthrie-Hubner Agency.
Albert, 18
Alberta, 144
Alexander McDougall, 117
Alger, Russel, 80
Alger-Smith Company, *75,* 80–81
Algoma, 144
Algonquin, 30, 31
Allouez Marine Supply, 190–91
Alworth, Marshall, 93, 121
Alworth, Royal, 93
America, 58, 109
American Federation of Grain Millers, 233
American Federation of Labor, 155
American Fur Company, 19, *19,* 21, 23, 34
American Grain Trimmers, 190, 249
American Hoist and Derrick Company, 220
American Ship Building Company, *112, 116,* 119, 165, 187, 215
American Steamship Company, 152, 240
American Steel and Wire Company, 217
American Steel Barge Company, 101, *112,* 115–18, *116,* 123, 147. *See also* Superior Shipbuilding Company.
Ames, Ward, 121
Ames, Ward Jr., 122
Anchor Line, 93, 112, 141, 143, 145
Anderson, Harvey, *197*
Anna C. Minch, 157
Antilla, Matt, 182
Armco Steel Corporation, 178–79, 238
Arthur M. Anderson, 187, 229, *239,* 240, *259*
Arthur M. Clure Public Marine Terminal, *8,* 183, 185, *193, 195,* 211–12, 220–21, 224, 234, 241, *244,* 248–51, *250,* 254, 256
Assiniboia, 144–45
Astor, John Jacob, 19, *19*
Athabasca, 21, 144
Atkins, Samuel, 182
Atlantic, 85
Atlantic and Gulf Stevedoring, 190
Austrian, Joseph, 88
Avafors, 229
Azcon Scrapyards, 240

B. A. Peerless, 146
Bacon, D. H., 64
Bacon, Henry, 38
Baker, Robert J., 190, 235
Baltimore, 28, 87
Banning, William L., 38–39, 41, 45
Bannockburn, 229
Barge 101, 113, 115, *115*
Barge 107, 117
Barge 109, 117
Barge 126, 114
Barge 127, 114
Barker, Charles S., 106
Barlow, S. S., 43
Barnes, Julius H., *121,* 121–23, 153, 166, *169,* 194, 196–97
Barnes Duluth Shipbuilding Company, 165–66
Bartholomew and Associates, 181
Baxter, Alexander Jr., 21

Bay Shipbuilding Corporation, 220
Belt Line Elevator Company, 139, 201
Benjamin F. Fairless, 165
Berghult, C. Rudolph, 182
Bergland, Bob, 233
Bernard, John T., 182
Berwind-White Coal Mining Company, 129, 176
Bessemer, Henry, 71
Bessemer Steamship Company, 118
Bethehem, Jones, and Laughlin Steel, 238
Bethlehem Steel Corporation, 178, 210, 219
Bibby, Richard D., *163*
Black Hawk, 24
Blatnik, Evelyn, *199*
Blatnik, John, 197–99, *199*
Blatnik Bridge, *199, 219*
Blodgett, Charles C., 83
Blodgett, Myron, 83
Blodgett, Omer W., 83, 169
Boilermakers and Iron Shipbuilders Union, 187
Boland and Cornelius Company, 190, 220
Bon Ami, 109
Bong, Richard Ira, 164
Boo, Ben, *199, 235*
Booth, Alfred Sr., 109
Booth Fisheries Corporation, 109
Borden, Mackenzie, 191
Boschwitz, Rudy, 237
Branch's Hall, *50*
Breckenridge, John, 35
British Shipbuilding Mission, 166
Broeker Hendrickson and Company, 187
Brooks, George, 111
Brooks, John W., 28
Browman, Sam L., *236,* 237, 251
Browning Line, 224
Brulé, Etienne, 16
Buckeye Steamship Company, 189
Buckeye Transportation Fleet, 159
Buhrmann, Bill, 226, 240
Burdick Grain Company, 201
Burke, C. Thomas, 221, 224, 226–27
Burlington Northern Santa Fe Railroad, 201, 220, 226, 229, 253, *255*
Burt, William, 26
Butler, Walter, *168*
Butler Taconite, 209

C. H. Graves, *87*
C. L. Austin, 179, 183
C. Reiss Coal Company, *181,* 220, 248, 257
C. W. Moore, 109
Cabot, John, 14
Cactus, 173
Cadillac, 164
Cadotte, Jean-Baptiste, 18
Calumet and Hecla Consolidated Copper Company, 95
Camenker, Norman, 190
Canada Steamship Lines, 145
Canadian-U.S. Deep Waterways Commission, 191, 193
Canadian Forest Navigation Company. *See* CanForNav.
Canadian Pacific Railway Company, 144, 253
CanForNav, 251
Capitol Elevator Company, 129–30, *195,* 201
Cargill, Inc., *156,* 190, *200,* 200–01, 205, *211,* 220, *224,* 234, 246–47, 254
Cargill, Sam, 201
Cargill, W. W. "Will," 57–59, 201
Carl D. Bradley, 229
Carnegie, Andrew, 65, 68, *70,* 70–71
Carnegie Coal Company, *129, 195*
Carter, Jimmy, 231, 233, 235–36, 240
Cartier, Jacques, 13–14
Cason J. Calloway, 187, *239,* 240
Cass, Lewis, 34

Castle, Lewis G., 194–95, *195,* 197
Cenex Harvest States. *See* CHS.
Ceres, Inc., 190, 213, 221, 233, 247–48, 251
Chabot, Marshall, 213, *213*
Champlain, Samuel de, 13–14, 16
Chapin, A. B., 93
Chapin-Wells Hardware Company, 93
Charles I, 14
Charles M. Beeghly, 223
Charles H. Bradley, 77
Chaska, 41, 111
Chester, Albert H., 63
Chestnut, Jack, 234
Chicago, Burlington, & Quincy Railroad, 211, 220
Chicago, Duluth, and Georgian Bay Transit Company, 143
Chicago, Milwaukee, and Lake Superior Line, 88
Chicago, St. Paul, Minneapolis, & Omaha Railroad, 52
Chicago & Northwestern Railway, 57, 61, 152, 201
Chicago Regional Port District, 227
China, 89, 141, 143
Chisholm, Alva S., 243
Chouart, Medard, Sieur de Grosseilliers, 16
Christiansen, Martin, 111
Christine, 211
Christopher Columbus, 118
Chrysler, 97
CHS, 200–01, *231*
Chun King Foods Corporation, 222
City of Bangor, 97
City of Buffalo, 36
City of Collingwood, 144
City of Duluth, 112
City of Fremont, 88, 111
Civilian Conservation Corps, *148,* 154
Clark, Morgan, 229
Clarke, Ed, 253
Clay, Henry, 27
Cleaveland, Moses, 23
Cleopatra, 86
Cleveland-Cliffs fleet, 164, 189
Cleveland-Cliffs Iron Mining Company, 26, 214, 239
Cleveland-Cliffs Steamship Company, 238, 240
Cleveland, Detroit, and Lake Superior Line, *33*
Cleveland, Grover, 191
Cleveland North Western Lake Company, 31
Cliff Mining Company, 26
Clifford F. Hood, 217–18
Cloquet Lumber Company, 77
Clure, Arthur M., 157, 182–83
Clure Public Marine Terminal. *See* Arthur M. Clure Public Marine Terminal.
Clyde Iron Works, 184
Coburn, R. G., 111
Colalillo, Michael, *170*
Colby, Charles L., 115
Colby, James L., 115
Colgate Hoyt, 110, 115
Columbia, 28
Columbia Transportation Company, 189, 226, 228, 240
ConAgra, 201
ConAgra/Peavey, 200
Congdon, Chester, 121
Consolidated Elevator Company, 130, 201
Continental Grain Company, 201, *205,* 205–06
Cooke, Jay, *38,* 39–41, 43, 45–46, 49, 63
Cooley, J. E., 109
Coolidge, Calvin, 149
Cooper, Jesse, 229
Corcoran, William Wilson, 35
Cornell, F. R. E., 43
Corning, Erastus, 28

Coulby, Harry, 243
Craig, Charles P., 192, 194
Crescent City, 36, 125
Crooks, Ramsay, 19
Cullen Stevedoring, 190
Culver, Joshua, 43
Culver and Nettleton Mill, 74
Cunard, 182
Cutler, Gilbert, and Pearson Mill, *74*
Cutler-Magner Company, 193, 248
Cuyahoga, 27

D. M. Wilson, *44*
Danielian, N. R., 194
Darling, John H., 106
Dart, Joseph, 49
Davis, Charles E. L. B., 107
Davis, Cushman K., 43
Davis, E. W., 176–77
Davis Works, 179
Defense Plant Corporation, 166
Delaware, *91*
Delaware, Lackawanna, & Western Railway, 89
Democratic Farmer Labor Party, 182
Deneweth, Charles, *199*
Detroit Atlantic Lines, 224
Detroit Edison, 220
Diamond, Jared, 24
Diamond Tool and Horseshoe Company, 164
Dionne quintuplets, *167*
Doering, Herman C., 211
Dominion Marine Association, 214–15
Donovan, William "Wild Bill," 197
Douglas, Stephen A., 35
Douglas County Street Railway Company, 101.
    See also Superior Rapid Transit Railway
    Company.
Dowling, Edward, 118
Drake and Piper, 184
Dry Dock Works, 111
Duluth, Missabe, & Iron Range Railway
    Company, *66*, *68–69*, 111, 210, 218, 241,
    245, 248, *248*, 257
Duluth, Missabe, & Northern Railway
    Company, 65, 67, 101, 103, 127–29, *131*,
    136, 150, 152, *154*, 159
Duluth-Superior Bridge Company, 101
Duluth-Superior Grain Trimmers, 190, 212
Duluth-Superior Pilots Association, 190
Duluth-Superior Ship Chandlery, 190
Duluth-Superior Shipping Agency, 190
Duluth & Iron Range Railroad, 64, 117
Duluth & Northern Minnesota Railroad, *78*
Duluth & Vermilion Railroad, 64
Duluth & Winnipeg Railway, 65, 67–68, 101
Duluth Aerial Bridge, *58*, *102*, *151–52*
Duluth board of trade, *127*
Duluth Central Labor Body, 155
Duluth Creamery and Produce Company, 194
Duluth Elevator Company, 52, 201
Duluth Imperial Milling and Capitol Elevator
    Company, 50, 129. *See also* Capitol
    Elevator Company.
Duluth incline railway, *158*
Duluth Iron and Metal, 218
Duluth Port Authority. *See* Seaway Port of
    Authority of Duluth.
Duluth Ship Canal, *39*, *58*, *77*, *99*, *105–06*, *143*,
    172, *189*, *198*
Duluth State Teachers College, 182
Duluth Storage and Forwarding Company, 90
Duncan, Kenneth, 183–84
Duncan and Brewer Lumber Company, 78
Dutch West Indies Company, 13

E. N. Saunders, 133
E. W. Clarke and Company, 39
Eames, Henry, 62

Eames, Richard, 62
Eastern Railway Company of Minnesota, 51–52
Easton, 109
Economic Development Corporation, 220
Edgar Thomson Works, 71
Edith, 112
Edmund Fitzgerald ("Fitz"), 226, *228*, 228–29
Edward L. Ryerson, *198*
Edward Y. Townsend, *119*
Edwin H. Gott, 219, *244*
Egan, James J., 43
Eileraas, Kaare, 213
Eisenhower, Dwight D., 181–82, 184, 195
Elevator Row, *53*, *219*
Ely, Edmund F., 35, 40
Emergency Fleet Corporation, 93, 122
Emergency Shipping Board, 123
Empire State, 86
Empire Stevedoring Company, 190, 212
Enders M. Voorhees, 165
Ensign, J. D., 43
Erickson, Ray, 203–04
Erie and Western Transportation Company, 93.
    See Anchor Line.
Erie Marine Division, 218
Erie Mining Company, 179–80, 206, 209
Erie Railroad, 92
Essayons, 184
Ethen, John, 246
Evans, Oliver, 49
Eveleth Taconite Company, 209–10, 220
Everett, Philo, 26
Exxon Valdez, 256

F. A. Patrick Company, 94
F. H. Peavey Company, 130, 139, 189–90, *195*,
    201, 204
Fairbanks, Erastus, 28
Fairbanks Scale Company, 28
Farmers Union Grain Terminal Association,
    161, 201, 203–05, *206*
Fashion, *150*
Federal Commerce and Navigation Company.
    See FedNav.
Federal Hudson, *259*
FedNav, 190, 224, 251
Ferner, Clinton, 245
Fillmore, Millard B., 28
Ford, Henry, 147
Ford Motor Company, 97, 187, 189, 209
Forest City, 55
Fossum, Ken, 176
Foster, Thomas P., 40
Frances Smith, *86*
Francis E. House, 128
Frank C. Fero, *42*, 43
Frank M. Rogall, 184
Frank Rockefeller, *114*. *See also* Meteor.
Fraser-Nelson Shipbuilding and Dry Dock
    Company, 187
Fraser, Robert M., 187
Fraser Shipyards, 187, *223*, *239*, 240
Fredin, Conrad "Mac," 212
Freeman, Alexander E., 185
Freeman, Orville, 182–84, *194*
Frick, Henry Clay, 65
Frontenac, 23, *191*, 238
Fur Trader, 21, 31

Garfield C & D, *250*, 254
Gates, Frederick T., 117
General Mills, *195*, 200–01, 247
General Motors, 97
George A. Stinson, 219
George G. Hadley, 124
George H. Russell, *69*
George R. Fink, *197*
Georgian Bay Line, 144

Gesick, Marji, 26
Gettysburg, 80
Giesler, Edward J., *186*
Glenlyon, *90*
Globe Elevator Company, 139, 201, 204
Globe Iron Works, 55, 61, 141
Globe Shipbuilding Company, 91, 111, 120, 123,
    165–70, 187
Gomonenko, Vladimir, *235*
Gordon, John Steele, 67
Goshawk, 77
Graff-Murray Mill, 78
Grandmaison, Jerry, 189
Grand Trunk Railroad, 93
Grant, Ulysses S., 38
Graves, Hollis Sr., 203
Great Lakes–St. Lawrence Tidewater
    Association, 192–94
Great Lakes Engineering Company, 143
Great Lakes Engineering Works, 165, 229
Great Lakes Storage and Contracting
    Company, 234, 249
Great Lakes Towing Company, *211*, *242*,
    242–43
Great Lakes Transit Corporation, 93–95
Great Northern Railway, *51*, 52, 59, 77, *91–92*,
    101, *127–28*, 141, 151, 164, 175, *176–78*, 199,
    201, 210, 220
Great Western, 86
Greeley, Horace, 31
Green Bay & Minnesota Railroad, 58
Greysolon, Claude, 16
Greysolon, Daniel, Sieur DuLhut, 16–18, *17*, 43
Grignon, Napoleon, 111, 168
Grignon, Peter, 168
Groveland Plant, 209
Gullick, Lewis, *232*
Guthrie, Alastair, 159, 189–90, *190*, 203,
    234–35
Guthrie, Germaine, 190
Guthrie-Hubner Agency, 235

Hagan, Charles S., 182
Hagen, Howard, 169
Haglin, C. F., 139
Half Moon, 13
Hallberg, Dennis, 249
Hallen, Eric, *213*
Hallett Dock Company, 248, *248*, 257
Halter Marine, 218
Hamonic, *143*, 144
Hanna, Daniel, 243
Hanna, Leonard, 243
Hanna Mining Company, 209
Harrison, Benjamin, 65
Harry L. Allen, 232
Harvest States Cooperative, 201
Harvey, Charles T., 28
Hattie Lloyd, *102*
Havighurst, Walter, 152
Hawser Eye, *171*
Head, George, 190
Hearding, William H., 38
Helberg, Davis, 203, 213, 222, *232*, 233–34,
    236, 237, 248–49, 251, 253, *254*, 256
Henderson, Ralph, 190
Hennepin, Louis, 17
Henry, Alexander, 18
Henry Steinbrenner, *156*
Herald, 189
Hibbing, Frank, *69*
Hibbing Taconite, 219
Hill, James J., 51, *51*, 68, 77, 91, 141
Hilleren, Chuck, 235, 238, 246–47, 250–51
Hiram R. Dixon, 109
Hitler, Adolf, 157
Hocking, Mark, *186*
Holmes, Donald S., 181

Home Smith, *105*
Hook, Charles R., 178
Hoover, Herbert, 153, 193
Houghton, Douglass, 25–26
Houston, D. C., 43
Hoyt, Colgate, 115, 117, 147
Hoyt, Elton II, 180
Hoyt, James H., 243
Hubbard, Jerry, 190
Hubner, Sven, *213*, 235
Hudson, Henry, 13
Hudson Bay Company, 18–19, 21
Hugo, Trevanion, 41
Hull-Rust-Mahoning, *56*, *180*
Humble, R. H., 125
Humphreys, A. A., 43
Hunter, 109
Huronic, 144
Hutchinson fleet, 189
Hyman-Michaels Company, 218, 240

Ilenda, Chuck, 233, 247
Illinois, 28
Illinois Central Railroad, 35
Imperial Leduc, *146*
Imperial Mill, 90
Independence, 31
India, 89, 141, 143
Indian, 157
Industrial Workers of the World, 155
Inland Steel Mining Company, 175, 189, 219
Inland Waterways, 170
Interlake Steamship, 240
International Duluth Seaport Corporation, 185
International Longshoremen's Association, 155–56, 234, 249, 251
International Milling Company. *See* International Multifoods Corporation.
International Multifoods Corporation, 201, 231–32
Interstate Bridge, *102*, *219*
Interstate Port Authority Commission, 226–27
Invincible, 21
Iris, 173
Irving S. Olds, 165
Isaac Ellwood, 125
Ishpeming, *42*, 43
Island Creek Coal Company, 129
Islay, 117–18

J. and H. Beatty, 89
J. B. Newland, *81*
J. F. McNamara Corporation, 190
Jack, 83, *122*
Jackson Iron Company, 26
James Nasmyth, 125
James R. Barker, 219, *255*
Janos, George, 190
Japan, 89, 112, 141, 143
Jay Cooke and Company, 39, 46
Jeffery, Bill, 217–218
Jogues, Isaac, 16
John C. Hay, 224
John Jacob Astor, 21
Johnson, Alan T., *236*
Johnson, Don, *185*
Johnson, Russell A. Sr., *206*
Johnson, Russell A. Jr. "Noonie," *206*
Johnson, Troy, 187
Joppa, Everett L., 184
Joseph, Burton, 182
Joseph H. Frantz, *96*
Joseph L. Colby, 117
Joseph L. Hurd, 88
Josephs, Hyman Y., 218
Juniata, 143, 145

Kakela, Peter J., 208
Kaner Brothers, *178*
Kansas City Bridge Company, 149
Keewatin, 144–45
Kelley-How-Thompson Company, 94
Kennedy, John F., 182, 206
Kennedy, Thomas E., 211, 249
King, *92*, 93
King Iron Works, 89
Kinsman Line, 189
Kirby, Frank E., *92*, 93
Kirby, Stephen E., 93
Kirscher Transport, 249
Knife Falls Lumber Company. *See* Cloquet Lumber Company.
Knudsen Brothers Shipyard, 183, 187
Koch Industries, 256
Kritikos, Christos, 213
Kubow, John, 249

Lackawanna Transportation Company, 89. *See also* Red Star Line.
Lady Elgin, *22*, 88
Lafarge Corporation, 248
Lafayette, 125
LaHacienda, 190
Lake Carriers' Association, 154–55, 214–15, 245
Lake Erie North Shore Line, 85
Lake Erie Transportation Company, 89
Lakehead Constructors, 249
Lakehead Pipeline Company, *146*
Lake Indian, *121*
Lake Ledan, *134*
Lake Markham, *121*
Lake Michigan and Lake Superior Transportation Company, 88
Lake States Lumber Company, *250*, 254
Lake Superior & Mississippi Railroad, 36, *37*, 38–41, *40*, 43, 45–46, 54, 90
Lake Superior Coal and Iron Company, 58
Lake Superior Consolidated Iron Mines, 68
Lake Superior Elevator Company, 50–51, *53*
Lake Superior Industrial Bureau, 184
Lake Superior People's Line, 88. *See also* Lake Michigan and Lake Superior Transportation Company.
Lake Superior Pilots Association, 234. *See also* Twin Ports Harbor Pilots Association and Upper Great Lakes Pilots.
Lake Superior Shipbuilding Company, 165–66
Lake Superior Shipping Company, 190
Lake Superior Transit Company, 45, 89
Lake Superior Warehousing, 249–51, 253
LaLiberte, Henry, 192–93
Land and River Improvement Company, 116
Land O' Lakes Cooperative, 201
Landon, Fred, 125
Langell Boys, *83*
Lapinski, Patrick, 187
Lee, Robert E., 38
Lehigh Valley Coal Sales Company, 59, 176
Lehigh Valley Railroad, 92
Lehigh Valley Transit Company, 93
Leon Fraser, 165
Leopold, Aaron, 88
Leopold and Austrian, 88
Leraan, A. W., *168–69*
LesStrang, Jacques, 196
Libby-Owens Ford, 212
Liberty, 109
Lightfoot, Gordon, 229
Lighthouse Service, 173
Lind, John, 191
Little, Peck, and Company Mill, *74*
Litton Industries, 218
Louis XIV, 16
Louis Dreyfus Corporation, 190, 205
LTV Steel Corporation, 238

Lucey, Patrick, *199*
Luoma, Ernest, 182
Lyder, J. W., 181
Lyons, Jack P., 227, 234

MacDonald, Donald B., 168
MacDonald, Donald C., 168, *169*
Mackin, W. J., 97
Mackinaw, 171
Madeline, 21
Majestic, 144
Majo, Albert C., 99
Mallet locomotive, *176*
Manhattan, 87
Manila, 125
Manistee, 88
Manitoba, 144
Marathon Oil, 238
Marine Fueling, 256
Marine Iron and Shipbuilding Company, 111–12, 165, 168, 170, 172–73, 187. *See also* Marine Iron Works.
Marine Iron Works, 111–12
Mariposa, *178*
Marquette gravity ore dock, *34*
Marquette Iron Company, 26
Marshall, Albert Morley, 93–94
Marshall-Wells Hardware Company, 93–94, *94*. *See also* Chapin-Wells Hardware Company.
Martin, Albro, 46
Mary Elizabeth, 21
Mary Woolson, *77*
Mason, Stevens T., 25–26
Mataafa, *123–24*, 125, 136, 229
Mather, Samuel, 243
Mather, William, 243
Mayflower, 85
McDonough, Andy, 253–54
McDougall, Alexander, 57, 93, 103, 112, *112–13*, 115–18, 120–23, 147, 166, 186, 194, 255
McDougall, Dugald, 112
McDougall-Duluth Company, 120, *120–21*, 122–23
McDougall, Miller, 93, 113, 122
McDougall, Ross, 112
McKenney, Thomas L., 33–34
McKnight, Sheldon, 87
McLean-Astleford Company, 184
McLean, Malcolm, 221–22
McLennan, Mark, *236*
McLennan, Stuart A., 190, *236*
McSorley, Ernest, 229
Meade, Joseph, 189
Meehan, Daniel E., 249
Meehan Seaway Services, 249
Merchant, 31
Merrill and Ring, 78
Merritt, Alfred, 35, 64
Merritt, Cassius, 64
Merritt, Hephzibah, 35
Merritt, Leonidas, 64–65, 67–68
Merritt, Lewis Jr., 64
Merritt, Lewis Sr., 35, 40, 64
Merritt, Napoleon, 35, 64
Merritt family, 35, 40, 64–65, *65*, 67–68, 111, 117
Mesabi Miner, 219
Mesquite, 173
Meteor, *36*, *47*, *86*, *114*, 255
Michigan Central Railroad, 85
Michigan Southern & Northern Indiana Railroad, 86
Mid-Continent Warehouse, 213
Midland Steamship Company, 234
Midwest Energy Resources Company, 227, 245–46
Milroy, Phillip, 187
Milwaukee, Lake Shore, & Western Railway Company, 61

Index

Milwaukee & St. Paul Railroad, 45
Mink, 21
Minnesota Aggregates, 248
Minnesota-Atlantic Transit Company, 93
Minnesota Canal and Harbor Improvement
    Company, 43
Minnesota Car Company, 79
Minnesota Iron Company, 64, 67
Minnesota Point Ship Canal Company, 43
Minnesota Ports Association, 251
Minnesota Steamship Company, 125
Minnesota Steel Company, 103
Minnesota Steel Division, 137
Minntac, 220, 239
Mississippi, 86
Mitchell and McClure, 78
Mondale, Walter "Fritz," *227*
Monticello, 31
Moore, Warren, 155
Mork, E. Clifford, 189
Morro Castle, 145
Moulton, Joseph, 52
Munger, R. S., 43
Munger, Willard, *194*
Munger and Gray, 74
Munger and Markell, 49
Murphy Oil Company, *244*, 256
Myron C. Taylor, 217

Napoleon, 23, 31, 35, 87
National Longshoremen's Association, 155
National Steel Pellet Company, 209, 229
Nelson, Byron, 187
Nelson, Donald, 162
Nelson, R. R., 43
Newman, Peter, 14
Newstrand, Bill, 251
New York Central Railroad, 93
Nicholson, Gary, *249*, 249–51
Nicholson Transit Company, *96*, *195*
Nixon, Richard M., 213
Nonsuch, 216
Norman, *40*, 43, 88
Noronic, 144–45
Norris Grain Company, *195*, 201
North American, *142*, 143–45
North Central Terminal Operators, 227, 234, 248
Northern Coal and Dock Company, 129
Northern Indiana, 86
Northern King, 92
Northern Light, 92
Northern Lumber Company, 77
Northern Navigation Company, 144
Northern Pacific Railway, 45–52, 57–59,
    62–63, 74, *87–88*, 89–91, *90*, 100–01, 112,
    116, 129, 132–33, 169, 185
Northern Queen, 92
Northern Steamship Company, 91–93, *140*, 141,
    143
Northern Wave, 92
North Land, 141, 143
Northland, 248
North Star, 92
North Star Steel, 220
North West, 141, *142*, 143, 145
North West Company, 18–19, 21, 27
Northwestern Fuel Company, *58*, 59, 129, 166
Northwestern Hanna, *195*, 218
Northwestern Leasing Company, 206
Northwest Growers Association, 201
Northwest Transportation Company, 89
North Wind, 92
Noyes, Gordon, 190

O'Konski, Alvin, *199*
Oberlin, David W., 212–13, *213*, 221, 234, 253
Oberstar, James, *246*
Occident Terminal Division, 130, 190, *195*, 201

Ocean, 31
Octorara, 143, 145
Office of Strategic Services, 197
Oglebay, Crispin, 178
Oglebay Norton Company, 178–79, 240
Ogontz, 88
Ohio Central Coal and Barge Company, 58
Ojard, Adolph, *256*
Old Hickory, 105
Oliver, Henry W., 65, 68, 103
Oliver Iron Mining Company / Division, 132,
    136, 180, 209
Omaha Road, 52
Onoko, 55, 61
Ontario Hydro, 196
Ontonagon, 88
Orba Corporation, 220
Orelands Mining Company, 132
Ortran, *219*, 220, 241, 246. *See also* Superior
    Midwest Energy Terminal.
Osborne-McMillan Company, 201, 203
Otter, 21
Overlakes Freight Corporation, 95

Paceco Economy Portainer Crane, 224
Paper Calmenson, 218
Passaic, 83
Paulucci, Jeno, 222, 231
Payton, Kimball, and Barber Company Mill, *74*
Peavey-Duluth Terminal, 139, 201
Peavey, Frank H., *138*, 139–40, 159, 201, 254
Peavey Company. *See* F. H. Peavey Company.
Peavey Steamship Line, 201
Peck, Elihu M., 55
Peerless, 88
Pella, Paul D., 227, 234
Pennsylvania and Ohio Coal Company, 59
Pennsylvania Railroad, 71, 93
Penokee and Gogebic Development Company,
    61
Perrault, Jean Baptiste, 18
Perseverance, 21
Peyton and Engler Company, 74
Pfeifer and Shultz, 184
Pharis, Leroy M., 181
Philadelphia and Reading Coal and Iron
    Company, 59, 129
Philadelphia & Reading Railroad, 67
Philip R. Clarke, 187, *209*, 221, *239*, 240
Phillipi, Tony, 249
Pickands-Mather Company, 132, 150, 152,
    179–80, 183
Pillsbury, Charles A., 48
Pittsburgh Coal Company, 129
Pittsburgh Steamship Company, 111, 124–25,
    136, 150, 153, 161, 165, 217, 243
Plymouth Rock, 86
Poe, Orlando M., 103–04
Poe Lock, *104*
Point Sur, 170
Porter, Gil, 173
Port of New York Authority, 221
Potlatch Corporation, 253
Power Authority of the State of New York,
    196
Presque Isle, 218–19
Privette, Thomas, 249
Pure Oil Company, 184
Puskarich, Frank, 248–49

Queen, 93
Quincy Mining Company, 95

R. A. Gray Company Mill, *74*
R. G. Coburn, 43
R. J. Reynolds, 222
R. L. Barnes, 122
R. W. England, 125

Radisson, Pierre Esprit, 16
Radosevich, Tony, 211
Ramon de Larrinaga, *188*, 189
Ramsey, Alexander, 37–38
Rankin, Bill, 218
Raymbault, Charles, 16
Reagan, Ronald, 257
Record, 115
Recovery, 21
Red Star Line, 89
Reiss Marine, 256
Remington, Jack, 190
Republic Steel, 179–80
Reserve Mining Company, 178–80, 183, 206,
    208, 209
Reuben Johnson and Sons, 187
Rice, Henry M., 35
Richard H., 157
Rico, A. F. "Tony," *213*, 227, 234
Riverside State Bank, 194
Road Machinery Supplies Company, 169
Robert J. Hackett, 55, 61
Rockefeller, John D., 68, 115, 117, 147, 243
Roger Blough, *214*, 215
Rogers Terminal and Shipping Corporation,
    190
Ronde, Denis de la, 21
Roosevelt, Franklin Delano, 153, 155, 157,
    161–62, 193
Roosevelt, Theodore "Teddy," 28
Ross, Emmeline, 112
Ruisi, Ed, 203
Russell-Miller Milling Company, 130
Ryan, J. C. "Buzz," 73

S. A. McLennan Agency, 189–90
S. B. Barker, 109
S.O. Co. No. 55, 147
S.O. Co. No. 75, 147
S.O. Co. No. 76, 147
S. R. Kirby, 58
S. S. Bethore, *163*
Sagard, Gabriel, 16
St. Lawrence Cement Company, 241, 248
St. Lawrence Seaway Authority, 194–95
St. Lawrence Seaway Development
    Corporation, 195, 197, 213, 221
St. Paul & Duluth Railroad, *52*, 77, 101
St. Paul & Pacific Railroad, 47
Sam Johnson Fish Company, *108*
Sandusky, *54*
Sargent, George B., 43, 62
Sargent Coal Company, 58
Sault Ste. Marie Military District, 162
Sauter, James C., 190, 212, *213*, 249
Sawyer, A. J., 52
Schoolcraft, Henry Rowe, 25
Schutte, Diederich, 111
Scott-Graff Mill, 81
Scott and Holston Lumber Company, 60, 78
Scott Misener Fleet, 189
Sea-Land Company, 222
Seafarers' International Union, 182
Sealanes International, 190
Search, 38
Sears, Clinton B., 104–06
Sears, Roebuck, and Company, 162
Seaway Port Authority of Duluth, 182–85, 201,
    210–13, 220–21, 233, 237, 241, 248, 251,
    253, 256–57
Segeza, *236*
Sellwood, Joseph, 61
Senator, *128*
Ship Canal Company, 28
Shusterich, Fred, *246*
Sibley, Henry Hastings, 37
Sielaff, Richard, 182
Simon Langell, *107*

Sinclair, James, 243
Sinclear, Lawrence, 212
Siskiwit, 31
Sivertson, Andrew, 109
Sivertson, Sam, 109
Sivertson, Theodora, 109
Skamser, Clarence, 167
Skelton, Ray, 258
Skillings, David, 165
Skuggen, George "Skip," 97
Slaughter, Edward L. "Buster," 155–56, *227*
Smith-Davis and Company, 112
Smith, Robert H., 211
Smith, Robert T., 182–83, *183*, 189, *194*, 210–12
Socrates, 242–43
Soo Line Railroad, 132–33, 184
Soo Locks, *27, 29, 110*
South American, 143–45, *145*
Southern Michigan, 86
SPAD. *See* Seaway Port Authority of Duluth.
Spencer, Albert T., 88
Spencer Kellogg Company, 201, 205
Spokane, 55
Standard Oil, 147
Steinbrenner, Henry, 189, 243
Stewart J. Cort, 212, 215, 217–19
Stone, George C., 62–64
Stone-Ordean-Wells Company, *87, 94*
Stuntz, George R., 35, 40, 62, 64, 99
Sundew, 6, 173
Superior, 54, 88, *181*
Superior Association of Commerce, 167
Superior Manufacturing Company, 192
Superior Midwest Energy Terminal, *219,* 246, 257
Superior Rapid Transit Railway Company, 101.
    See also Douglas County Street Railway
    Company.
Superior Shipbuilding Company, *118–19,*
    119–20, 123. *See also* American Steel
    Barge Company.
Svensson, Theodore W., 190, *225*
Svensson and Baker Agency, 190
Swallow, 31, 87
Syncrude UE-1, 253

T. H. Camp, 109
Taylor, Harry, *185*
Theobald, Leonard, 182
Thomas W. Lamont, 150
Thomas Wilson, 114, 124–25
Thorp Marine Supplies, 190
Thye, Edward, 195
Tionesta, 84, 143, 145
Tip Top Market, 190
Titanic, 121
Tito, Marshall, 198
Toledo-Lucas County Port Authority, 212
Toledo Shipbuilding Company, 171
Tower, Charlemagne Jr., *63*
Tower, Charlemagne Sr., *63,* 63–64, 67
TransErie, 204
TransMichigan, 204
Trelford, Thomas H., 182
Truman, Harry S., *170*
Twin Cities, 93
Twin Ports, 93
Twin Ports Harbor Pilots Association, 234. *See
    also* Lake Superior Pilots Association
    and Upper Great Lakes Pilots.

Uncle Tom, 31
Union Improvement and Elevator Company,
    49, 200
Union Towing and Wrecking Company, 243.
    See also Great Lakes Towing Company.
United Parcel Service, 213
United States and Dominion Transportation
    Company, *144*

U.S. Army Air Corps, 197
U.S. Army Corps of Engineers, 33, 43, 51, 90,
    99, 103–04, 106–08, *123,* 124, 153, 168,
    181, 195–98, 210–11, 215, 226, 255, 257
U.S. Army Quartermaster Corps, 93
U.S. Coast Guard, 162, 168, 173, 187, 229
U.S. Department of Agriculture, 233, 235, 237
U.S. Department of Transportation, 241
U.S. Economic Development Agency, 224
U.S. Maritime Commission, 165–66
U.S. Naval Reserve, 157, 182
U.S. Navy, 187
U.S. State Department, 237
U.S. Steel Corporation ("Steel Trust"), 111, 125,
    132, 136–37, *137,* 153, 178, 180, 209–10,
    217, 219, 231, 238–41. *See also* USX.
U.S. Supreme Court, 46
U.S. Topographical Corps. *See* U.S. Army
    Corps of Engineers
U.S. War Department, 43, 99, 162
U.S.S. Dubuque, 157
U.S.S. Paducah, 157
U.S.S. Sacramento, 157
University of Minnesota, 176
University of Minnesota–Duluth, 182
University of Minnesota School of Mines, 183
Upham, Williams, and Company, *51,* 111
Upper Great Lakes Pilots, 227, 234
USS Great Lakes Fleet, 187, 226, 240
USX Corporation, 219, 238. *See also* U.S. Steel
    Corporation.

Valiant Nikki, 234
Van Brunt, Walter, 43
Van Horn, Jay, 203–04
Vermont, 242
Victoria, 19
Viking, 80
Vision, 253
Volpe, John, *199*

W. B. Morley, 102
W. H. Knox Mill, 80
W. Wayne Hancock, 224
Wabash Railroad, 89
Wagenborg, 250
Wahnapitae, 80
Walk-in-the-Water, 23
Walli, Ken, 251
Walter Butler Shipbuilders, *161,* 165–66, *166,*
    168, 170
Wanvick, Arne, *194*
Ward, Samuel, 87
War Production Board, 162–64
War Shipping Administration, 95, 165–66
Washburn, Cadwallader C., 43, 48, 201
Washburn Crosby Company, 201
Wedin, Russ, 234, 251
Welland Canal Company, 192
Wemyss, R. J., 116
Western Land Association, 46
Western Transit Company, 93
Western World, 86
West Superior Lumber Company, 78
Wetmore, Charles L., 67–68, 115
Wetmore, Russell C., 147
Weyerhaeuser, Frederick, 77–78
Wheeler, Henry W., 73
Wheeler, J. B., 38
Wheeler, Samuel, 35
Wheeler Mill, 74
Wheeling-Pittsburgh Steel Company, 238
White, Peter, 28
White, Trevor, *186,* 187
Whitefish, 21
White Line Transportation Company, 90
Whiting Refinery, 147
Wicker, Howard, 211

Wilbur, John S., 214–15
Wilfred Sykes, 175
William B. Davock, 69, 157
William Brewster, 21
William Bursley, 170
William Clay Ford, 187
William H. Gratwick, 90. See also Glenlyon.
William H. Truesdale, 128
William J. Bennett, 256
Wilson, Jack, 28
Wilson, Thomas, 115
Wilson, Woodrow, 119, 127
Wilson Marine Transit Company, 97, 112, 115
Winslow, 45, 89
Wolfe Stevedoring, 190
Wolff, Julius F. Jr., 125
Wolvin, Augustus B. "Gus," 152–53, *153,* 201,
    243
Woodrush ("Woody"), 172, 173
Works Progress Admnistration, 154
Wyard, Willis, 185

XY Company, 18

Yetka, Lawrence, *194*
Yetter, Keith, 257
Youghiogheny and Lehigh Coal Company, 59
Young, Telford, 182
Youngstown Sheet and Tube, 238

Zachau, August, 73
Zalk, Max, 218
Zalk-Josephs, 218
Zenith Dredge Company, 165, 168–70, 172–73,
    184